The Second Infantry Division
in World War I

ALSO BY GEORGE B. CLARK
AND FROM MCFARLAND

*United States Marine Corps Generals of World War II:
A Biographical Dictionary* (2007)

*Decorated Marines of the
Fourth Brigade in World War I* (2007)

*The Six Marine Divisions in the Pacific:
Every Campaign of World War II* (2006)

*United States Marine Corps Medal of Honor Recipients:
A Comprehensive Registry, Including U.S. Navy Medical
Personnel Honored for Serving Marines in Combat* (2005)

*Hiram Iddings Bearss, U.S. Marine Corps:
Biography of a World War I Hero* (2005)

The Second Infantry Division in World War I

A History of the American Expeditionary Force Regulars, 1917–1919

GEORGE B. CLARK

McFarland & Company, Inc., Publishers
Jefferson, North Carolina, and London

All photographs appearing herein are from the author's collection

LIBRARY OF CONGRESS CATALOGUING-IN-PUBLICATION DATA

Clark, George B., 1926–
　　The Second Infantry Division in World War I : a history of the American Expeditionary Force Regulars, 1917–1919 / George B. Clark.
　　　　p.　　cm.
　　Includes bibliographical references and index.

　　ISBN-13: 978-0-7864-2960-8
　　softcover : 50# alkaline paper ∞

　　1. United States. Army. Division, 2nd.　2. World War, 1914–1918 — Regimental histories — United States.　3. World War, 1914–1918 — Campaigns — France.　I. Title.
D570.32nd .C53　2007
940.4'1273 — dc22　　　　　　　　　　　　　　　　2007021905

British Library cataloguing data are available

©2007 George B. Clark. All rights reserved

No part of this book may be reproduced or transmitted in any form or by any means, electronic or mechanical, including photocopying or recording, or by any information storage and retrieval system, without permission in writing from the publisher.

Cover illustration: The 5th Marines fighting in shattered Belleau Wood

Manufactured in the United States of America

McFarland & Company, Inc., Publishers
　Box 611, Jefferson, North Carolina 28640
　www.mcfarlandpub.com

TABLE OF CONTENTS

Preface   1

Introduction   5

1. Organization of the American Expeditionary Forces   11
2. Training   14
3. Toulon   22
4. Chateau Thierry   37
5. Soissons   95
6. Marbache   113
7. St. Mihiel   118
8. Blanc Mont   133
9. Meuse-Argonne   157
10. Occupation of Germany and Return Home   179

Appendix A. Pedigree of the Division and Its Units   185
Appendix B. Second Division Register   193
Appendix C. Major Awards to 2d Division Personnel   221
Chapter Notes   237
Bibliography   249
Index   255

To my wife,
Jeanne Clark

Preface

Shortly after completing my book about the U.S. Marines of the 4th Brigade, 2d Division, American Expeditionary Force, I began to consider expanding upon the division itself. Whereas the 4th Marine Brigade had no real written history, the published history of the infantry, artillery and assorted support troops was likewise deficient. The only published written history of that arguably "greatest division of the United States Army" is over sixty-five years old and badly dated. Details are sparse, vagueness is rampant (and, consequently, few hurt feelings) and maps, especially, are atrocious. Hopefully, the maps in this volume are somewhat better or at least readable. The Division fought the good fight, arguably better than all the other divisions in France, and it deserves more from history. Besides, it was an anomaly, sometimes called the "Marine Division" because half its infantry was composed of United States Marines. At several early battles many of the junior officers in the Marine Brigade were U.S. Army officers and several of the senior officers of the division and its units were Marines.

Marines have served honorably with the U.S. Army in many wars the nation has been engaged in during its brief history. But this was the greatest concentration up till that time and two Marine general officers were its commander at one time or another, the first and the last.

While working on what became *Devil Dogs: Fighting Marines of World War I*, I naturally had to perform some investigation into what the other "half" was doing. My book, at over 500 pages, was much longer than expected and left little room to tell the entire story of the Division.[1] Part of the story was, for obvious reasons, included but certainly not with enough material to honor those men of so many years before. Consequently I began to collect data and hoped to be able to correct that imperfection.

So, why not write an updated history of that division with all its glories and warts? With an open mind and a desire to propagate the memory of that fine outfit, I have taken pen in hand (actually my computer keyboard) and begun to fill in the blanks. What follows is one man's opinion, and certainly not that of the advocates of the other divisions. I have been accused of being opinionated, so why not continue that honorific and bring down the wrath of reviewers once again?

Here is what that Division did in France and Germany between 1917 and 1919. I have tried to tell its story better than it has been told previously. Heavy concentration is on the "players," the most important element, in my opinion, in describing history. Only the reader can judge the success of this attempt. The details are as accurate as I could make them based upon official documents, but early records of the division are extremely limited. Only the multivolume set *Records of the Second Division*, though generally unavailable, is of value.

Unlike its predecessors—the 1st, 26th Division, and 42d Division, which were formed in the United States—the 2d Division was approved in the United States but took form after its arrival in France. The portion about the 4th Marine Brigade has been derived primarily from my own book, which many people seem to consider the definitive source. The portion about the 9th Infantry benefits slightly from its wartime history. Additional material provided by Rolfe Hillman III, son of a soldier of that fine regiment, has aided me immeasurably. The rest of the Division is mainly derived from the multivolume history of the 2d Division. The latter has been my mainstay and without it this volume would have been near impossible to complete as it is.

Several times during this history the reader might well wonder what happened to some of the units that don't receive heavy coverage, while others do. An example of this will be in the coverage at sector Chateau Thierry. For most of the month of June the Marine Brigade was busy, very busy. The position before the 4th Brigade was considered by the French command to be most important and the Marines were the anointed. Consequently, the 3d Brigade did not advance very much. The division commander and his chief of staff made the decision not to "fight more than one brigade at a time"—rightfully so, I believe. Because of that the Marine activity was much greater than the infantry activity. Their reports are more exciting or interesting, and are much better in describing the war then being fought. Many messages and reports from the 23d or 9th Infantry were dull. These units took casualties, but mainly from the German artillery and especially from gas shells. Very few reports exist for the artillery brigade and the engineers were continually working, by companies, for the various infantry units so had little organizational history in official records. The trains were there but few are even mentioned. The machine gun brigades were always active but, like the engineers, they too were serving the infantry by companies and, consequently, not much appears in official records. But they were right there all the time and fighting the big fight every bit as much as their "ground pounder" comrades were.

Appendix B is titled "Syllabi of the Second Division" and includes, in one place, all the pertinent details of everything that happened to that division by units, as well as most of its commanding officers. It has been retrieved from a postwar publication and, generally, is accurate. Each unit provided its own entry and you can notice the slight differences in format. Also, the few errors have been allowed to remain because correct data exists within the body of the work. An example is when the 3d Brigade entry states that at Chateau Thierry the brigade advanced on 18 July. Of course that is incorrect, and the typist was really referring to Soissons. What the correct date should be is probably 1 July, when the brigade attacked Vaux and its environs. It is effectively a resource for data in one location which may be scattered about throughout the pages.

There are a few implants added. Namely I have added an asterisk following a hero's name when he received a major award for deeds accomplished during that battle. This was usually a Distinguished Service Cross, Army, Marines and Navy, and most of the Marines also received a Navy Cross issued after they returned to the States. As best as I have been able, I have added names of individuals, primarily officers, to the story rather than simply their unit name and number. Unfortunately, enlisted men aren't as well identified. It has been easier to complete more information about the Marines, my collection of data being much more complete, but I've done fairly well with all members of the division where possible. Additions of commanding officers' names are usually in brackets, such as (Capt. Bailey M. Coffenberg). See most other abbreviations listed below. The word "Marine" is generic. It means an individual, or a unit, and on occasion a regiment. Frequently the general term "infantry" also means Marines as well as 3d Brigade soldiers.

The terms used to describe foreign (i.e., French or German) units is generally by their divisions. The definition is always "21st French DI" which means the 21st French Division of Infantry. Some of the following change if taken from a quote, depending upon the source:

Abbreviations and Symbols

Army	(alpha or numeric)	Tenth	or 10th
Corps	(Roman)	XI	
Division	(numeric)	2d	
Brigade	(numeric)	4th	
Regiment	(numeric or alpha)	9th Infantry/Ninth Infantry	
Regiment	(numeric or alpha)	5th Marines/Fifth Marines*	
Battalion	(numeric)	1/6	Bn
Machine Gun Battalion	(numeric)	4th	MG Bn
Company	(numeric or alpha)	18th or	L Co
Field Artillery	(numeric)	12th	FA
General	Gen.		
Lieutenant General	Lt. Gen.		
Major General	Maj. Gen.		
Brigadier General	Brig. Gen.		
Colonel	Col.		

*The usage of the term "Marines" in describing a regiment did not officially come to pass until the early 1930s. Practically everyone, however, including soldiers, sailors, and marines, used that term in France to describe a regiment of marines. Therefore that term is utilized herein.

Lieutenant Colonel	Lt. Col.
Major	Maj.
Captain	Capt.
First Lieutenant	1st Lt.
Second Lieutenant	2d Lt.
Sergeant Major	Sgt. Maj.
First Sergeant	1st Sgt.
Gunnery Sergeant	Gy. Sgt.
Sergeant	Sgt.
Corporal	Cpl.
Private First Class	PFC
Private	Pvt.
American Expeditionary Force	AEF
Center of Resistance	CR
Commanding General	CG
Commanding officer	CO
Company	Co.
Headquarters	Hdqs
High explosives	HE
Infantry Division (foreign)	DI
Skipper	CO of a Marine company (not official but commonly used)
Dates	24 April 1918
Time	1830 (hours)

Many individuals, some friends, and numerous comrades in World War I history, and others, helped me over the years. There are too many to cite all, but I must thank a few by name, alpha: Jerry Beach, Col. Ronald Brown, USMCR (ret), Cmdr Neil B. Carey, USN (ret), Patrick Clark, Stan Clark, Patrice and Caroline Demenais, Col. Walt Ford, USMC (ret), Gy Sgt. Richard "Dick" Gaines, USMC (ret), Joe Gorin, James Hallas, Col. Richard Hemenez, USMC (ret), Col. Douglas V. Johnson, II, USA (ret), Dan Kennedy, Giles Lagin, James T. McIlwain, MD, Patricia Mullen, Peter Meyer, Brad Omanson, Col. Peter Owen, USMC, Sgt. Maj. Robert Singer, USMC (ret), Harry Tinney, and Peter Zischke. There are millions more (thousands? hundreds? lots!) I haven't room for. My thanks to all.

INTRODUCTION

This is the story of a fighting division of the U.S. Army. The members gave themselves the nickname "Second to None." They were that; they were arguably the hardest fighting division in the "Great War." After their early learning experiences they plugged a big hole and blocked the further advance of the best army then in Europe: the Germans. It was their first major effort and its successes, while small in comparison to the events then going on, were, to paraphrase Sam Spade, the stuff that "dreams are made of." The French were overjoyed at seeing their nation spared defeat by young foreigners barely dry behind the ears. For defeat it would have been had the German army managed to continue its advance upon Paris in May and June 1918. At the Chateau Thierry Sector, the 2d Division (Regular) and the 7th Motorized Machine Gun Battalion of the 3d Division (Regular) built the stone wall the German army ran into.

The 2d Division (Regular) was formed along the lines of Pershing's recommendations of 17 July 1917 to AGWAR (Adjutant General, War Department), in Washington. He recommended the composition of American divisions to be "square." Two infantry brigades of two regiments each with one machine gun battalion, and one brigade of artillery with three regiments, two of field guns and one of howitzers. Along with engineers and ancillary services, Pershing's division would be composed of approximately twenty-eight thousand men. The European divisions were generally about fourteen thousand, and much less after suffering severe casualties. The AEF staff that developed this "square division" concept believed that the larger infantry base would provide more than double the firepower and hence have more staying power when the going got rough. They were right, and they were also wrong.

On 20 September 1917 in Washington the army chief of staff approved the formation of the 2d Division (Regulars) and two days later it became official. The division headquarters was opened at Bourmont, France, on 26 October 1917 and Brigadier General Charles A. Doyen, USMC, the senior officer present, assumed command. Two weeks later, the designated officer to command, Major General Omar Bundy, USA, arrived and relieved Doyen. Unlike the other American divisions, the 2d Division was conceived and formed overseas mostly from units already in France. As you will read, the division engaged in a modest training period, and in March entered the trenches in a combat zone for additional training. From then on, especially after they effectively stopped the German drive on Paris in early June 1918, the Division was, until the Armistice, continually engaged in combat with the enemy forces every month. Basically, they were the first American unit to engage the enemy. On the morning of 11 November 1918, when the Armistice became effective, they were still fighting. Of the entire AEF this Division was the most actively engaged during the final year of the war. Proponents of the other great divisions will be shocked at that declaratory statement and react accordingly. Regardless of opinions to the contrary, it is a fact.

What did the Division's opponents, the Germans, and their comrades of the French army think of the 2d Division? We have included some statements by leading figures of both the German and the French armies. The quartermaster-general of the German forces, Erich von Ludendorff, had some positive and some equally negative things to say about the AEF. He quoted the German Supreme Command, in July 1918, as stating: "In general, the fighting value of the American divisions, considering their limited war experience and insufficient training, must be considered as good. When on the defensive, even the youngest troops gave a good account of themselves. The American soldier proves himself, brave, strong, and skillful. Casualties do not daunt him. Nevertheless, leadership is still inferior." About the 2d Division he wrote:

> Of one of these crack units, the 2nd Division ... must be considered as a very good one, perhaps even as a shock unit. The material of the rank and file is very good indeed. They are healthy, physically well-developed men from eighteen to twenty-eight years of age. Their morale is inexhaustible, and they are imbued with a spirit of implicit confidence. Significant are the words of one prisoner: "We kill or get killed." All the attacks in Belleau Wood in July [sic] were executed briskly and without hesitation. Their nerves are still strong and they are well fed.[1]

Ludendorff added some statements about the attack by the 3d Brigade at Blanc Mont that were less favorable:

> The 2nd Division, AEF, is considered a crack unit. This division has been twice cited in the Order of the Day. Its achievements, however, according to our German standard, do not entirely warrant the high opinion with which this unit is generally regarded.[2]

He then criticized the advance by the infantry between St. Étienne and Orfeuil: "the infantry charged briskly, utterly disregarding our artillery fire. However, as soon as the attackers met with resistance in the German trenches, in the form of rifle and machine-gun fire, their charge quickly ceased and they even faced about."

There were many less favorable responses, especially about the later arrived divisions, which admittedly were not prepared to fight upon arrival in France. Ludendorff was, however, unlike Pershing, laudatory about the 26th "YD" and its CG, Clarence Edwards. Other observers were more positive in their exclamations about the 2d Division, especially the French. One, Gen. Eugène Savatier, chief of staff of the French army and later CG of the 34th French DI, mentioned a captured French officer commanding a battalion of Zouaves who said, "What does it matter? Just wait until the Americans get into the fray." Mostly they were laudatory of what the 1st and 2d Divisions performed at Soissons. In fact, so were the Germans. They are reported to have stated about the 1st, Moroccan, and 2d Divisions, "I may state here that the enemy *only at this very spot* succeeded in obtaining results worth while" (emphasis added).³

General Joseph Hellé, chief of staff for Gen. Charles Mangin, said, "What of the Americans? The outcome of the Great War, the very fate of the world depended on them in the early summer of 1918." He mentions the arrival of the 2d Division at Belleau Wood (which he identified as Bois de la Brigade de Marine):

> The 2nd U.S. Division was also to distinguish itself at that date (1st of June)—a fact that did not surprise those who, like myself, had seen it enter the sector. General Harbord, former Chief of Staff of General Pershing, commanded the famous 4th Marine Brigade, the flower of the Corps. The 3rd Brigade (General Lewis) and the 23rd Regiment (Colonel Leroy Upton and Colonel Malone) [sic] were anxious to outdo the Marines.⁴

General Hellé wrote, after the Soissons campaign, "The two American divisions were in marvelous form, and their conduct gained for them the following appreciation in an official (French) document of July 22, 1918. Their offensive spirit is indisputable; it has, in fact, been noted by the enemy in a written document found a month ago, referring to the 2nd D.I.U.S." ⁵

The 2d Division was as good as, or even better than, the Germans and the French believed. Hopefully you, too, will believe when you read about their history in France during 1917–1918.

Before we get into the history of the 2d Division it might be well to sketch out a brief outline of why the division was formed. What happened that caused the United States to send soldiers across an ocean to fight a nation with which we always had a reasonable relationship? In fact it was the first time the U.S. had involved itself in Old World affairs since the Barbary Wars in the late 18th and early 19th centuries. That was basically a naval war, with no U.S. Army and but a few Marines who landed on North Africa. Why was World War I different?

In the late summer of 1914 a man and woman were shot on the streets of Sarajevo in Herzegovina. They were not American, nor French, nor British, nor German, nor Russian; they were Austrian. That, however, was the excuse needed by those nations that were looking for a fight. Austria–Hungary wanted to beat up on Serbia, and this assassination gave them an excuse, because the gunmen were Serbian nationals. Wilhelm, the German kaiser, gave the Austro-Hungarians carte-blanch, in effect saying, "we'll back you one hundred percent." Russia sided with Serbia, a fellow Slavic nation,[6] and France, allied with Russia, was just looking for an excuse to get even with Germany. Russia mobilized even when Germany requested that they cease and desist or Germany must also mobilize. Russia did, then so did Germany and then France. Britain wanted to curtail an overly aggressive German nation whose industry and trade now far exceeded theirs. Additionally, the naval fleet being built to back up the German mercantile fleet was a threat to Britain's dominance on the seas. So Britain jumped into the conflict. Other nations were inveigled to come in, on either side, and it soon became a world war.

The first year was the worst; hundreds of thousands of soldiers on each side were killed, wounded or permanently disabled. France suffered the worst because of an ill-conceived military policy which called for *revanche*— revenge — for their disastrous defeat by Germany in 1870–71 and subsequent loss of two provinces, Lorraine and Alsace, both of which had been part of German states two hundred or so years before and conquered by the French king Louis XIV's army. The way the French army went about getting revenge cost them 25 percent of the entire combatant force just in the so-called Battle of the Frontiers in 1914. They wore beautiful uniforms: Blue coats and bright red trousers. The Germans wore drab green. What a target the French, brave as they were, became for the Maxim guns and the Krupp artillery.[7]

The British came into the war to "save poor little Belgium from the Hun"[8] and they were soon following the lead of the French. Within the first year they too took terrible losses for the small numbers they had engaged. Aggressive advances against machine guns and artillery tore up the formations as they crossed the scarred fields of Flanders. The Germans also suffered severely but soon learned to save manpower by digging in, limiting their advances, and relying heavily upon artillery to destroy their enemies. From August 1914 until the spring of 1917, the loss of soldiers on the various fronts was running into the millions. Austria had mainly faced the Russians and they, too, suffered horrendous casualties along the Eastern Front. Worse even than the French were losses to the czar's army. Italy came into the war in 1915, primarily to take land from Austria. They were soon joining the casualty club, trying to outdo the other warring nations and catching up rapidly. The year 1917 was the major turning point. Russia, in the throes of revolution, dropped out as an active participant. That freed up a multitude of German divisions for the Western Front and Austro-Hungarians to turn on Italy. The French army, commanded by Gen. Robert G. Nivelle, launched a disastrous assault in April 1917 which cost almost as many troops as were lost in 1914. French army morale fell apart and several divisions mutinied. The British launched another attack which helped to subtract hundreds of thousands more from Haig's army. April 1917 was also important because the United States modified its so-called neutrality when President Thomas Woodrow Wilson asked the Congress for a declaration of war against the German empire. The excuse was the German navy's reinstatement of unrestricted submarine warfare.[9]

The Allies had been working toward the goal of getting the United States into the fray since the war began. Finally they managed to drag the completely unprepared U.S. into that foreign war but were shocked to learn that the nation had nothing to fight with. They apparently expected many divisions to just hop over the "pond" and relieve the battered Allied armies. When two separate military missions from France and Britain learned the truth in Washington, they suggested that the U.S. send them men and they would train and feed them into their depleted ranks. That way the Americans could fight as French or British and learn the latest techniques, the same used on the Somme and at Passchendaele, or like Nivelle's plan to "smash the German line at one blow of a gigantic fist—brutal and quick." Instead he smashed the French army, which Haig seemed to be doing to the British army. Some recent American historians have suggested that Pershing, Secretary of War Baker, and President Wilson were at fault for not blending American troops in British and French formations. Those three had many faults but that wasn't one of them. It was the best thing they ever did—keeping Americans under the American flag and control. Otherwise they would have been the spearhead of continual attacks until they, too, were decimated and their morale destroyed.

The French mission, led by Joffre, realized that the American army had nothing physical to offer so they suggested, rather begged, that the Americans send a token force as soon as possible. Baker agreed and by June the brand new 1st Division (Regular) was shipped to France. It was an amalgamation of regular army soldiers and some draftees hastily gathered together to "show the flag." That was about the extent of their abilities at that moment. The unwanted 5th Regiment of Marines managed to get over to France at the same time. Upon the arrival of the Americans, the French were bewildered. They thought that several hundred thousand men would be shipped across, not 20,000. The division landed with all the equipment they had available—Springfield .03 rifles and perhaps a few Lewis guns or outmoded Colt "potato-digger" machine guns, certainly not much more. They paraded in Paris and the French observers were dismayed. Their formation was not much better than civilians strolling down the avenue. Basically, many were just that.

It was obvious that the U.S. could never get its arms requirements up and running fast enough to do any good in France. Another source had to be found. Generally speaking, France became the arsenal and the U.S. government soon had a system in place for purchasing needed equipment. Practically everything the AEF needed was supplied by France, at a price; they, in turn, received most needed raw materials from the United States. Therefore, the 1st Division began to be supplied with the necessaries so they could fight the war and the same thing happened to all other divisions coming over.

The next complete divisions to get across the ocean were, in order, the 26th "YD" Division, 6 September 1917–2 January 1918; 2d Division, 22 September 1917–30 March 1918; and the 42d Division, 18 October 1917–8 December 1917.

If one selects the 5th Marine Regiment as representative of the 2d Division, that puts them second in line. The rest of the divisions followed in no particular order but most came over during 1918. Consequently, those five divisions were the American units showing the flag. In mid–March the 2d Division entered the lines for training with the French near Verdun in Sector Toulon and remained there until mid–May. The 26th Division met the enemy at Seicheprey on 20–21 April 1918. Pershing's premier, and favorite, 1st Division clashed with the Germans at Cantigny on 28 May. Of the AEF, General Bundy's 2d Division was the first unit to seriously engage the enemy and that was in early June. Then it was the big one. All the previous collisions were mere child's play in comparison.

Eventually over forty American divisions made it to France. Some were regular, but most were national guard and national divisions, the latter mainly composed of draftees. Somehow, and with the famous American know-how and some British transports, the U.S. managed to get all those men to France. This feat was accomplished without a serious mishap over 3,000 miles of submarine infested Atlantic Ocean. That was possibly the greatest victory of the war. It was one which the Germans had not expected when they resumed unrestricted submarine warfare in January 1917. And it was the victory that ensured the Allies wouldn't lose the war.

1

ORGANIZATION OF THE AMERICAN EXPEDITIONARY FORCES

The American division developed to fight the war was constructed from results obtained by the so-called Baker Board and its subsequent report, that is, a group led by Col. Chauncey B. Baker, Quartermaster Corps, visited "training camps and other military establishments, both in the zone of the interior and the zone of operations." The latter meant that they also inspected what they considered were important locations in Great Britain and France and their observations of what the U.S. Army should do to improve the administration, organization, supply, training, and transportation of the nascent U.S. Army. The group took six weeks in June and July 1917 and came back with their answers to Maj. Gen. Tasker Bliss, the chief of staff.

While so engaged they visited British and French schools, observed operations at the front, studied organization, regulations, and methods and had intensive discussions with their counterparts. They came back with a detailed study from which the final organization of the AEF was developed. Most, if not all, of their recommendations became part of the final structure. Examples abound but, essentially, one of the most important was that which established the infantry company, and which declared that each company should be composed of 6 officers and 250 men, including a proper proportion of noncommissioned officers. The company was to be formed of:

    4 platoons of 50 men each (200 total)
    a captain's group of 31 (company headquarters)
    combat train group, 5
    field train group, 3
    officers, 6
    1st Sgt., 1
    casualty margin, 10

It was suggested that each company follow the British example: establish a 33 percent margin to remain behind as a base to rebuild upon in the event that the company was shattered in a battle. In actual fact, the Americans would consider 20 percent to be adequate for that purpose.

From the company they would next develop the battalion. The Baker Board recommended four companies for each battalion, which totaled 1,024 officers and men. That number was to become pretty much standard, sans casualties, of course. With the establishment of a three battalion regiment the final numbers became 3,072.

Each regiment would have one machine gun company. Those numbers would be set at 172 men each, with 12 guns, plus 4 spares, in each company. A battalion machine gun unit would total three companies.[1] The board also recommended a regimental supply company of 4 drivers and 10 privates as stable orderlies.

On 10 July 1917 a report authored by Brig. Gen. Hugh A. Drum, based upon a general conference concerning the original report, recommended the following (slightly modified):

> A four division corps with two replacement divisions per corps; a fighting force of 20 divisions, plus replacement divisions; the infantry established in four company battalions, three battalions per regiment and two regiments per brigade, so either could be replaced when necessary. The increase of the infantry company to six officers and 250 men is required in order to reach the absolute minimum effective strength considered necessary by both the French and British.

The combat strength of a division would be 25,484 officers and men including 16,546 infantry. One important point not generally stated or identified was the decision to go to a "square" division. That meant that two brigades would have four, rather than the usual "triangle" of three regiments. The major reasons the decision was made to go that route were because the U.S. Army officers were not experienced in modern war and a larger personnel base would allow consequently longer staying power in combat. Consequently, fewer trained officers were required to manage more men.[2] There would be changes as the war went along but, generally speaking, the final result remained somewhat consistently as shown above.

Later in France it was decided that more machine guns than provided for were necessary for each division. It was finally agreed to provide a machine gun company per regiment and one machine gun battalion of four companies for each brigade. One additional MG battalion would be part of the division. In the 2d Division, it was the 4th Machine Gun Battalion; the 5th was for the 3d Brigade and the 6th for the 4th Brigade. All machine guns were of French manufacture.

Each division had a Brigade of Artillery numbered as the division. The 2d Artillery Brigade had three regiments: the 12th with 75mm field guns, the 15th with 75mm field guns and the 17th with 155 howitzers. All were of French manufacture. Each artillery regiment had 1,337 officers and men including medical personnel. It would later be established that one of the two regiments with light guns (75mm) would service one of the two brigades. Generally, it was the 12th with the 4th Brigade and the 15th with the 3d Brigade. But, like any well ordered military unit, that wasn't always the case.

The other primary fighting organization with the division would be a regiment of engineers. In this case they would be numbered the 2d Regiment of Engineers. The regiment would aggregate 1,098 officers and men in two battalions. Each enlisted man would pack an .03 rifle and the officers the usual pistol. Frequently during this war the 2d Regiment of Engineers would be engaged in infantry work during the day and construction most of the night. They were very highly regarded in both infantry brigades, for good reason.

There were quite a few subordinate service units. Few saw active fighting service but most were of the highest importance in a "modern" war. Though the 2d Military Police Company was usually way back "guarding roads, etc.," they too had casualties, mainly from the enemy's artillery fire. The division had a hospital care group identified as the "2d Sanitary Train" which served the medical needs of the army. The Marines, however, had their usual support provided by the navy. Their "Sanitary Train" was listed as the "Navy Medical Detachment." Six of their number were recipients of the Medal of Honor.

All details of the division formation and organization, plus commanding officers' names of each unit, in chronological order, will be found in the appendix listed as *Syllabi of the 2d Division*. That section has been taken, nearly intact, from the booklet issued while the division was on occupation duty in Germany. I have made minor changes but nothing which alters the original context. Mostly, changes have been made to bring each unit entry into a common style. Since the entries were provided by the clerks of each unit, the variation in each could overwhelm any reader.

2

TRAINING

The 2d Division was officially organized at Bourmont, France, on 26 October 1917. Brigadier General Charles A. Doyen, USMC, assumed command of the Division and on that same date Lt. Col. Logan Feland, USMC, was appointed his chief of staff.[1] The divisional commander designate, Maj. Gen. Omar Bundy, arrived and assumed command on 8 November. He would retain command until, following the Battle of Belleau Wood in the Chateau Thierry Sector, he was reassigned to command a corps. Meanwhile, Doyen would revert to command of the 4th Brigade.

When the first men arrived in June, especially the members of the 5th Marines who were assigned various laboring duties, no training was engaged in for some time. Experiences of the Marines were less than military in nature and caused some morale lowering in the regiment. Organization of the AEF was still not perfect, if it ever became so, and the men were barely half fed most of the time, with huge quantities of food remaining in warehouses. In effect, the 5th Marines were pretty much ignored, even though they were probably the best trained American unit then in France.[2]

Bourmont, the 3d Training Area, became the 2d Division's area when a detachment of the 5th Marines arrived at Damblain on 24 September 1917. Within a few days the 23d Infantry and elements of the 9th arrived from St. Nazaire. Although the infantry went directly to the training area, unfortunately for the Marine units, they were still scattered throughout the AEF area protecting and unloading ships. As an example, the 8th Machine Gun Company of the 5th Marines was sent to protect AEF headquarters at Chaumont. Another company of the regiment, the 67th, was even sent to England to provide service for the incoming American troops there. They would not return to the division until late March 1918. Consequently, they all lost many hours of training in France, if indeed they ever had any.

The Marines weren't alone in their diversion from the training required. The 2d Engineers had been engaged in construction work in divisional areas and it wasn't until 10 December 1917 they were "sent to its proper station in the 2d Division." Later, in March, the 2d and 3d battalions of the 9th Infantry

A shattered French village. What the members of the Second Division saw as they neared the front.

were sent to do guard duty and railroad construction. So they, like the 5th Marines, lost valuable training time. Both battalions would return in time for their assignment to the Toulon front later in the month. Essentially it was the 23d Infantry units and most of the machine gunners that were engaged in training.

Bernard McCrossen described the early days after arrival in France as being a period when the 23d Machine Gun Company, 23d Infantry, was getting used to their Hotchkiss machine guns. They also had their first payday in two months on 9 November and with "Boo Koo" francs everyone who could get away went out on the town for "Oeufs," "Toot Sweet," with "Boo Koo" beer to wash it down." The next morning there were "only fifteen men in the barracks and only half of these turned out for reveille. The other half was unconscious."[3]

At first all training was in the hands of the French army.[4] On 10 October, thirteen French infantry officers were assigned for that task with both the 2d and 26th divisions. Additionally, one French officer was also assigned to liaison, with the infantry, engineers, and one each for the artillery regiments, or eighteen in an American division in all. Brigadier General James G. Harbord, Chief of Staff for the AEF, mentioned in a letter of request to the French Mission to the AEF how well the critique system had worked with the 1st Division. That meant training for trench warfare but the overall concept was soon

Marines in training. A skirmish line firing their rifles.

dropped. Major General John J. Pershing, and many of his staff, had decided some time before that American troops wouldn't fight from trenches as the Europeans had been doing. His determination was for his army to fight "standing up and going forward," maneuver warfare in its most basic design. It was a good idea, but not well thought out at the time. The list of casualties would provoke much criticism.

What was interesting, during this period, was a training memorandum issued by (and possibly prepared by?) Gen. Pétain. In it, mention is made of the instructions in force since 30 December 1917 which discussed operations on stabilized lines, but also advancing on open ground. It stressed mobility and speed over open ground, specific but brief orders to small units; flexible formations and general directions to larger units. The balance of the instructions were equally aimed toward the Pershing idea for open warfare, which meant that the French high command was coming around to the only obvious way to end the war; up and out of the trenches and flexibility in place of previous rigidity.

Colonel Albert J. Bowley, commanding the 17th Field Artillery, was also in charge of artillery training at Le Valdahon, at least in January. His report of events told of his own regiment beginning their firing on 14 January, which

2. Training

"continued daily except Sundays for the rest of the month." He explained that the 15th FA was also so engaged and for the same period. Finally, the "12th Field Artillery arrived at this post January 30, 1918." Another artilleryman tells of how liaison officers with the French were selected. "Who can speak French?" Col. Merrill asked and our hero Kean raised his hand. He later wrote home, "I have been appointed a liaison officer—there only being five in the regiment (12th FA).... I do not know what I am to be liaison with—but all the French officers say it is sure to be a good job," possibly because it would be out of the direct line of fire.[5]

Chaumont made the decision that each of the divisions would undergo a three month training period in the art of war. Training commenced with small unit problems, beginning with platoons and up to company level. Many of the lieutenants and captains were new at the job. Some were newly promoted sergeants, especially in the Marine units; others were recent volunteers whose only qualification was three or four years of college. Consequently, they too were learning. For the most part, they learned quite well and did a decent job of it when their time came.

After the low-level training it was decided that battalions then would

The French training a 75mm battery of 2d Division artillery.

interact with French divisions in a quiet sector. The infantry would gain the absolutely necessary experiences of nearness to an enemy that trench warfare in a quiet zone could provide. It was also relatively safe. Artillery would train separately, with their newly acquired French guns at fields prepared for gunfire. They would also be trained in how the French were using said guns along a front, methods of firing, tactical usage and handling, and actual firing to develop skills. When infantry and artillery had completed that second month they would then reassemble and in the third month train as a complete division.

During late January and the month of February the concentration of the 2d Division, less artillery, was completed. By 13 March the division, still less artillery, moved to the area of the French Second Army, near Sommedieue, perhaps a dozen miles southeast of Verdun-sur-Meuse. That devastated city was still a bastion of French determination and courage. This was the area in which the division would begin and end its trench experiences. Fortunately, it was now a relatively quiet area.

Meanwhile, U.S. Army schools were in the process of being established, in both divisional and army corps. These schools were for officer training, non-commissioned officer training and others that were important for the style warfare to be engaged in. Army schools were developed for training staff officers, officer candidates and specialists of various kinds. All were developed with the concept of fixing and controlling the tactical doctrine agreed upon, maneuver warfare, and all were considered important. Few of the British and French senior officers working in tandem with the Americans agreed with the decision and attitude of the Americans. As far as they were concerned, they had been fighting the war for three plus years and were more knowledgeable as to how to defeat the Germans, even though, so far, they hadn't been able to. The attitude of many of the Americans was, "If so, why haven't you?" General Pershing made the rifle a near holy relic in the hands of an American soldier. In fact he was quoted as saying that "the most dangerous weapon in the world is a Marine and his rifle." This was hardly likely, with machine guns and artillery causing most deaths. But the leadership of the AEF was less than prepared. Fortunately some of the junior staff officers were.

There were pros and cons to both philosophies. Men, who had relied upon as much cover as was available, couldn't (or wouldn't) easily get up out of moderately safe trenches and go straight toward a line of an army pouring automatic fire at them, with artillery shells falling all about. That style was retrograde back to 1914 and the Allies were still doing the same thing. What Pershing was calling for was to not get under partial cover in trenches but to go forward under protection of all available cover and fire support. The Germans had begun engaging in alternative fighting, and were most frequently successful when they did. They called it *Sturm*, or assault. It was developed to get away from the horrors of static trench warfare, but for some reason the Allies paid little attention to what began happening to them because of it.[6] Bands of German soldiers, including a few officers, would assault an enemy position, usually a trench, and often overwhelm the men defending the position. The assault would be as silent as possible and as limited in time as was possible in order to reduce the danger of counterattack. The intent was not to gain ground so much as to disturb the enemy lines and prepare them for a major attack. Essentially, Pershing was more forward thinking than Haig or Foch, and later, in 1918, both Allied nations would begin to see the light and also begin to change their tactics.

At the time, the Americans were basically promoting pretty much the same thing as the Germans, but entirely independently, without, it appears, any connection to what the Germans were doing. Essentially it was a warfare that relied heavily on individuals and their independent actions. That was not something that Europeans generally could accept. Rigid discipline was still being enforced because they believed that was the only way you could control an army. That the German army was promoting individuality was a fascinating alternative to the common concept of their inbred rigidity.

One of the primary problems of the trench mentality was the difficulty in getting men to move out when they were under modest protection. Getting them "over the top" was difficult, but getting them to move as far forward as desired, under terrible fire, was extremely difficult. In maneuver warfare the troops frequently would find cover but that might be illusory and subjected to concentration of enemy fire anyway. Consequently, they would move, perhaps hoping for better cover. In any case, the idea of digging in was alien to Americans; besides being too much work, they didn't like the idea anyway. Pershing was right, the end of the war came because everyone got up and went forward when the Germans began to fall back. However, many Americans would pay the supreme price to make his concept successful. That was, however, because of the lack of skills in carrying the ideas forward in the AEF.

Unlike the infantry, the U.S. Marines were having little problem with their men in France. Even their relative newcomers, all of whom had gone through boot camp, had been exposed to Marine discipline and esprit, and that effectively eliminated much of the difficulty. There were the occasional troublemakers but, as a whole, the preparations before going to France had sufficiently instilled in the men what was expected of them. But it was not so with the infantry. Many, even those in the so-called regulars, had little discipline instilled in their basic training. Partly it was the lack of experienced trainers and partly the inexpert system used in the rapidly expanding army. Whatever the problem, the 2d Division infantry units were experiencing growth pains before leaving the U.S. and especially after arrival in France.

Some of the men, mainly draftees in the 9th Infantry, were becoming more difficult, as were the conditions. Especially arduous was 3/9. For some reason the officers had been unable to effectively discipline the many foreigners, most of whom were still having difficulty with the English language. Although most of the men were barely obeying daily orders, others were stretching the thin patience of their leaders, especially that of the regular officers. For some reason that situation continued for some months and took some overtime exercises to weed out the problems.

After the Division's arrival in France, the problems seemed to be expanding rather than settling down. It became so difficult that Gen. Bundy became personally embroiled. As a long-term regular army officer, he was particularly angered that his officers couldn't seem to control the men. Obviously there couldn't be a blanket court-martial for the malcontents. For some reason he decided that the Marine Brigade wasn't having trouble so he investigated and began to make plans accordingly.

The Marines in France were top-heavy in field ranks. Majors were plentiful and unoccupied battalion commands were scarce. There were several Marine majors who had managed to get "over the pond" without combat commands. Two of them, Maj. Harry G. Bartlett and Maj. Hiram I. Bearss, were available for battalion command in the AEF. The former was most recently in Haiti chasing the Caco bandits and had been a Marine officer since 1905. Bearss was a man of longer service, entering the Corps as a 2d Lt. in 1898. He was a legend in the Corps and had a recommendation in the Philippines for the Medal of Honor, which was eventually bestowed in 1934. He was a fighter in an organization noted for that quality. And he was tough, real tough.

Both men were relatively free of command responsibilities and Bundy obtained the services of both for his troubled 9th Infantry. Bartlett went to 1/9 and made a fine reputation for himself as battalion commander. Bearss went to 3/9 and immediately angered officers and men. The story is told in his biography of how he trained them, officers and men, until they were ready to assassinate *him* instead of the Germans. Expecting the usual German style of attack, Bearss turned almost exclusively to night training. He was, of course, expecting *Sturmtruppen* and was well aware that these officers and men would be helpless before such an attack. For weeks he trained them, including forming raiding parties against each other. As a result of many complaints, Gen. Bundy went to see Bearss and asked him to describe what he was getting into and how he could solve the problem. Bundy warned him that it appeared to be a mutiny in the making in 3/9.

Somehow Bearss survived, as did most of 3/9. His training was skillful preparation for what was then happening on the Western Front. The Germans were trying and perfecting their new tactics. Hiram was well aware of what they were doing and he was preparing 3/9 for their moment in the sun. That moment would come while the division was at the Toulon Sector and would generate commendations for the Division, Regiment and the officers and men of 3/9 from the likes of John J. Pershing himself.[7] When Bearss was transferred most of the officers of 3/9 came to him, hats in hand, with profuse thanks and apologized for doubting him.

Like most of the Division, the engineers were basically fabricated from new

2. Training

Map 1. The Second Division zones in France. This map represents the Second Division zones of occupation while in France, except for a few locations where the division was in training or in rest billets. The asterisks indicate a general location where the division fought each of its five major battles in France. They are the *Aisne-Marne Defensive (Belleau Wood); the Aisne-Marne Offensive (Soissons); St. Mihiel; Blanc Mont;* and the *Meuse Argonne.* The dates are approximate periods in which the division was engaged in battle. The large, bold line indicates the approximate location of the German and the Allied forces at the beginning of June 1918.

men, including numerous draftees. This was brought about primarily because the companies expanded from about 160 men each to the required 250 men of the Pershing divisions. Most of this happened after arrival in France when 400 replacements arrived from the 116th Engineer Replacement Regiment. The 2d Engineers later complained that their training in France was pretty much limited to the post-construction period beginning in mid–January 1918. From 14 January, when the entire regiment was assembled at Bourmont, until they left for the Toulon Sector, it was five weeks of infantry training and little else. That was a good thing, too, because they would become important helpmates to all the infantry regiments during the bad times ahead. Yet, the official history complained that the newer men were lacking in any training, especially in rifle firing. The 1st Battalion was detached from the regiment on 27 February 1918 and sent to join the 1st Division (Regulars) in the Toul area. This was done to support the 1st Division engineers constructing various sawmills and the like in the rear areas. The battalion remained in that assignment until 9 May when it rejoined the 2d Division near Bar-le-Duc. The engineers later became an important asset to the infantry units of the Division, and required training in rifle usage skills, which some of them lacked. Somehow, someplace along the line, they picked up the necessaries and were lauded by Marines and Infantrymen.

3

TOULON

General Vandenberg, commanding the French X Corps, wrote that he was prepared to welcome the American 2d Division to his zone for a period of one month's training. On 14 March he ordered that the division spend its time with three French divisions in the lines, the 33d, 34th and 52d DI (Divisions of Infantry). This area has been commonly termed the Verdun Sector but in reality it was officially the Toulon Sector. Why it had that name isn't known; there being no town of that name nearby.¹ However the name came about, it was a bona fide front line position where the Americans would be exposed to German fire. Better yet, it was, as the French say, "a bon sector." The enemies facing each other weren't rocking the boat; no one intentionally shot at the other side. The Americans, however, would soon change all that, upsetting the German and the French by their aggressive behavior. That was, however, why the Americans were in France — to finish the war.

Rail movement for the 2d Division began from Bourmont on 13 March and the last train left Le Valdahon on 21 March with the big guns and division personnel. On 16 March division headquarters was established at Sommedieu with the ammunition depot at Heippes² and railhead at Suippes. The latter town was quite a distance from the sector and would be the site of a very important campaign fought by the division in October.

Movement of a division was trying. The train personnel all spoke French, of course, and were under French orders. There were American Railway Transport officers who were technically in command and fortunately this move went relatively smooth. Of course, the going was not the most pleasant for the men, who were crowded into the "*40 hommes*" but at least without the "*8 chevaux.*" Officers managed to ride in a coach, however, and were somewhat less uncomfortable. Actually, the cars were designed for 40 Frenchmen, who overall were a bit smaller than most American males. The cars were extremely uncomfortable for the taller Americans. Joe Rendinell, 97th Co, 3/6, complained that his "legs were so numb I could not stand up because 3 Marines laid on them." Somehow he figured out how to make it to another car with "8 mules & 5 of us Marines." From then on, for him it was better, more room and with straw for comfort. One private seeing the lettering for the first time commented that he didn't know the teams but it was a rotten score. Another man from M Co., 23d Infantry, later described the horrible and slow train ride from Bourmont to their destination. He was one of several to note that the inhabitants of the very slow train were able to hop off and back on again with new greenery to wear for Saint Patrick's Day.

Men of the division began arriving at Dugny and Souilly on 14 March. The heavier than usual rail traffic was noted by the ever watchful German observers and the station at Dugny was heavily shelled on the 15th and 16th. Dugny is a town located just south of Verdun and right on the Meuse and consequently very few miles from the German lines. All subsequent trains went instead to Souilly. The 23d MG Co was one of the first arrivals at Dugny. From there, they were marched to Genicourt, a distance of about 6 miles, in the rear of the third line of trenches. They remained there for three days, always out of sight of the German planes flying constantly overhead. They left Genicourt at dusk on 17 March, "St. Patrick's Day," shouted Sgt. Bernard McCrossen, and headed to the front lines.[3]

Not satisfied with an initial learning experience, shortly after arrival two men from Co A, 1/23, went out after a German sniper that had been bothering their company. At the German wire they ran into a hornet's nest. Two dozen Germans came out after them but the infantrymen made their way back under cover of Chauchat fire. Nonetheless, the game was beginning to get heavy. Both sides had requested artillery support and shells were dropping all over the place. Private Stanley Dobiez of A Co., 1/23, remained in his outpost with his Chauchat. He refused to fall back, becoming the first man of the division killed in action.

Another diarist was Cpl Harry F. Collins, probably a private when this entry was written, and a member of the 82d Co., 3/6:

> March 15: Reach town near Verdun front. Roofs and walls caved in by shell fire. Marched about seven or eight miles from town. Stopping in a French camp for a few days. French soldiers very friendly. Roar of cannons very plain from here. Front is about four miles distant. German aeroplanes sail over camp. Fired at by French anti-aircraft guns.[4]

His entries were always brief but his experiences were common for each of the men arriving in the area. Another man who kept a diary and converted it to a brief but excellent book after the war was Martin Gus Gulberg.[5] Sergeant Gulberg was with the 75th Co., 1/6, and was a survivor. He describes a "funny little incident" during an inspection before they left Bourmont. It seems that "it was St. Patrick's Day and, of course, our Irish blood had to celebrate." Some, perhaps many, of the men had loaded their canteens with *vin rouge* before falling in and the inspecting lieutenant smelled someone's breath. At first he accused Gulberg and then found out that "the Irishman" was innocent, but nearly everyone else wasn't. He and his company were satisfied and pleased when upon their arrival at "the railhead of Suilly [sic]" the French Red Cross, more civilized than their American counterparts, gave them coffee "laced with rum." Upon arrival that evening at Sommedieue they were well greeted by the French soldiers. Not too long afterward they managed to gather together some bacon grease to fry their hardtack, stole some potatoes to French-fry, bought *vin rouge*, and had a splendid repast.

The divisional artillery were also moving up. One of the best descriptions of life with an artillery regiment is that written by Robert W. Kean, he of the 15th FA.[6] Their trip to Souilly was slightly different than the lowly infantry. Their French 75mm field guns were too heavy to lug; consequently, they also moved by train, and their enlisted men traveled "40 & 8." This trip, he and his advance party left on 18 March and arrived the next morning at Lemmes, which was near Souilly. From there they went to a "well-built French rest camp" near Ancemont. He and the rest of the advance party were to prepare for the arrival of the main body due on 20 March, the following day. "It was a pleasant set-up ... attractive little huts ... a little gardening ... but the camp was swarming with rats." He went on to describe his unhappy experiences with the brazen little creatures who ate all his chocolates. Next came the description of the various battery's positions in the Bois de Bannoncourt. He was with C Battery at this time and all were on the west side of the Meuse.

The 3d Battalion, 17th FA, arrived at Lemmes on 20 March and soon after marched to the "shell-torn little village of Villers-sur-Meuse." According to the unit "history" they identified themselves as making their first appearance "on the battle-front" as the second battalion of the 17th, Batteries D, E, and F.[7] Upon arrival on 21 March, Battery A was located at Camp Nacrillon " some three or four kilometers in the rear." They told us in their brief history that the first shot fired in anger was on 1300 on the afternoon of 25 March. Sergeant Walter F. Graham commanded the firing piece, Cpl Roman J. Szopinski was the gunner and Pvt. Thomas A. Greenwood, Jr., was "Number 1."[8]

The 2d Battalion of the 2d Engineers traveled to the *Toulon* Sector with the rest of the Division in mid–March. Company D, however, lost three men to German shell-fire while they were engaged in constructing machine gun nests on the front line. These were the regiment's first casualties. Other construction projects included dugouts or deep shelters of one kind or another. The work was mostly hand labor since equipment was not available in the trenches. The men worked eight hour shifts. Several shifts were in daylight and consequently dangerous. Auxiliaries, as they were called, were gathered from nearby French or American infantry. Those men usually did the bull-work of bringing up materials or removing earth. The 1st Bn, 2d Engineers, was still temporarily employed with the 1st Division down south of Nancy.

As can be seen from the area map, the positions of the French at Toulon were covered by two armies, the Eighth covering the St. Mihiel Sector and the French Second Army beginning at Maizey, north to the fortress town of Verdun and beyond. This latter was the Toulon Sector, and the French general, Auguste Hirschauer, commanded. In his command the X Corps occupied the right flank, from Maizey to Verdun. This was where the 2d Division would reside. The French held the northern flank of the St. Mihiel Salient stretched in, generally, a northeast direction to les Eparges. From there it curved northward to Haudiomont then toward Verdun and the Meuse River, where the Allied line took a decided westward turn. The river ran northward behind the position six or seven miles to the west. It protected the southern flank of Verdun and the northern flank of the salient. At the time, the section was called the Côtes [hills] de la Meuse (and perhaps still is). The salient had been held by the Germans since the early days of the war. It was seen by Pershing and his staff as the likely spot for the Americans to hold the line. In fact, almost immediately after their initial settlement in France, they began a plan to retake it.

Upon arrival of the 2d Division, each sector was held by a French division; the 33d DI held the north end of Toulon; the 34th DI held Rupt and the 52d DI held Troyon. The agreement was for a battalion from each infantry regiment, including Marines, to relieve a French battalion and to occupy that portion of the line on a rotating basis. The Americans were to have some time to reconnoiter the territory they were to hold before relieving their French comrades. The 5th and 6th Marines, supported by 1/12 and 2/12, were positioned with the 33d DI in the Toulon Sector in the north. The 23d Infantry, supported by 1/17 and 2/15, were placed in the Rupt Sector, with the 34th DI. At the bottom along the northern line of the salient was the 9th Infantry in the Troyon Sector. They were supported by 1/15, less a battery, plus 2/17 and the 2d Trench Mortar Battery.

The location to be held by the 3d Brigade, 2d Division, was in fact divided into two subsectors. One was called Rupt, after Rupt-en-Woëvre, a small town in the central part, and the other Troyon for a village on the river. Rupt was further divided into subsector Ranzières, center of resistance (CR) Riga. Troyon into subsector Rouvrois, CR Coralie. Those troops along the Troyon Sector were close to the river and the divisional artillery was forced to locate on the west side.

The 4th Brigade's area was also divided into two subsectors: Bonchamp, CR Mont-sous-les-Côtes, and Les Éparges, with CR at Montgirmont. The Plains of Woëvre were opposite the 2d Division but under German control. Later, after taking St. Mihiel Salient, that sector would become a central part of the American plan. It would allow the American army to drive hard into the plain and onward to take important rail lines and mines in that area, including, especially, the city of Metz. However, Marshal Haig managed to throw a monkeywrench into that concept and the bloodshed of the Meuse–Argonne Campaign resulted. (See Meuse-Argonne.)

As soon as the soldiers and Marines began filling their new positions, it became obvious to even the lowest ranked man that something was wrong. The

The Bois de Rupt, near the devastated city of Verdun.

space allotted to the American companies was much too small. The twice as large American formations were over-filling the space left by the smaller French formations. In fact, they were packed in like the proverbial sardines. Among other things, indirect shell-fire on their trenches would cause more casualties and create havoc; therefore immediate plans were promulgated at Division to reduce the excess numbers. The Germans actually made the plans for Division. They began a major offensive against the British positions on the Somme on 21 March. That forced the redirection of some French divisions to proceed north to bolster their Allies. The French leaving the Toulon Sector meant great vacancies and American men needed to fill the gaps. The 2d Division was considered practically good enough to hold the line. It didn't quite come to that but the Division did take over more territory and assumed the appropriate responsibility.

With the departure of the French relieving units, the X corps lost the 34th DI, and the corps on its left lost the 131st DI, forcing it to take over Moscou Sector, extending its left boundary from Eix by five miles. The 52d DI CG was asked to extend his lines northward incorporating part of Rupt. This enlargement of the Troyon Sector caused the 9th Infantry to send a second battalion into the line, taking over the Bizerte CR. The same thing happened to the 23d; they spread out and took control of Maria Louise CR. The 5th Marines and a French regiment moved in to take over the Moscou Sector. That would be headquarters for the 4th Brigade. The 5th and 6th Marines and several French regiments spread out to fill the gaps required by the adjustment. By 2 April the two Marine colonels, Neville for the 5th and Catlin for the 6th, were each given command of subsectors. On 2 April, Brig. Gen. Charles A. Doyen issued 4th Brigade Field Order No. 1, which described the moves that his marines would take to occupy their new positions. The 4th was to take control over subsectors Moulainville (5th) and Ronvaux (6th), with two battalions in line and one in reserve.

A few days later both Malone of the 23d and Upton of the 9th were also assigned command over their respective regiments and the positions they occupied. The French senior officers were forced to recognize that, though they were new to the front, these were regular U.S. Army and Marine officers with years of command experience who could be expected to perform satisfactorily.

On 23 March, 2d Lt. Moses E. Taylor, E Co., 2/9, was mortally wounded leading a patrol. His body was left behind and the Germans identified him as an American.[9] This was the way most intelligence about recently arrived units was gathered. But as late as 24 April the Germans still didn't have common knowledge that Americans were in the line opposite them. For some reason, possibly because of the uniforms and especially the helmets, they were sure it was British troops opposite them. The Germans were convinced that the Americans would not easily, if at all, make their way across the German submarine controlled Atlantic Ocean. How wrong they were.

During this period the Division personnel participated in the usual activities required in trench warfare. Conditions in the trenches were unpleasant, to say the least. Everyone who spent time in them complained, then and many years later. Captain Roy C. Hilton of the 9th Infantry MG Co. provided the following description of daily life:

> The trenches, being prepared for long service, were supplied with duck boards for the floors and sand bags for the parapets.... Doors to dugouts opened into the trenches and were well reinforced as were the trenches themselves with timber. The dugouts were constructed to accommodate from ten to fifty men.... Bunks were built with one section above another ... all dugouts were infested with lice, better known to Americans as "cooties." There was difficulty in bringing up food and supplies through the trenches.... [10]

Each night patrols would go out into "No Man's Land" and usually beyond the American wire. Frequently there was action, sometimes firing, sometimes grenades thrown; other times artillery or trench mortars laid their progeny out across the front. Usually the men were out there against their will. The Germans were always on guard and being on patrol meant you were always subject to death or wounding. But even those men on patrol dreamt of being back in their nice, safe, lice-ridden bunks with all their warm clothes on.

Sergeant McCrossen had some helpful hints as to how to "soften" the advent of cooties. One suggestion was to take off all clothing and explode a hand grenade among them. Another was to sprinkle all clothing with salt: "Then get to the nearest pond and spread garments.... In a short time, owing to the heavy feast of salt, the little beasts will make a mad dash for the water to quench their thirst." Then, he emphasized, one must grab the clothing and "beat it before the little darlings return." It isn't clear that he successfully tried either, but he acknowledged that he was given a shower and had his clothing deloused on the second day out of the lines.

"Life in the trenches is real hell," so said Gulberg. He described duty as being "two night watches, half the platoon being on from 6:00 P.M. to midnight, and the other half from midnight to daybreak." He told of constant artillery duels and gas attacks. Nightfall brought patrols into enemy country, everyone cutting enemy wire, establishing "listening posts" and making great efforts to capture prisoners without losing any to the Germans, who were also very active.

It was early spring and still cold on many days and most evenings. As was usually the case, the AEF was barely able to supply ammunition, let alone warm clothing. Food was another commodity in very limited supply. In Warren Jackson's[11] memoir his most common complaint was about the lack of food. When he was on guard duty, back in the rear, he wondered why so much food was available in the warehouses but so little for the troops.

Corporal Frank W. Anderson, M Co., 3/23, wrote in his memoirs about how his battalion was moving up to the lines after dark on 2 April:

> My company started for the front line trenches, Captain Joe Green in command and Lieut. Alband in charge of my platoon.... Of course there was mud; there always is.... Three miles from the front lines the mud became deeper.... When we were a half mile from the reserve trenches, shrapnel came over and barely cleared the column, bursting and throwing their deadly steel balls into the woods by the side of the road.[12]

He further describes how the French soldiers guided the neophytes in to their positions and "showed us our bunks" in the dugouts. The described conditions had been the same for all soldiers, of each army, since the armies went into trenches back in 1914 and 1915.

Jackson's memoir of being a Marine in 1/6 goes into more detail about everyday life in the trenches near Verdun than is commonly seen. His observations are exceedingly perceptive and descriptive. He goes into especial detail about one issue that concerned him mightily: food, and the lack of it. The description of how the troops went about bringing the chow forward and under what conditions is worthy of a look. Men were selected at random, so he thought, and given the unenviable task of traveling many miles to get the goods. After obtaining the rations, they then had the agony of bringing them back a distance through twisting trenches, to the front lines. The rations were in large cans hooked onto long poles, which two men would carry. The cans would swing and the "slum," which it was usually, spilled over. Twists and turns made

A Sixth Marine dugout behind the lines near their Toul Sector.

the trip even more difficult. The full cans would be half empty upon arrival and the bearers would be cursed by the always underfed men. The cold food would then be dealt out by an always ravenous sergeant who managed to get several helpings for himself. In those days, sergeants were usually physically bigger than most of the men. That helped them when the hungry men would curse and threaten the sergeants with bodily harm.

This being the first time the American men had been up front, at first they seemed genuinely surprised at the condition of what had once been villages. Shell-fire over the years had managed to destroy everything above the front steps of every building. An occasional shell of a building, one wall or less, would stand out but they were few and far between. It wasn't long before the men grew accustomed to the devastation and accepted it as normal.

Most memorists, however, complained of rats, rats, and more rats. Rendinell commented, "These rats are terrible. We can't lay down without them starting in to nibble at our legs. They are nice and fat from eating dead Frenchmen & Germans. Now they want American meat. Those babies will find it pretty tough, I bet."

General Doyen made trips around his front-line positions, an eight mile circuit, every day. Undoubtedly Gen. Peter Murray, and after him Gen. Edward M. Lewis, of the 3d Brigade, did the same thing. It wasn't easy. They were older men and the going, especially in that rainy season, made the trip extremely difficult. The mud was always slippery and ice pockets caused many slips and sliding for everyone. Additionally, the weather was very cold that winter, making any exposure difficult and unpleasant for everyone, regardless of age or rank. According to one Marine reporter, some company officers continually remained below in their relatively warm dugouts.[13] The men grumbled but little could or would be done to correct the leadership failures. A continuing factor that never seemed to have been corrected for the Marine Brigade, and most probably for everyone else in the AEF, was the constant hunger. Men ate the modest emergency rations that were "to be eaten when hungry" because, as one said, he was always "in a delirium of hunger." Some were court martialed for the offense, but nevertheless, eating the rations continued all during the war. Emergency rations were to be eaten in an emergency and every day was such for the men in line. Corporal Harry B. Field of the 18th Co., 2/5, blamed the problem on the distance the food had to travel in order to be eaten. Other complainers described the cooks in the rear area as being more concerned with their own skins than with the bellies of the men. Memoirists have been especially unkind to the cooks and bakers: "always slum for food and gun-cotton for bread" was the common complaint.

Being in trenches and in such close human proximity during the two months' experience caused personal differences to fester and in some cases explode. Officers and men occasionally died from "friendly fire." Fights broke out and a common occurrence was cursing each other and especially the army (or Marines). Several memoirs written by men who were obviously malcontents make it clear that not everyone was enthusiastic about the war at this point. Several hated everyone, especially their officers. One had nothing good to say about his. According to him, they were all cowards, or worse. Some were, of course, but most weren't. They were like everyone else, scared for their own well-being. Patriotism was just a word by this time. Many of the "patriots" who had joined up at the declaration of war were wishing they could turn their decisions upside down, or inside out.

Easter Sunday was on 31 March that year and the food, for the officers at least, was "bon." The officers in 3/6 had gotten together and bought some local turkeys for themselves. Several of the enlisted Marines stole one or two. Cpl William A. Sweeny kindly fed the cook a bit of *vin rouge* while Rendinell burnt his fingers as he swiped a bird from the oven. The latter rejoiced in telling of this great victory over cooks and officers.

Reports dated 7 April for the one day of 6–7 April described how the 9th Infantry and the 23d Infantry were both subjects of German attention the previous twenty-four hour period. The enemy raided "without result" the 9th and the same night attempted to discourage the 23d but both attacks were broken up by rifle fire. On the morning of the 6th, platoon leader 1st Lt. William D. Meyering* of the 23d Infantry took effective methods to defeat an enemy attack

3. Toulon

The trenches occupied by members of the Second Division in the Toul Sector.

upon his positions. He handled his men well until he was wounded and was forced to seek medical attention, walking safely through an enemy bombardment and machine gun fire to a dressing station.

The greatest disaster at Toulon, insofar as the 2d Division was concerned, happened on 13 April. The 74th Co, of 1/6, had successfully repulsed a German raid on their position near the town of Trésauvaux. There were four casualties to the Germans and Marines each. However, soon after, when the company went into reserve at Camp Fontaine about a mile behind the lines, the German artillery launched a heavy load of gas shells. This happened just after the exhausted men arrived and bedded down. Not many of them managed to put on their gas masks and the casualty numbers were horrific. Basically the company was all but wiped out. All the officers were evacuated in serious condition as were at least two hundred twenty of the men. Later, forty of them succumbed, but most of the others were finished as far as active service was concerned. Warren Jackson describes the condition of several of his friends of that company who were returned to active duty and his description isn't kind to the doctors who released them nor the officers who accepted them.[14]

The infantry soon recognized what the German *Sturmtruppen* were able to do: hit anyplace at anytime because of their mobility. Colonel Paul B. Malone, and probably his headquarters staff of the 23d Infantry, prepared and submitted a plan to Division to organize similar special units of independent assault battalions of six companies each. The plan was approved and Capt. Otto F. Lange, a German speaker, was designated to command nine officers and one hundred fifty men. The detachment was composed of officers and men culled from the entire regiment. They spent six days rehearsing and on the night of 21 April they went over. They raided an enemy trench which unfortunately was empty, and the only benefit derived was the training.[15]

During this period the Germans intensified their artillery action along the line. Both the 9th and the 23d regiments were subjects of their attention. The commander of French artillery sent a warning down the line that the infantry could expect a *Sturmtruppen* assault very soon. On the morning of 14 April, at approximately 1245, the Germans launched the largest demonstration against the Division since the Division's arrival in the area. It was against the 9th Infantry and both the 2d and 3d battalions were on line. That previous day of the 13th had seen heavy enemy artillery activity which portended a night raid by the *Sturmtruppen*. Sure enough, that night, what Lt. Col. Hiram I. Bearss, USMC, had been training 3/9 to expect happened, and they were fully prepared.[16] Over the Germans came, dressed in French uniforms, as Hiram said they would be, and yelling "Gas!" in English. The American soldiers responded with what Bearss expected and smashed the German attackers. Companies L and I even surprised themselves. There were reports back at regimental headquarters that both companies had been wiped out. They weren't, they gave back as good as they got and in some cases, better. They lost a few men wounded and some captured but when the Germans tried to exit the area, the artillery shelling made the passage back extremely difficult and most of the Americans that were prisoners escaped. One of I Co.'s privates, Charles Schmitz,* with his Chauchat, advanced through the German forces, found five of the enemy in a shell hole and killed or wounded all. Captain Henry H. Worthington,* of Hdqs Co., 3/9, held his men together during the major part of the enemy assault even though heavily outnumbered, and inflicted severe casualties upon the Germans. Even though he was severely wounded, the men drove the Germans out of the trenches and back where they came from. The captain was forced to evacuate but not until the enemy had been dispersed. Worthington paid the ultimate price for his aggressiveness and courage.

The losses to the 9th Infantry were seven killed, 3 officers and thirty-six men wounded, nineteen 9th Infantry men plus one medical officer and six hospital attendants were captured. The German loss was one officer and sixty men killed plus eleven captured. The Germans managed to retrieve all their wounded. This was the first time most of the 9th had been subjected to hostile action by experts and they fared well. Rightfully so, they were quite thrilled with themselves. They were cited as a unit in Division orders. After that, Hiram Bearss could do anything with them. He became their beloved "Hiking Hiram." Beginning on 5 May Hiram was signing off on the regimental War Diary in place of Leroy Upton. He was, for at least until 25 May, tem-

Burying division dead behind the lines at the Toul Sector.

porarily in command of the Ninth Infantry. But sometime after their arrival in the Chaumont-en-Vixen area, old Hiram was transferred once again, but remained within the division. This time he went to the 6th Marines.

In the meantime, the Marines were also hit by aggressive German infantry. On one patrol, on the evening of 22 April, the 18th Co., 5th Marines, was rushed by superior numbers of the *Sturmtruppen*. Corporal Wolcott Winchenbaugh* displayed exceptional coolness before and after his patrol leader, intelligence officer 2d Lt. August L. Sundval, U.S. Army, one of many serving with the Marines, was badly wounded and being dragged home by the Germans. Winchenbaugh grabbed the body of Sundval, pulled him free, and, dragging and half carrying him, successfully reached his own lines.[17]

As would be expected, both infantry brigades, including medics, machine gunners and engineers, took the daily brunt of trench living and unpleasant exchanges with the Germans. However, the artillery rained shells upon their enemy and received counter-battery in kind, suffering the usual casualties. The 17th's howitzer fire was directed toward the second and third line German trenches whereas both the 12th and 15th FA fired flat trajectory at the nearest

From left, Maj. Holland M. Smith, Col. Charles A. Doyen, CO, 4th Brigade, Lt. Col. Frederick Wise, CO, 2d Bn, 5th Marines, at Toul.

enemy machine gun nests or other obvious strong points. This activity continued until it was determined that the Division had experienced war and could be pulled out of the lines to refit and recover. The dates had been planned well in advance and the move out began in mid–May. Various units within the Division were relieved by French units. By this time, the officers and men of the Division were proud to have served at Verdun but happy to be getting out of the damp and muddy conditions in trenches.[18]

French Gen. Eugène Savatier pointed out upon the relief of the 2d Division that when they had arrived the sector was quiet. But upon their arrival, all that changed: "They were irrepressible! If the night relief took place without a hitch and in the deepest silence, as soon as the sun was high enough some of the doughboys, who had no place in the front line, wanted absolutely to see and kill the German. They climbed the highest trees and began to fire on the enemy sentries or on the platoons which ... they could see running between the first and second line trenches."[19]

The senior-most officers of the Division were changed during this period, especially the brigadier generals. Murray of 3d Brigade was replaced by Lewis on 7 May; the day before, Harbord replaced Doyen in the 4th Brigade; on the 20th of April, Irwin of the 2d FA Brigade was briefly replaced by Cruikshank, then again by Chamberlaine on 11 May. At regiment, on 5 May, Lt. Col. Thomas E. Merrill turned over command of the 15th FA to Lt. Col. Joseph R. Davis. Last, but certainly not least, the new divisional chief of staff was Col. Preston Brown, who had relieved Col. Tebbetts on 6 April. The latter was competent but, unlike Brown, less attention-getting.

Each unit left their positions as they were relieved, some heading back to Bar-le-Duc, others to waiting trains, most to eventually arrive in the Chaumont-en-Vexin area, north and west of Paris. The artillery regiments were sent to locations such as Lattainville, northeast of Paris. Men of Battery A of the 17th nearly exhausted themselves by marching 44 miles to Vanault. After resting two days they then marched 14 more to Revigny. They entrained from there and on 20 May detrained for a hike of 18 miles to Chaumont. They didn't have to drag their guns all that way but would only have 11 days to train and rest before the next major exercise.

Meanwhile, everyone in the Division expected, or at least hoped, to obtain passes to the grandest city in all the world, Paris. Only a few officers and a few men going "French leave" made it. Some soldiers that traveled by train managed to get a glimpse of Paris as their vehicle passed on its outskirts. Others traveling by camion bypassed the "City of Light" but not far enough away to keep soldiers and Marines from taking a leap from the moving vehicle. Some eventually were picked up by the ever-present military police patrolling Paris, while others made their way back and faced some kind of punishment. They were needed and usually the punishment was loss of pay.

The Division would now train for the next encounter with the Germans. But in the meantime administrators went on about their business. Before arrival, on 20 May, the assistant chief of staff, Col. Charles H. Bridges, issued directions of where, upon arrival, the units were to obtain wood for their cookstoves. The French service intendance at each wood dump would give receipts for the volume of wood received and the reader was warned that "the necessity of economical use of fuel is imperative." Obviously a colonel was required for such important duties. Fortunately for the division, the chief of staff, Col. Preston Brown, was busy with more important matters. He would be by far the best chief of staff of the Division during their war in France.

The division anticipated next relieving the 1st Division up north. The 1st Division had been slightly battered on 28–29 May in their successful assault on, and defense of, Cantigny. A motion was inaugurated along those lines when Field Order No. 3 was issued by 2d Division on 30 May,[20] a holiday (then called Decoration Day) for the troops. A national holiday, it had been a relatively easy day for the men, possibly the only one they had enjoyed while in France. Each unit was authorized to send out advance billeting parties and to stand by for transport. Most did, but that order was soon abrogated by another, very different Field Order No. 4, dated 30 May at "9:30 P.M." issued by Col. Preston Brown. It read simply (with modifications), "1. The division moves to another area.... 3. Embussing and entraining begins 31 May, Annex 1.... 5. Duration of journey, one day.... 10. Division Headquarters closes at hour of departure of last train. Advanced echelon opens 31 May, 4:00 P.M. at a point to be communicated verbally to General Officers. By command of General Bundy." That was it. The order was somewhat delayed in being delivered and some units didn't learn of the changes for many hours. But, as the saying goes, none of the 2d Division men ever missed a train. Early on the morning of 31 May, infantry units from both brigades were "up and at 'em" and, soon after embussing the camions, on their way eastward.

4

CHATEAU THIERRY[1]

The heading of this chapter is the name of the sector in which the 2d Division next served and where it imposed its will upon the German army. In reality it was a relatively small engagement, hardly noticeable in the overall scheme of things. What set it apart from most other battles was that it established, once and for all, that not only would the Americans fight but they would fight like hell! Effectively, the 2d Division stopped the Germans cold. The Germans were trying to reach Paris and this was the one route easiest for them. Some say the Germans weren't stopped, "they were tired and slowed down for a few days," which was possibly true. They did slow down and gather their collective breaths, but they could never get on the move again. The Germans would never again run around in France and work their will. Their days were numbered and this battle was the victory the people of France had been looking forward to for nearly four years. It regained, for France, its collective will to defeat the Germans. The only people not surprised by what happened were the American civilians, soldiers, and Marines.

Thursday 30 May 1918

The troops had enjoyed the one day holiday, Decoration Day (now called Memorial Day), and were expecting that the morrow would see them on their way north to relieve the 1st Division at or near Cantigny. At 1700 hours, however, a rapidly moving French automobile, covered with dust, pulled up in front of 2d Division headquarters. A French staff officer got out. He gave Gen. Bundy and Col. Brown a short summary of the critical situation on the front before Paris. The officer hand delivered orders for the division to start for Meaux, located on the Marne River, about twenty-five miles west of Chateau Thierry and a good fifty-five miles from Chaumont-en-Vexin. Trucks, or rather camions,[2] were to be provided for the infantry; no transportation for other troops or division trains. Later another French staff officer brought word that the troops would go by rail except the division's motor transport, which would move by its own power. It was one more set of confusing and contradictory messages to join several more that would help create confusion and organizational difficulty for the division. And this was just the beginning.

Work was at once begun preparing the necessary march tables. To save time, instructions were sent to the troops by telephone and courier, in the form of Divisional Field Order No. 4.

Friday 31 May

The troop movement began at 0500 on the morning of the 31st. Most of the officers and men had been awake since 0330 and, from all reports, appeared raring to go. The Americans were anxious to get into the "Big Show," which they realized was not going to wait for them forever. Just the previous night they had prepared to move north to relieve the 1st Division, and that was cancelled, adding to the frustration. There was more disappointment when they were kept waiting for the camions. Sergeant McCrossen of the 23d Machine Gun Company wrote of how his company had been expecting to mount up and

Second Division troops boarding camions for their rapid trip toward Chateau Thierry.

move out as soon as they were ready. As he wrote, "We were fooled." They, like most of the members of the division, waited for what seemed like forever before they began their move eastward. Finally he and his company started off "on our long and tedious hike." That would be a serious problem when the machine guns were badly needed, as they were marching somewhere along the line.

The 6th Machine Gun Battalion was rather more fortunate. The personnel mounted up on camions and made the voyage rather easily, but without their guns. The gun carts and mules went with the supply train and at Chars entrained between 1400 and 1630. The men arrived at May-en-Multien and bivouacked at approximately 2300 hours. Division artillerymen marched the whole 23 mile distance to near Cocherel, their assembly point. The big guns traveled by train arriving upon the field on 3 June. When the French were in a hurry, they reacted in haste and to blazes with the consequences.

The 2d Engineers tell in their official unit history that they were shaken awake at 0130 and soon were ready to go. By the time they arrived at their bus stop they had to wait until at least 0800 or later, so the rolling food wagons were sent for. At 0700 the troops received a hearty meal "that was the last real cooked meal for many days."[3] At 1000 the trucks arrived, "driven by French and Chinese [Vietnamese] drivers."[4] At about dark, they reached Meaux. They had been driving through crowds of refugees, who would frequently, when the camions stopped, give the men water and their sincere prayers. Possibly not one of the French civilians expected that these untrained Americans could stop the dreaded Germans, but they undoubtedly hoped for the best; most likely none expected them to survive. There was little reason to expect survival; the Americans had been in the war since April 1917 and had not as yet fought to any extent.

Colonel Preston Brown, chief of staff of the 2d Division, went ahead by automobile to prepare for the arrival of the troops at Meaux. On the way he stopped in Paris, went to the American provost marshal's office and from there reported the new dispositions by telephone to Colonel Malin Craig, chief of staff of the I Corps, at Neufchâteau. He requested that rations, ammunition and hospital supplies be sent immediately to Meaux, for this move separated the troops from their trains.

At Meaux, Colonel Brown met the Division Adjutant, Lt. Col. William W. Bessell, who had already established a temporary office; then he went on to Trilport, two miles further east, to report at headquarters of the French Sixth Army. This headquarters, according to him and others who witnessed it, was a complete mess. No one located there seemed able to explain clearly the situation or to give any definite orders. The French seemed to be in a complete state of shock. In fact, Brown learned that no one knew that the division was coming and had no plans for receiving it, nor to deploy it.

Finally he found General Denis Duchêne, the French army commander, and reported that the troops of the 2d Division were on their way. He pointed out that the roads were filled with an ever increasing stream of refugees and that there would be great confusion if the vehicles carrying fifteen thousand American infantry ran into Meaux. Instead he suggested that the camions bypass that town to the north through May-en-Multien where the troops could setup a defensive line on Clignon Brook, facing northward toward Soissons. The Germans were expected to come from that direction. Orders from General (later Marshal) Henri P.O. Pétain had been delivered to Sixth Army telling Duchêne to prepare an elastic defense in depth, which he overlooked and instead put all his men on line. With all in line they were, of course, overwhelmed and were rapidly falling back in great disorder. There was no telling where the Germans were located at that moment, but everyone knew that they were on their way westward, to Paris.

According to Brown, Duchêne was as badly off as his subordinates. At first he told Brown, "Things are very bad," adding that he couldn't give any orders "just now." Brown insisted that something had to be done about those fighting men coming to meet the oncoming Germans. Duchêne would first deliver an order for the location and formation of the 2d Division, then rescind that, followed by something else. Finally, the Frenchman agreed to allow Brown to set up wherever he wanted to. His final question was "Would the Americans hold?" Brown responded, "General, these are American regulars. In a hundred and fifty years they have never been beaten. They will hold." And once again Brown was right on target; they did hold.

The artillery was shipped via trains every hour on the hour beginning at 0530 the morning of 31 May. Later in the morning the machine gun companies' equipment began to leave, followed by the infantry and engineers' baggage. Infantry was sent via camions, the 23d Infantry leaving first followed by various units and lastly by 1/5, 3/5 and the 2d Engineers.

Late in the afternoon of a hot sweltering 31 May the infantry of both brigades began arriving at May-en-Multien and by midnight all had been accounted for. New orders came in to move further north but, after a few units got on the road, those were soon rescinded. Pressure from the Germans had become apparent at Chateau Thierry instead of from Soissons. Because of this, the division's reporting line changed from VII Corps to XXI Corps. The division adjutant, Lt. Col. Bessell, had prepared a report that indicated the general condition of the division. The total manpower was 1,064 officers and 25,614 men available for duty. Perhaps half that number were available to fight.

Late in the day, Field Order No. 5, issued at 1940, read as follows:

1. A strong enemy attack has developed on the line EPIEDS — ETREPILLY — BOURESCHES
   The Division passes from the 7th Army Corps (French) to the 21st Army Corps (French) as reserve.
2. It will be concentrated at once in the area MONTREUIL — DHUISY — BEZU — COUPRU.

3. (a) 3d Brigade. In the zone MONTREUIL — DHUISY — MARIGNY — LA FERTE — CHATEAU THIERRY Road. Headquarters — Montreuil-aux-Lions.
   (b) 4th Brigade. In the zone LA FERTE — CHATEAU THIERRY Road — COUPRU — BEZU — CHARMOST.[5]
   (c) 2d Artillery Brigade. — In zone of LIZY — COCHEREL ROAD — LA FERTE — CHATEAU THIERRY ROAD.
HEADQUARTERS — COCHEREL.
   (d) Engineers — to MONTREUIL-AUX-LIONS.
       Hdqrs. Trains & M.P. to MONTREUIL-AUX-LIONS.
       Ammunition Train — to COCHEREL.
       Supply Train — to MEAUX.
       Engineer Train — to MONTREUIL-AUX-LIONS.
       Sanitary Trains: 1 Ambulance Co. — to COCHEREL.
       1 Ambulance Co. — to BEZU.
       Remainder to DHUISY.
   (e) Hdqrs. Troop — MOUNTREUIL-AUX-LIONS.
       4th Machine Gun Bn. — MONBERTOIN.
       1st Field Signal Bn. — MONTREUIL-AUX-LIONS.
4. The signal corps will connect Division Headquarters with the 21st Army Corps and the brigades and trains.
5. Division Headquarters — MONTREUIL-AUX-LIONS.

Members of the Fifth Marines marching on the Paris-Metz highway toward Chateau Thierry.

The 167th French DI was located south of Lizy-sur-Ourcq, with headquarters at the Beaurepaire Farm and surrounding Hill 204 on the west, which meant that they were positioned along the north bank of the Marne to deflect any effort by the Germans from the south. The French 43d DI was positioned north of Lizy-sur-Ourcq facing eastward along Clignon Brook. Essentially the 2d Division was to be between both divisions. This created a long, rather narrow salient, east to west, with the 2d Division at the point of impact.

Saturday 1 June

The 23d Machine Gun Company of the 23d Infantry marched 12 hours straight with just the usual ten minute break every hour. By 0830 they stopped for breakfast: "a boiled potato, a piece of bacon and coffee." They had already marched nearly thirty miles and would soon reach a fifty mile march in 17 hours with but two hours' rest. That was a good stretch of the legs.

This day the infantry troops were up early and on the road to glory. The Ninth Infantry, less 3/9, which had been slowed down by defective vehicles, was leading the column. The Sixth Marines, who had left Chaumont-en-Vixen last, arrived late, and because of that, had never been diverted to May-en-Multien.

Second Division supply trains on the Paris-Metz highway.

4. Chateau Thierry

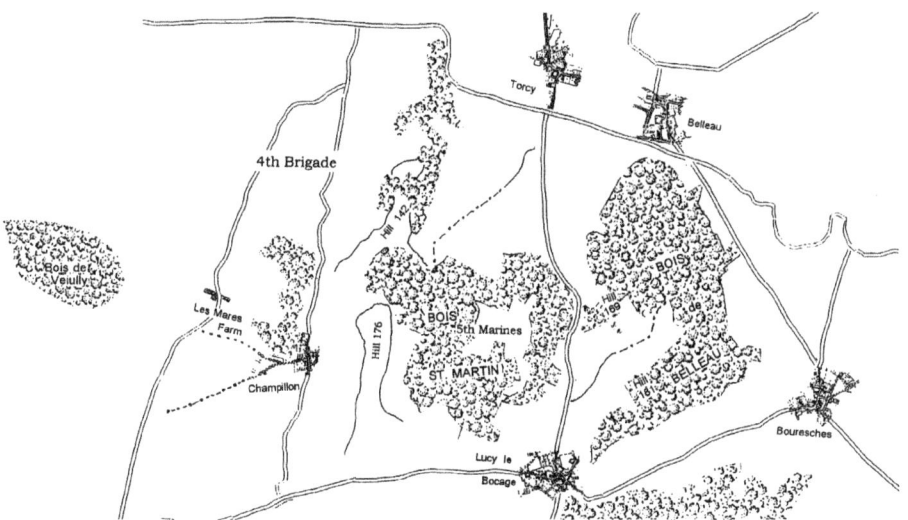

Map 2. Northwest of Chateau Thierry (Belleau Wood), 1 June to 5 July 1918.

General Harbord, who had been riding in his car pressing the divisional supply train onward, grabbed a group of trucks just as they completed unloading and took them back along the road toward Montreuil. There they loaded up the last battalion of the 6th Marines. Then Harbord, leading the trucks, raced toward the front. In the meantime, the leading two battalions of the 9th Infantry, led by Col. Leroy S. Upton, arrived at le Thiolet, a village of a few buildings located on the Paris-Metz highway. There he was directed to turn off the Paris–Metz road, to the right.[6] The regiment moved down the dirt road toward the wooded area known as the Bois de la Marette, which was located on high ground just above the much larger town of Monneaux.

Soon after, the camions bearing 2/6 pulled up and the men were disgorged. Major Thomas Holcomb, the last Marine battalion commander to arrive in France, was leading the first Marines to arrive on this battlefield to be. Holcomb and his men were directed down the line of the Bois de la Cense[7] toward La Cense Farm. For some reason the order of battle was now the reverse of what was listed on FO 5. Marines were now north of the road, the army was south. Each regiment dug in, in what were then known as rifle pits, what or were just beginning to be called "fox-holes" by the newly arrived AEF infantry forces. There were as yet no artillery and not even machine guns, if later complaints were listened to, they were coming overland by "slow boat." At first this American action would be just a rifleman's war.

Holcomb was directed to continue northward and eventually his battalion stretched out through Triangle Farm northwest to Lucy-le-Bocage; a very long stretch. Not long after arrival, Maj. Maurice Shearer, with 1/6,[8] marched on the field and extended the American line north on the Torcy road to St. Martin's Wood.[9] Next to arrive, also by camion, was the 6th Machine Gun Battalion. They unloaded near Hill 201. Under Maj. Edward B. Cole's command they immediately moved and within a few minutes took up positions at the Montgrivault-le-Grande Farm, on the hill just opposite Lucy-le-Bocage. About this time, Col. Albertus W. Catlin led Maj. Bertram Sibley's 3/6 off the road at Paris Farm and into headquarters at the crossroads village of La Voie du Châtel, less than two miles west of Lucy. When Sibley's Marines arrived, a lad from the 83d Company asked where the line was, and a grizzled sergeant said, "Hell there ain't none, we's gonna make a line right near here."

The entire march on the Paris road had been one of constantly moving off the road to allow the civilians and numerous French soldiers to continue making their way westward. Continual cries from the passing French soldiers of "*Le Guerre est finis*" did little for the American morale. If the war was finished what in hell were they doing there, they might have asked, if there was anyone who knew. Besides, like their comrades in the rest of the Division, the men of the 9th were exhausted. They had not eaten in thirty-six hours, had little rest on the trip east and were now expected to prepare positions. Let the engineers dig the holes, only there weren't enough of them to go around. Moreover, they were going to be needed in a forthcoming fight. The infantry could always count on the engineers to give a good account of themselves in a scrap.

Headquarters of the Ninth first established itself at Les Aulnois-Bontemps with 1/9 on the right and 2/9 to the left. The "lost battalion," 3/9, arrived about noon and went into regimental reserve. Companies K and M were selected for a redoubt on Hill 201, and I and L were posted at the Regimental Post of Command (PC) in the northeast corner of the Aulnois Wood.[10] The PC for 1/9 was located at La Nouette and for 2/9 at La Croisette. These were about halfway toward the Monneau–Bonneil line. French cavalry was up forward in the Bois de la Marette and had the good fortune not to receive any German guests. Consequently, for the Ninth Infantry, all was quiet the rest of that day and they settled in.

Later in the afternoon the 23d Infantry arrived and took up positions on the left and rear of the 9th Infantry, across the Paris–Metz road. Earlier that morning, a message timed at 0300 from French Gen. Victor Michel directed Col. Paul Malone to take his regiment and join with the French 43d DI up along the Clignon in the vicinity of Coulombs-en-Valois, roughly eight miles to the west and north to the town of Brumetz. Upon arrival he was to dispatch several battalions hither and yon, wherever they could locate French troops, to plug a hole. It wasn't quite that bad, but close to it. What made this a slightly different connection was that, soon after, he was directed to take 1/5 (Maj. Julius S. Turrill) with him. Malone was a good man, so the Marines had no kick on that score. They would also be served by the 5th Machine Gun Battalion and C Company of engineers. Their problem wouldn't become serious until 6 June, when it would be very challenging for 1/5.

In the meantime, the Marines of the 4th Brigade had completely arrived and were taking up their assigned positions. Colonel Wendell Neville and his 5th Marines moved north off the well traveled Paris-Metz highway and moved about a mile up the Marigny-en-Orxois road. There Neville established his first headquarters at what was then known as Pyramide Farm. The regiment setup camp in the open field opposite. There, "we all did it shipshape and by the numbers," according to 1st Lt. Elliott D. Cooke, USA, of the 18th Company who wound up becoming a genuine Marine before the war was over. He soon began talking the slang and when he wrote his memoir, many years after, it was leavened with the salty talk of the regular marine.[11] He was one of sixty, perhaps more, U.S. Army officers loaned to the 4th Brigade when the personnel expansion took place and the Corps was deficient in 2d lieutenants but the army wasn't. All in all, they each served the Marine Brigade exceptionally well during the earliest battles.

The 6th Marines were spread out covering a large area. They were even opposite the Bois de Belleau, which would loom very large for the Marines in the ensuing days. French troops, making a last stand along this line as the Germans weighed heavily on them, came through the American lines as they fell back under the pressure. One reported that a bruised and battered Poilu "showed me his rifle.... The butt had been shot away and he had been hit in the shoulder. 'Beaucoup d'allemands' and he hurried away."[12] Gulberg wrote that he was sure the Frenchman was convinced that the Americans would soon be following him. At midnight Maj. Shearer, still commanding 1/6, reported that his unit held the line from Hill 142 (not actually all of that hill) to Lucy-le-Bocage.

The 2d Engineers were also arriving along with the infantry units. The 1st Battalion was first to arrive and was assigned duty with the 3d Brigade. Company A was assigned to 1/9; B Company to 2/9, while C was assigned to the 23d Infantry, which was divided into four platoons. The 1st and 4th platoons went with 1/23 and the 2d and 3d with 2/23. The 2d Battalion went with the 4th Brigade. That night they arrived in the area covered by the 6th Marines, without maps or any guidance. Company F went before the town of Lucy while D and E companies were at Triangle Farm. That night the four platoons of D were each assigned to a company of the 6th Marines. There they remained until the morning of 5 June when Co D was reassigned to the woods near La Voie du Chatel.

Sunday 2 June

Col. Preston Brown sent Col. Paul Malone an order repeating that from Gen. Michels the previous day, namely that he and his regiment plus 1/5, the 5th MG Battalion (Maj. Harry T. Lewis) and Company C of the engineers would bolster the French forces along the Clignon Brook. The German army had been putting great pressure upon that line, most of which was held on the north bank.

Neville decided to move his PC northward to a quarry at Carrières which was less susceptible to German artillery fire. While these changes were taking place Lt. Col. Frederick "Fritz" Wise received orders to take 2/5 and defend Les Mares Farm just north of Champillon. He was to also tie up with Marines on Hill 142 and thinly spread himself westward to the Bois de Veuilly. This was an area much greater than one battalion should have been required to fill. But 2/5 went to it and was soon situated around and about the farm. They never seemed to make contact, nor did Shearer with Wise, who was still "occupying" Hill 142.[13]

The Les Mares Farm location was clocked at thirty miles from Paris and would be the closest the Germans would get to Paris until 1940. Their voyage, however, was stopped at this farm and its environs on 3–5 June. Someone later called it the "Bloody Angle of the AEF," in a magazine article. It was one of the most important victories of the 2d Division northwest of Chateau Thierry. Had the Germans punched through 2/5 they would have been well within and behind the 2d Division, which would then have been cut off. Needless to add, the road to Paris would then have been wide open.

The battalion had several visits from the Germans that day but none of severe intensity. Some noise was heard out front of the farm buildings. Corporal Francis J. Dockx* and three other men went out to find the source. They found enough Germans digging in to start a small war of their own. Soon, the firing brought more Marines out front and Gy Sgt. David L. Buford* and two more Marines added their firepower to the clash. Buford, a superior pistol shot, hit seven Germans by himself. The Germans had enough and took off for their lines. Dockx and Buford both rightfully earned a DSC for their part in the disagreement.

To the west, 23d Infantry had moved into place behind the rear of the 43d DI. Turrill's 1/5 took up position in the Bois de Vaurichat and spread out to their right, into the Bois de Veuilly. Major Charles B. Elliott's 3/23 assumed positions north of Germigny-sous-Coulombs and 1/23 on the high ground west of Brumetz. The 2d Bn of the 23d was held in reserve. The machine gunners of the 5th MG Bn and the engineers were assigned directly to the French forces. This group of Americans were under the direct command of Gen. Michel, commander of the 43d DI. German forces had been attacking and piercing all along this line. Around Torcy they had managed to break through across the Clignon Brook and were now scattered along the south side of that stream.

Shearer's 6th Marines suffered several casualties, officers and men, wounded only. Mainly 1/6 took some artillery shells into their positions in St. Martin's Wood. Captain Oscar R. Cauldwell of the 96th Co took shrapnel in a leg and he was out. The Germans launched several probes that morning which were handily turned back by the gunners of the 6th MG Bn. The 3d Bn., 5th Marines, were still in reserve.

The 4th MG Bn, Maj. Edmund L. Zane, commanding, reported their presence, "(less Fords [autos])" but plus the 1st Field Signal Bn and Headquarters Troops which "arrived at 11:30 A.M. and are now unloading." He had requested 16 three-ton trucks to move the 4th MG Bn to May-en-Multien: "We have no transportation and cannot even march afoot." Somehow they made it.

Things along the 9th Infantry front were relatively quiet but in the afternoon the rear areas were taking a shellacking from well-registered German guns. The French cavalry, however, remained in the Marette woods without interference. Major John G. Livingston was relieved from command of his 1st Battalion by Col. Upton "because of his inability to read a map and inefficiency." Major Franklin L. Whitley was his successor. Upton also called for seven ambulances with extra litters to evacuate 26 wounded. German artillery was making serious trouble for Upton.

That day the French artillery had used up their "heavies," running out of 155mm ammunition. They commandeered a recently arrived 32-truck ammunition train and had them race back 45 miles to reload, then back another 45 miles to unload their essential cargo. The total trip took thirteen hours and all 32 trucks managed to make the entire voyage without failure. It was fortunate because in the next few days the division infantry would especially require that heavy "stuff."

At 1630 Harbord advised Neville that Turrill and 1/5 were being recalled to become 4th Brigade Reserve, thereby relieving Maj. Benjamin Berry and 3/5 to become corps reserve. In his message he also told Neville that the regimental 8th MG Company was marching overland and still had thirty miles to go. they were expected "tomorrow night some time" but were trying to obtain trucks to carry men and guns much sooner. Late that afternoon, about 1800, Turrill was instructed by Malone to prepare to move with the company from the 5th MG Bn assigned to him back to Les Glandon. At about midnight, 1/5 was relieved[14] by 2/23 and proceeded back home but without their engineers, who were reassigned to 3/23, Maj. Charles B. Elliott's outfit.

That day, the French loss of Belleau and Torcy was a disaster for the 43d French DI, which forced them to retire behind the 2d Division lines. That was even more serious and, in a few days, would be troublesome for the 4th Brigade.

Monday 3 June

At 0100 Gen. Michel sent word to the 2d Division that French soldiers were going to "retake the positions they have just lost [in the Bois de Belleau]. The American troops will maintain at *ALL COSTS* the line of support they occupy...."[15] The message was passed along to all units in the 4th Brigade with Harbord's added admonition "at *all costs.*" For some reason the French had deserted those woods which provided much cover and protection for the defending force and were now going to try to regain it. Their attack upon the now completely occupied woods began at 1300 and German resistance was intense. The 43d DI was not successful and was subjected to heavy losses in the failed attempt. This failure would cause the 4th Brigade, especially, and members of the 23d Infantry enormous casualties in the coming weeks. It would also delay the French release of command control to the Americans over the area.

Colonel Malone of the 23d was able to send messages that two separate German attacks upon Germingy and environs had been stopped and broken up by his regiment. In messages to his battalion commanders, Malone emphasized the destruction German tactics were having upon the line as a whole. The Germans were using ravines and woods and other obstacles to vision to get small elements behind the lines. Then, when the frontal attack was launched, the defenders' flanks and rear were overwhelmed. Malone's instructions were to "guard all ravines and establish an outpost line." He also mentioned that the 23d MG Co, without guns, had arrived the previous night but hadn't as yet been utilized. According to Sgt. Bernard J. McCrossen, things were rather slow for them the entire time the company was in the sector.

Turrill and 1/5 were relieved at midnight and in his message to Neville he indicated that one of his men had been killed and eleven wounded. He had been directed by Harbord to become brigade reserve. He and staff were then located in farm buildings and two companies, the 49th and 67th of his battalion, were in the nearby woods. This was opposite the Pyramide monument. Wise had requested support for his position at the farm and Harbord had assigned two of Turrill's companies to 2/5. They were "dropped off" on the trip back and Wise still retained the 17th and 66th companies, both of which would soon be reassigned to duty with the French.

Early that morning messages were being sent around to the various infantry units advising that their machine gun companies were marching through Montreuil. Until they arrived the honors were entirely upon the brigade and division machine gun battalions. Two companies of the 5th MG Bn had been busy supporting the 23d Infantry and 1/5 while that infantry in turn backed up the 43d DI. The 6th MG Bn had done their duty helping to hold much of the extensive front of the 6th Marines. The divisional 4th MG Bn at Langue Farm had been in Division reserve since arrival in the area the previous day and would continue to be until 15 June. After that time, some small detachments would be sent around to the infantry units carrying rations or helping the engineers. The unit remained, however, in Bois Gos Jean, near their original site.[16]

That morning the 12th FA was still on the road, but moving from Montreuil east to their appointed positions. Brig. Gen. William Chamberlaine, commanding the 2d Artillery Brigade, reported to G-3 that 1/17, with its 155mm guns, was in position. At 0830 Col. Joseph R. Davis, CO of the 15th FA, received directions from Chamberlaine to contact Brig. Gen. Edward M. Lewis, CO of the 3d Brigade, to select positions for batteries. Chamberlaine was very insistent that he receive definitive plans as to location of batteries. Both Marine regimental machine gun companies, the 8th and the 73d, arrived that day and were warmly welcomed, especially by the now very tired men of both the 5th and the 6th MG battalions, both of which had been carrying the burden of automatic fire for the division.

During the day, the French retired even further back and in so doing lost Bouresches, Bussiares, Torcy and the town of Belleau. Late in the afternoon they also lost Veuilly la Poterie and were forced back through the lines of 2/5 at Les Mares Farm. At this time a French officer gave written orders to Capt. William O. Corbin, adjutant of the 51st Company to retire with his troops. Corbin referred the officer's message to Capt. Lloyd W. Williams, the senior officer present, who in turn conferred with a another officer and then wrote a response to Wise: "I have countermanded the order — kindly see that the French do not shorten their artillery range." What he said to the French officer, according to his officers and men was, "Retreat, Hell! We just got here." Others have later laid claim to making that statement, but most everyone in attendance agreed that Williams was the man. Arguably, it best said what most Americans would have said had they received that order. According to Harbord in a message to Catlin he said, "Am very glad Captain 82d declined retire"[17] when ordered to by a French officer. Disobedience to orders from the French was evidently widespread.

In any event, all the lost ground would have to be retaken by the Marine brigade before the campaign was over. Those lost positions would be harder to retake than they were to lose. All were in the area covered by the 4th Brigade and many Marines would be cut down before they were retaken. The French army was fighting a different kind of war than they had previously. Now, no losses at all was their philosophy. They had suffered huge personnel losses for three plus years and, according to Pétain and Foch, France had no more blood to shed. So it was to be up to the Americans to do the job and lose the blood. They did both.

Malone was terribly concerned. He had just learned that the gap between his 2/23 and the 5th Marines, supposedly upon Hill 142, was in reality 3 kilometers wide. He admitted to division that he couldn't fill the void with his men. Something had to be done. An hour later, at 1950, Malone advised division that the CO of 2/23 could see Germans advancing and seemingly headed directly toward that position that wasn't filled by Marines in the Bois de Veuilly. Unbeknownst to Malone or Neville, the retreating French had filled that gap. Later that night the Germans would help the French to evacuate the town of Veuilly-la-Poterie but, temporarily, the French would continue holding the nearby woods.

Late in the day, following Malone's message to Bundy, 3/6, less two companies, the 84th and 97th, which had been held as regimental reserve, was ordered to move into position to close the gap between 2/5 at the farm and 1/6 in St. Martin's Wood. They were to wait until dusk and occupy Hill 142, which was an extension along the northern edge of the St. Martin's Wood. The 4th Brigade was finally brought together. That, however, didn't do much for the 23d Infantry, which was still out there, separated from other 2d Division units.

In another hour, by 2035, the CO of 2/23 could report to Malone that his right flank in Bois de Veuilly was now occupied by the left flank of 2/5. That was prompted by the arrival of two companies from 3/6. The 82d arrived first and later came the 83d with one platoon from the regiment's 73d Machine Gun Company. These two companies would serve Wise and 2/5 very well in the following days.

During the day, Division had decided to apply modern techniques to a modern war. Each unit of the division was detailed a code name which, possibly, didn't change during the war. Division was named "Custer," while 3d Brigade became "Boston," 4th Brigade, "Moscou," and the 2d Artillery Brigade, "Custer A." Each regiment had a name tacked on: 9th Infantry was "Harp," 23d Infantry, "Bear," 5th Marines, "Plan," 6th Marines "Form," 12th FA, "Loan," 15th FA, "Calf," 17th became "Walk" and the 2d Engineers became "Bore." Each company or battery received a specific number by which they were identified. The numbers issued were from 31 to 50 and began with "A" company or battery. Thus, A Company, Ninth Infantry, was "Harp — 31"

Additionally, each commanding officer, *except for the infantry units*, was assigned a numeric designation, beginning with Gen. Bundy as "No. 1." There were 32 in all and most do not concern us here. Perhaps the AEF in general had a similar system and the plan made a lot of sense at the time. At least Bundy, ably assisted by Brown, was on top of things. Another decision was made by those two. It was to fight but one brigade at a time. That would make a great difference to the 4th Brigade, since they were holding ground opposite what the French army demanded be retaken — Belleau Wood. Effectively, and for the first few weeks, all attacks were launched by the Marines. The army would hold their ground and defend and do that well, with substantial losses to the 23rd. But still, the losses wore most heavily on the 4th Brigade.

Meanwhile, as we have seen, two companies from 1/5, the 17th and 66th, were assigned to support 2/5. Both were positioned along the northern edge of Bois de Veuilly and they would remain there for several days. Wise would use them well and he then assigned them to the French, who would be reluctant, when it became necessary, to lose them back to Maj. Turrill. This would cause serious trouble for 1/5 on the morning and afternoon of 6 June. (See below.)

Adjutant Bessell was reporting substantially the same numbers available for duty even though several units had sustained a few casualties. He notes, "90 casualties have passed thru Div. Dressing Stations and have been evacuated thru MEAUX. Not included in above report," which didn't made a lot of sense. He also reported that the men had reserve rations for one day, with 2 more days' rations in the supply trains.

Tuesday 4 June

That morning, effective at 0800, the 2d Division was ordered to assume command over the entire sector and the French 43d DI withdrew from the Clignon line behind the 2d Division lines. French cavalry in Bois de la Marette, which was temporarily assigned to the 2d Division, remained where they were. Early that morning, before 0500, 1/9 left its place as right flank of division and was replaced by the 30th Infantry, of the nearby 3d Division.[18] The French 10th Colonial DI was on that division's right flank down to the Marne River. The 2d Division area of responsibility was now extensive. No longer could the Americans count upon the French artillery nor any of its other experienced forces before them. The division's right flank began from just above the village of Monneaux, located at the base of Hill 204; to Le Thiolet on the Paris–Metz Road; northwest to Lucy-le-Bocage; continuing on to Hill 142 and finally to Les Mares Farm. Now there was nothing between the Americans and the Germans.

Major Benjamin Berry's 3/5 was removed as corps reserve to become 4th Brigade Reserve. In a couple of days they would have their opportunity to engage in the war. The 6th Marines were still generally holding the front for the 4th Brigade, with 2/5 doing their share at the division's extreme left flank.

This was the day that 2/5 would stop the farthest advance the Germans were to make. After a period of shelling, two battalions of German infantry approached Les Mares Farm from the north, right down both sides of the road and in the adjacent wheat fields. Wise had an aggregate of different units assisting and four well positioned companies of his own. Several Marine officers and men would make considerable reputations for themselves this day, and at least one would eventually become commandant of the Marine Corps.[19]

On their first pass, the advancing Germans suffered heavily from the aimed sustained rifle fire which enabled the Marines to send many Germans down, even at 600 to 1,000 yards. It was accurately aimed shooting by individuals that the war hadn't witnessed since 1914. It certainly impressed the war-hardened German veterans, who would remember this kind of killing long afterward. They retreated more rapidly than they had advanced, leaving the field to 2/5.

Meanwhile, to the south, the entire 9th Infantry was now on line, with no reserve. It was slightly better further north where two battalions of the Sixth, 1/6 and 2/6, were on line with only two companies, 3/6 in reserve. Lt. Col. Wise's 2/5 was still holding the northwestern end of the 2d Division's line, and 3/5 was now in brigade reserve. During the night, the 23d Infantry and associated troops were relieved from their positions by the French 167th Division and Malone reported to Lewis that he was on his way "home" to become division reserve.

Lieutenant Colonel Walter S. Grant, of the 2d Division general staff, reported to Brig. Gen. Fox Connor at I Corp in some detail about the day's activ-

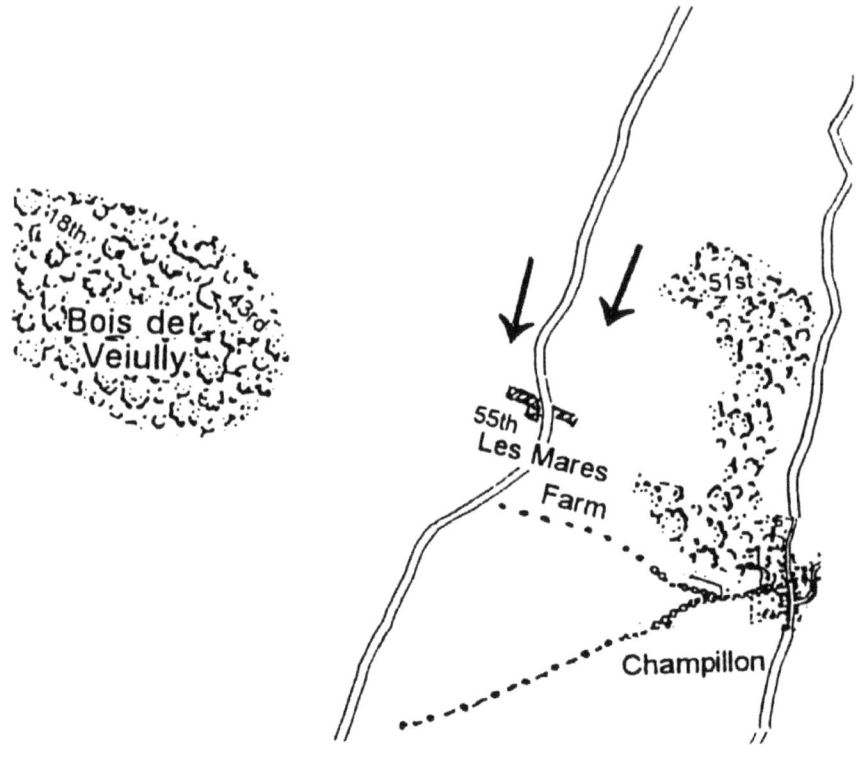

Map 3. Germans advance upon Wise's 2/5, at Les Mares Farm on 3 and 4 June 1918.

ities. He mentioned that the early morning saw more 2d Brigade Artillery firing exercises than previously, plus heavy French support. The Germans got around to replying at 0225, "putting down a heavy barrage for a few minutes" at the junction of the 23d Infantry and the 5th Marines. Harbord was pleased to enter into the day's War Diary, "The Brigade Headquarters were honored this afternoon by a visit from the Commander-in-Chief [Pershing]."[20]

Wednesday 5 June

With the arrival of the 167th DI on the left, the 2d Division's boundary, effective at 0800 that morning, moved back east to the brook at Champillon. This was a day when the infantry units of the division had a rather "soft time." The Germans weren't trying to kill them and the Americans were acting kindly in response. Instead of fighting, the entire division lineup was reorganized.

However, the 3d Brigade remained on the division's right flank, and the 4th on the left. Regimental locations, from the right to left, were the 9th

Infantry, the 23d Infantry, the 6th Marines and the 5th Marines. The moves required to make the change in the lines weren't complete until the night of 5–6 June, and even then some problems remained. The French cavalry in the Bois de Marette were relieved by 2/9. Tommy Holcomb's 2/6 was relieved by two battalions of the 23d Infantry. From right at Le Thiolet to left at Triangle Farm, inclusive, went 1/23 and 3/23. That shortened the Marines' total coverage in a constantly active front. From here on the 23d and the Germans would be very busy entertaining each other. Meanwhile D Co., 2d Engineers, was relieved from duty with the 6th Marines and retired to the woods near La Voie du Chatel.

Major Ben Berry's 3/5 would replace 1/6, from Lucy-le-Bocage north to the eastern slopes of Hill 142. The following morning, 3/5 would assist 1/5 by covering part of its right flank during its attack. Major Berton Sibley's 3/6 would be replaced in the Bois de Champillon after midnight. In the meantime the relieving force, still composed of just two companies from Julius Turrill's 1/5, wouldn't be near the woods until after midnight.

A decision was made by both the French Sixth Army and XXI Corps that the 167th DI would advance northward and retake the hills south of the Clignon between the village of Veuilly la Poterie and Champillon Brook. Their advance would begin at 0345 on 6 June. Orders were sent to Maj. Gen. Bundy to assign a flanking unit. He assigned that role to 1/5, which was in reality just a half battalion composed of two companies. The "battalion" was to advance down Hill 170 to Hill 142 and then into the woods south of Bussiares to, essentially, cover the flank of the 167th. The orders from Bundy/Brown to Harbord must

The First Signal Battalion erecting lines in the Belleau Wood area.

have gotten lost someplace because the orders from Harbord to Turrill didn't arrive until after midnight on 6 June. Turrill was miles from where he was supposed to be and was required to be there to "jumpoff" at 0345 that morning. Worse, neither he nor any of his officers or men had even seen the ground they were to go over and take. Additionally, the French ordered an attack upon Belleau Woods as soon as possible after 1/5 had completed their task.

Colonel Preston Brown's Report of Operations indicated that the day was "QUIET, except for increased artillery activity and abnormal enemy aviation." He added that the enemy had made a small attack upon Hill 142 but it was broken up by artillery fire. "One company of 6th Marines, considerably annoyed by a German machine gun, sent out a patrol of 12 men about 1:00 P.M., killed all the Germans and brought back the machine gun."

Thursday 6 June

This would be the big day for the 4th Brigade. At 0300 Wise and 2/5, less the 51st Co, and the two companies from 1/5, 17th and 66th, were relieved by the French and the latter began their trek homeward. In the meantime, Turrill with his orders, sent and received after midnight from brigade headquarters, was struggling with his two companies to make the deadline imposed for 1/5's assault upon Hill 142. He had at least two miles over broken ground, un reconnoitered in daylight, to get to his jumping-off post. When he arrived he had barely minutes to launch his attack over territory heavily defended by well-entrenched Germans with a multitude of Maxim machine guns, and with half of his battalion missing.

Somehow, the two companies made their way to Hill 170. At 0345 the 1st Sgts., out before their companies, blew their whistles, waved their sticks over their heads and down, and the line moved forward.[21] Down the hill they went, yelling rebel cries and everything else Americans had been screaming for many years to frighten their opponents. Their opponents had faced nearly everything imaginable in nearly four years of death and destruction and yells didn't penetrate. Only bayonets and bullets did that. The Germans stood their ground, at least for a few minutes.

The 67th Company (1st Lt Orlando Crowther,* temporarily skipper) was on the left and the 49th (Capt. George W. Hamilton*) was on the right. Companies D and E, plus elements of F of the 2d Engineers, were in the second line as support. They participated completely in what was to happen to 1/5 in the next few hours.

Some Germans were entrenched on the downhill and those were rapidly overrun and driven back down the hill. When the Marines arrived on the flat surface of Hill 142 the enemy was strongly entrenched within the wood line facing them. Twelve well-situated Maxims caused many casualties in both com-

Map 4. Two companies, of Turrill's 1/5 advance upon Hill 142 and beyond, 6 June 1918.

panies. Some guns were facing immediately out of the wooded area, others were within. Crowther took one machine gun by himself and as he started on a second he was gunned down and was dead before he hit the ground. His crowd continued on and further down off 142 into the ravine alongside, successfully driving all Germans out. Later, failure of the French to advance on that flank would cause more trouble that the 51st Co, 2/5, would be forced to address.

Hamilton and his men were soon facing the defended woods at the north end of Hill 142, with but one other officer still standing.[22] But Hamilton turned out to be a one-man army as far as the Germans were concerned. Nothing was going to stop him; he continued his routine all day, leading what was left of the two companies and driving the enemy from the hill and down toward Bussiares and Torcy. In fact, Hamilton overshot his target and had to retire in order to conform to the later orders he received, which told him to pull back to Hill 142.

Heroes were a dime a dozen that morning and that is a positive statement. Several enlisted men were commissioned and many received awards. Some were the ultimate: Gy Sgt. Charles F. Hoffman,*[23] armed only with his bayoneted .03 charged a group of German machine gunners, stuck two and routed the rest, killing and wounding several others in the process. He received the Army Medal of Honor and later the navy equivalent. Major Turrill* was up front and was also commended, receiving a DSC and Navy Cross for his consummate leadership in the assault.

Within three hours the entire Hill 142 was cleared of any Germans but casualties. Hamilton, now fully in charge of both companies, formed a line and set up his captured guns and those of the supporting 10 guns from the 15th Company, 6th MG Bn. He was the lone officer of the 49th. The other five were casualties. There was also one surviving officer from the 67th Company, four others falling that day. It was later calculated that at least 50 percent of the enlisted Marines of the two companies were dead and wounded.

Later that day elements of the 17th and 66th companies had managed to join their comrades and it was just as well. Capt. Lloyd Williams, with three platoons of his 51st Company, also reported as ordered by Lt. Col. Logan Feland,* assistant regimental commander of the 5th Marines. At about 1400 that afternoon 6 guns of the 81st Co arrived and were properly placed to defend Hill 142 against anticipated German counterattacks.

The two assaulting companies had paid severely for their success, yet the day was not over. The enemy launched several assaults against the sparsely held hill but each was turned back with severe losses to the enemy. In the final analysis, 1/5 was about all done. They wouldn't face another disaster such as this taking of Hill 142 until 4 October 1918 at Blanc Mont. The exhausted battalion would remain in this position nearly until the sector was secured at the end of June. The chief of staff, Preston Brown, and the War Diary both reported, "Our casualties were light." Perhaps accurate reports hadn't yet become standard. Meanwhile, the Germans were expecting further attacks so they launched a heavy volume of artillery fire at Lucy, Champillon and the farm at Montgrivault for the balance of the day.

Harbord was overjoyed at the news of their first real success. He sent the following message to Col. Neville at 0900: "I congratulate you and the 1st Bn. and the 3rd Bn. on doing so well what we all knew they would do." The performance of the brigade would enhance Harbord's career, leading to command of the division. He had every reason to be thrilled. Meanwhile, Turrill was literally begging for ammunition and asking Neville, "Can't they [the French] be persuaded to come up to our left?" The French artillery had laid down some fire and hit on their own 115th Infantry, which then intelligently hauled themselves out of their position. The Marines left flank would remain open for some hours to come. Fortunately the enemy failed to recognize the hole and fill it. Turrill also mentioned that Ben Berry and 3/5 were "fighting in the woods on my right." The enemy had launched small attacks down the Torcy–Lucy road which were beaten back.

Williams and his men of the 51st Co were taking the left position and the recently arrived Capt. Roswell Winans and his 17th Co. were cleaning out the woods to Turrill's immediate right. With Winans' arrival, Berry and 3/5 had moved farther to their right. This all happened before 1000 hours that morning. Hamilton reported to Turrill, who then passed the message along, that 1/5 held the nose of Hill 142 but was terribly exposed. Hamilton had four machine guns in place, had been attacked several times and "our casualties are *very* heavy. We need medical aid badly, cannot locate any hospital apprentices (probably all dead or dying) and need many. We will need artillery assistance to hold this line tonight." He added that the line was held by a mix of the 49th, 66th and 67th Companies. Later he begged for ammunition, which was getting desperately low.

At 1300 Turrill advised Neville that "a strong attack on our right would finish us." He added, "No signs of Berry on our right." What he was saying was that his salient, that is, the right of the nose of Hill 142, was completely open. Winans' 17th was now up on the hill and there was nothing on his flank. The French had returned on the left, so that side was basically safe, for the moment.

Meanwhile, the 23d Infantry adjutant was complaining to Col. Malone that the regiment rations hadn't arrived and, worse, the last issue was on 4 June. An hour later the colonel was ordering changes to correct the complaints. Essentially he stated, "I have ordered kitchens filled and cooking to begin...." His tone reads as though he was somewhat angry. The CO of the 15th FA received a message from Malone about his location at Domptin and asked, "What batteries are supporting me?" He was quickly informed by Lt. Col. Joseph R. Davis* that 2/15, located at Coupru, was his battery.

Malone was also advised that when the Marines advanced on his left flank, later that day, his regiment must conform to their lines and retain liaison. His dispositions along this line ran from Le Thiolet on the Paris-Metz highway northwest to Triangle. There they met the 6th Marines.

Major Benjamin Berry* and his battalion, 3/5, had received orders a few hours earlier in the day to attack the main target, Belleau Woods, at about 1700. He had with him the remaining 6 guns and men from the 81st Co of the 6th MG Bn. The attack went off as scheduled and the slaughter began. No reconnaissance of any kind had taken place beforehand. No artillery was placed on the woods because Brig. Gen. Harbord did not wish the Germans to be aware that an attack was coming, even though Berry's battalion was visibly forming up on the hill opposite them. If a reconnaissance had taken place the general might have learned that the place he selected as Berry's attack location, with the woods on the three sides, was a veritable armed encampment. Maxims occupied almost as much ground as the German infantry. Because the planning was nil, another battalion of Marines would pay an extreme price for leadership negligence and incompetence. Additionally, 3/6 would also suffer bitter casualties as they were covering Berry's right flank going into the woods. This inability by Brigade headquarters to understand modern warfare would generate a one day destruction of four battalions of marines, something that no one else had managed in 143 years.[24]

Exactly at 1700, 3/5, in what was later termed "splendid formation," went down the wooded hill on the west side of the Lucy-Torcy road, across and into the wheat field lying before them. They went in a column of platoons. This attack was supported by 2 guns of the 81st Co, 4 guns from the 6th Marines own 73d MG Co, and 4 guns from the 77th Co, all supervised by 1st Lt Jack S. Hart* of the 81st Co. Almost immediately the Maxims opened up, even though the Marines were still a half mile from the wide open space and another half mile from their target. Within a few minutes the casualties were horrendous. The guns were in the woods on both wings of the maw and had a clear shot at the advancing men. The Marines' only saving grace, and not much of that, was the growing wheat partly hiding their bodies. The 45th Co (Capt. Peter Conachy), late in arriving, was on the left with the 16th (Capt. Robert Yowell) next, followed by the 20th (Capt. Richard N. Platt) and, on the extreme right, the 47th (Capt. Philip T. Case). The entire affair was rather clouded by bad communications. Second Lieutenant George V. Gordon, USA, later described how fouled up his company was. He and 1st Lt William Duckham, both of the 16th Co, were watching the advance from their hill. Captain Henry L. Larsen, company adjutant, ran up to them and told them they and their platoons were supposed to have advanced a few minutes before.[25] The battalion would eventually make it to the far end and some men would actually enter the woods, but by then it was much too late. Berry and his battalion were a thing of the past. Berry had been badly wounded, losing a hand, which was shot off by

A view looking east toward Belleau Wood as seen from the Bois St. Martin.

Map 5. Berry's 3/6 advance on Belleau Wood, at 1700 hours on 6 June, and Holcomb's 2/6 advances on Bouresches

machine gun fire.[26] Elements of the 20th and 47th companies would remain in the woods to the right for a few days to come.

Sergeant Merwin H. Silverthorn, of the 20th Co., described later how his unit was enfiladed on two sides and forced to go into the nearby woods, far from the designated objective. With about 52 men left they tried to cross into another section of the Bois de Belleau and only "six people got across the first 75 yards. All the rest were killed, wounded, and pinned down."

The 3d Battalion, 6th Marines, based around Lucy, didn't have to advance very far to get into the woods — a couple of hundred yards and then turn north into the southern portion of Belleau Wood. In the advance they were assisted by the 23d Co's (6th MG Bn) machine guns, which fired two barrages — one before the attack and another covering 3/6's advance. They were also supported by B Co. of the 2d Engineers. The battalion, after hard fighting and several hours, made it east to the rocky slope in the woods just west of Bouresches, where their advance was stopped.

Meanwhile, Harbord had decided to use 2/6 to provide right flank support for Sibley but along the southern edge of the woods along the road to

A view looking east toward Belleau Wood as seen from the Bois St. Martin.

Bouresches. Holcomb and his battalion were directed to jumpoff at 1730, a half hour after Sibley. Holcomb's task, besides supporting Sibley's left flank was to take Bouresches. He directed Capt. Bailey Coffenberg to use his 80th Company to provide close flank support. That officer, while performing as directed, would receive his baptism by fire, which was a bullet in his leg, before the day was finished.

The 96th Co, led by Capt. Donald F. Duncan,* was selected to lead across the relatively open ground; they were to be backed up by three platoons of Capt. Randolph T. Zane's* 79th Company. At 1830 off went the 96th followed by the 79th. It was another bloody mess. Before they even got to the outskirts of Bouresches, most of the 96th Co. was down, with many of them dead. This included Duncan, who though badly wounded was killed by a shell exploding as several men were removing him from the field. One of Duncan's buddies from back home, Gy Sgt. Aloysius P. Sheridan, described the incident in which he was hit as he entered the town. A German bullet hit his cartridge belt and exploded three bullets. He survived that but later succumbed to a gas attack. Second Lieutenant Cates* was knocked down by a bullet but managed to get up and lead men forward. When they got into the town, 1st Lt James F. Robertson,* who had taken over command at Duncan's demise, ordered Cates to remain with the 18 or 20 Marines in the town while he went back for reinforcements. Cates and his men managed to hold it against several desperate counterattacks by the enemy. They were eventually supported in the town by Zane and the remnants of the 79th Co, whereupon Zane assumed command of the Marines defending the town. During the night of 6–7 June they were reinforced by A Co of the engineers and elements from both 2/6 and 3/6.

One of the first casualties for the 6th Marines was its commanding officer, Col. Albertus Catlin, hit by a bullet from a machine gun or sniper, which no one really knows for sure. A newspaper correspondent with him took one slug in his eye and would be left lying where he fell, presumably dead. Later his last "previously prepared account" went out to the world and earned him and the Marines international renown. His name was Floyd Gibbons and he described an old-time Gy Sgt. who led his company yelling, "Come on, you sons-a-bitches, do you want to live forever!" That, of course, was Marine legend Dan Daly.*27

For some reason, Harbord was made to believe that Berry and Sibley's attacks upon the woods had been successful, so at 2055 he ordered the balance of the 6th Marines to carry out the next phase of his orders. When it was brought to his attention that he was a bit premature, that order was cancelled. In fact, the order was about three weeks early. Sibley's message of 2045 to his new regimental commander, Lt. Col. Harry Lee, Catlin's replacement, reported:

> Unable to advance infantry further because of strong machine gun positions and artillery fire. Have given orders to hold present position at far edge of woods. *Losses already heavy.* Await instructions. Sibley (emphasis added).

One participant, Private Raymond T. Riffle of the 84th Company (Capt. Frederick W. Karstaedt), 3/6, who would earn a Silver Star that day, reported many years later that his squad was on the extreme left of his company, in liaison with the 83d Company (1st Lt. Alfred Noble). Riffle continues and describes, "the enemy fire was severe, about two feet off the ground." Corporal Patrick P. Donohue was badly hit and fell on Riffle's Chauchat, knocking it from his hands. Riffle picked it up and then a bunch of hand grenades fell near him. With that, he skedaddled behind some boulders. He soon realized he was the only man left out of his squad, and his company had progressed further, about a half mile, toward Bouresches. He observed that even though the skipper of the 83d Co. put him in for a medal, his own skipper cancelled it, stating that all men performed at a high level and not one man should be singled out. Riffle was a recipient anyway.[28]

Meanwhile, the rest of the division was not sitting on their collective hands. According to Col. Malone, "at 5:00 P.M. the Marines were seen advancing in splendid order. The spectacle was inspiring." Major Edmund C. Waddill* had received instructions from Malone to keep up with the Marines, letting their eventual position govern his left. At 1900 Major Waddill (1/23) went forward and personally directed his battalion. As Paul Malone reported, "A fight thus spontaneously resulted and was conducted with great dash and courage, without adequate artillery support as the supply of artillery ammunition was running low and it was absolutely necessary to conserve the supply for the next morning when an attack was expected."[29] The lack of artillery support has been an article of contention since that date. Field Order No. 2 for the 4th Brigade allowed Brig. Gen. Chamberlaine the discretion to determine "the artillery preparation," which of course never came off: "The Marine attacks on Belleau Wood ... had not been too successful because they had been made *without proper artillery preparation* and as a result they had suffered terrible casualties"[30] (emphasis added). The only support mentioned is that of the 77th Co of the 6th MG Bn and that only for the attack by 2/6 on the Bouresches railroad station.

Malone describes the fighting spirit of the men of his regiment and how they exceeded the limits because of "enthusiasm and by the desire for combat" far beyond where they could be supported. He reports that he had many casualties and many heroes to commend. In the report he described the actions of an "isolated group [which] attacked a machine gun group [and] killed all the members thereof except for a lone prisoner." At that time he knew of the loss of 27 killed and 225 wounded and missing, concluding that "more accurate data may be secured." Later it was determined that it was the far right, K Co, 3/23 (Elliott*), that suffered the most casualties. The battalion had managed to advance a good mile east of Triangle Farm. At 2000 Elliott's right flank was counterattacked by the Germans at Hill 192, and there he suffered severe losses. The 23d Infantry was reported, by engineers, to have had their right flank overwhelmed. That report was untrue. The regiment stood their ground all along the line, giving as well as receiving from very aggressive Germans. At midnight both battalions of the 23d were ordered to fall back to their line of departure. This, unfortunately, left the right flank of Marines and engineers at Bouresches completely exposed.

After the war, there was some controversy regarding the 23d Infantry's advance that day. It appears that Col. Malone and Maj. Elliott were not in agreement about the whys and wherefores of 3/23's advance. According to the records, at 1615 Col. Malone ordered Elliott's battalion to advance his left at 1700 and take and hold Hill 192 as Elliott's objective. There were, according to Elliott, no preconditions, other than that his right should maintain its current position; in other words, 3/23 would wheel to their right. About 15 minutes later Malone went north to Waddill's PC where he gave instructions for 1/23 to advance at 1700, keeping liaison with the Marines he would see to his left.

The Marines he might have seen to his left could only be the 78th Co, 2/6, who were just readjusting their positions but not moving forward. Consequently, Waddill remained in his position. Elliott, believing that his orders called for him to move forward and take Hill 192, proceeded to try to do just that. Bursting out from the Bois de Clerembauts the battalion went rapidly forward under very heavy machine gun and artillery fire. Hill 192 was quite a distance forward and, when 3/23 approached it, concentrated German fire from Bouresches to Vaux poured in upon them. The German small arms fire was such that a hurried resupply was called for when they ran low. It had been many years since the German infantry had expended so much small arms ammunition.

Obviously, 3/23 was in trouble, but Elliott managed to report to Malone that, though his losses were heavy, he was managing to hold his ground. His battalion had Companies M and K on a portion of the hill though his right was completely in the air.

Col. Malone, due at brigade headquarters for a meeting, rushed to make the contact. Upon arrival he learned that his regiment was not to have moved forward and that he must immediately stop all aggressive activity. Upon return to his PC he issued orders to Maj. Elliott to "use utmost endeavor to restore the situation and get your battalion back to its original position by dawn." It is quite possible that this message, which originated at Coupru, did not reach Major Elliott before midnight.

At about the time it was issued, 1/23 and the left of 3/23 were readjusting their lines in less advanced positions, and digging in under fire, some distance east of Triangle Farm. At 11:30 pm, 2 companies of the Brigade Reserve were sent forward under Maj. Alfred C. Arnold.

The final phases of the action are obscure. Both battalions were fighting on ground that they had never seen before, and their location descriptions were consequently indefinite. It is evident, however, from the German records, that 3/23 was able to occupy the western part of the Bois de la Cote 192, on the front of the 47th Regiment, and at 0100 the 47th German Regiment counterattacked from the north and forced the Americans out of the woods and back upon the Hill, capturing 4 soldiers of the 23rd Infantry. Following this attack, it was reported that the line of the 23rd Infantry was broken; but the Germans did not press the attack beyond the recovery of their own positions, and moved 2 battalions of the 6th Grenadiers up as reinforcement south of Bouresches.

Records of the 9th Infantry's activities that day are sparse.[31] Late that evening an effort was made on the division's right flank by the French 10th Colonial Division and the 30th Infantry of the American 3d Division. The object was Hill 204 and they managed to obtain a foothold before they were stopped. The 9th Infantry had orders to keep liaison and 2/9 reached its objective, establishing a line on the high ground just west of Bourbelin. In so doing they lost seventy-six men, chiefly from artillery fire.

The following morning Preston Brown's Report of Operations for the division submitted a total of "30 officers ... and 900 men killed and wounded."[32]

Many of those were in the 4th Brigade, but a large number were from the 23d Infantry. It wasn't just the 4th Brigade that was having leadership problems.

Friday 7 June

During the night, Maj. Sibley went about his own area and the contiguous areas to determine how best to arrange his battalion, making a few changes in the process. They had been fortunate in receiving support when Maj. Milo P. Fox of the engineers arrived with two companies, which were assigned to a position just to the rear of the 82d Company, adding considerable support to that badly weakened line. One of their main problems was the constant shelling, of both HE and gas. The latter was even more serious because it remained lying at ground level in that wooded area for many days, causing 3/6 much discomfort. This would badly afflict 1/6, which would also occupy these same positions a few days later.

Major Alfred C. Arnold of the 9th Infantry had led two companies from his regiment in support of the 23d Infantry the previous day. He received directions from Malone to remain where he was until just before daylight, unless something developed, and then to return to his "billets."[33] Malone reported casualties for 3/23 of 8 officers and 165 men, and at another time 8 officers and 58 enlisted men for 3/23 on 6 June. The regiment experienced serious casualties during the entire period but sixteen officers on one day seems excessive. Possibly the second message was really sent first, followed soon after by a revised message.

According to the division history, "June 7th was quiet," and "the 4th Brigade was preparing a resumption of its attacks on Belleau Woods," while several German divisions were pretty much used up and being replaced or retired. Factually, the 4th Brigade was in no condition to do anything except save itself. However, at 0200, 2/5 was moved forward into the St. Martin's Wood and placed to the right of 1/5 and the left of 3/5. A couple of hours later they repulsed a vigorous Germans attack and in early afternoon replaced 3/5 in line. Men and guns of the 23d Co., 6th MG Bn, helped to repel this dangerous attack from Torcy. At some time on this day a platoon of engineers from B Co., had been provided to Capt. Roswell Winans of the 17th Co. to prepare trenches in the first line. The 2d Engineers also had a busy day. Their personnel officer, 1st Lt Alexander Kennedy, Jr., reported casualties of five killed and nineteen wounded.

At 1700 two companies of 3/5, the 45th and 16th, launched an attack northward toward Torcy, capturing a small wooded area about a half mile southwest of that town. They were able to extend 1/5's right flank down Hill 142 and continue the defense line southeast, opposite Belleau Wood and toward Lucy.

Sibley's position came under heavy artillery attack and later, at about 2330, the Germans launched a heavy attack upon them. Three/6 managed to successfully repel this and in the morning was able to distinguish numerous dead Germans before their lines. That night another, also unsuccessful, attack was launched against Bouresches. The accurate rifle fire of Marines and engineers broke it up before it even got into the town. The right flank 23d Infantry was also hit hard, on its left flank where they met the 6th Marines, suffering severe losses. The enemy attacks went down the line as far as the 9th Infantry. All three regiments, however, managed to contain the Germans.

Down south on the extreme right of the division, the 9th Infantry lost contact with the 30th Infantry on its right. Somehow the French on the other flank also lost contact with the 30th. Several hours later, that was corrected. Late that night 2/23 relieved 3/23 at Le Thiolet. Otherwise, most units remained where they were. Report of Operations declared that 2d Division casualties totaling 410 passed through the dressing stations on 7 June.

Saturday 8 June

Fifteen minutes after midnight the 23d Infantry was slammed by a heavy barrage of German artillery and then attacked across its entire front by German infantry. The attack was repulsed with severe losses to the enemy. Fifteen minutes later it was the turn of the 9th Infantry. This was also repulsed and with substantial losses to the enemy. Casualties to the 3d Brigade amounted to about 6 men, while there were at least 100 enemy losses. In another hour they tried another attack upon Bouresches, which was also turned back with heavy losses to the Germans, but very few to the Marines and soldiers defending the place.

At 0500, 3/6 plus the 80th Co. (Capt. Egbert T. Lloyd) of 2/6 and B Co., engineers, attacked in the woods. Sibley's men were attacking Maxims and each taken was covered by another as deadly to the men and officers of 3/6 as all the others. The advance was limited and at 1500 they fell back and 3/6 remained pretty much where they initially had been. Men were dying on both sides, but more Marines than Germans. It would remain that way for weeks to come. One wounded Marine from the 82d Co. made it to Bouresches and told his listeners, incorrectly, that Sibley had taken all but one Maxim and probably had that "by now." Captain Randolph Zane told Maj. Frank E. Evans, adjutant of the 6th Marines, that he had been able to hear Americans in the woods shouting and mentioned one yelling, "Get that son of a bitch," obviously an American). Meanwhile, the enemy guns, 77's, 105's, 150's and even 210's, pounded Marine positions in the woods and they especially worked over the 23d Infantry line. It went on for much of the day but seemed most concentrated late in the afternoon, intensifying at approximately 1725. The 2d Brigade artillery fired counter-battery but didn't seriously affect the incoming.

At 1027 Maj. Berton Sibley had the unpleasant obligation to convey a dis-

Marines of Weapons Company, 5th Marines, firing their one-pounder while supporting an attack in Belleau Wood.

tress message to Maj. Evans, which in turn was passed along to everyone to be affected, including Paul Malone, whose men were flanking the 6th Marines. In it Sibley said:

> They [Germans] are too strong for us. Soon as we take one M.G. the losses are so heavy that I am reforming on the ground held by the 82d Co last night. All of the officers of the 82d Co wounded or missing and it is necessary to reform before we can advance.... These M. Guns are too strong for our infantry. *We can attack again if it is desired*[34] (emphasis added).

That message read like Sibley was hoping he would not be ordered to attack once again. A few hours later he complained that his men had not been fed for several days and at 1355 he added, "Regret to report officers and men are too much exhausted for further attack or strong resistance until after several hours rest." That message should have sent a strong message which brigade headquarters would have understood.

Meanwhile, unbeknownst to Sibley, the Germans were genuinely concerned about the 2d Division. General headquarters directed that as much damage as possible be done to the Americans before them. One intelligence officer announced to his officers and men:

> Should the Americans on our front even temporarily gain the upper hand, it would have a most unfavorable effect for us as regards the morale of the Allies and the

duration of the war.... We are not concerned about ... this or that unimportant wood or village, but rather with the question as to whether Anglo-American propaganda, that the American Army is equal to or even superior to the German, will be successful.[35]

That night those in charge finally smelled the smoke and 3/6 was withdrawn from its tenuous position in the southern part of Belleau Wood, ostensibly to safely allow the 2d Artillery to plaster the woods. Sibley's message is evidence that he and his fine battalion, what was left of them, were worn out. They had suffered from artillery fire, HE and much gas, plus machine guns located among the many boulders and hunger and exhaustion during two and a half days they were perpetually exposed. No one immediately replaced them. There was no one available. But Harbord had sent orders to Capt. George A. Stowell, temporarily in command of 1/6, which had been in corps reserve, to "relieve Sibley." That was at 1822, and 1/6 was many miles west of Belleau Woods. In a message to Holcomb at 2115, Harbord apologized for being unable to relieve 2/6 and added, "taken out the Sibley battalion tonight and not replacing it." Trouble was, when 1/6 arrived Sibley would be several days out of the woods, and no one knew what the Germans had done about that or had any idea where they were now located.

In the meantime, headquarters finally had Capt. Henry Larsen relieved. Major Maurice Shearer was the man and almost as soon as he arrived Harbord sent him a message[36] telling him to "go over to Bouresches tomorrow morning and familiarize yourself.... Your battalion will relieve his [Holcomb] tomorrow night." In the War Diary Harbord wrote complaining of what his command was doing wrong. One item read:

> 6. Dispersion of troops is the fault of beginners as pointed out by all military authorities, and has in our Brigade, with the length of our line, deprived us of the necessary echelons in depth.[37]

Harbord did not attempt to answer this particular problem. He also listed the lack of support to be expected and that during the first week they were used up "at a rate not to be expected hereafter." The next entry is even more telling:

> 9. The heavy losses of officers compared to those among the men are most eloquent as to the gallantry of our officers, and *correspond nearly to the proportions suffered by both the Allies and the enemy in 1914–15.* Officers of experience are a most valuable asset and must not be wasted[38] (emphasis added).

Sunday 9 June

Major John Hughes,* CO of 1/6, had been away at school and in his absence Capt. George A. Stowell, nominally skipper of the 76th Co, briefly had the command of 1/6 following Maurice Shearer. Stowell received brigade orders to bring

1/6 to Lucy and he attempted to obey. That was late evening on 8 June. Meanwhile, Hughes had returned and was at Brigade headquarters getting synchronized and awaiting his battalion to arrive before joining them.

At about midnight Stowell and 1/6 were making their way eastward by a path through a gully, a rear portion of the battalion made the wrong turn and went north instead of east. When that was discovered, it took several hours to rearrange the battalion and Stowell was very late as 1/6 crossed open fields now in daylight, well within sight of German artillery observers. The shells falling managed to scatter the battalion and collecting them together took the better part of the morning. That happenstance made the relief of 3/6 impossible and left the bloody ground of the southern woods bare of Marines. By midday Hughes had managed to get his exhausted battalion under wooded cover just south and east of Lucy and there they were to wait until 10 June.

Meanwhile, during the night, three companies of 3/5 partly relieved 2/6 at Bouresches, completing the change early the following morning. Shearer had received orders directly from Harbord to leave one company in the woods southeast of Lucy as regimental support for the 6th Marines. We can assume that Lt. Col. Harry Lee was aware of and comfortable with that arrangement of his regiment and support units.

Sometime that day Harry Lee reported to the Maj. Gen. commandant, George Barnett, that the "raw replacement troops" received the day before were superlative, "Among it a large majority who were enlisted two months before...." Lee continued in the same vein, describing in detail what a great job Barnett was doing. We can trust that the commandant was happy to learn of this success, but how Lee found the time to write this is a mystery. Harbord added his compliments to Barnett about all the replacements being of the same quality.

Monday 10 June

Hughes sent a message that he was pleased to report that he was "in position" at 0245. In the meantime, artillery fire was working the woods over. At 0430 that morning, the attack upon the southern part of Belleau Wood by Hughes and 1/6 was initiated.[39] They crossed the open ground and made their way well into the woods with minimal casualties.[40] Harbord was thrilled at this news. Finally, he believed he had a Marine battalion "mid-way up into the woods."[41] His plans for the next few days would all be based upon this miscalculation. Hughes would proclaim the woods "mince-meat" from artillery pasting, which proclamation was slightly premature. Later, when writing his memoir, Warren R. Jackson would allude to that continued artillery pasting he and the others of 1/6 received, but it came from the Germans. At 0910 Paul Malone sent Lee "hearty congratulations upon work of last night."

Major Edward B. Cole,* commander of the 6th MG Bn, taking some guns

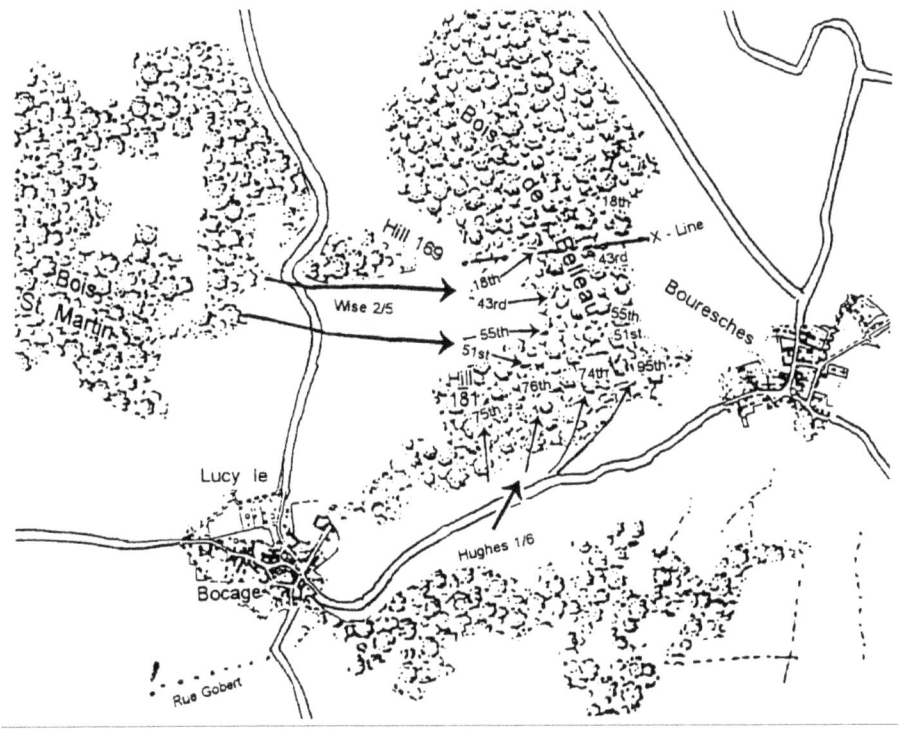

Map 6. Hughes 1/6 attacks Belleau Wood 10 June as does Wise's 2/5 on 11 June 1918.

and crews along, went over with Hughes. After arriving safely in the woods he was the target of a grenade thrown by one of the Germans and was badly wounded. He, in fact, would die of those injuries on 18 June. His temporary replacement was Capt. Harlan E. Major,[42] skipper of the 15th MG Co.

At a bit after 1000 Harbord, still thrilled with Hughes' success, asked his opinion on what was above him in the woods and whether he could take the balance of the woods with his battalion.[43] He also let the rest of the division in on "what my Marines have accomplished." German artillery continued to plaster the "mince-meat" all day, all night and for many days to come. Gas was their specialty. The resultant cloud of gas fumes would lie for weeks and make life even more miserable than ordinary day-to-day agonies. During that day Hughes suffered about forty more casualties from Maxims and the next morning another two dozen while cleaning them up. But the German line, as hit by Sibley, was still intact. Nothing had been gained except more casualties.

In a report to Gen. Bundy dated 0800 10 June to 0800 11 June, Harbord described what had happened, as far as he knew. One of the entries reiterated the error that Hughes was at "the narrow part of the wood at 261.7." Another, and even more important, was his plea that follows:

> I desire to call attention ... that this Brigade has been in the line since June 1st ... and has been almost continuously fighting. Its line has receded nowhere and has everywhere advanced. Officers and men are now at a state scarcely less than *complete physical exhaustion*. Men fall asleep under bombardment and the physical exhaustion and the heavy losses are a combination calculated to damage morale, which should be met by immediate arrangements for the relief of this Brigade.... I cannot too strongly urge that immediate arrangements be made for its relief to enable us to rest and reorganize[44] [emphasis added].

Harbord also mentioned that the French army believed that 5 or 6 days' continual fighting was sufficient excuse for them "to fall back before the enemy." Yet, that night he ordered 2/5 to "take the woods" effective 11 June. Wise later complained that "[I] was dumfounded, all my plans were up in the air." In his memoir he stated that he believed that he and Harbord had agreed on an entirely different attack plan, one in which his battalion would not enter the "jaws of death" but rather circle to the north and enter the woods just below and to the west of the village of Belleau.

Bundy didn't sit on his hands after receiving Harbord's report. In a telegram to "COMMANDER-IN-CHIEF, AEF, CHAUMONT," he added strong words in the same tone and added that a regular brigade should be its replacement so the 4th could go "well to the rear for repose." The message was apparently ignored, possibly because of Fox Connor's reaction to it. (See below.)

Tuesday 11 June

Regardless of exhaustion, Harbord's orders would stand. At 0430 the whistles blew, the canes went up and over the shoulders and 2/5 went to its reward. For some reason, possibly because the Germans were getting sick and tired of slaughtering Marines, the casualties, while heavy, weren't bad enough to stop Wise and his men. Once into the woods, they were to have turned northward. But, because the enemy were firing heavily into their right flank, the Marines tended to head in a southeast direction instead. As he entered the wood Hughes' 76th Co, led by 1st Lt Macon Overton*, was to follow 2/5 as it entered the woods and protect their right flank. He missed the boat and because of it, William's 51st Co took a very bad shellacking.

Wise and most of his men made it into the narrow part of the wood and began to reorganize the remnants. Captain Charley Dunbeck,* with his 43d Co, was at the northern end and nearly at once that consummate professional began setting up defensive positions. Dunbeck, however, had been wounded, and Williams was killed in action. The following day, the day's total loss was reported as 7 officers and 222 men, mostly from 2/5. In fact, 2/5 was unable to keep going because they were in such bad shape after breaking into the German lines within the woods. In one dozen days just one battalion, 1/6, was still in combat shape, and they were getting gassed out of their positions. Harbord could be thankful to Providence for the almost daily replacement drafts made available from the Marine Corps.

Harbord actually reported Wise located at coordinates along the northwest line of the woods, where Wise declared he originally wanted to go. Harbord wasn't aware of just where Wise and 2/5 were located on 12 June.[45] The division report stated clearly, "4th Brigade attacked the *north half* of the BOIS DE BELLEAU and *captured the entire woods*" (emphasis added). At any rate, regardless of Harbord's misinformation, 2/5 stayed the route and were able to provide the wherewithal for the eventual American retention of the woods. In early afternoon Harbord sent Wise congratulations for capturing "the biggest thing in prisoners that the AEF has yet pulled off. We are delighted." He added that 1,000 replacements had just arrived. Otherwise, the night was relatively quiet, giving the battered battalion and Germans a bit of rest. That evening Capt. George H. Osterhout, who had made his way up from the battalion supply train, replaced Harlan Major in command of the 6th MG Bn.

Wednesday 12 June

The 9th Infantry had been busy the previous night and this early morning, moving about in replacing front line units with reserves. German attacks had ceased being serious and the Germans had lain dormant since 6–7 June. Each night, Col. Upton made sure that a company at a time was replaced, "It being impracticable to relieve more than one company at a time on account of the violent shelling...." The regiment had established a redoubt on Hill 201 which ensured the constant attention of German artillery, but they held on.

Wise was ordered to brigade headquarters to attend an early morning meeting. At the conference, Wise told Harbord and the other attendees that he believed that the Germans held the northern tip of the woods "very precariously." He was feeling better and braver, having received 150 replacements and 2 companies of engineers. He further espoused the theory that with some artillery support he could take the whole thing.

His suggestion was accepted and orders were forwarded to the 12th FA to begin bombarding the northern portion of the woods for one hour, 1500–1600. At 1600 Wise and 2/5 were to move northward. They had spread across the narrow neck by companies. What would happen when they arrived where it branched off to the west and greatly enlarged doesn't seem to have been written anyplace. The shelling began as planned but Wise declared that they had barely made an effort and he asked for another hour. He claimed that the Germans just waited for the end and then returned with their guns to their old positions to wait for the attack. Another hour went by and the results were the same. So off went 2/5 and more destruction.

Wise found that the Germans were entrenched much closer to him than had been believed and that the light .75 mm guns of the 12th FA barely impacted upon the dense woods. He ran into a whirlwind of fire and soon his casualties were making progress difficult. When the front broadened, his relatively tight organization fell apart. Additionally, officers went down and noncoms replaced them, then privates replaced noncoms. Groups congregated under a leader and went forward again. German machine gunners were having a field day until the tables were turned. As always, it then became "*Kameraden*" when the gun was out of ammo or destroyed. Some went the way of their guns, others became prisoners.

The Marines and surviving engineers somehow penetrated the German lines and some made it to the northeast end of the woods. A large group of German soldiers, cut off by 2/5, surrendered en masse and their wounded officer let Wise know the Germans had planned a massive counterattack the following morning. Wise was wise enough to realize he couldn't possibly hold all he had taken, because he lacked sufficient manpower. Neville was so informed and the news went up to Brigade. It wasn't very long before the return of the Germans that day and their pressure pushed much of 2/5 back. But they fell back along the eastern line rather than moving very far south. They now had their backs against the far eastern edge of the woods, with their line running north to south. This became known as "The Hook." Hughes had sent some of his companies forward, providing Wise with some additional support to hold the line across the narrow portion.

Losses were again heavy: 2/5 was down by another 150 and Hughes lost 54. However, they captured at least four hundred prisoners, sixty machine guns and ten minnenwerfers. No numbers are available about the dead and wounded Germans but they too must have been substantial. Wise still had about 300 officers and men while Hughes had 700.[46] Total strength of both battalions should have been about 1,200 officers and men, Wise's message to Harbord was simply, "Men in fine shape and line is holding but getting thinner.... About out of officers." With that he requested artillery support. In fact, all that day and into the evening the same cry was read in messages from 2/5. Even the company commanders were sending Wise the same messages: "Lines getting thinner" and "We may not be able to hold if there is a serious attack" or words to that effect. Wise to Neville: "P.S. This is a different outfit from that of yesterday." There were lots of warnings but little response.

Colonel Paul Malone, ever thoughtful and professional, sent Harbord a message at 1430 stating, "Hearty congratulations on the splendid work of your brigade. It will inspire all Americans." He added that he had a small slice [of the action] but wished he had more and soon: "We rejoice in your victory." Harbord replied, "Many thanks.... The Marine Brigade is certainly a superb lot of officers and men.... All you need is the opportunity, which I hope you may soon get."

The 23d Infantry had been engaged in attacks and counterattacks along the line near Bouresches. They would suffer continual losses the whole time in the lines at this sector. Their sister regiment, the 9th, fared slightly better but they would get theirs later in the month. Early that morning Maj. Elliott reported his inability to relieve a portion of the 6th Marines at Triangle because they had no knowledge of being relieved. Malone told Lewis at 3d Brigade, "request Marines be informed," and that he be informed when their "proper representatives may be seen near Triangle." In the meantime, Maj. Waddill was communicating with Maj. Shearer at Bourseches asking if the Marines were still there, which was answered in the affirmative. In his reply Shearer answered that he would be getting details about how many Germans were in the town and advise Waddill at 0630.

Sometime during the night Sibley, then in reserve, received orders to relieve 1/5, which had been nearly a week in the lines since taking Hill 142. Hughes was asking for food and especially "hot *strong* coffee" for his battalion. In the message, he mentioned having about fifty casualties (which, incidentally, included 2d Lt Edgar Allen Poe[47]), to which regimental adjutant Frank Evans responded," Impossible to get coffee or water up to you tonight."

The 2d Division report of this date clarified a mistake they had made the previous day. In it they acknowledged that only a portion, but a large part, of the woods had been taken the previous day: "Our losses are approximately 50 wounded, generally slight wounds," perhaps in the rear areas.

Thursday 13 June

The survivors of the original Marine Brigade were now two weeks in combat with no relief, except from their comrades of the 2d Engineers, who were also in combat for two weeks. Even some of the replacements had almost as much time in the front lines. As seen on the 10th of June, efforts were being made by Bundy and Brown but they were running into a bit of trouble. Back at Pershing's headquarters his G-3, Fox Connor, is quoted as saying in reply to Bundy's telegram, "The reports we have show that conditions are not very bad." He, of course, was back at Chaumont, eating and sleeping reasonably well, so he didn't see any problems.[48] The division report would allow that the numbers of officers and men of all units were approximately 90 (infantry) to 97 (machine guns) percent with just two exceptions: the engineers (85) and the ammunition train (86). Perhaps those percentages weren't known in the four infantry regiments and brigade machine gun battalions.

Shearer and 3/5 were still holding Bouresches though the town had been attacked numerous times since 6 June. He reported about 55 German casualties in and about the town. Someone erroneously told Malone that the Germans were in the town at about 0400. But that was refuted by Shearer. At 0512

A view of the shattered condition of Belleau Wood in mid-June 1918.

Malone directed his battalion commander, Maj. Waddill, to "protect your left flank. Maintain constant liaison with the Marines and report situation every 15 minutes."

At noon Sibley, now at Hill 142 where 3/6 replaced 1/5, reported to Neville, sending along a report of his patrol activity. The Germans had dug in just before Torcy, and Sibley was making every possible attempt to preempt any hostile moves toward his position.

On the night of 13–14 June the 9th Infantry moved to their left, relieving the right company of the 23d Infantry at Triangle Farm. They remained at the same eastern limit as previously. The 9th Infantry was kept moving to the left to take up the slack caused by the continuous losses to the 5th and 6th Marines and the 23d Infantry.

During the night, the German artillery had been really giving that part of the line a working over. During the course of it, heavy gas was launched along the line where the 6th Marines and the 23d joined. Both units were plastered and the losses were significant. The 1st and 2d battalions of the 6th Marines had 450 men gassed while 3/23 had another 150. The 78th Co, 2/6, stated in their semi-official history that "all but twelve men ... were killed, wounded or gassed." That part of the line, usually the weakest point, was in bad shape. Meanwhile Holcomb, commanding 2/6, had orders to go into the woods and support Wise.

Friday 14 June

Early that morning Holcomb advised Neville that his command was "pretty well shot up" and that he would be delayed in relieving Wise. The entire brigade was exhausted and functioning on "sheer nerve alone." This had been so since at least the 10th of June and still there was no relief in sight. Fortunately for the brigade and division, the 3d Brigade lengthened their line to include the town of Bouresches, which reduced the 4th Brigade's responsibility. In the meantime, both Marine regiments were pretty well mixed up. At the top of the line was 3/6 at Hill 142, followed to the east by 1/5, then 3/5 in reserve in and around Lucy. Wise and 2/5 in the woods were supported by 1/6 and expected the arrival of Holcomb's 2/6. Lee held command of some of the mixture and Neville the others.

When Holcomb was finally able to make his way to Wise, the latter saw about 150 miserable wretches and realized that a relief by that sad outfit was not possible. On his own he decided to remain at his post and amalgamate the tormented into the line with 2/5, advising Brigade of what he'd done. Knowing the Germans would probably not be able to attack a wood so thoroughly gassed, Harbord had Wise pull back from the eastern edge to the narrow western side. He did this even though it was learned that the German division facing the woods, the 237th Division, was down to about 50 officers and 1,500 men. They had, since 4 June, lost at least half their manpower. Both flanking divisions were in the same shape and there were no reserves. Harbord also made the decision to combine the three Marine battalions in the woods under the command of Lt. Col. Logan Feland.

One of the Marines relieved was discovered to be in tough shape. The man, Pvt. Andy Peters of the 95th Co., was shaking like a leaf. He had been on burial detail back on 5 June and the sight of decomposing mangled bodies of Marines and French soldiers, especially those where heads and other portions of their anatomy were missing, destroyed his effectiveness. The very sound of artillery being fired was the catalyst. There were many like him and most, when discovered by doctors, managed to receive treatment behind the lines. It was then, and later, called "shell-shock." Other casualties in France became addicted to morphine. It was the drug of the era and was used for almost any pain. One doughboy was quoted by 1st Lt. Laurence T. Stallings, of the 47th Co., 5th Marines, also a casualty (losing his foot at Belleau Wood) who was experiencing the pains of withdrawal from that drug. The doughboy, in a humorous aside to make the other patients laugh, said, "Nurse, can I have a aspirin?"

The French Gen. Dégoutte relieved Duchêne at Sixth Army and Gen. Naulin replaced the former at XXI Corps. Naulin could do nothing for the 4th Brigade but he recommended that it be relieved and placed in reserve and that the 3d Brigade replace them. Bundy reacted rapidly and advised the Corps commander that he didn't want to lose a relatively fresh brigade and, since the 3d U.S. Division was close by and inactive, why not pick on them. Naulin vacillated but

Portrait of the commanders of the 5th Marines. Seated in front, from left, are Col. Wendell C. Neville, CO, with Lt. Col. Logan Feland, assistant CO. Officers in rear are unknown.

Bundy demanded relief for the 4th Brigade. It was decided to send him the 7th Infantry under Colonel Anderson, only the officers and men of one battalion each night. The total relief time would take three nights. The auxiliary services would be left behind — machine guns, kitchen and water carts — for the 7th. The first battalion was to be relieved beginning "tonight." The relief didn't begin all that soon and it was to last for six days. The 7th would fall under the command of 4th Brigade Headquarters, i.e., Brig. Gen. Harbord. Three of the Marine battalions relieved would assume the old positions of the 7th and the fourth would be retained within the division area as reserve.

Saturday 15 June

During the night, the 9th Infantry had some excitement. While the usual company relief was going on, 1st Lt William H. Zwicky, with a patrol from 1/9, crossed more than a half mile of No Man's Land, ambushed and killed two German sentries and returned with valuable information. From this the division learned that the relatively fresh 444th Infantry Regiment of the fresh 232d German Division was now operative opposite the 2d Division.

In the morning, efforts were being made by Feland and his mini-battalion to drive the remaining Germans out of the northern portion of Belleau Wood. There were too many machine guns and a direct assault upon their strong positions was deemed not feasible. Attempts to encircle the Germans also failed. Consequently nothing of note occurred. Hughes and his men were withdrawn mostly out of the southern part of the woods due to the heavy concentration of gas all about.

Early that afternoon Lt. Col. John P. Adams, commanding 1/7, and four officers of the 7th reported to Neville for a reconnaissance of the positions they were to occupy. Adams acknowledged that he was thoroughly aware of the inherent problems caused by the German machine guns in the woods. So the relief could begin as soon as Col. Thomas M. Anderson, Jr., CO, 7th Infantry, thought advisable.[49] Soon after dark 1/7 entered the woods and relieved 2/5 and 2/6. Needless to say, Wise's and Holcomb's officers and men were overjoyed. To say they were exhausted might be understating the situation. Wise later said his officers and men "were past physical limits. Traveling on naked nerve."

Harbord had instilled in Adams, before the 7th went into the woods, his words of wisdom: "You must hold the woods at all costs." Adams positioned his men along line 262.0, in the northern section of the woods. It just happened that the Germans were being relieved at the same time and they and 1/7 got into a bit of a scrap, nothing terribly serious but it was reported as a major setback for the enemy. Shearer and his 3/5 were still in the Bois St. Martin, acting as reserve. Sibley and 3/6 were withdrawn when relieved this night by a battalion of the 174th French Infantry. The Marine line continued to shrink back.

Division reported a casualty total for the day of 793, of whom 745 were due to gas.

Sunday 16 June

Hughes and 1/6 were relieved the following day by 2/7 commanded by Capt. Patrick J. Hurley, and his battalion tied in with the 23d Infantry to their right. Major Jesse Gaston, with 3/7, moved into the area covered by 3/5 and extended across the road into Belleau Wood to tie in with Adams. Hurley had his men continue installing the barbed wire that 1/6 had begun days before.

Harbord's Report of Operations signified that the day was "relatively quiet." Yet he mentioned German artillery work on various roads within

Engineers of the Second Division stringing wire in Belleau Wood.

the brigade sector and especially noted that "ten German planes came over.... Allied planes are seldom seen...." He added, "Nothing else of importance to report."

Division reported that "the men are beginning to sicken at the French canned [monkey] meat, and, in general, do not like the French ration. Some diarrhea is beginning to appear.... Request is made to supplement the ration with fresh meat or at least a portion of the American ration." Division also received 9 officers along with 233 men as replacements.

Monday 17 June

Adams reported a serious attack, and Harbord minimized it with this entry: "Attack repulsed; probably German patrols." He added that German planes were very active and "it is almost impossible to make a move in the area without coming under the eye of a balloon observer." Sarcastically, he added, "Our aviation is either passive or non-existent." At 0810 Col.Malone raised the universal question: "The Marines are being relieved, are we going to be also?" Then he added "If not, I'm going to have to replace Capt. Charles E. Moore and

I Co in Bouresches, because the strain is more than they can stand for long." The colonel was right, of course, the town was constantly being shelled and attacked by the Germans. It was a key point which both sides recognized, perhaps the Germans more than the Americans.

During the evening hours, the 7th Infantry tried another attack, which failed and forced the men back to their starting line. Meanwhile the 23d MG Co, 6th MG Bn, supported the 7th Infantry with a barrage. During this period, the remnants of the 4th Brigade rested and many found to their dismay that their packs had been violated by troops in the rear. Many personal goods had been purloined, and valuable, irreplaceable mementoes were gone. This same thing would happen to all AEF front line troops one or more times during the war.

From this time forward the 7th Infantry would continue to try its collective best to remain in the woods and not lose any ground. The Germans continued to pressure them and each time the 7th saw a modest loss of hard-earned ground.

Tuesday 18 June

That previous evening Maj. Elliott, 3/23, recommended that Malone not consider trying to straighten the line so as to bring Bouresches within his firm control on the south end. He recommended instead, "Hold the town as it is or give it up altogether ..." the latter course not being a likely exercise, Malone had to consider continuing the salient exposure of his men within the town. He was also receiving pressure from Maj. Elliott for a relief of his battalion. They had all been serving in the combat zone and were getting very tired, even with occasional but minimal relief.

Captain James O. Green reported to Maj. Elliott that the trenches dug upon the hill overlooking the Bouresches-Vaux road weren't worth the exercise. "They are dug in a sandy soil which would offer little resistance to heavy shelling from high explosives.... They are in full view of the hills held by the enemy and are open to direct artillery and machine gun fire from there." In other words, the place was useless, like most of the area occupied by the 2d Division. Malone sent Green's report through to Preston Brown with no comment.

In Gen. Bundy's daily report to Chaumont he gave figures for losses suffered by 2/5 to date. The battalion began 31 May with 36 officers and 1,051 men. As of 18 June their losses were 20 officers and 617 men, more than half of both.[50] Nonetheless, 2/5 recovered slightly when they received 2 officers and 122 men as replacements. A couple of days later Turrill's 1/5 was described as suffering 544 enlisted casualties out of 1,040 and the loss of 16 officers of the original 27. On the next day's report, Holcomb's 2/6 was in even worse shape, mainly because of the various gas attacks they had suffered. Their casualties stood at 21 officers out of 31 and 836 men of the original 941. Four officers replaced the 21 and 361 enlisted replacements brought those totals up to nearly half the original strength.

Wednesday 19 June

Early in the morning, Capt. Starr Sedgwick Eaton,* CO L Co, (see 1 July) described to Elliott how his positions were arranged. His men weren't in a continuous line, as there weren't enough of them to cover the entire ground that way. Consequently he broke them up into teams. Their "rifle pits were in groups" with 6 to 10 men in each group. The foxholes were spaced at least ten, and more often 30, yards apart. He had also arranged his automatics so as to cover his entire area. It appears that Malone wished to replace his men by platoons, which, under the circumstances, Eaton explained, was not doable for L Co.

Later in the afternoon a French liaison officer name Villaret sent a message to Col. Malone that "There is nothing new to report; all is unusually quiet." However, the Germans didn't know that. They continued in their shelling and patrol activity all that night.

Thursday and Friday 20–21 June

Other than the continual German artillery practice upon the lines of both the 9th and 23d infantry regiments and occasional patrols to and from the lines, this day was relatively quiet for the 2d Division. Captain Moore offered to remain where he was since K Co was full of new men who were "uncomfortable" and their sergeant had to turn in to sick bay. Moore's message to Elliott was clear and somewhat detailed. He said there were 150–175 new men and Capt. Valentine, CO, was willing to come but "has no confidence in his men, as they are." He admitted that he and his men were tired but it wouldn't get any better until they were fully out of the line. He reckoned that they could last another five days or so: "When I leave this place I want to keep on going until I get entirely out of it and never see it again."

Malone sent a message to Elliott in which he stated, "It is a joy to have such a man [Moore] guarding my left flank. Please convey to him my appreciation." Later that afternoon Maj. Elliott was obviously fed up with various staff members. His response to Col.Malone indicates that 3/23 was starting to get very testy from exhaustion. The report is included in detail because it makes good reading:

Requests, orders, and reports of some of the staff are so absurd, ludicrous and in many cases impossible I request that the following officers visit my C.P. as soon as possible to see the situations for themselves. Regt. Gas Officer, I[ntelligence].O., Sig[nal]. Officer, Surgeon. For instance to receive instructions that "no one will sleep within 1200 yards of the front line unless in a gas proof dugout and with gas sentries over each dug-out" would keep us all awake all of the time...."A man exposed to mustard gas should have a warm bath with soap and change of clothing," when as a matter of fact we don't get enough water to wash regularly and some are about to fall through their clothes even though requisitions were submitted some time ago. We are supposed to have two O.P.'s [out posts] — doubtful if they can be found. Liaison with left company by lamp, telephonic communication with light wire in shelled areas and a few other things which sound fine theoretically.[51]

After that Elliott continued in the same outraged vein, complaining that these instructions were "doped" out of a book: "The *actual defense* of this position ... takes some time each day." In other words, stop bothering the troops. The following day Malone responded as could be expected: "I have absolute faith in your judgment.... Don't be worried over the 'dope' sent out."[52]

Captain James O. Green of M Co was now on different ground and well dug in with assistance from a few 9th Infantry platoons. The new location was south of the Lucy-Bouresches road. His description pleased Malone and he passed along his regards and thanks to Maj. George C. Bowen of the 9th Infantry.

Elliott was still upset the following day. Then he blasted the officer in charge of sending hot meals: "The one hot meal is only *one* meal. What becomes of the other *two*?" Then he mentioned that some of the food had spoiled and was thrown out. He wanted Lt. Stokely to work over the mess sergeants to make them "*think* and act" as if that one meal was all they were going to get.

At 0945 the 9th Infantry was pushing their lines forward and Malone advised Maj. Waddill of 1/23 to move with them to keep the lines constant.

The only other activity was that of the 7th Infantry in Belleau Wood. They and the Germans were still exchanging unpleasantries. At daybreak 1/7, without artillery preparation, tried an attack and within minutes the German machine guns forced them to retire to their original positions. In fact, according to Lt Villaret, French liaison officer, in a report to Malone, "The enemy counter attacked and succeeded in increasing his position in the northern part of these woods." Malone's response was, "We have to accept small knocks and smile. Better luck next time." That afternoon Malone sent a message from Adams to his intelligence officer that a "suspicious character" was going around in an "F.A. officer's uniform. Issue stringent order" to apprehend. Harbord's reaction was not very pleasant to Lt. Col. Adams in his response to the latter's report.

At a very late hour Capt. Russell Beall sent Col.Upton a message informing him that there had been a heavy shelling of the entire position of the 9th Infantry and casualties had been heavy. In fact 6 enlisted men were killed and

15 wounded. Only two of the wounded were returned to duty, the balance being evacuated to hospitals out of the area.

That night 3/7 spread their flanks eastward into the woods while 1/7 withdrew about 600 yards and division artillery sprayed the northern end of the woods once again, to little avail. In the morning at 0315, 1/7 tried again. The advance was stopped within a few feet and they were forced to retire to a line farther back than that which they took over from the Marines on 15 June. The battalion commander reported 170 casualties in the attempt.

Back near Montreuil, Maj. Littleton W.T. Waller, Jr., son of the famous Littleton W.T. Waller, arrived to assume command of the 6th MG Bn, replacing Osterhout, who returned to command the 23d Co. The French corps changeover occurred on 21 June. Corps XXI was replaced with Corps III. General Naulin was relieved and his replacement was Gen. LeBrun.

Saturday 22 June

Marines reentered the lines on this date. The infantry in the northern part of the woods was relieved by Shearer and 3/5 during the night 21–22 June, after which the Marines settled into the new line.[53] That day and evening was spent in patrolling the front to ascertain the German positions. Otherwise it was relatively quiet. One member of the 20th Co., Sgt. Merwin H. Silverthorn, complained about the food supply. He mentioned that the only decent food they had was taken from dead French, German, or 7th Infantry soldiers' packs. Some of that was "monkey meat," better known as dried beef in cans. No one seemed ever to like it but they would eat it because they had little else.

Upton complained to Malone about his men going out before darkness and bringing down artillery fire upon the 9th Infantry. Malone passed along the message and added, "Put on sentinel and stop circulating. Allow no movement for water ... until after dark."

His 2d platoon leader, unnamed, sent a message to Capt. Moore that his men had today buried "George L. Young, U.S.M.C. #271810, probably killed June 6/18." Young had actually been lying there since 3 June and the corpse must have been in bad shape. Malone sent Moore a very nice supportive message late that evening in which he stated, "Your gameness and leadership are winning you a place in the history of the regiment. I am proud of your achievement and appreciate the task you are accomplishing." He added that Maj. Gen. Bundy had also sent his regards.

That day Col. Jacques Aldebert de Chambrun[54] sent a message to Gen. Bundy explaining what the French could and would do when and if the 2d Division made a decision to assault and take the village of Vaux. That, of course, would come early in July, therefore few arrangements had been made at this point in time.

Notice went around the 23d Infantry that some patrols with slips of paper would be going out during the night. Another message said: "Patrols to dispense *educational literature* among the Germans will be sent out tonight between 11 P.M.–1 A.M." [emphasis added]. Obviously, this was propaganda.

That night Maj. Berton W. Sibley and his fighting men of 3/6 reentered the lines and relieved 2/7 in about the same spot from which they had vacated the woods. The soldiers had increased the defenses by nearly completing the wiring job originally assigned to 1/6. In addition, they had buried the Marines lying about as well as the German dead.

Sunday 23 June

As soon as it became light enough, 3/6 expanded their position to make contact with 3/5, further north in the woods. Finally relieved, by B Co, 4th MG Bn, the 77th Co, 6th MG Bn, then marched back to a wooded area just east of Montreuil to join the 23d Co for a few hours' rest. The machine gunners had been working straight through, nearly the entire month.

Sometime during this day, Lt. Col. Frederick Wise was relieved of command of 2/5,[55] being replaced by Maj. Ralph S. Keyser.* Later this evening and early morning, 23–24 June, 2/5 would assume the division's westward most position and relieve 3/7.[56] Hill 142, formerly the extent of the left flank, was now held by a French infantry unit. Because of heavy losses the territory held by the 4th Brigade had been reduced significantly during the month of June. On its right flank, the 23d Infantry, which had also suffered considerable casualties, had its territory reduced with the 9th Infantry taking up their slack.

Lieutenant Colonel Carey H. Brown, now commanding the 2d Engineers, requested that the 5th Marines return two of his men, Pvts. Ballard and Pennington of E Co. They had been sent as support on 6 June to Hill 142: "Haven't been heard from since." There is no record of the response or whether they were still alive.

At 1900 an attack was launched by 3/5 against the ground still held by the Germans in the northern part of the woods. Machine guns mowed the Marines down. Their fire was so interlocked that even though the Marines knocked some out others were positioned to cover those. The ground was rocky and such that no one could dig in. German artillery added to the misery. By 2320 the attack was stalled and 3/5 was back in its old positions but with additional losses of over a hundred Marines. Neville reported to Harbord, "Things are rather bad. One company almost wiped out." He was writing of the 16th Co led by Capt. Robert Yowell, which lost an officer and 75 men. The 20th Co, Capt. Richard Platt, lost at least another 26. Both were in the center of the battalion's advance. The Germans were still not ready to leave Belleau Wood. They would have a few more days left to occupy those woods.

Monday 24 June

This was a day of mourning and rest. As soon as the clock moved beyond midnight the Germans began a very heavy gas attack against the 3d Brigade. The 23d Infantry suffered a total of 162 casualties and the 9th Infantry were hit for at least seven straight hours, mainly with mustard gas and some high explosives. The division reported a total of 339 gas casualties, which meant that the 9th suffered at least as many casualties as the 23d. Third Brigade solicited 2d Artillery Brigade counter battery, which was supplied.

The Division history stated, "It was evident that the task [taking the entire woods] was one that could not be accomplished without strong artillery support." It had taken numerous casualties and more than three weeks for the various principals to arrive at that decision. The 5th Marines, the 6th Marines and, to a certain extent, the 7th Infantry, had all been shattered in Belleau Wood, before the leaders arrived at that conclusion. Consequently, a conference was held which included Harbord and staff, 4th Brigade, Chamberlaine and the colonels of three artillery regiments, Neville and Feland plus the three battalion COs, and appropriate officers representing French artillery. It was decided to really work over the northern end of the woods that day and evening into 25 June.

Tuesday 25 June

This was, as the Germans would say, *Der Tag*. For most of the day, from 0300 to 1700, artillery pounded the woods. The heavy artillery, American and French, worked at the northern part of the woods, firing at least 2,300 rounds on that compact area. An unknown number of rounds were sent over by the 75's. At 1700 3/5 went "over the top." They also were supported by the 83d Co, 3/6, which went with them. The Germans were in tough shape. The big guns had made them very unstable. But many were still ready for the Marines that were to come.

Nearly an hour after the jump-off, Shearer reported a few casualties but very little enemy machine gun fire. Marines didn't throw themselves at machine guns in frontal assaults, as they had for three weeks. Many guns were not working, because their German operators were out of action — shell-shocked, dead or wounded. For comparison, the 11 June firing was a mere 700 rounds of light stuff. This time the Marines' artillery support gave them a fair chance to succeed and they did.

By 2130 Shearer's 3/5 held most of the woods with just a smattering of Maxims and their gunners still holding ground. Messages from 3/5 rolled in: "47th Co. gained objective — 20th and 47th digging in. 45th still in reserve but will occupy positions just as soon as things settle." The first two companies sent an estimated 150 prisoners back to Brigade headquarters. Yowell's 16th Co was

Illustration portraying the 5th Marines fighting in shattered Belleau Wood.

the only one finding stiff resistance. The 47th was counterattacked and Shearer asked for two platoons from Keyser, his next door neighbor: "Please keep artillery and machine guns going to stop reinforcements of the enemy." Then an hour later he sent this: "Need replacements badly to hold on" and "counterattack would be fatal to us in present condition." At 2312 "*We have taken practically all of the woods but do need help to clean it up and hold it.* Do we get it?" (emphasis in original).[57]

Keyser had orders to expand his right to the woods and to keep pace with 3/5's advance. He did so and made contact with 3/5 late in the evening. The Marines' line now ran from just below Hill 142 eastward through the woods and south to 3/6, which was positioned near 3/23 still located in Bouresches.

Harbord told Neville, "I have no fear of a counter attack by the Germans tonight," which meant that Shearer could set all his worries aside. Harbord also told Neville that he had ordered Keyser to send a platoon to aid the 16th Co. He was still bypassing the chain of command.

In the meantime, the French Sixth Army was planning combined attacks upon the Germans at the eastern portion of the 2d Division front. The objective for the French III Corps lay just before the 9th Infantry's front. The line would be from the northern edge of Bois de Cote [Hill] 204 down into Vaux up to the Bois de la Roche and to the Bois de la Cote 192. The date of attack would be announced later.

On the following day, headquarters reported a total of 7 German officers and 302 men made prisoners by 3/5, plus numerous captured machine guns and large quantities of material.

Wednesday 26 June

By early morning 3/5 was in command of most of the woods; Shearer's losses, dead and wounded, were totaled at 4 officers and 119 enlisted men. Overall the Marine Brigade suffered 250 casualties that day. The few Marine prisoners taken by the Germans earlier in the day were released before they were removed from the woods.

One Marine private, Henry P. Lenert, a runner, was stopped by Germans in the woods after he had delivered a message. After questioning which Marine units were where, Lenert told him the entire 6th Marine Regiment was now in the woods, a consecrated lie. The German major decided that was more than they could handle and asked if he and his men could turn themselves over to Lenert as prisoners, after which the Marine private hauled his load of seventy-eight Germans (some say as many as 100) back to brigade headquarters, asking an American officer standing there, "Hey bud! What will I do with these prisoners I've just captured?" This story went all the way up to Chaumont, where it was discounted as "more Marine propaganda."[58]

This evening Lt. Col. Thomas Holcomb and 2/6 relieved 3/5 in the woods and the latter were sent back to the Bois Gros Jean for a well-earned rest. At the same time 3/23, overwhelmingly exhausted at Bouresches, was relieved by 2/23. While there, 3/23 had withstood numerous German attacks upon their positions in and around the town, but nary once were they driven out.

Thursday to Saturday 27–29 June

During these three days the major alterations to the line were in and around Belleau Wood. Harbord sent 1/6 in to the southern portion of the woods to relieve Sibley and 3/6 and to back up Holcomb. Eventually, the 6th Marines assumed complete control over the woods and the 5th Marines moved westward to join the French 43d Division's right flank on Hill 142. On the 27th, the French 39th Division relieved the French 10th Colonial Division, located on the 2d Division's right flank.

Additionally, plans, based upon orders from the French Sixth Army, were firmed up. Because they were specific and important to the outcome of the next few days, they will be covered in some detail here. Provisional Field Order 18, from 3d Brigade, was issued on 28 June but was to be slightly altered on 30 June. Essentially this plan showed a great deal more thought and planning than had the one hurriedly issued by division and 4th Brigade some three weeks earlier.

Sunday 30 June

The order began: "The Third Corps [French] will attack the line HILL 204 — VAUX — Woods North and Northeast of HILL 192 on J day at H hour." The French 10th Division had managed to occupy Monneaux on 6 June and two days later were partly up on the southern part of Hill 204. The 9th Infantry had pretty much retained their original positions during the month. In fact the semiofficial history reads:

> During this period of fighting for the Bois de Belleau, the front of the 3d Brigade, with the exception of the movement of the 23d Infantry on June 6th, had been comparatively quiet.

It then goes on to explain that "the brigade had not been inactive," and gives some information about digging trenches and aggressive patrols which dominated the enemy front. Many of the casualties of the 9th Infantry occurred from 23 June forward. Overall, the 3d Brigade losses during June were given as "17 officers and 302 enlisted men killed, and 36 officers and 1414 enlisted wounded."[59]

In addition to the 3d Brigade the French 39th Division, part of the XXXVIII Corps on their right, would also advance. Both would be supported by 2d Division, and French III Corps, and XXXVIII Corps artillery and air service. The 23d Infantry would mainly be left flank, assigned to take the Bois de la Roche, located to the north of Vaux, to help take the town itself. The 9th Infantry's zone of advance, on the right flank, was relatively narrow but the regiment would be primarily involved with taking Vaux. Third Battalion, 23d Infantry, B Co, engineers, and D Co, 5th MG Bn, under command of Maj. Elliott, was assigned to the lead role for that regiment. Major Arthur E. Bouton* would lead 2/9, A Co, of the engineers, and the 9th MG Co and would take Vaux. The lineup formation and movement east was from south to north. The town was a hotbed of resistance, the Germans having occupied and strengthened it for more than a month. The Brigade Reserve, 3/9, A Co, 5th MG Bn, were all under the command of Maj. Alfred C. Arnold.

Fortunately during this period the many patrols and regular daily observation gave many clues as to what the problems would be and the 9th and 23d were primed and ready. The town was down at the bottom of a ravine, but the

Germans still occupied most of Hill 204, the highest ground, and would support the defenders from there. It was a substantial spot, with a copious panoramic view. The buildings in Vaux are generally of stone and located on both sides of the main road from Paris into Chateau Thierry. It wasn't going to be easy no matter how much external support the infantry could expect.

Later that day the 3d Brigade learned that 1 July was "J Day," and "H hour" was selected to be at 1800. Brigadier General Lewis went over the high points of the assault with Col. Upton of the 9th and Malone of the 23d and Col. Albert J. Bowley of the 17th FA who now commanded the 2d Artillery Brigade, Chamberlaine having been promoted and relieved on 27 June.

Late in the day, perhaps right at 1800, the artillery began playing their tune. According to the records it went on for 24 hours and most likely became tiresome to the Germans long before that.

Monday 1 July

Malone was having minor problems. As late as 0830, the officer commanding D Co, 5th MG Bn, hadn't shown up, and Elliott was having a fit. Also, Malone requested that Upton supply the officer required by both regiments for liaison between them. Malone simply stated, "I'm so short of officers I cannot send one.... Please send an officer." The message traffic, especially from Malone, was especially heavy during that day. He, obviously angry at being sidetracked, let his command know that from 1400 on he would not give orders: "Gen. Lewis is in command."

The artillery fire was doing its job; by noon the town of Vaux was entirely engulfed in fire from the artillery. By 1700 Malone had his units in position, mostly in the Bois de Morette. Major Bouton had his battalion arranged as follows: two companies in line, one in support and the fourth in reserve. The first two were to plunge ahead following the barrage to their objective and with the engineers consolidate their position. The support company would take Vaux and then defend it against anticipated counterattacks. Major Elliott had three companies on line and the 4th in reserve. They, of course, were going against the woods and would be in the open for a much longer period. The Germans would have clearer fields of fire over relatively open ground and the casualties were expected to be much greater.

At 1755 the barrage commenced and in two minutes lifted and moved forward a hundred yards. That rate would continue during the advance. At 1800 off went the infantry closely following the barrage. The Germans were in bad shape, the attack seemed to have been completely unexpected.[60] The few that stood their ground and fought back were rapidly taken in flank and wiped out if not captured. Within an hour the Yanks were on their objective and the Germans were either dead, or wounded and captured. At 1815, Company F of

Battery F, 15th Field Artillery Regiment, firing in support of the 23d Infantry near Belleau Wood.

the 9th Infantry was apparently the first unit to enter the town. After some hard fighting the town was taken and the engineers and infantrymen went about setting up their defenses. A half hour later Lewis of the 3d Brigade was thrilled to advise Division of the great success of his brigade: "Attack complete surprise.... Behavior of men splendid." Col. Upton forwarded to Lewis a message from Elliott of 3/23 which stated, "All the front is secure. Many machine guns captured."

Several members of infantry and artillery regiments wrote letters home after the fact describing the events as they saw them. All agreed that 1 July was a viciously hot day and the men suffered accordingly. One man complained that they were wearing several layers of clothing, including oilskin pants and coats, rubber gloves and gas masks: "We looked more like fishermen than soldiers." The Germans were in dugouts, usually in the cellars of the buildings at Vaux, and only the gas shells permeated and caused them numerous gas casualties. Undoubtedly the shelling caused the German defenders severe shellshock, which effectively knocked out many men during the war.

Later that evening several serious attempts were made by elements of the

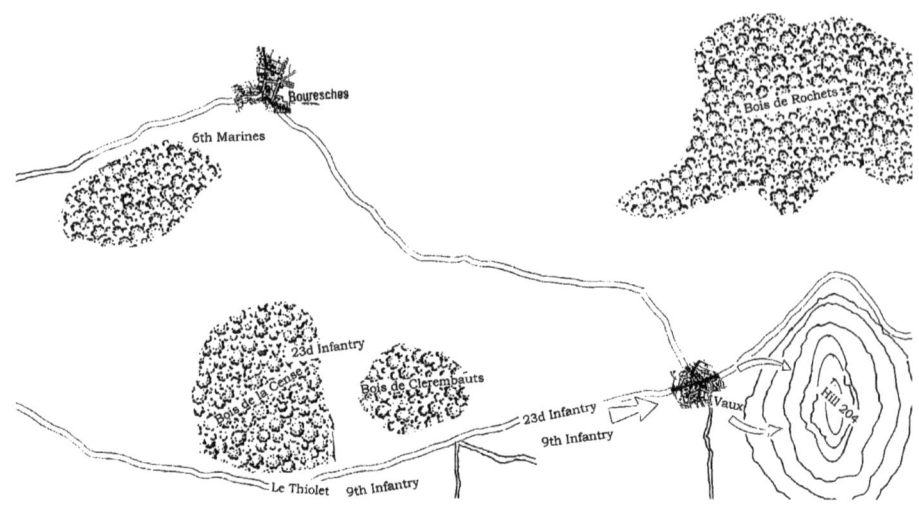

Map 7. Northwest of Chateau Thierry (Vaux), 1/2 July 1918.

401st German Infantry to regain control of Vaux but all failed and the regiment was recalled by the regimental commander. The rest of the regiment defended the crest of Hill 204 which the French 153d Infantry was in the process of trying to take. They had run into severe resistance in that narrow neck held by nearly all the 401st. French soldiers didn't make it and were forced back nearly to their original starting line. Because of this, for a time the right flank of the 9th was exposed to German fire. The left flank, held by the 23d, was in decent shape and had little difficulty but had suffered many casualties. Total losses for the 3d Brigade were grave. One officer and forty-five men were killed and six officers and two hundred sixty four wounded, plus one officer and eleven men missing. The losses were primarily to the 23d Infantry. The German losses totaled 926, most of whom became POWs.

Tuesday and Wednesday 2–3 July

Just after midnight, Elliott advised that he had to put his reserve company on line and requested a company from 1/9 to replace them. Two hours later "Harp One" (Upton) advised Elliott that he would receive two platoons from 1/9 "within an hour." Major Franklin L. Whitley sent Elliott a message at 1425 telling him the two platoons of C Co were now his. The latter was still looking for the two companies as late as 2000.[61] That night, however, 3/23 was withdrawn and 1/9 took its place.

During the day, orders were issued throughout the division to select a company from each regiment to send to Paris for the 4th of July parade and celebration. The French decided to rename the entire 2d Division sector *"Pas fini,"* possibly at the request of some American connected as liaison with the French. The phrase was taken from the Yanks' reply to *"La guerre est fini"* from the retreating French. The war wasn't finished yet, as long as the Americans were in it. Or, as some would say, "Retreat, Hell! We just got here."

Thursday through Sunday 4 to 7 July

The front of the newly named sector was occupied by the division from Vaux through Bois de la Roche to Bouresches and ended at Bois de Belleau. The latter was soon to be officially renamed the Bois de la Brigade de la Marine. The breakdown was the same: 3d Brigade on the right and 4th Brigade on the left, and no trenches as such, but a series of strong points with at least one battalion across the rear of each regiment as support. There were to be no more attacks for the 2d Division, at least for a few days or more. Somehow food managed to get to the front lines and the men began to eat on a fairly regular basis. They no longer needed to pilfer the packs of the French and German dead, nor eat the reserve rations, which everyone already had, even upon pain of charges being brought against them.

As early as 2 July orders were received that notified the French and Americans that the I Corps under Maj. Gen. Hunter Liggett, USA, would take over the line as of 4 July. That same day the 2d Division headquarters were recipients of a message which indicated that the 26th "YD" Division would replace them. The 52d Brigade would be brought up in trucks and on 4–5 July the 4th Brigade would be replaced. Two days later the 51st Brigade would come up and replace the 3d Brigade. Second Brigade artillery would also be relieved beginning on the night of 5–6 July. The well informed German intelligence service sent over a message in English on 4 July: "Goodbye, Second — Hello, Twenty-sixth." The YD was a very active and well-trained division and it wasn't long before they easily moved into their new surroundings. In July it would become their task to advance beyond the farthest line attained by the 2d Division in conjunction with a major attack all along the line.

Though the troops of the 2d Division were relieved in the frontlines, they remained close by for the anticipated German counterattack. The 3d Brigade, interestingly enough, was assigned to the rear of the line previously occupied by the Marines. The Marines took up positions on the south side of the Paris-Chateau Thierry road. They managed to actually swim in the Marne once or twice. It was several more days before the troops were effectively sent a little further out of the line of fire for rest and relaxation. That was to last only a few days, less than a week. Trouble was being stirred up about fifty miles further north and the French, who planned most activity for the Americans, had need of good American troops. The 2d Division (Regular) were good American troops.

Group portrait of the remnants of the 2d Battalion, 6th Marines, after the Belleau Wood campaign.

Following the one month exercise, most often titled "The Battle of Belleau Wood," many comments on Belleau Wood and Vaux were expressed by different people, some but not all by observers of what went on during June 1918. Here are three, one American, one German and one French. They are representative of all:

> Supreme War Council, American Section, Versailles, Fr. July 1, 1918.
> To Gen. J. J. Pershing, CinC, AEF.
>
> Frequently remarks have been made to me by French officers of all ranks, by French civilians, and by my British colleagues, plainly expressing their belief that the American troops in the vicinity of Château-Thierry stopped the German drive, and very possibly saved Paris.
>
> (Sgd) TASKER H. BLISS, General, U.S. Army, American Permanent Military Representative.

In March 1923, there was a public controversy on the subject of the Allied occupation of the Ruhr district between Herr Gessler, German minister of defense and General Dégoutte, French occupation commander in the Ruhr. It was reported in the Associated Press. In a rejoinder made by Herr Gessler reported in the *New York Times* of March 2, 1923, the following sentence appears:

4. Chateau Thierry

In the summer of 1918 France was saved only by the fact that an American division revived the fighting, and at the last moment prevented the taking of Paris.[62]

French inhabitants of the region where the 2d Division operated expressed their gratitude. On July 10 the mayor of the Meaux District *(Arrondissement)* sent to the Division a resolution passed by all the mayors of the district. It reads:

> Voted in a Congress of the Mayors of the Meaux District who were eye-witnesses on the 25th of June, 1918.
> The Mayors of the Meaux District who were eye-witnesses of the generous and efficacious deeds of the American Army in the stopping of the enemy advance send to this Army the heartfelt expression of their admiration and gratefulness.
>
> Meaux, June 25th, 1918.
> The President of the Committee,
> G. Lugol

Not much more need be added to the above to explain that this battle was the most important one fought by American troops in the war. It was that which stopped the Germans from any further advance into France. Though both the 26th Division and the 1st Division had fought earlier battles, none were so effective in proving the will and ability of Americans to stay and fight and their determination to win — one month and the Americans not only stayed the rout

German trenches in Belleau Wood, after eighty years.

but beat the mightiest army then in existence. The Germans learned that lesson almost as soon as the French. It was sufficient knowledge to make them aware that the war was truly now lost for Germany.

During this period, the Second Division suffered a total of 7,876 casualties, attached units suffered another 375. The division began the battle with 26,063 effectives and on 30 June, after replacements, it had 24,042.

5

Soissons

Members of the 2d Division were encamped in quiet zones, more or less, for the better part of two entire weeks. There were several interruptions, the one most pleasant was that which required representatives from each unit to parade in Paris on 4 July 1918. Otherwise, other than guard duty and the normal everyday exercises of a military force such as obtaining food, health care, cleaning of persons and clothes, and other human endeavors, it was rather tranquil. Some members managed to swim in the great Marne River, engage in minor athletics, write letters home and read some that had finally arrived. That was a good thing: the officers and men were worn out and needed plenty of rest and relaxation.

Serious plans to disrupt that paradise were being made by the French army, however, and the division was included in those plans. On Bastille Day, 14 July 1918, orders were received at division headquarters at 1900 advising that it had been placed at the "disposal" (a superb word choice for the ultimate outcome) of the French Tenth Army. Additionally, the artillery brigade had orders to move fifteen miles further north to Betz,[1] and at 2100 moved out for their destination. Their commanding officer, Brig. Gen. Albert J. Bowley, moved ahead of his artillery columns to their destination of Chantilly, arriving at nearly midnight. There he reported to Tenth Army headquarters just after midnight on 14–15 July, at which time he was instructed to return the following morning to meet with the Tenth Army's commander, Gen. Charles Mangin.[2]

That morning Mangin gave him his basic outline and orders. The news arrived at 1300, however, that the division artillery was to return to the 2d Division command. So, preparations for the reassignment began, but those orders were cancelled at 1400 — fun and games in France. Then the 2d Artillery Brigade received orders to march for the Villers-Cotterêts forest about a dozen miles north of the town of the same name. On the way they endured traffic congestion, many French troops moving to the front. It took the brigade slightly more than a day to arrive at their destination.

The 4th Brigade was now, and would be but briefly, commanded by Col. Harry Lee.[3] As his replacement, Lt. Col. Thomas Holcomb had briefly assumed command of the 6th Marine Regiment, while Col. Logan Feland commanded the 5th Marine Regiment. Lt. Col. Hiram Bearss, who had been Lee's second in command, had become seriously ill and had been transferred to a hospital in Paris. Colonel James F. McIndoe had just been promoted to IV Corps engineering officer and was replaced in command of the 2d Engineers by Col.William A. Mitchell. At Division staff, Col. Arthur L. Conger was replaced by Lt. Col. George A. Herbst. Maj. Gen. Omar Bundy, considered deficient by AEF headquarters, was promoted to command the newly activated VI Corps (but sans any troops), and Brig. Gen., promoted to Maj. Gen. (15 July), James G. Harbord moved up to command the 2d Division. However, as we shall see in the days ahead, the latter had little chance to actively command the division. Essentially, the French army took the division away from American command and directed them during the combat phase. It was not a good time for the American command and worse for their troops.

Back on the Marne, the division infantry and assorted support services were still trying to recover from their month long ordeal. In mid-month, heavy fighting was taking place up the Marne River east of Château Thierry. The Germans launched a major assault against the untried 3d Division (Regular), that latter appellation a rather nebulous term with some of the United States Army divisions. The attack began on the morning of 14–15 July. At first the enemy crossed the river and made modest gains in some places. But, to most everyone's surprise, the Americans met the Germans coming over the river and for the most part stood their ground and gave back as good as and then better than they received. Two of the infantry regiments, the 30th and the 38th, did very well, particularly the latter, which earned and deserved the nickname "Rock of the Marne" for their stand while being assaulted on their front and both flanks. They gave the Germans hell and vice versa, but they didn't give ground.

Up north the French had been engaged in making plans. The enemy had moved into the Soissons area during their major attacks in the spring. But now the French were determined to make arrangements for the territory's return to their ownership. Unfortunately for the two main divisions to be engaged, both American, the 1st Division (Regular) and the 2d Division (Regular), they were generally kept as much in the dark as was the enemy. What was worse, so were their commanders. The French added a very used up North African division composed of Moroccans and Senegalese to be in the middle with the 1st Division on their left and the 2d Division on their right.

The French gave the 1st Division a bit of time to arrive within their proposed striking area, but for some reason arrival of the 2d Division was to be on the run. On the evening of 15 July, at 2030, a French staff officer arrived at Chamigny, division headquarters, and said that the division infantry would move, somewhere, not stated. Division headquarters would close at Chamigny at 1000 on 17 July and reopen at the same time and date at Carrefour de

Nemours. A division staff officer was directed to Marcilly to find further orders. He arrived but the orders hadn't. It was that kind of war.

Harbord, now back with the division, and his chief of staff, Col. Preston Brown, closed division headquarters down on the afternoon of the 16th and reported at Headquarters, Tenth Army. Mangin was up front and no one else knew much of anything, except that the 2d Division was now a part of the French XX Corps. For the most part, that is about all they would learn for the next few days. Their division was, effectively, no longer theirs. Later, in his memoir, Harbord wrote, "A division of twenty-eight thousand men, the size of a European army corps, had been completely removed from the control of its responsible commander and deflected by marching and truck through France to a destination unknown to any of the authorities responsible either for its supply, its safety, or efficiency in the coming attack."[4] He had more to add but that was more of his resentment coming out in print many years after the events.

The division infantry were taken for a ride, and what a ride it was. Worse, when they arrived at their destination in the Fôret de Retz, they were given a few hours, very few, to rest up and then make their way to the jump-off line, many miles ahead. The 3d Brigade had it somewhat easier, not a whole lot, but they were located nearer to where they should be. The 4th Brigade was further

Troops of the Second Division mounting their camions for the journey to Soissons.

away, about fifteen miles further back, and would have a terrible trip through a monstrous traffic jam to the front on foot.

The French general Hellé wrote: "My late chief, General Mangin, was delighted to receive American divisions to coöperate in his offensive." Then he adds, "It was with the greatest spirit of sacrifice, that the Marine Brigade and the 3rd Brigade, forgetting their fatigue, hastened to the forest of Villers-Cotterets and went through it, despite the greatest difficulties."[5]

The advance was to begin on the early morning of 18 July, at about 0435. There were no reserves for either Marines or soldiers. The formation of the division was to be as follows: The 23d Infantry was on the division's right bounds with its left flank covered by the 9th Infantry, the 5th Marines were to have the left bounds of the division, their right flank covered by the 9th Infantry. In fact, their frontage was as large as the other two regiments combined; because only one Marine regiment was included the 5th would have to cover the ground, three regiments to go forward abreast on a very wide front with an extremely sharp swing to the right after passing Translon Farm. Whoever planned that movement is probably still rotting in hell. However, since no one would have an opportunity to reconnoiter the field, and maps were nearly nonexistent, the 5th Marines went slightly astray. Most of the officers involved later stated that they had not seen, or had barely seen, a map, singular. But few officers owned one. In the meantime, the 6th Marines, and the 6th Marine Machine Gun Battalion were in corps reserve, while assorted service units, like the 2d Engineers, were the division reserves. This is discussed further below.

Because of the width of the division front, they were each to have a two battalion front, with one battalion in support, but, again no reserve. The 1st (Turrill) and 2d (Keyser) battalions of the 5th were to advance and 3/5 was to be the support. Unfortunately, the latter had been chewed up at Belleau Wood late in June and had not yet received replacements. Therefore, they were down to below 500 officers and men and would be unable to provide much service if required to replace an attack battalion. First Lieutenant Elliott D. Cooke, skipper of the 55th Co., 2/5, was one of the best reporters of events at Belleau Wood and Soissons. He tells in his memoir of how, on the night before the Fifth Marines were to launch their attack, he and the other officers of the battalion were briefly told by Major Keyser what their role would be on the morrow. Hardly anyone got a look at the one map available and no one had any weapons which the French authorities described in their attack order. Worse, Keyser directed that each company CO select one officer and twenty men to leave behind. Cooke complained that he only had 160 men and needed all. Keyser replied, "They will be needed as a nucleus to build new companies on, after the attack." Cooke said, "I wish[ed] I had kept my mouth shut."[6]

The 5th's neighbors would be the usually venerable North African Division, but not tomorrow. Gen. Hellé wrote about the 2d Division, "I do not wonder they got out of touch with the Moroccans. We were quite unprepared for such fury in the attack."

Because of the fragmentation, and French diversion of the 2d Division from its normal organizational structure, and the fact that when his troops were desperate for leadership Col. Logan Feland would find himself, much like Maj. Gen. Harbord, outside the command structure of the 2d Division, basically it would be the battalion commanders directing the attacks.

Thursday 18 July

Of the three regiments slated to advance, only the 9th Infantry was in position when the rolling barrage began. Somehow it had managed to avoid the congestion and take its place in line early. However, the infantry brigade's newly assigned commander, Brig. Gen. Hanson Ely, was less well disposed toward the CO of the 9th Infantry, Col. LeRoy Upton, and made his uncertainty known.[7] Regardless of Ely's concern, Upton's 9th would do its duty against an increasingly desperate enemy. In fact the 9th Infantry would garner numerous major awards on this day. The enemy was, surprisingly, taken completely unawares. At least that was the case early that morning and the Allied advance was made less disastrous because of their being unprepared. That in itself was the major part of the ultimate French victory.

Later, Marine Capt. John W. Thomason, Jr., in a written monograph for the U.S. Army Historical Section, stated, "There was the haste and confusion incident to the last-minute concentration for the attack — all made inevitable by the French Army and Corps instructions wherein order and deliberation were compromised to the end that a surprise might be achieved. Thus, no reconnaissance by the American officers was possible ... changes of direction in the course of the action, especially on terrain without prominent natural landmarks, are difficult under the most favorable circumstances and to the best trained troops."[8] Obviously, Thomason didn't think too highly of the French leadership style at Soissons.

The 23d Infantry, and its CO, Col. Paul B. Malone, had to race forward over a mile, and were slightly out of breath when they too went forward following the barrage. That morning, at 0115, Malone had sent a message to the CG, 2d Division: "All my battalions are enroute to their posts. The roads are blocked with traffic," which turned out to be a common complaint for all divisional units. At 0600 he reported that 2/23 was in the lead followed by 1/23, which he was with, and that "friendly troops" were in Vauxcastille.

The 5th Marines, also exhausted from a day and a half in transit, had an even longer course to make before reaching their jump-off position, possibly as much as fifteen miles through that traffic jam. And they were forced to march rapidly much of the way because they were a great distance from where they

Methods used by the Second Division to communicate with its far-flung units, before effective radio contact.

were supposed to be. The sleep-deprived Marines were without food when the 5th was made to double-time for possibly a half-dozen miles in order to make the jump-off on time. Though they were slightly late, a few minutes, they advanced not too far behind the artillery barrage. The barrage had started when they came close and they were forced into a dogtrot to catch up. French planning was not of the highest order.

By 0610 Keyser was reporting to Feland that he was at Verte Feuille Ferme (farm) and had established his PC: "We went well to the first objective... They [2/5] were on the way to the 2nd objective ... 30 minutes ago." Turrill and 1/5 had also managed to move quite rapidly and by 1000 had established a PC in a vacated German dugout at the east end of Laie-du-Translon Ferme.

The 5th Marines' pattern of advance was to move, on the extreme leftflank of the division, in a northeasterly direction. then, at a certain point, to turn an oblique to the right and move southeasterly. The turn to the right that the Marines were supposed to make didn't happen as anticipated. There were no distinguishable marks anywhere and their lack of maps hindered them further. Very few of the company commanders had even seen a map, and perhaps none of the platoon leaders had either.

So, 1/5 continued rapidly moving (to catch up with the rolling barrage) in a northeasterly direction. Because the 5th was running behind they were slightly aft of the advance of the 9th Infantry. Consequently, the 9th, taking fire on their left, naturally bore to their left and began assaulting the Germans and also advancing to the north as they did so. Their history described it this way: "The First Battalion meeting hot fire straight ahead, was unable to expose its flank to make the change of direction." The Moroccans had not kept up with the 2d Division's advance, and therefore had not removed those Germans in their sector. Two companies, the 17th (Capt. LeRoy Hunt) of 1/5 and the 55th (1st Lt Elliott D. Cooke, USA) of 2/5, even managed to take Chaudun, a major town well into that Moroccan sector. The Marines were assisted in that endeavor by elements of the 9th Infantry that had also gone straight forward, not making the planned oblique right turn.

Elliott D. Cooke, a U.S. Army 1st Lt who had been with the Marine Brigade since Verdun and had been leading the 55th Company since early June, told the best-reading story of the taking of Chaudun. His account, and map, indicated that he even saw elements of the 18th Infantry, a 1st Division regiment, plus Africans, arrive at about the same time the town was taken.[9] One of his lads, a man from Buffalo, New York, apparently really had it in for German machine guns. Frank Barcsykowski,* with the aid of a couple of his buddies, charged three machine guns, killing the crews and turning the guns on the enemy, thereby opening up a lane for his comrades to advance. Frank had done something similar back at Belleau Wood on 11 June when he and a buddy took out a machine gun that had been killing his pals. He was awarded a distinguished Service Cross (DSC) at Soissons and an Oak Leaf Cluster for Belleau Wood. He would also be awarded two Silver Stars and a Navy Cross after the war.

Both units were by now clearing the enemy out of the path of the tardy Moroccan division. After the town of Chaudun had been taken the elements of both 1/5 and 1/9, engaged in that capture, made their way south to rejoin their regiments as best they could.

In the meantime, Capt. Charles Speer* had been leading 1/9 but was wounded and evacuated less than a half hour after the advance began. His leadership included capturing an enemy artillery battery (where he was wounded) and leading his men in crossing a ravine. His battalion, however, continued their attack and soon, with support from 1/5, had taken Verte Feuille Farm and 1/5 Maison Neuve Farm. Following as support to Speer was 2/9 led by Maj. Arthur E. Bouton* and it was followed by 3/9 in reserve, led by Capt. Henry H. Worthington, who had earned a DSC at Toul. Bouton was another casualty early on, but his was final. He was awarded a posthumous DSC for his leadership, courage, and dash in leading his battalion against machine guns under terrific artillery fire. The 3d Battalion, 9th Infantry, was well represented in leadership positions but suffered accordingly. Meanwhile, most of the balance of the 3d Brigade and some companies of both 1/5 and 2/5, generally speaking, made the oblique southeasterly turn, and continued their eastward advance, pushing the Germans back many paces well in advance of the rest of the Tenth Army. They took several well-defended positions along the way. Company M, 3/9, with severe losses, took Beaurepaire Farm. Their left flank was still hindered by the lack of Americans on their left flank, which was caused by the non-arrival of the Moroccans.

Upton was not sitting in his PC as a regimental commander would be expected to. He decided that being up front with his troops would give him a much better appreciation of the real situation. Therefore, leaving most of his staff behind, Col. Upton* made his way to Beaurepaire Farm, through many stragglers and malingerers. He, according to his own words, threatened to shoot some of them, especially those hiding and pretending to be wounded. When he arrived at his destination he expressed shock at the devastation and the discovery of so many dead and wounded. There were many other men of the Ninth who earned at least a DSC that day.

Malone's 23d Infantry had, like the 5th Marines, double-timed to their jump-off positions and had left their automatic weapons behind, because of their weight. They were expected to advance, keep abreast of their right flank liaison, the 38th French Infantry Division, and eventually take the town of Vierzy, located in a ravine about a mile east of Vauxcastille. This part of France seems (to a foreign observer) to be composed entirely of rivers, streams, ravines and woods. The part of ground assigned to the 2d Division was mainly the latter two configurations, and the enemy utilized them extremely well. Vauxcastille sits atop a cliff looking down a ravine at the east end of which lies the town of Vierzy. In the ravine are a series of large man-made basins filled with

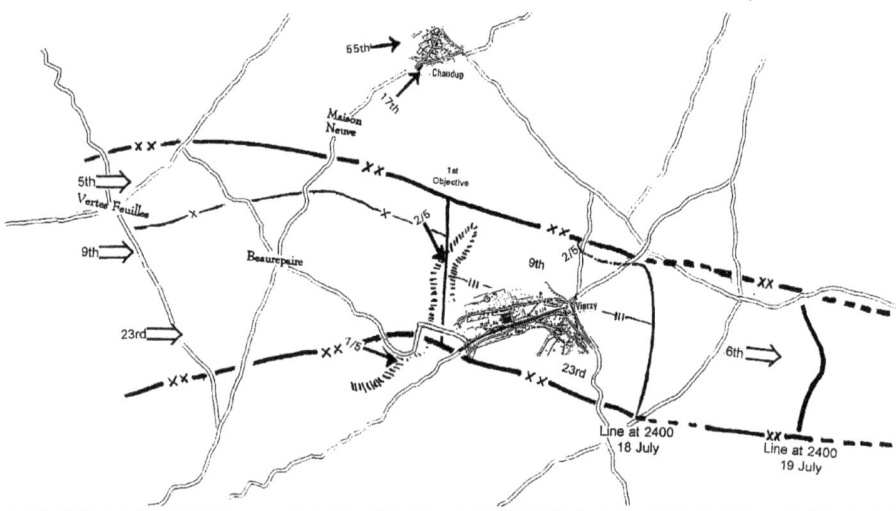

Map 8. Advance of 2d Division at Soissons, 18 and 19 July 1918.

water, all of which would interfere with easy movement by advancing troops, forcing them to the several roads. The Germans had numerous machine gun nests within this ravine and they took their toll of the brave men that tried to advance toward Vierzy. A corporal of K Company, 3/9, Clyde A. Fritz,* a resident of Kokomo, Indiana, along with nine other soldiers, went down into that furnace. He and another soldier were the only survivors of the group, the others all dead or wounded. However, they managed to silence enough guns to make a further advance by 3/9 possible. New York born Robert Hassard,* another corporal, in E Company, 2/9, was wounded three times in that attack upon Vierzy, but refused each time to go to the rear. During the day he provided his platoon leader with valuable services in preparing the line for the anticipated counterattack. He remained with his squad until they were relieved that night. The French thought so highly of his courage and ability he was also the recipient of their *Médaille Militaire.*

Malone soon made Brigade aware of his weapons shortage and the limits that imposed. His men had left their Chauchats behind, probably under his orders, and even though the weapons were obstinate and bulky they did throw out a lot of lead. Malone was a short man in height but large in fighting stature. He was able and willing to provide anyone within hearing a detailed explanation of his complaints. French Renault tanks had been assigned to support the advance of the 23d but Malone was soon informed that, because of the ground, among other reasons, they were not usable. The tanks were stuck in a ravine and couldn't be counted upon for the future. Malone's efforts to take Vierzy would obviously be costly in manpower.

Robert Kean, liaison officer from the 15th FA, advanced with the 23d Infantry and noted that he "encountered a Major of the 23d ... [and] I attached myself to him for a short time, but he was very rattled. He only had one or two runners, had completely lost control over his battalion and did not, in fact, know where his own troops were."[10] Kean also told of how the infantry of the 23d would use his body as a shield, lining up in a row behind him, as they were advancing across the wheat fields. Of course, Kean might have been boasting of his reputation for courage, as opposed to the common soldiers' lack thereof.

The 5th Marines had become somewhat scattered, far off their assigned track, and soon, after capturing Chaudun, 1/5 and 2/5, becoming aware they were offtrack, began moving in a southeasterly direction, across the advancing lines of the 9th and even the 23d Infantry regiments. It was, obviously, quite disconcerting to everyone concerned, perhaps even to the Germans. Two Marines from the 66th Company, 1/5, Sgts Louie Cukela* and Matej Kocak,* both born in what was then Austrian territory, took out machine gun nests that were delaying the advance of 1/5. Both men were later awarded the Medal of Honor, though Kocak's was posthumous.[11] Kocak gathered together about two dozen Moroccan soldiers who were wandering around the field and led them on to take out more German machine gun nests. Cukela, later to be consid-

French Renault tanks badly handled by German artillery at Soissons.

ered quite a character of the Corps, succeeded in getting behind the German machine gun nests chewing up his company and killed the Germans in each nest then knocked out their interconnecting units with rifle fire or hand grenades.

Keyser's 2/5, continuing alongside much of the 9th Infantry, made it to Clancy Ravine but were forced to halt there because the German machine guns were too heavy to take head on. After taking numerous losses in trying to take them, they waited for their French tanks to come up and help. At 1330, with the frontage narrowed down somewhat, 3d Brigade took the lead and the 5th Marines were assigned to support them as directed by Brig. Gen. Ely. Turrill's 1/5 and the 15th MG Company, 6th MG Bn, was assigned to support the 9th Infantry. Keyser's 2/5 and the 23d MG Company went to the 23d Infantry for the afternoon's advance. More confusion would reign.

Meanwhile, PFC Salvatore DiCarlo,* from Los Angeles and a member of B Company, 4th Machine Gun Bn, ran forward and personally knocked out three machine gun nests, killing some but capturing 8 German prisoners while so engaged. He later cared for and assisted the wounded from the battlefield. The division machine gun battalion provided support for all three regiments. The 6th MG Bn had difficulty, some of which was forced marching instead of riding in camions, and they were late in arrival. The 15th Company and 1/5 were assigned duties in support of the 9th Infantry at 1800 on the afternoon of the

18th of July. It was 2100 when the 23d MG Co managed to support the 23d Infantry. In other words, the battalion was in about the same condition as the rest of the 2d Division.

At 1400 Malone reported to Ely that portions of three companies of 2/23 plus attached Marines of 1/5 had attempted to take Vierzy from the north side of the town but the heavy enemy gas and machine gun fire drove them back. All the same, infantry of the division continued their advance against increasing resistance, but finally, by late afternoon, moved to a line east of the village of Vauxcastile in the south and Clancy Ravine in the north. The fighting had been fierce but the leading companies kept up the pressure and gave the enemy little rest. Major d'Alary Fechet,* CO of 2/23, was, with his name undoubtedly French but born in Washington, DC, one of the tough men of the 23d Infantry. He had already been wounded by a shell fragment in his neck but returned to duty and his "energy and personal heroism were material factors in his battalion's successful attack upon the strongly fortified town of Vierzy." Another hero of the regiment was Cpl Edward F. Phelan* of Braintree, Massachusetts, a member of E Company. Phelan left the assaulting waves of his company and singlehandedly went out and killed or captured the entire crew of a machine gun, giving his buddies a safer right flank. That allowed his company to continue moving forward toward Vierzy.

Meanwhile, the Moroccans and 1st U.S. Division were still far behind where they were supposed to be and would be so at the end of the day. All day the 2d Division's left flank, mainly Keyser's 2/5, was greatly exposed to German attack and infiltration and badly hurt because of it. That situation would continue into the following day. In fact, it would be several days after the 2d Division was pulled out of the lineup that the 1st Division and Moroccans would reached the same forward position.

The Germans had been recovering from their initial shock of the morning and were slowly but effectively mounting defenses and at the end of the day the Americans were finding it hard going. Much worse was the near breakdown in communications throughout the 2d Division. By noon, Harbord had received orders for the morrow that prescribed an early morning jump-off from a location far ahead of his division's present positions. He personally ventured forth to pass along the less than happy news to his subordinates. In order to make up the difference, they were to plan a continuance of the attack to begin at 1700 hours that afternoon.

In the meantime the troops were working to earn their keep. Five fighting men[12] of Company G, 2/9, took on a party of more than 60 Germans, and in an intense and desperate hand-to-hand fight, succeeded in killing 22 of the enemy, and capturing 40 more plus 5 machine guns. Sergeant John B. Brewer,* Co. K, led his platoon against a strong machine gun position and at the same time encountered heavy shell fire, but he, severely wounded, pressed on. His second wound took him out of the fight. One of his men, Cpl Herbert A.

Brown,* took out a machine gun nest that was slaughtering his company, thus driving the enemy gunners out. He then took the gun and laid a heavy and withering fire upon the retreating enemy.

By mid-afternoon elements of the 23d Infantry were in the western part of the Vierzy Ravine but finding the going increasingly difficult especially because of the defenses of that town. The 5th Marines had been placed under Ely's command for the duration of the attack that day. However, in a field message at 12:15 P.M., Upton advised Ely that he had told Turrill, "[I] don't need him." He would later on. The efforts of truck driver Pvt. Charles Phillips of Company A, 4th Machine Gun Bn, provided the necessary ammo for his unit, who were covering the advance of the 23d upon Vierzy. Twice that day he drove a truck loaded with ammo to and later through Vierzy under heavy enemy shell fire each time. He would also provide a similar service on the 19th. (See below).

The 9th Infantry history tells us that "Although the battalions were very much reduced in strength and nearly all the officers killed or wounded, the Colonel [Upton] received orders for a further attack to be made that evening to be carried on beyond Vierzy." It describes the advance beginning at 1909 with "the Second and Third Battalions leading and the First in support." They traveled "South of East" at 10 degrees where they crossed Hill 132. They were soon overtaken by darkness and were forced to halt and take up defensive positions.

Turrill had some difficulty. At 1715 he received orders to report to Ely at his PC, located on the Paris-Mauberge highway, which was located about four direct miles from where Turrill was located. Turrill wrote in his operations report, "As soon as possible I started for Vierzy." He brought along his battalion headquarters and on the way they were subjected to sniper fire which wounded two of his men. He met Capt. John Fay, skipper of the 8th Machine Gun Company, who told Turrill that he had just then received his guns and ammo and was heading forward to move with the evening attack. He finally made contact with Ely, who was put out at the delay, since he didn't arrive until 2000. Ely demanded to know where he'd been and "His excitement and anger gave me the impression that there had been some miscarriage of plans and the person responsible therefore had not been ascertained."

Turrill was ordered to take the town of Vierzy. He explained that he had so few men, some with pistols, and none with rifles nor automatic weapons. Ely has been quoted as replying, "They are Marines, aren't they, major?" The Marine grudgingly agreed that was true. After a very bitter exchange Turrill is quoted as saying, "We then took the town."[13] After 1/5 had pushed about three-fourths of the way through Vierzy, elements of the 23d Infantry came in at the north edge of town and continued the advance, taking numerous prisoners. The 2d Division had begun its advance at roughly 1700 hours, though others mentioned 1900 hours, and continued driving past the Virezy line.

During the afternoon, Maj. Keyser had managed to get together three of his four companies. They were the 18th, 43d, and 51st companies, but missing the 55th. He would advance in three lines on a 500 meter front when the time came. His later operations report stated, "The 9th Infantry was on my right, and no one on my left. We had no tank or artillery support." A bit later the 55th Company came up and joined Keyser during the advance. Keyser hadn't gone far when he began receiving heavy fire to his left. Pushing a short distance further, he was forced to retire to "some old trenches" and it was then that he decided to remain where he was for the balance of the night. Not long afterward he sent a message to Col. Upton of his inability to continue forward. He mentioned his losses and the condition of his men, who, like the balance of the division's infantry, had been exhausted in the previous several days and without food, and that his ammunition supply was drying up.[14]

Meanwhile, late that evening, 2d Lt. Joseph A. Molloy* of Charlestown, Massachusetts, was leading his 23d Infantry platoon in a patrol when a shell landed in the middle of them killing 15 men and wounding a like number. Shaking off the shock to himself, despite the darkness and the interference of wearing a gas mask, Molloy began providing medical attention. Though the terrific shelling made his situation more difficult, he managed to help all the wounded, and got them on their way to the rear.

It was getting late; the three regiments were almost completely out of ammunition and casualties had been extremely high for each. In effect, the three took defensive positions where they were and later, after dark, the 6th Marines came up to join them. The losses were considerable and for that reason the three regiments would not be able to even provide support for an advance on the 19th. On the morrow, only one regiment of infantry was available for the division and that was the 6th Marines. Of course the 6th Machine Gun Battalion and the 2d Engineers would be in support but it was to be a 6th Marine's exercise. The 18th had been a tough day, but it would be as nothing compared to the 19th.

Meanwhile, the Germans had taken the offensive when they launched an attack at 0400 the next morning. That forced the Moroccan division back but the remnants of the three regiments held their ground and soon stopped the Germans with heavy fire.

Friday 19 July

During the 18th, as they remained in reserve, the 6th Marines and the 6th MG Bn were reasonably well fed and rested. Consequently they should have been a solid bet to continue the destruction of enemy forces as begun on the 18th. Yet, one regiment occupying the same frontage as three was quite different and how they managed to continue an advance, with no coverage on their left flank,[15] against an enemy now much better prepared, is the story of heroes.

The 6th Marines had been moving forward to the positions behind those held by the other three infantry regiments and by early morning were pretty much in forward locations for the morning's attack. Because of the usual lack of coordination between various units, especially between American and French units, the attack went off in two main parts. The artillery began the barrage at approximately 0630 and the Marines were still making their way forward to the division's established frontline. Their orders were to cross the line of demarcation at 0700. They would continue moving up until about 0900. Artillery barrages were intended to provide a covering fire usually about 100 yards in front of the advancing infantry so the enemy would keep their heads down until the attackers were in upon them. But, this morning, by that time the barrage was well on its way and the German defenders had managed to duck until the barrage passed and then prepare for what they knew was coming. Obviously it was a disaster in the making.

The regiment, 2/6 [Holcomb] leading, 1/6 (Hughes) following and 3/6 (Sibley) in support, left Beaurepaire Ferme at 0630 and made its way to Vierzy without undue loss. They were to make their way directly to their objective, the Chateau Thierry — Soissons highway. At the railway station in Vierzy Lt. Col. Lee issued orders as follows: the two lead battalions would move abreast,

The remnants of the Sixth Marines in the late afternoon of 19 July 1918.

1/6 (Hughes) on the right and 2/6 (Holcomb) on the left and Sibley in support. All three would be torn to pieces, including 3/6, which was also well within enemy artillery range. The regiment would suffer casualties beyond reasonable expectations. In fact, after a brief period and because of the terrible losses, two companies of 3/6 were sent forward as close support. Holcomb's battalion was stopped after about a brief kilometer "because we had nothing left with which to continue the attack." Hughes sent a message through Sibley that his losses were considerable and he needed replacements, indicating "nothing less than a regiment sufficient." The 6th Marine Regiment was not able to take the town of Tigny, lying a bare kilometer before its objective, and very late that night the regiment was replaced in the line by a French regiment. Losses were reported as between 40 and 50 percent but in actual fact the regiment went in with 2,450 Marines and a few hours later crawled out with 1,150. Total losses for the 6th Marines: 1,300 officers and men.

One well explained example of the terror and destruction was written by Maj. Robert L. Denig,[16] in a letter. It is as good as can be found and is included here for the best telling of 19 July 1918.

> At 8.30 we jumped off with a line of tanks (French) in the lead. For two "kilos" the four lines of Marines were as straight as a die, and their advance over the open plain in the bright sunlight was a picture I shall never forget. The fire got hotter and hotter, men fell, bullets sung, shells whizzed-banged and the dust of battle got thick. Overton (John) was hit by a big piece of shell and fell. Afterwards I heard he was hit in the heart, so his death was without pain.
>
> A man near me was cut in two. Others when hit would stand, it seemed an hour, then fall into a heap. I yelled to (Pere) Wilmer that each gun in the barrage worked from right to left ... looked for Hughes way over to the right; told Wilmer I had a hundred dollars and be sure to get it. You think of all kinds of things.[17]

Stories of the disaster abound. The 74th Company, 1/6, briefly stated, "Here [Soissons] on July 19 we struck the enemy a hard blow and suffered many casualties."[18] Sergeant Arthur R. Ganoe's story, related by Catlin, tells of being hit just as the 74th Co. jumped off that morning. He told of being in "the land from which only cooks and chaplains return." He thought he'd lost a leg but found out he was still whole.

The history of the 80th Company described their part with a bit more detail: "We went over the top at 8:00 July 18th [sic] advancing with the 96th Company in support of the 78th and 79th Companies (also 2/6). Our objective was two hundred yards beyond the Chateau Thierry—Soissons highway. The French tanks were with us but were a drawback, the enemy capturing one and turned it on us, but it was later retaken. We missed our objective due to heavy casualties from artillery and machine gun fire so that after an advance of four kilometers there were not enough [marines] left to proceed further."[19]

The 78th Company, also 2/6, told of going "over the top, assisted by French tanks" at "10 o'clock ... without a supporting barrage we advanced across a wheat field and out into a beet field, capturing a few prisoners and driving into a woods beyond. For the time it lasted, this was one of the bloodiest battles the Seventy-eighth Company was ever in."[20] Corporal Joseph Rendinell of the 97th Co., with the aid of journalist George Pattullo, was one of the most erudite reporters of what the 6th Marines faced on that day. He described what happened to the men on each side of him as they tried to advance. Basically they crumpled while grabbing their wounds, those that could still grab: "I passed a lot of dead and wounded. It was terrible to hear the wounded moaning and crying, 'First Aid! First Aid! First Aid men here.'"[21] It wasn't long after that Rendinell himself was wounded. That was the end of the war for him and many others of the 6th Marines.

The regimental history added many more scorching details such as, "What remained of the regiment took shelter in a line of semi-complete entrenchments constructed by the Germans, where from 10:30 A.M. until dark the regiment was subjected to the enemy's artillery, one-pounder and machine gun fire."[22] This meant that the regiment was only able to move forward for perhaps a half hour before being nearly decapitated. They were in bad shape in their holes and were unable to send out water details, on a very hot day when the canteens were already empty, nor could they replenish ammunition, nor obtain food. The losses were heavy, 2/6 with but three company officers remaining, Hughes' 1st Battalion with three officers killed in action and one captain and seven lieutenants wounded. Third Battalion lost about 40 percent of their officers. The 6th had entered the battle with twenty-eight hundred Marines, three hundred and fifty were not engaged (as part of the usual hold-back), and of the 2,450 in the battle they lost 1,300.

In the meantime, a few of the support units were taking hits as well. Pvt. Charles Phillips, of Company A, 4th Machine Gun Bn, whom we met earlier, again drove his truck as far forward as his company had advanced. In so doing, this time loaded with food, his truck was nailed by German shell-fire. He survived and managed to find another truck that he could take back to the division lines. Phillips was rewarded with a DSC for his courage and initiative during both days. Two more men from the Co. A, 4th MG Bn., Pvts Antonio Aiello* and Albert E. Beeby* (also shown as Henry H.), climbed out of their relatively safe hole and brought in a wounded 6th Marine.

Many years after the fact, Private Raymond T. Riffle, whom we met at Belleau Wood, described his experiences on this day: "My company (84th) was in the second wave and my platoon was over loaded with several replacements who had just joined us." In other words, they were not trained or experienced in that kind of war so couldn't have been expected to add more than just bodies to the veterans. He went on to state that his platoon was "a round sixty men, double our usual strength. We leaped the front wave about 2 P.M. and our Captain (Mark) Smith was wounded at once." Apparently the Germans were finished because he tells of how many surrendered as the 6th Marines continued to advance. He mentioned that they had 43 prisoners and there were only

16 Marines left. The casualties were horrendous, and a few men managed to make it back by supporting the walking wounded. Who could blame them?

General Hellé had written, "I was anxious to have the Americans relieved. They had been under a strain for days."[23] About midnight the 6th Marine Regiment was relieved by French forces, Algerians, when they were able to move forward. The 6th was pulled back and the division was relieved by the 58th French Infantry Division in the early morning of the 20th. The 1st Division (Regular) and the Moroccan Division still hadn't reached the forward line attained by the 2d Division. But now it mattered little to the survivors of the 2d Division. Yet they were receiving heavy shelling in the reserve areas, and additional casualties for the four regiments continued.

Robert Kean of the 15th Field Artillery later related a story about his finding several bodies from the 23d Infantry, including two officers, on the ridge east of Vierzy on this day. Their pockets were turned out and he later learned that the Moroccans had been through the area and had literally plucked the pockets of money the men had been carrying. Possibly the reason they weren't keeping up with the 2d Division advance was so they could relieve the Americans of their francs.

Saturday 20 July

Effective this morning the division passed from the control of the XX Corps to Tenth Army. The division was in collective recovery in a forest some distance from the frontlines but during the night of 20–21 July they were continually pelted with rain and shelling with HE and gas explosives along with huge broken oak branches that fell upon the weary men, killing some and wounding many more. Certainly many of the soldiers and Marines must have believed that their purgatory would never end. The 2d Battalion, 6th Marines, were sent to Nanteuil, arriving on 25 July. Then, the following day they spent the morning in "close order drill, bayonet practice, and Chauchat instruction. The afternoons (27th to 30th) were devoted to rest and recreation." The division did move, however, when on 31 July it was removed from that area.

It was about this time that Gen. Pershing decided that he desperately needed Gen. Harbord in an administrative post, managing a badly managed Service of Supply, though no one has mentioned or commented, in writing, upon the exchange of positions.[24]

In the meantime, Brig. Gen. John A. Lejeune, USMC, had just been transferred into the division to command the 4th Marine Brigade on 25 July. He, however, lasted in that post but three days and was assigned to replace Harbord as the CG of the 2d Division on 28 July 1918.[25] This assignment, Pershing must have hoped, would squelch any efforts by Maj. Gen. Barnett, Marine commandant, to create a Marine division in France.

Churches were often used to house wounded. This was taken after the battle at Soissons.

The Second Division suffered a total of 4,392 casualties during the period of Soissons. The division began the battle with 24,042 effectives and on 31 July, after replacements, it had 20,297 available, which fact, according to the authors of *Soissons, 1918*, made it seem "very successful during the period."[26] The Ninth Infantry seemed to have had a specially bad day on 18 July. They lost 14 officers and 463 enlisted soldiers killed or mortally wounded. The usual percentage of dead to wounded seems to be about one to two, which would add up to nearly nine hundred enlisted or a total out of the regiment of more than 50 percent.

No wonder they were in no condition to help the 6th Marines on 19 July.

6

MARBACHE

The Battle of Soissons was over and the division was once again in bad shape. For a few days it would try to catch its collective breath while at rest at Nanteuil-le-Haudouin. It and the 1st Division, now also out of the line, were assigned to the III Corps (American) commanded by Maj. Gen. Robert Lee Bullard. As we have seen, Maj. Gen. Harbord was relieved of the division when he accepted Gen. Pershing's request that he take over the badly organized and badly functioning Services of Supply. Brigadier General John A. Lejeune, USMC, had managed to get appointed to command the 4th Marine Brigade, but within three days he had been promoted to major general and assumed command of the 2d Division on 28, July 1918.[1] Colonel Preston Brown continued as chief of staff, Brig. Gen. Bowley the 2d Artillery Brigade, and, since 15 July, Brig. Gen. Hanson Ely the 3d Brigade. Col. Leroy Upton commanded the 9th Infantry until promoted to brigadier general when he assumed command of the 57th Brigade, 29th Division. Col. Malone, of the 23d Infantry, was promoted to brigadier general and assumed command of the 10th Brigade, 5th Division. Their immediate replacement commanders were both brief and then Upton's replacement at the 9th Infantry was Col. George W. Stuart and Malone's was Col. Edward R. Stone. Colonel Wendell C. Neville was promoted to brigadier general and assumed command, once again, of the 4th Brigade. In late July, Logan Feland was promoted to colonel and was assigned to command the 5th Marines. Lieutenant Colonel Harry Lee still commanded the 6th Marines, and was still a light colonel.

Replacements began arriving, about a thousand officers and men, but 7,000 more were required to "remove the tourniquet and stop the bleeding." On 29 July the division received orders to prepare to move on the following day, but the destination was not mentioned. It proved to be near Nancy and the division was placed under the command of the 8th French army, Maj. Gen. Augustin G.A. Gérard commanding. Upon arrival they were informed of their assignment to the XXXII French Corps, Maj. Gen. Fénelon F.G. Passaga commanding, although administrative control would be with the IX American Corps, Maj. Gen. Joseph T. Dickman, commanding. The 1st Division was also part of the same corps, as was the 82d American Division, and for now all three divisions were in a quiet sector. The 2d Division was mostly based at the minor French town of Pont-à-Mousson, although headquarters would remain at Marbache. This would be a nice, more or less safe sector after the bruising received at both Belleau Wood and then Soissons.

More changes occurred in the division. Col. Manus McCloskey of the 12th FA was promoted to brigadier general and moved to command the 152d Field Artillery Brigade, 77th U.S. Infantry Division, on 26 August. According to the division history, Col. John R. Kelly replaced him at the 12th FA and Lt. Col. John A. Holabird assumed command of the 17th FA on 30 August.[2]

Within the assigned territory, the division boundaries were structured as follows: The 9th Infantry occupied an area including Seille, Flamecourt-Beauzard, and the Landremont districts, the 23d Infantry was in adjoining districts, Lesménils and Schweble, the 5th Marines abutted them at Fausson, Facq West and Merivaux Farm, while the 6th Marines had Bourgogne and Cartonnerie Cuite. As usual, the 12th FA supported the 4th Brigade, the 15th the 3d Brigade, and the 17th FA was in general support of the entire division. Machine gun companies were attached to each battalion, as was the custom.

During the relief of the French forces, a modest problem occurred at 0200 on 8 August when a party of Germans approached the Mousson district where the 2/5 had assumed control the night before. The small raid was discovered by the Marines, and the Germans were driven off. Artillery support was called for and the 12th FA delivered fire as did the 6th Machine Gun Bn, both for an hour. Command passed from the French to the 2d Division at 0800 on 9 August.

Generally the stay in this sector was agreeable and the small number of encounters with the Germans was usually hardly worth reporting. Only the various patrols seemed to alter the almost pleasant ambience. An example of a less than satisfactory patrol was one led by 2d Lt Stephen M. Richardson, of Company G, 9th Infantry, on the night of 11–12 August. They were looking for a suitable crossing point for the River Seille. At some point the patrol leader allowed two corporals and five privates to leave the patrol. Following that reduction the patrol of one officer, one corporal and six privates was completely surprised when attacked by an estimated twenty Germans. The American losses were heavy. The officer and one private returned safely. The others were either killed or missing. The lieutenant's report stated, "Behavior of men: The men carried out a good patrol and certainly showed good American scrap in what little chance they had."

Another, but much larger, relief patrol, led by 1st Lt George E. Parker, Jr., Co. F, was sent out by the 2/9 on 16 August, with five officers and thirty-six men. They crossed the Seille River and came upon a sergeant from the 325th Infantry, 82d U.S. Division, who had wandered from his patrol when it came upon a force of Germans. He told Parker that his "whole patrol has been shot to pieces" and his lieutenant had sent him to look for help. Not long after, Maj.

Hawkins of the 325th came out of the woods leading a group of about five enlisted men. Hawkins was not able to supply much information and indicated simply that his unit had scattered.

Parker and his relief went looking and even went through the Germans' wire, but had little success until 0420 when Sgt. Quinn of the 9th went further and located the wounded Lt. Wood of the 325th and brought him out. After that 2d Lt George W. Hezzelwood, Hdqs Co., 2/9, and two men made a reconnaissance, learning nothing. It was then that Parker and his five officers decided to penetrate enemy territory further, looking for anymore wounded, and the lead units were also attacked. The casualties were quite severe, twelve wounded, four severely, including Hezzelwood. The remnants returned with little else to tell headquarters.[3]

The 23d Infantry had several encounters when their rather large patrols went out and, in some cases, cut the German wire. They provided several descriptions in their operations reports but nothing of serious consequence and with minimal losses. The 5th Marines had a report from Col. F.M. "Fritz" Wise, temporarily CO of 2/5, which indicated that the regiment was having a like experience, as was the 23d Infantry. One mildly exciting adventure was reported by Logan Feland, when Pvt. Lester L. Danley of the 23d Machine Gun Company, 6th MG Bn, crawled out into No Man's Land to investigate a fallen French balloon which German planes had shot down. Instead he found numerous pipes stuffed with explosives lying under the division wire, obviously to enhance a later attack on the 5th Marines, which never came off.

During this period a request was made, at least to the officers of the 2d Artillery Brigade, for volunteers to go home and serve as instructors. A few officers considered it, among whom one was 15th FA officer, 1st Lt. Robert W. Kean, a DSC man at Soissons. He, and two others, went to headquarters and answered the call; the other two went home but, "he couldn't spare me."[4]

This, nevertheless, was what the period at Marbache was like for the front line units. Not much of anything serious happened, other than nightly patrols, some of which were dangerous but all in all, there were few casualties. The artillery brigade sent over a few rounds, and incoming was at about the same level. The division, however, really needed this "catch up" time. Its infantry and support units like the engineers were depleted, requiring serious replacement and rest.

On or about 15–16 August the 82d Division was to replace the 2d Division in line and the Division was to retire to the town of Colombey-les-Belles, south of Toul, an area the French had set aside for it. By the 20th of August the division, save the artillery, had pretty much assembled at that town. The artillery joined the rest of the division within two days. Upon arrival near the town of Toul, the 2d Engineers were immediately put to work making the so-called French shooting range into an American range. According to the unit history they had their work cut out for them. It was a mess. They worked from daybreak until at least 2100 most every day. At the end of five days they had constructed 80 usable targets. Lieutenant Colonel Thomas Holcomb, 6th Marines, who had a national reputation, having been a member of the USMC national rifle team, was placed in charge of the range and every unit of the division was able to complete the course.

According to the division commander, Maj. Gen. John A. Lejeune, "the hardest kind of work was ahead of us." He adds that the division strength "was reduced to approximately 20,000 men, about 8,000 below the authorized complement." He added that most of the loss was in the two infantry brigades and that their numbers were reduced by half. The 4th Brigade received 1,000 men, which made them still 2,500 short and, he added, "there were no more Marine replacement battalions in France." AEF Headquarters told Lejeune that unless Marine replacements were forthcoming they would provide U.S. Army personnel to fill the void. Lejeune cracked up at that and demanded that the Marines in France, serving in various noncombatant roles, be sent to reinforce the brigade. There were several companies which had been assigned as guards to the AEF and some of those were made available to Lejeune, but nowhere near enough to make the brigade adequate in strength.[5]

From this period on, the division prepared to serve as part of the newly created 1st American Army, commanded by Maj. Gen. John Pershing. The planning of the reduction of the St. Mihiel salient was prepared by notables who would later become some of the U.S. Army's top leaders as late as World War II. There was, of course, the usual "down time" for the enlisted men. Some required dental work and others had aches and pains in their bellies or other portions of their anatomies. One member of the 95th Company, 1/6, described his three day dental foray which ended when the dentist left before he was taken care of; his teeth still bothered him.[6]

During this later period there was a large parade for the various decorations awarded to members of the division. Seventy-five medals were to be pinned on the sixty recipients in the presence, on parade, of most of the division. It was on a Sunday, 25 August, and Maj. Gen. Hunter Liggett was Pershing's representative. The awards were the Distinguished Service Cross, the French Médailles Militaire, and the Croix de Guerre. Liggett pinned the awards on each man while the citation was read, then shook hands with each. One lone German plane visited the area but was shot down by antiaircraft artillery, which prevented interference and casualties to the assemblage.[7] During this visit, Colonel Preston Brown was promoted to brigadier general, but he, fortunately, would remain with the division as chief of staff.

Preparation for the oncoming major campaign continued and even the few replacements were virtually becoming "veterans," or so some of them probably thought. There was a major rehearsal with most units of the division participating in which the various units moved over ground similar to what they would be on in the next fight. Division was ordered to join the I Corps, U.S. Army, on 27 August, and on 1 September moved to Francheville where, on 3 September, the 9th Infantry entered corps reserve. In a few days, the entire division would be moving toward their place in the lineup for the next push at St. Mihiel.

7

St. Mihiel

First Corps issued its field orders on 8 September and 2d Division was given a dual role. Its mission was to take Thiacourt and also to assist IV Corps by reducing Bois d'Euvezin and Bois du Beau Vallon. I Corps set the Division's boundaries as: right, Remenauville, Bois du Four, Bois d'Heiche, crossroads 306.6, Bois de Bonvaux (exclusive) and Rembercourt-sur-Mad (all others inclusive), left boundaries, Limey, east edge of clearing between Bois du Beau Vallon and Bois d'Euvezin, Thiacourt, Xammes (exclusive), Charey (all others inclusive). Objectives were: immediate, north edge of Bois des Saulx, Tranchée de la Loge, first phase, north edge of Bois d'Heiche, point 242.6. first day, north edge of Bois du Fey, point 277.7 to point 264.5. Possible objective, first day, was: crossroads 266.2, high ground between Jaulny and Xammes, second day: the army objective (same), exploitation line: Bois de la Perriè and Charey (inclusive).

Additional units assigned to the Division included three light (Renault) tank companies with forty-five tanks, plus eighteen medium tanks, the 1st Aero Squadron, 1st Balloon Company, and a detachment of gas and flamethrower troops. The medium tanks were to penetrate the enemy wire and the light tanks to reduce hostile points of resistance (primarily machine guns).

On the night of 9–10 September the 2d Division marched and motored to the woods north of Noviant-aux-Prés and Manonville. There they relieved elements of both the 89th and 90th U.S. Divisions in what became known as the Limey Sector. It was located in the part of France known as Lorraine, which had been a German possession since the end of the Franco-Prussian War.

The front line of this sector, on the south face of the St. Mihiel salient, gave the division a bit more than a mile frontage from southeast of Remenauville to about a half mile north of Limey. The 5th U.S. Division was located to their right and the 89th U.S. Division on the left. The 2d Division was the left flank of I Corps and the 89th was the right flank of IV Corps.

When Pershing arrived in France in June 1917, he and his staff promptly decided that they wanted to assume responsibility for the extreme right of the French line, or at least a large segment just south of Verdun. When additional

7. St. Mihiel

On their way toward St. Mihiel, troops take a ten minute break near Limey.

American troops arrived, the latter was, or was expected to be, within their capacity. That was when they also assumed that the French authorities would cooperate and that the AEF would have satisfactory docking facilities and railroads to run in supplies and troops from the coast. In the meantime, as the going got rougher, though Pershing had to allow the French, and to a lesser extent, the British, to utilize American doughboys fighting the enemy, the St. Mihiel salient was never set too far out of their view. Planning for that action never ceased, and by mid-summer, when the Americans were literally piling into France, Pershing and staff decided it was about time to organize the American forces into the First American Army and seriously plan to retake that ground lost by France in 1914.

The plan for the advance would place the most divisions on the southern face, where the most severe difficulties were anticipated. When they wheeled eastward the division located farthest to the west would have the greatest distance to travel. The 1st U.S. Division, in order to advance northeastward, to reach the 26th U.S. Division coming in from the north, would form the left flank of the 1st U.S. Army's advance. In the lineup, west to east after the 1st, would lie the 42d U.S., the 89th U.S., the 2d U.S., the 5th U.S., the 90th U.S. and, at the southern shoulder, the 82d U.S. Division.

The 2d Division did not have to wait long after their arrival in the area. On the night of the 11th the infantry brigades began moving in and about Limey into what had been French trenches, each regiment taking over about a half mile of front. In a few hours they wouldn't be sitting still. Corps had planned for the Division to advance in a column of brigades, with the 3d leading followed

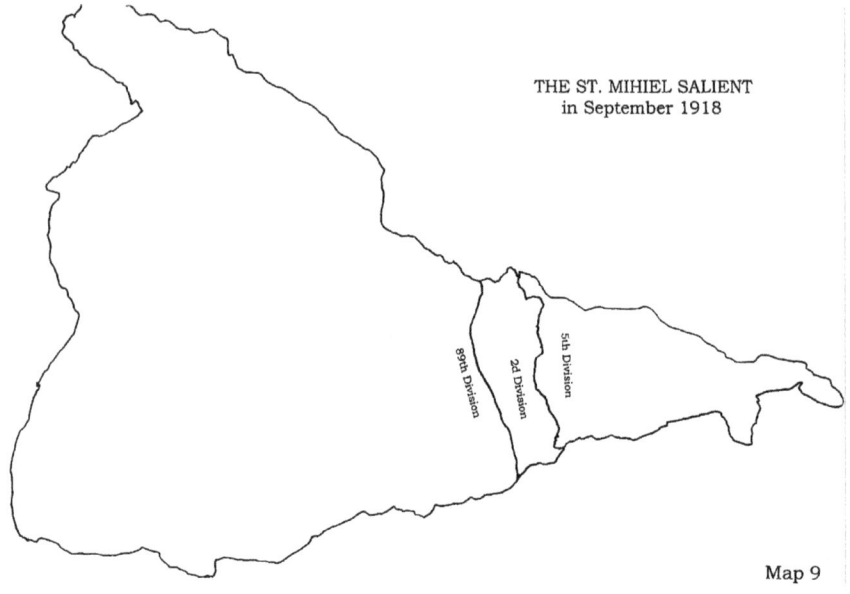

Map 9. The St. Mihiel Salient in September 1918.

by the 4th in support. At 0100 the artillery of the entire 1st Army, including the 2d Artillery Brigade and its three attached French artillery regiments, two of 75's and one of 155's, opened fire and many sources, German, French and American, later claimed it was the most powerful bombardment they had ever heard during the war. It went on for four hours, shattering nearly everything in its path. As McCrossen stated in his memoir, "We started 'over the top' at daybreak when the fire became a rolling barrage; and it was a dandy, the most effective fire we had ever seen."[1]

Thursday 12 September

In the meantime, the 2d Division Infantry, both brigades, were in a column of battalions, to each of which, as was usual, was attached one machine gun company. The division's 1st objective, Thiacourt, lay almost directly north. The 9th Infantry was on the right flank, with 3/9 in the forefront and led by a Marine, Maj. Robert L. Denig.[2] Captain Frank C. Foley followed with 1/9 in support and Maj. George C. Bowen with 2/9 in reserve. Corporal Michell Mebreski,* Co I, 3/9, leading his squad of about a dozen men, started the battalion off with style. They flanked a machine gun nest and then captured a German ammunition dump and 69 prisoners.

The 5th Marines followed the 9th in support. Their order of battle was

Illustration showing the 9th Infantry jumping off on 12 September 1918 at St. Mihiel.

as follows: 3/5 led by Maj. Maurice Shearer, Lt. Col. Julius Turrill and 1/5 in support; and the newly appointed CO of 2/5, Maj. Robert Messersmith, in reserve.

To the left, along the Corps line, stood the 23d Infantry lined up with their comrades of the 9th Infantry. Two/23 was leading (Capt. Farragut F. Hall) with 1/23 (Lt. Col. Edmund C. Waddill) in support followed by 3/23 (Maj. Peyton). Their left liaison was with the 89th U.S. Division, which would pretty much keep up with the veteran 2d Division during the advance. In fact, that day the American divisions, of which there were seven on this southern face, would all arrive at their objective for that day and, in fact, exceed it. The two French divisions, a portion of the 26th and to its right, in liaison with the 1st U.S. Division, the 39th, would move forward less rapidly. Admittedly, they were at the portion of the salient opposite the town of St. Mihiel, and street fighting slowed them down considerably. Also, the liberation of French people, kept hostage by the enemy for more than four years, by French troops was a matter for celebration. On the opposite face of the salient, at the northern face, was the balance of the 26th French Division followed eastward by the 2d French

Dismounted Cavalry Division and lastly, at the northern shoulder, the estimable 26th U.S. "Yankee" Division.[3]

Following the 23d Infantry in support were the 6th Marines. Their formation was 3/6 led by Lt. Col. Berton Sibley, then 2/6 with Maj. Ernest C. Williams in support. Major Frederick Barker with 1/6 had been lent to the 23d Infantry to maintain Corps liaison with IV Corps. Liaison skills became necessary for the American divisions to learn as they began moving in large numbers with other American and foreign units to their flanks. Mostly, to date, except to a limited extent at Soissons, the Americans were a single unit with limited flank support.

While not denigrating the achievements of the 1st U.S. Army, it must be mentioned that the Germans had been preparing a withdrawal from their advanced sector almost since their initial occupation of the salient, back in 1914. However, they didn't seriously begin planning or moving until they observed the American development opposite them during the previous few weeks.[4] So when the advance began, the enemy was not standing and fighting fiercely as they would a few days later on. Therefore, the advance by the 1st Army on the southern face was comparatively easy, meaning that for once the 2d Division had a relatively easy time of it.

The guns of the 2d Brigade of Artillery gave the infantry a four hour preparation and the advance began at 0500 behind a rolling barrage. Denig's men of 3/9 encountered no appreciable opposition in the first line of German trenches and enemy counter-barrage was nonexistent. When they arrived at the Bois du Four, about a mile forward, the doughboys knocked out the few machine gun nests, and continued doing so in the Bois la Haie l'Evèque, which lay a few hundred yards to their left. The battalion passed its immediate objective at 0700 and the first phase objective, the northern edge of the Bois d'Heiche, by 0930. They had by now advanced two and a half miles against modest impedimenta. The German troops were still pulling back and those defending did so reluctantly.

In the 12th FA, especially Battery E, when caught in enfilading fire, the entire crew on gun number one became casualties. Captain Robert B. Hood* quickly ordered a supplementary crew to put the gun back into action. Six men, led by Sgt. Donald F. Green,* quickly assumed positions after removing the casualties and put that gun back into action in 4 minutes. Each man was awarded a DSC for courage and capability that day. Besides Hood and Green they were Pvts Monroe Ellet,* Robert E. Geyer,* and Angelo Gillotti* plus PFCs Matthew W. Forsyth, Jr.,* and Frank J. Settle.*

Onward went the 9th Infantry and soon they reached their main objective, Thiacourt. Denig's 3/9 had a group of soldiers from M Co. Pvts Tony Wagner,* Stanley Mazurkevczk,* and PFC Hyman Lashiwer,* plus attached medic Bronislaw Kacprzyzki,* who voluntarily went out and helped bring in the wounded in front of the lines, all the while under heavy enemy fire. At about

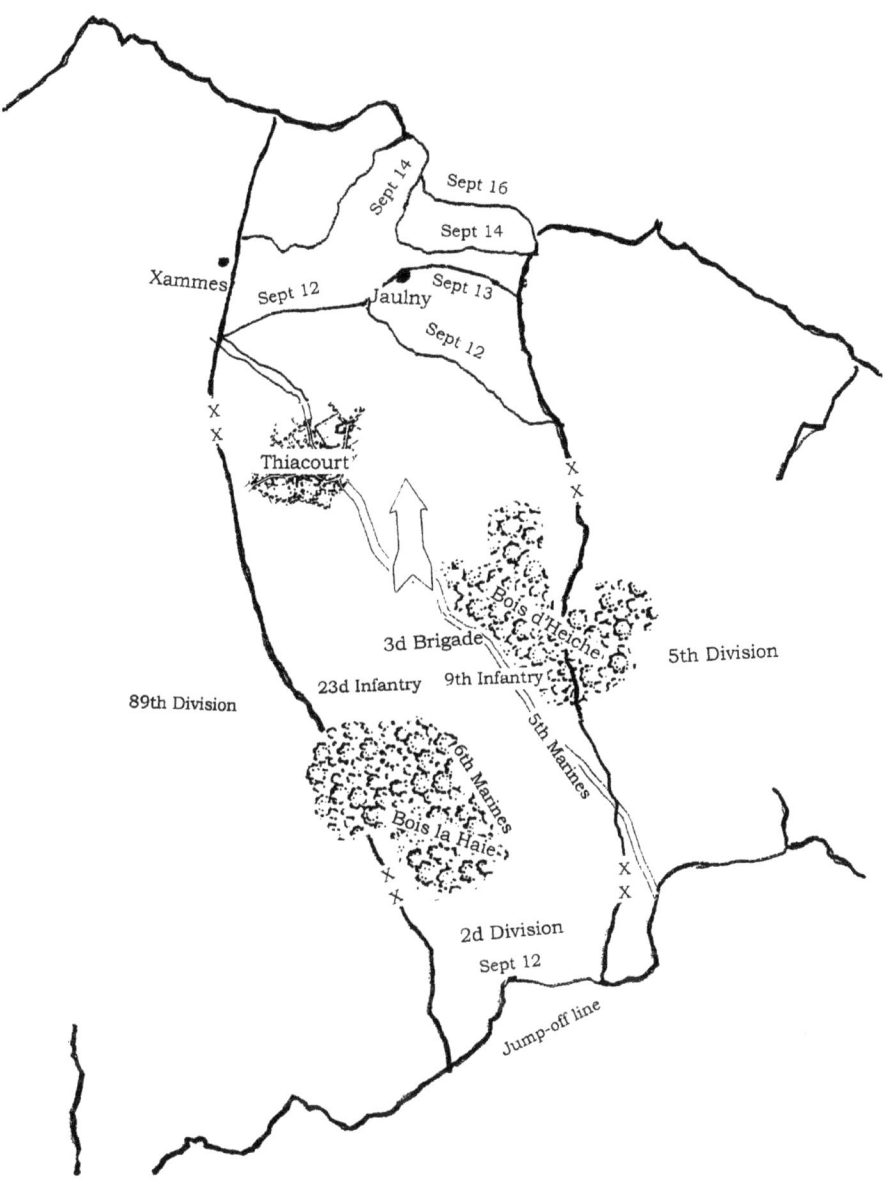

Map 10. The advance of the 2d division at St. Mihiel 12 to 16 September.

this time their front opened up, from the narrow 1 kilometer to about 2 kilometers. Thus the two supporting battalions moved forward, 1/9 to the left (even into the territory assigned to the 23d Infantry) and 2/9 to their right, while 3/9 dropped back and followed in support. The 5th Marines continued in support of the 9th Infantry. It was at about this time a wounded soldier of the regiment strolled back through the 5th Marines heading for an aid station. A young

Marine replacement, anxious to learn what fate had in store for him asked, "Hey, buddy, how's things goin' up there?" The response was "Aw, Hell, son, goin' fine. We're goin' through 'em like a dose of salts through a tall, thin woman."[5]

While advancing, 1st Lt. Walter J. Kimball,* Co. B, 1/9, was forced to spread his men over a wide sector into a thickly wooded area in order to maintain contact and liaison with 2/9 on his flank. While so engaged he managed to knock out several machine gun nests, and routed the enemy. He also managed to capture another gun and its crew. Another soldier of 1/9, Co. D's Pvt. William A. Tierce,* left his safe hole to get a better position for his Chauchat. He operated it, causing destruction in the enemy formations, until a shell landed nearby and broke both his hands and disabled his gun.

The 9th Infantry continued its attack. Pushing to the northern edge of the Bois du Fey, 2/9 extended to the right as far as crossroads 306.6 and managed to hold a line along a road tilting slightly forward on the left but slightly reverse to the right, following the line formed by their next door neighbor, the 5th U.S. Division. By 1330 the 9th Infantry had reached the "1st Day Objective," passed that and soon after also the "Army Objective." At this point the troops began to dig in. They were a half a mile from Jaulny, which would be their next objective.

During the afternoon and early evening, the Germans attempted several "half-hearted" counterattacks, none of which succeeded. The 9th Infantry on the ridge north of Le Rupt de Mad Ruisseau withdrew temporarily to the reverse slope, and here the attack was repulsed. The last one, at 1900, decimated the attackers. The regiment re-occupied all the ground taken that day, holding it all night, including the quarry and trenches half a mile to the west. That evening patrols were in contact with the 5th Division. According to the 9th Infantry operations report, artillery support for the Americans that afternoon was half-hearted.[6]

Captain Claude Burlingame of C Co., 23d Infantry, described a mess when his company of the support battalion, 1/23, was missing two platoons, the 3d and 4th, which were misdirected. Soon after, the 1st Platoon and 2d Platoon became separated, whereupon Maj. Edmund C. Waddill, CO, 1/23, halted them. At 0520 the two other platoons, 3 and 4, went forward. Meanwhile Burlingame, who was with the first two platoons, became "disconnected" but he then collected together about 300 stragglers and proceeded ahead. It appears as though 1/23 didn't get entirely back together that day. As the regiment neared Thiacourt, 2d Lt George H. McGay* gathered together about twenty soldiers who had become separated from their units and under heavy machine gun fire attacked a strong enemy position. They took the post, though greatly outnumbered, capturing at least twenty-five soldiers and 4 machine guns. Meanwhile, Capt. Eldridge G. Chapman, Jr.,* of the 5th Machine Gun Bn, standing before his men, bravely pointed out targets to his gunners even though the enemy had launched a violent attack upon their positions. He was credited with causing the failure of the enemy to capture his emplacement.

During the early morning, about 1000, a runner from the regiment brought along a message for 1/23 and 3/23 (Maj. Peyton) to pass through 2/23 and continue to attack. The runner met 1st Lt John T. Kibler, CO of A Co., who, like the runner, had no idea where anyone else was. He did send the message forward and made preparations to come through 2/23. While so doing A Co. went in and captured Thiacourt, and in the process gathered in a large number of unresisting prisoners. They then took a hill just north of the town and decided that was as far as they wanted to go that day.

The missing two platoons from C Co. joined them later in the day. The 3d came in with the 9th Infantry and the 4th had teamed up with the 353d U.S. Infantry of the 177th Brigade, 89th U.S. Division. A later report described what had happened to the 3d and 4th platoons, and why they were in such disarray. Just prior to the jump-off a shell landed between the two platoons killing 2d Lt Richard R. White and three enlisted men and wounding another ten enlisted men. This, according to Burlingame, completely demoralized the 3d Platoon which was composed heavily of recent arrivals or, as the report stated, "more or less green at the game, it being their first time under fire." The report further adds that, when the rear platoon was out of the trenches and past the bodies, "they behaved like veterans." Captain Burlingame gave credit to two officers and two privates for their coolness and good judgment. They were 1st Lt Martin G. Griffen, 1st Lt William A. Dobson, and Privates John J. Doyle and Wilbert E. Lockwood. Griffen, Dobson, Doyle and Lockwood would all be decorated at Blanc Mont in October but do not appear to have been recipients of awards at St. Mihiel.

One tough Hungarian, Sgt. Joe Farkas,* E Co., 2/23, was leading his platoon when a bullet hit him in the eye, which, besides creating great pain, blinded him. Regardless of losing much of his sight Farkas continued to lead his men forward. He and his men flattened a machine gun nest, about two hours after he was wounded, and only then did he seek medical treatment.

Two/23 reached the first phase objective by 1000 and at that point 1/23 and 3/23 were ordered to pass through the lines. Three/23 had not been able to keep up with the rapid movement of 2/23 so 2/23 would continue in the lead, but with 1/23 as its neighbor.

Meanwhile, Colonel Stuart of the 9th Infantry had requested a couple of companies from the 5th Marines to reinforce his left flank. The 16th (Capt. Robert Yowell) and 20th (1st Lt Jonas H. Platt), both from 3/5 (Maj. Maurice Shearer), went forward at approximately 2040 and remained with the 9th Infantry until 2100 on the 13th.[7] The other two companies, 45th (Capt. Peter Conachy) and 47th (Capt. Philip T. Case) were scattered around someplace and caused Shearer great distress because no one seemed to know where they were located.

Orders were issued at 1850 to the 6th Marines to send 2/6 over to take a flank position for the night on the high ground north of Thiacourt. This was followed by the movement of several other elements of the 4th Brigade to a close support position behind the center of the Division line. There was some patrolling by the 3d Brigade that night but no contact with the Germans. The day had been very successful and by day's end Division had reached the second day's 1st objectives.

Friday 13 September

Early morning patrols from the 9th Infantry investigated Jaulny, the Bois de Rupt and Bois de Blainchamp, finding no German presence in any of them. On the 12th, elements of the regiment had wandered into the zone occupied by the 23d Infantry and were recalled that morning. By noon 1/9 and 3/9 were located in the ravines in Bois du Fey as support and in reserve. According to a Distinguished Service Cross citation, two members of A Co., 2d Engineers breeched Jaulny on the 12th with wire cutters being the first Americans in that town. One was Cpl Thomas D. Saunders* who wasn't deterred by the heavy machine gun fire he and his comrade, Pvt. Alfred Wilkerson,* encountered. They also were not concerned too much with the snipers and remnants of the enemy still occupying the town. After capturing 8 Germans in a dugout they searched the caves in that town and took an additional 55 prisoners. In the afternoon 2/9 advanced to deny the enemy his present position around Jaulny. By mid-afternoon the 9th held the territory around Jaulny in most directions.

The 5th U.S. Division, on the 2d Division's right flank, was attacked in force by the enemy that afternoon and the Second braced for the same kind of treatment. Denig's 3/9 was called upon to provide the division's flank protection by ordering it into position southwest of the Bois de Bonvaux. It would remain there until 0400 on the 14th when it would be recalled, not having met the enemy during that period.

In the later afternoon, orders were forwarded to the 4th Brigade to begin relieving the 3d Brigade in the front lines by midnight. Reports coming in to the 4th Brigade indicated that battalions of the 5th Marines were describing minor activity. Captain DeWitt Peck, skipper of the 55th Company, 2/5, sent his battalion commander, Messersmith, a message at 1900: "*Our* artillery is shooting all around us. Fragments landing in our lines" (emphasis in original).

One of the gallant officers of the 9th, 1st Lt. Cylburn O. Mattfeldt,* hopped on a horse, rode across an open field in full view of the Germans and told the battery firing upon the marines to cease and desist. It was later determined by Brig. Gen. Bowley of the 2d Artillery Brigade that the firing was coming from Battery E, 20th FA, 5th Division, which unit promised never to do it again.

Photograph of the 17th Field Artillery (105 Howitzers firing support for the infantry going forward at St. Mihiel.

Colonel Stuart of the 9th, however, reported this evening that the artillery supporting their next door neighbors (most probably the 5th U.S. Division artillery) dropped a barrage "into my area on two occasions and caused a loss of five killed and several wounded." He went on "it suggests a serious condition, possibly disloyalty in its personnel." These are strong words, and it's not known what facts he based that remark on. The previous evening Col. Feland had complained that 2d Division artillery had dropped a few rounds on his regiment and they too had suffered several casualties. This was a common complaint from the AEF troops during most of their campaigns in France. The artillery officers always dismissed the accusations, but the troops continued dying. Meanwhile, Sgt. James A. Claflin,* medical detachment, 5th MG Bn, in an area swept by two German artillery batteries, managed to save several of the wounded and superintended their safe removal. While Claflin went about his business a private of the same battalion, Scotsman Patrick J. Clark,* voluntarily carried messages through intensified enemy machine gun fire, and later volunteered to carry more through that heavy artillery fire.

The missing two Marine companies, the 45th and 47th, were still not accounted for at midnight on 13–14 September and Shearer was loudly complaining about it. Later it would come out that the two were in positions before the location of the 16th and 20th when they were acting as reinforcements for the 9th Infantry, although "how and why" aren't clear in the divisional history. It must have been a concern of the "troops." In fact, in a message to Shearer late that night, Yowell, after requesting that "a hot cup of coffee would put new life in everybody," also asked, "Have you found the 45th and 47th?"

As part of the overall relief of the 3d Brigade, at 1830 the 6th Marines moved forward and relieved the 23d Infantry, which nevertheless remained in that general location the following day. Late that night the CO of K Co., 3/9, and a volunteer, PFC Robert E. L. Kilby,* went forward to locate a German trench. When they reached it, they found it occupied by one German officer and seven enlisted men. Kilby cleaned out the position, saving his captain's life.

Saturday 14 September

At midnight the 9th Infantry was relieved in the front lines by the 5th Marines and withdrawn to the Bois d'Heiche. The total relief was completed by 0400. The new CO of 1/5, Lt. Col. Arthur J. O'Leary, and his troops remained in their outpost positions, just north of Jaulny, for the next few days. Messersmith and 2/5 went into support positions and 3/5, Shearer, hopefully with the recovered two companies, went into reserve. On their right, the 5th Marines were level with where the 9th Infantry had been, and on their left, with the 6th Marines.

The 6th Marines fed their 3/6 (Sibley) into the outpost position followed by 2/6 (Williams) in support and 1/6 (Barker) as reserve. The 6th Marines were about even with the town of Xammes to their left, which was held mainly by the 89th Division.

During the early morning the 5th Marines were ordered to establish an outpost line from the northern end of the Bois de Hailbat to the northeast corner of the Bois de Montagne, from right to left. This put the 5th considerably forward of their flank support, most of which on their left was exposed because the 6th Marines weren't also ordered forward.

Sergeant Karl McCune, of the 55th Company, 2/5, while still bivouacked in the Bois de Bonvaux (actually in Blainchamp), described an interesting sidelight to the campaign. It seems that a German aviator flew low over their area and "quickly every man with a rifle or pistol and the machine gunners directed fire upon him and brought him down. The aviator was made a prisoner and the machine picked to pieces for souvenirs." Undoubtedly, the Marines of that company never forgot the excitement, and possibly also the German aviator as well.

That afternoon division ordered the 4th Brigade to push out reconnaissance patrols toward the general line of Rembercourt–Charey, right to left, about a mile forward of the current line. Or, as Neville was directed, "as far as they can go." This position would practically bring the 4th Brigade into contact with the vaunted Hindenburg Line, which was very near Charey. At 1630 the 45th and 47th companies advanced patrols before the 5th Marines, establishing outposts in the Bois de Hailbat and in the Bois de Rupt but continuing to maintain contact with the 6th Marines to their left.

The 82d (Capt. James H. Johnston) and 83d (Capt. Alfred H. Noble) companies, 3/6, relieved the 84th (Capt. Louis M. Bourne, Jr.) and 97th (Capt. Thomas T. McEvoy) companies in the front lines mid-afternoon. Late in the day, however, at 2340, the latter two companies were pushed forward through the former and by midnight the battalion's line extended east of Xammes astride the Thiacourt–Charey road. During the early evening, at 1830, 1/6 received orders to push two companies north and place an outpost in the Bois de Montagne. Both the 74th (Capt. Robert H. Shiel) and 76th (Capt. Macon C. Overton) companies advanced as directed, and the former established a contact with the 47th Company, 3/5, to its right.

Sunday 15 September

The night of 14–15 September was marked by heavy artillery fire from the Germans. The Americans were beginning to get close to the Hindenburg Line and had to expect this change in added resistance. The going had not been too difficult the first few days but it was going to be tough from now on. That morning Maj. Ernest Williams and 2/6 were pushed through the line to occupy the Bois de Montagne and the movement brought intense enemy artillery fire. Regimental movement was brought to a halt with a message from Lee (signed by his second, Sibley) when a message to the 84th and 97th companies admonished them to stay where they were on the "Army Line." He didn't know exactly where Barker and 1/6 were; "up front in the Bois de Montagny [sic]" someplace. Wanting to know where, Sibley wrote, "Send forward a patrol from each," meaning the 84th and 97th companies. He also added that 2/6 had been split into two units, one under Williams and the second under Maj. George W. Martin, and he wanted to know where both parts were now located. In other words, the 6th Marines were scattered and Lee and Sibley were not in control.

While the regiment was in action they were ably, as always, supported by their navy "docs," one of whom, Phm3d Oscar S. Goodwin,* established a position behind the lines that day and worked through the ensuing bombardments administering to the wounded. He was serving with USN Lieutenant Gordon A. Grimland,* who was in the same location serving the same comrades, under direct artillery fire all day. Another doc, who had earned plaudits at Soissons, Hap 1st Bernard W. Herrman,* was equally distinguished on this field on this day. While attached to the 76th Co., 1/6, Herrman was conspicuous for his coolness under heavy fire while removing the wounded from the fire zone. One of his colleagues, Phm3d John R. Litchfield* with the 74th Co., lost his life while engaged in removing the wounded to the rear. Another, Phm3d James E. Manning, also of 1/6, was tending to his wounded Marines when a shell hit the dressing station and wounded the Marine in two more places. Manning dressed the new wounds and while so engaged was struck in the back and knocked over by another shell explosion striking the station. Manning refused to be evacuated until "his" Marine was removed from the scene. Then another shell destroyed the station by completely gutting it but Manning and the other docs managed to survive — a good thing because the 6th Marines were very busy this day and needed all the help they could get.

One of the companies of 1/6, the 75th, was led by 1st Lt Henry E. Chandler,* who fearlessly exposed himself to the heavy enemy fire, sniper, machine gun and artillery, while locating enemy strong points and machine gun nests. He then led his company forward and crushed the nests. One of his privates, Grover N. Chatman,* by himself pushed forward and voluntarily crossed open ground covered by enemy sniper fire and knocked out three of the worst who were doing great damage to his company. The 73d MG Co, supporting the 6th Marines, had Cpl Lyle C. Houchins* and Cpl Casey V. Loomis,* who, during an enemy counterattack, left their relatively safe position and set up their gun in the open. There they managed to break up the attack within 100 yards of the Marines line. Houchins, however, paid the supreme price for his courage.

Williams' battalion got caught up in a fiery German counterattack. For some hours they were hit by everything the Germans could throw at them and suffered casualties. But the Germans were taking their hits too. One group that attacked the 80th Company (Capt. Bailey M. Coffenburg) met Gy Sgt. William Ulrich,* and most wished they hadn't. When the Germans came in towards them Ulrich, with three Marines, charged them through intense enemy machine gun fire. The Germans began to retreat and Ulrich, using his personal knowledge of the German language, convinced over fifty of them to surrender. Unfortunately one of the Marines then began firing at them and off they went. Ulrich chased after them and again screamed in German, and almost the entire line turned and surrendered to him. A few more Ulrichs and the war would have been over much sooner. There was another fighting Marine in that company, Pvt. Donald M. Parker,* who voluntarily joined with an officer and the two men went out and silenced a strong machine gun position menacing the left flank of the 6th Marines. He remained and held the position under strong enemy attacks until killed by a sniper.

Serving 2/6, the 81st MG Co, 6th MG Bn, moved forward about 0400. Soon after, Pvt. Patrick J. Moran* was passing from gun to gun, at great personal danger while carrying ammunition to his guns. He spotted his badly wounded skipper, 1st Lt Jack S. Hart,* as Hart was hit. Leaving a relatively safe location, Moran went out and picked him up, carrying Hart to a dressing station. Before that Hart had been doing just fine. He had advanced with his guns looking for favorable locations, assigned them and continued his reconnaissance. Locating a German Maxim he attacked it single-handedly and, though seriously wounded in the attempt, managed to capture the position and crew before he went down. Moran must have aided him in bringing in the prisoners though Hart's citation doesn't mention that.

Other men of 2/6 earned fine reputations that afternoon, one being a Chicago lad, Pvt. John Joseph Kelly, who will be later recognized, especially at Blanc Mont, a great battle to come. But at St Mihiel, as at Verdun, Belleau Wood and Soissons, this young man was at the forefront of fighting and leadership, assisting in capturing a machine gun nest.[8] He convinced a senior sergeant, Henry S. Brogan,* to pull together his 78th Company after it had been shattered and all officers were down. Kelly had done this same thing before but then he had assumed the leadership role. Another fighting Marine of 2/6, Pvt. Albert Meyer* of the 79th Co, while on duty as a stretcher bearer, rushed into the open to rescue another Marine threatened with capture, in the face of a large force of advancing Germans. He immediately killed two of them and brought the wounded Marine to safety. Another 79th Co. man, Cpl Edward J. Wollert,* at the risk of his own life went to the aid of a captured wounded Marine officer held by six Germans. With his pistol he shot two of them while the officer killed two more, then Wollert forced the other two Germans to carry

After their success at St. Mihiel, the 9th Infantry are carted away.

the wounded officer back to their lines. Further proof of individual valor is the story of Pvt. Lester H. Nutting* of the 96th Co, 2/6, who voluntarily went forward toward the enemy lines, sitting machine gun nests and signaling the message back to his comrades, who immediately set to work wiping each of them out. Nutting, however, was killed while returning to his company lines.

At the end of the day, further advance became difficult because the Germans were now fiercely holding their positions, and the 2d Division ended their advance. The 1st and 2d battalions, 6th Marines, were still in the front line. By nightfall the 5th and 6th Marines were being relieved by the 309th and 310th Infantry of the 78th U.S. Division. Command of the sector passed to the 78th at 1000 on 16 September. The 2d Division artillery remained in the sector to support the 78th until 18 September when they too were withdrawn. All divisional units were moved to the general vicinity of Toul, about fifteen miles south of Limey. There they would rest a bit and gather in more replacements, but not many.

During the entire period that the division arrived and remained in the area, from 8 to 19 September, division casualties were rather modest in comparison to those of the two previous brutal campaigns, Belleau Wood and Soissons. In all, less than 1,500 officers and men were killed or wounded. Oh, that the improvement would continue; but it wouldn't. The next battle was to be the worst, yet it is hardly known today, perhaps because it was directed by the French army.

The Second Division suffered a total of 1,487 casualties. The division began the battle with 26,003 effectives and on 30 September, after replacements, had 26,897.

8

Blanc Mont

On 26 September 1918 the American First Army, jointly with the French Fourth Army, launched their attacks against the southern German front, the former from the Argonne Forest east to the Meuse River, and the French located in an area about 23 miles to the east of the city of Reims and nearly the same distance from the Argonne Forest to their right. Overall, this was called the Meuse-Argonne campaign and would be the final effort of the war. The most punishing part of the enemy line was to be at Blanc Mont Ridge, in the French sector.

The French had been trying to retake that very important ridge since 1914. Possession of that high ground had given the Germans unlimited observation of the ground that any attack must come across. Every attempt by French forces to take that all but impregnable height had ended with severe losses and in complete failure each time. The French XXI Corps had recently managed to gain modest ground against the strongly entrenched German forces in the area, advancing about three miles along the front. In so doing, they had successfully taken several German positions but all on the lower ground approaches. As had always been the case, eventually the Germans drew up in their well-prepared positions, just north of the town of Somme-Py, and there on 30 September they once again stopped French progress. French forces were exhausted, and were frustrated at their losses and lack of accomplishment. It boded ill and French leadership realized that the overused French troops would not make a serious effort again.[1]

Earlier in September the French high command, recognizing the disastrous condition of the Fourth Army, and anticipating great difficulties in their coming Champagne offensive, had, on 16 September, requested the loan of American troops from General Pershing. As we have seen, Pershing assigned the 2d Division and the 36th Division to be used by Marshal Foch in whatever manner he saw fit. With a simple phone call, later put in writing, the 2d Division was officially transferred to French control on 23 September.[2]

Under orders, the 2d Division entrained on 25 September and arrived at its destination, detraining in the vicinity of Châlons-sur-Marne, about 21 miles south of Somme-Py, where it became the reserve division of the French Group of Armies of the Center.

Major General John A. Lejeune, the 2d Division commander, had, on 21 September, received notification from his Corps commander, Maj. Gen. Hunter Liggett, that his unit was in the process of being transferred to the French High Command. Subsequently, when General Henri J.E. Gouraud summoned him to the headquarters of his Fourth French Army on 26 September, Lejeune assumed, without having any written confirmation, that his division had already been reassigned to Gouraud's army. Upon arrival at Gouraud's headquarters at Marie-sur-Marne, he was informed that Gouraud requested his presence at his personal headquarters in Châlons-sur-Marne as soon as possible.

Lejeune tells us that he was "greeted most cordially." During their lengthy discussion Gouraud told Lejeune "that he, too, was a Marine, as indicated by the khaki-colored uniform which he wore...."[3] Lejeune says he was impressed by Gouraud, sensing that "he was a man of power with a will of iron, but kindly withal. I acquired confidence in his judgment and ... justness."[4]

The brief "get acquainted " conversation over, Lejeune returned to his headquarters. There, on the following day, 27 September, Lejeune's chief of staff, Col. James C. Rhea, USA, passed along a disquieting rumor that upset Lejeune greatly. Rhea told him that plans were being considered by Fourth Army Headquarters to break up the 2d Division and assign each infantry brigade to a French division. Assuming that the report was true, without first requiring confirmation, and taking no chances, Lejeune took the first opportunity to interrogate Gouraud concerning the rumor.

Gouraud, in his office, at first held the conversation with Lejeune strictly on matters he wished to discuss. These matters were the current efforts of the Fourth Army and what plans Gouraud had for the near future. He told about how the French advance had been stopped but the Fourth Army was now holding Somme-Py westward to Ste. Marie á Py, a distance of about 2 miles, and then south to the Suippe River. Gouraud explained that the Germans were strongly entrenched in a fortified range of hills known locally as "Les Monts." About 2½ miles north of Somme-Py lay another and more difficult target: "Le Massif du Blanc Mont" dominated the entire area. The ridge had been, and would continue to be, dangerous to any attacking force, even on its sloping offshoots, including those about Médéah Farm and the village of Orfeuil. Gouraud further advised Lejeune that:

> If I could take this position by assault, advance beyond it to the vicinity of St. Étienne à Arnes, and hold the ground gained against the counterattacks which would be hurled against my troops, the enemy would be compelled to evacuate 'Notre Dame des Champs and Les Monts,' thereby freeing Rheims which he has been strangling for four years, and fall back to the Aisne, a distance of nearly 30 kilometers.... My divisions, however, are worn out from the long strain of continuous fighting and from the effects of the heavy casualties they have suffered, and it is

doubtful if they are now equal to accomplishing this difficult task unless they are heavily reinforced.[5]

Lejeune had no difficulty catching Gouraud's broad hint. It was obvious, to Lejeune, that Gouraud was suggesting merging the Americans into the badly depleted French forces. To forestall what he perceived was coming, Lejeune offered to accomplish the "impossible" by taking "Blanc Mont Ridge, advance beyond it, and hold a position there" if Gouraud would promise not to break up the 2d Division.[6] Gouraud, however, told Lejeune that he had no intention of breaking up the division and that in fact it wasn't a part of his army anyway, but belonged to Foch and Pétain: "I will, however, bring to Marshal Pétain's attention what you have just said."[7] Lejeune admitted to being caught somewhat off guard and his hasty reaction and ill-conceived promise were to cause very serious repercussions for the division in the days ahead. Lejeune's miscalculation was apparently what the French were hoping for and they instantly took full advantage of it. The American had made a commitment and therefore it had to be, and would be, honored.

Later that day Lejeune was advised that at Gouraud's request Pétain had assigned the division to Gouraud's army. Orders were then being prepared for the 2d Division to move to a forward position in the Souain-Suippes area, which was located about 3 miles south of the village of Somme-Py. Previously, under separate orders by the French Army, the 4th Brigade had been moved near Toul, in the Verdun Sector. They were now recalled and moved by rail to Châlons-sur-Marne to rejoin the division.[8] The order that Gouraud issued on 28 September put the entire division on the move once again, this time by camion. On 30 September the 2d Division was designated as the reserve of the French Fourth Army.

The German 12th Saxon Corps, led by Gen. of Cavalry Krug von Nidda, was the German unit holding Blanc Mont. It included the 14th Reserve Division of Infantry (DI) located on the west facing the French XI Corps, the 200th DI facing the area of the 2d Division, and the 7th DI facing the French XXI Corps' eastern flank. It was known to the German High Command that ten American divisions were, or soon would be, in place and that "must be reckoned with."[9]

Von Nidda also gave an estimate of the situation on 1 October that came close to what actually happened. He predicted that untold numbers of troops crossing the Py Brook, plus the numerous tanks, indicated that "on October 2, a hostile attack is to be expected...."[10] He was incorrect by date but close enough to be well aware that something was about to happen. In other words, the Germans would be ready.

Meanwhile, the 4th Brigade received a divisional field order, dated 29 September, specifying that it would be the van of the 2d Division in its move to Suippe. The FO directed the two Marine regiments to move by camion but, as

A view of the area around Blanc Mont, looking toward the Bois de la Vipère.

frequently happened, the division machine gun battalions and regimental machine gun companies would march with the assistance of animal transportation. When the Marines arrived at their destination, the brigade would be located so as to be a single night's march from Somme-Py.[11]

Tuesday 1 October 1918

On 1 October orders from the Fourth French Army formally assigned the 2d Division to the XXI French Corps. The division had previously served under the command of XXI Corps (Maj. Gen. Stanislas Naulin) in June in the Chateau Thierry Sector, so it was not too difficult getting settled in. Headquarters officers of each unit knew many of the others. The first order issued, verbally, was for division to relieve the exhausted 61st French DI in the front lines on the night of 1–2 October. The 4th Brigade easily complied during the early morning hours. The written order, however, was not received at brigade headquarters until 0440, long after the relief was completed. Confusion reigned.

Second Division trains headed toward Somme-Py to support the two brigades in their attack upon Blanc Mont.

The assigned position in the trenches for the division took up approximately two miles. When eventually the 3d Brigade arrived on line, each brigade would occupy one mile, the 3d on the right, the 4th on the left.[12] The French 21st DI, a part of the French XI Corps, occupied the territory left of the 2d Division and the French 170th DI, part of the XXI Corps, the 3d Brigade's right flank. It was planned that when orders were issued to advance each French division was to advance in liaison on either flank of the 2d U.S. Division. At least, that was the concept. It didn't quite happen that way.

The 4th Brigade occupied the trenches just north of Somme-Py between the Boyau de Custrine on the right and Boyau de Bromberg on the left, about a half mile in length. The 5th Marines on the right and the 6th Marines on the left were supported by the guns of the 6th Machine Gun Battalion. The actual layout was:

Left	*Right*
2/6 and the 81st Machine Gun Company	1/5 and the 8th Machine Gun Company
1/6 and the 73d Machine Gun Company	2/5 and the 23d Machine Gun Company
3/6 and the 15th Machine Gun Company	3/5 and the 77th Machine Gun Company

The Germans were still located just before the Marines, in a series of trenches called Pacha, Elbe, and Essen. From there the next line of trenches to the north was located on Blanc Mont Massif.

Meanwhile, the 3d Brigade was down near Suippes as Corps reserve. General Lejeune, nearby at Wagram, his post of command (PC), sent an "inspiring order"[13] to his division, about which, he later exclaimed, "The order had an excellent effect.'" It gave few details as to what the division would do in the forthcoming days but was heavy with vague historical references in the first part and was terribly mawkish in the second. The message in effect called upon the division to fall upon the enemy "and once more gloriously defeat" him.[14] Lejeune added that the order had fallen into the hands of the Germans, had been translated into English and dispersed amongst their troops. The statement, indicating the sorrowful state of Germany, greatly troubled the German soldiers, according to Lejeune.[15]

Early that afternoon, 4th Brigade's Operation Memo No. 9 spelled out the brigade's responsibility, which was to move forward that night and be in readiness to attack on the morning of 2 October.[16] Regardless of the order, from the very beginning there was great confusion at Naulin's corps headquarters. Division attack orders for the morning of October 2d were not issued until 2350 hours on 1 October. Those orders stated that the 21st French DI, in liaison with the 2d Division on their right, "will attack at 1150 hours after an artillery preparation, the duration of which will be fixed later."

Von Nidda was well aware that a serious attack was coming. This day he sent out a message to his local commanders giving his estimate (which proved to be right on target) of the situation. He recognized where the main attack would be launched (against the ridge) because of the "numerous reserves" coming in a northerly direction "in an uninterrupted flow throughout the day" and crossing the Py Brook.[17]

Though there was no attack upon the Group Py (von Nidda's), the French II Corps, to the right of the XXI Corps, launched an attack against the German 42d DI (part of the Group Perthes) at 1000. It was repulsed, as had been so many others. That evening at 2040, Headquarters, Group Py, issued the following orders:

> The 200th Infantry Division, 15th Bavarian Division, and 3d Guard Infantry Division will maintain their positions; the 7th Infantry Division will withdraw its lines as far as the line of Tor Hill — along the main line of resistance as far as Altona–Mulde–Stallmulde–the strong point at the east slope of Helenen Hill.[18]

The orders continue to describe the location of each German unit along the entire front. The units identified were the 199th and 203d DI, which were to "withdraw from the lines." Both would fall back to support positions. The regiments of the 203d, the 406th Infantry, would be at Orfeuil (see map) and the 409th at Médéah Hill, and the 410th at Bémont Ferme. The 7th DI would be relieved by the 51st Ersatz Division. The Guard Fusilier Regiment of the 3d

Guard DI would be relieved by a regiment of the 199th DI, with all changes to be carried out that evening.[19]

Wednesday 2 October

The next morning Lejeune was called to Naulin's headquarters and he brought along his two brigadiers, Ely and Neville. They were at Corps Headquarters "presumably for orders." The exact sector to be occupied was, "of course, unknown." Naulin pointed out that the French army had been battling this "fortress" without success and with severe losses since 1914. It was a time when the French soldier was no longer willing to be sacrificed to the demands of the French high command. Therefore, the French command felt it necessary to bring new forces into the attack on that heavily fortified position.

While discussing the forthcoming attack, Gen. Naulin suggested a plan, which Lejeune, supported by Ely and Neville, rejected out of hand. Asking for a few minutes to get their heads together, the three men came up with a countersuggestion which Lejeune described. This suggestion was to launch the assault in a two brigade front, the 4th on the left, and the 3d on the right. Each brigade would advance in a regimental front, the 6th Marines on the left and the 9th Infantry on the right. Their front would not be contiguous (see map). The plan called for the 3d Brigade to come together with the 4th at the ridge. The latter would come in at an oblique angle. A wooded area, known locally as the Bois de la Vipère, would separate them and would be bypassed to be taken later when the ridge had been attained. In other words, both brigades would have an exposed flank, the 4th to their right and the 3d to their left. At the very least, each could expect light weapons fire from German infantry in those bypassed woods. For some reason the attack on 2 October did not come off as scheduled. Counter orders were issued to instead advance on 3 October as had been proposed by the Americans.

Lejeune tells us that the task on 2 October for both the 2d Division and the French 21st DI was to clear out the still occupied Essen and Elbe trenches at their front. On that day the Americans were successful in cleaning out their section, Elbe, but the French at Essen were not, a situation which did not bode well for the next day's attack.

The 6th Marines lost fifteen men from fire emanating from the Essen Hook, at their left flank, but the 5th Marines on the right had a relatively easy time taking the German trenches lying just before them. Colonel Harry Lee of the Sixth Marines reported to division that a reconnaissance of the Elbe and Essen trenches, directly to his regiment's front, had found them to be unoccupied, but the strong points northwest of the subsector occupied by the 6th, notably the Essen Hook (i.e., located in the 21st French DI sector) was able to completely control any ground that the regiment would advance over. He added that for his troops to attempt to overcome these strong points, before the advance scheduled for the following day, would do irreparable damage to his lead battalion. He suggested that the position be neutralized by artillery fire when his troops were in their jump-off positions.

Members of the 6th Marines were active that day, managing to drive out most, if not all, the Germans in the trenches lying before the Regiment. Newly commissioned 2d Lt. Hugh Kidder* of the 78th Co., led a small patrol into the enemy's trenches on the morning of 2 October and captured two machine guns and crews that were threatening his platoon. He would hurl his gauntlet in the Germans' face again on the morrow but they would hurl it back at him.

Fourth Brigade field orders were issued at 1820 hours on 2 October and, among other directions, gave a brief description of where heavy weapons should be placed in the forthcoming fight. It also explained that Maj. Gen. Lejeune's headquarters would remain at PC Wagram, near Suippes. Lejeune would direct his division from his PC, about eight miles from the division's objective. Those were the days when radio and telephone communication was almost nonexistent. Eight miles from the action might not appear very conducive to good management but there he was and there he stayed.

The plan was finalized for the 6th Marines to be in the van, followed at a

The 17th Field Artillery near Suippes, firing their 155mm howitzers at the Blanc Mont Massif.

discreet distance by the 5th Marines. Colonel Harry Lee had Lt. Col. Thomas H. Holcomb as his second in command. Battalion commanders were, Maj. Frederick A. Barker, 1/6; Maj. Ernest C. Williams, 2/6; and Maj. George K. Shuler, 3/6. Major Littleton W.T. Waller, Jr., commanded the Sixth Machine Gun Battalion.[20]

The formation of the 4th Brigade as assigned for the attack to be made on 3 October in a column of battalions was as follows:

> Front
> 2d Battalion 6th Marines and 81st Machine Gun Company.
> Twelve light French tanks.
> 1st Battalion 6th Marines and 73rd Machine Gun Company.
> Twelve light French tanks.
> 3d Battalion 6th Marines and 15th Machine Gun Company.
>
> Rear:
> 2d Battalion 5th Marines and 23d Machine Gun Company.
> 3d Battalion 5th Marines and 77th Machine Gun Company.
> 1st Battalion 5th Marines and 8th Machine Gun Company.

Leaders of the 5th Marines were as follows: 1/5 Maj. George Hamilton; 2/5 Maj. Robert Messersmith; 3/5 Maj. Henry Larsen.

Plans for the formation of the 3d Brigade were not yet finalized. In fact no orders had yet been issued to bring the 3d Brigade up to their jump-off point, another example of French disorganization which would cause needless sacrifice of troops, this time Americans.

At 2000 a highly agitated Lt. Col. Harry Lay, USMC, liaison officer between the French command and 2d Division, was making every effort to reach Brig. Gen. Ely in order to pass along information that the assault details on the morrow had changed. Artillery preparation would begin 15 minutes earlier and the two brigades would begin their advance 40 minutes earlier. A bit later Neville received orders from Col. Rhea to send a battalion to counter the effects of the continued German occupation of the Essen trench on the advance of the 4th Brigade on 3 October. The French 21st DI had been unable to evict the Germans in their sector and now the Marines would have to face that challenge to their left flank.

During the night, Col. George W. Stuart, 9th Infantry, with indefinite instructions from the French command, led his formation forward over bad roads made worse by German intermittent shelling. In all, the regiment had 104 officers and 3,344 enlisted men. In a diary entry, Capt. Roy C. Hilton, CO of the 9th MG Co., described the nine mile march: "A French guide was to meet us after we had gone five kilometers (3 miles), but he did not arrive and we passed practically all night locating our new position."[21] His company, lugging their heavy French Hotchkiss guns and ammunition, began at 1800 on 2 October and the trip didn't end until 0500 on 3 October at which time, less than an hour before the jump-off, "the men were exhausted."

Captain Aaron A. Platner,* CO of 1/9, was actually able to relieve the French Chasseurs with his battalion. Although some of their outposts were left in front, Platner was not notified of their presence. Two/9, Lt. Col. Alfred C. Arnold,* and 3/9, Major Robert L. Denig,* USMC, both came up later that night and were sent off to woods nearby to await the morning attack. Their orders were to pass through the French line in the morning attack. Just before darkness set in, the 23d Infantry, Col. Edward R. Stone,* CO, arrived and took position just behind the 9th Infantry.

The 3d Brigade would have an unpleasant undertaking just to make the 0500 jump-off on the morrow. Upon arrival near their jump-off site, they would find that the Germans had retaken those trenches from the French and would have to be evicted before the 9th Infantry could go forward as planned. This would also stall the 23d Infantry in their support positions, creating, thereby, a serious problem for the 3d Brigade to reach its objective, the ridge, and keep liaison with the 4th Brigade when it reached their target, Blanc Mont Massif.

Thursday 3 October

At 0550, after five minutes of artillery preparation, the two brigades jumped-off. The 3d Brigade had a fight on its hands even before they could advance up towards the ridge. The Germans who had retaken the trenches stalled the infantry advance for a short period. Meanwhile, the Jägers at Essen Hook withstood everything the French 21st DI could throw at them. Because the French 21st DI could not eradicate the Germans from Essen Trench, the 6th Marines endured heavy fire emanating from the left. The 5th Marines, with orders to protect the left flank, had waited until the 6th Marines had cleared their departure area before progressing. Then the last battalion in line, 1/5, sent the 17th Co. (Capt. Leroy P. Hunt) to relieve the pressure on the left flank. Hunt had 2d Lt Arthur Wilkinson, with his 1-pounder squad, move forward and selected four targets, all Maxims, to be eliminated. Wilkinson and his lads wiped out the four guns and crews. Hunt and men then assaulted the Hook, but before much more could happen the Germans decided to surrender, and by 1030 the position had been completely taken. The captured Hook and prisoners were turned over to the French of the 21st DI and then the 17th Co. followed the 5th Marines up the hill.

However, the 21st DI had not advanced with the 2d Division and essentially remained at the starting gate. That afternoon the Germans counterattacked the 21st DI and the Hook was quickly retaken. The whole left flank of the 2d Division had been and continued to be exposed all that day and well into the next. As could be expected, this caused the 4th Brigade enormous casualties. Third Brigade's right flank was well covered by the French and they had to fight Germans only to their front, and that was tough enough.

The 3d Brigade, however, had a difficult time making it to their assigned jump-off position. Ely and his brigade had a march of 3 1/2 miles that early morning in order to get there. Just after 0300, Brig. Gen. Ely would complain to Col. Rhea, division chief of staff, that French guides from the 170th DI, had not met his 23d Infantry and he was not yet in communication with Col. Stuart of the 9th. Meantime, German artillery blasted them as they approached and 1/9, which was to lead off, was instead briefly dispersed. Alternatively, Stuart, not having heard from Platner after the dispersement described above, assigned 2/9 to the lead, and 3/9 to follow as support and, "after its reorganization," 1/9 would follow as reserve. Platner and his company officers rapidly pulled 1/9 together and relieved French Chasseurs in line. Placement was as follows: Companies C and D were in the front line, with A and B in support. The machine gun platoons from Hilton's company were placed with Companies C, D and B.

Now two battalions were in the lead. At 0830 the regiment consolidated and 1/9 spread out to their left to cover the entire brigade front. Two/9 rearranged itself and took up support positions and 3/9 went into the reserve position, five hundred yards further to the rear. The 3d Brigade continued its ascent up the hill, with 1/9 still in the lead.

In the advance, as C Co. of 1/9 was being held up by enemy machine gun fire, New Yorker Pvt. Frank J. Bart,* company runner and reckless like most of his breed, grabbed a Chauchat and ran out in front of the line. He silenced one machine gun nest and then regained his post by his CO. Shortly after the advance continued it was held up once again by more machine guns. Bart took his trusty Chauchat along when he went out and knocked off another machine gun nest. Those actions by a brave runner earned him the only Medal of Honor awarded to the 9th Infantry during the war. The French paid him honor with a Médaille Militaire, their version of the highest of the high American awards.

According to one of the gunners, the 2d Artillery Brigade began firing at 0100 and "we blazed away for two hours. At 3.00 A.M. we lifted our barrage; our infantry went over ... [We learned] at 6.00 A.M. that the Germans were offering severe resistance. The German troops opposing us had a division of Bavarians, mostly all young men; they surely fought every inch. Our infantry captured the hill twice and were forced to withdraw. We couldn't fire to assist them as they expected to try again."[22]

Off the 9th Infantry went, with the French 167th DI[23] on their right flank and the Bois de Viperes on their left. Up the hill, and even though they were slightly late in the beginning, by 0840 1/9 had taken the first objective, the Médéah Ferme—Blanc Mont Road. There, they joined with the 6th Marines, who had also reached their objective atop the hill. Patrols were sent by 1/9 to the farm itself and it was found that the French of the 167th DI occupied that position. The 9th Infantry moved forward and held this position for the rest of that day and night. An officer of the 9th Machine Gun Co., Capt. R.C. Hilton, wrote:

> The objective was Medeah Farm which was reached without halt and where our line was organized. From here two machine guns from our company fired into hostile artillery stopping the artillery and causing them to change positions. Here we were receiving German artillery and machine gun fire from both flanks and the front, as the French had failed to advance on our right, and there was a gap on our left. They finally came up about four days later, but we had many casualties before this time."[24]

Several men of F Co., 2/9, Cpls. William Curlee,* Harry Osborne,* and Elmer Zeiler,* helped by Pvts William Y. Allen* and Andy Toblini,* charged a machine gun nest with three guns, taking the site and 20 German prisoners. At 1015 a battalion (not identified) of the 23d was sent to assist Maj. Frederick Barker of the 6th Marines to resist a counterattack.[25]

The Marines also had a tough climb and suffered heavily on their left flank from German fire. At times the various platoons and even entire companies ventured over into the territory of where the 21st French DI should have been and killed, or drove out, the Maxims and gunners. Along this route "Johnny" Kelly,* a runner for Capt. James McB. Sellers, skipper of the 78th Co., advanced before his company and the division's rolling barrage by at least 100 yards and took out a Maxim gunner and his assistant and then captured another eight Germans, making them prisoners. Marching them back to his company through the barrage he yelled "See! I told ya I'd do it." His reward was a Medal of Honor.[26]

The 2d Battalion of the 6th had been taking a rough handling from the Germans on their left and much of their fighting had been along that flank. They did manage to get up that hill to the massif and by 0830 had taken most of the exposed part of the ridge. The worst part of it was that the left side, which sloped down the hill and held many machine guns and infantry, was still in the hands of the Germans. This fight would take all the balance of the day and much of the next with the 6th Marines digging the Germans out, one by one. During this period, Cpl John H. Pruitt,* also of the 78th Co., captured two Maxims, killing their gunners and taking forty prisoners. He too was awarded a Medal of Honor, but posthumously, having been killed by shell fire soon afterward. Many more good men would die before this battle was over.

Men of 2/6, commanded by the irascible Ernest N. "Bull" Williams,* were going at the Germans with a vengeance. Williams was awarded his Navy Cross for "bravery and skill" in keeping his battalion obtaining their objectives on time through heavy artillery and machine gun fire. Williams had already been awarded a Medal of Honor in Santo Domingo in 1916.

When their 78th Co., 2/6, was held up by Maxims, four privates, Julian W. Alsup,* Roy H. Beird,* Richard O. Jordan,* and Bruce H. Mills,* went forward and wiped out the enfilading fire from a machine gun nest. They made a flank attack with hand grenades and rifle fire, killing 3 Germans and capturing 3 guns plus the 25 members of the nest.[27]

The 6th Machine Gun Bn was well represented in this climb. After their gun was upset by a German grenade, Corporal Olin J. Butterfield,* with assistance from Pvts Fred Haefliger* and Grannis L. Syverson,* calmly set it up again even though Butterfield and Haefliger were wounded. When the advancing Germans were within 20 feet the Marines opened fire and drove them from the field in disorder.

Within 600 yards, the 5th Marines followed the 6th and also had a rough time of it. The German balloons above the lines were radioing artillery positions and the guns worked over the infantrymen as they climbed: "Here comes machine gun fire from the left. We drop and lay perfectly still in the grass and weeds; someone from the extreme left will be sent after the machine guns."[28]

The division artillery was well placed and with powerful support. To it was attached artillery from several French divisions, the 28th, 61st, a battalion of

Illustration of wounded troops being brought to a dressing station near Blanc Mont Massif.

120's and two battalions of 155's. As usual, the 12th FA was firing for the 4th Brigade and the 15th FA for the 3d Brigade and, though they only fired for five minutes, it was intense. Then they began the rolling barrage fired at 100 meters in advance, moving up every four minutes. From available records, it was professionally performed with no "friendly" casualties.

Atop the hill the 6th Marines were heavily engaged in cleaning out the various dugout positions and the German 2d Jäger Brigade headquarters now abandoned the Massif after some members had been captured by the Marines. Several feeble attempts were made by the enemy to organize a serious counterattack but each failed. By 0900 the 6th Marines were walking around as "Kings of the Hill" but still German troops occupied numerous dugouts within the hill and the 6th begged Corps headquarters for assistance before those too had to capitulate. In fact, at 0920, the German operator notified headquarters that the "Americans are demanding surrender" but before a response could be made the line went dead. The entire artillery headquarters and the 200th German DI advanced station were captured.

General Naulin was quite unhappy that the advance had slowed down and demanded that Lejeune continue forward. Lejeune explained that the French on the left had not advanced and the Germans were still occupying that flank, even clinging to the west side of the Massif, which, of course, required that the Marines clean that out before advancing further. Nevertheless, in early afternoon FO 36 prescribed that the 5th Marines pass through the 6th Marines and continue the advance toward St. Étienne.

Meanwhile the 3d Brigade front changed. The 23d Infantry pushed through the 9th Infantry at about 1700, an hour later than ordered, and the 9th followed in support. The 23d moved forward rapidly and though the 9th followed, an extended area began to develop between them. The 23d had been moving toward their left gaining about a mile, and soon the 9th found no Americans before them on their right. The 15th Bavarian DI were thrust in to attempt to stop the Americans. Exhausted from previous exploits, their 31st Infantry (Maj. Reiss) could only assemble 120 men, however, 80 more from the two other regiments joined them in their efforts. It was a German total of less than one American company to hold back a regiment.

The 1st Bn, 23d, pushed way out, but was stopped from a further advance by fire from both flanks about a half mile from St. Étienne. The regiment was now located in the 4th Brigade sector. However, two battalions of the 9th Infantry came up to fill the gap on their right and met the French at Médéah Ferme. Meanwhile, as the 23d advanced, Messersmith's 2/5 assumed the left front from the 6th Marines and finally at dusk succeeded in pushing the enemy back and connecting with the 10th Bn of the French Chasseurs on their left.

At 1830 that evening, 3/5, followed by 1/5, moved to their right and forward up the Somme Py–St. Étienne road to connect up with the 23d Infantry.

8. Blanc Mont

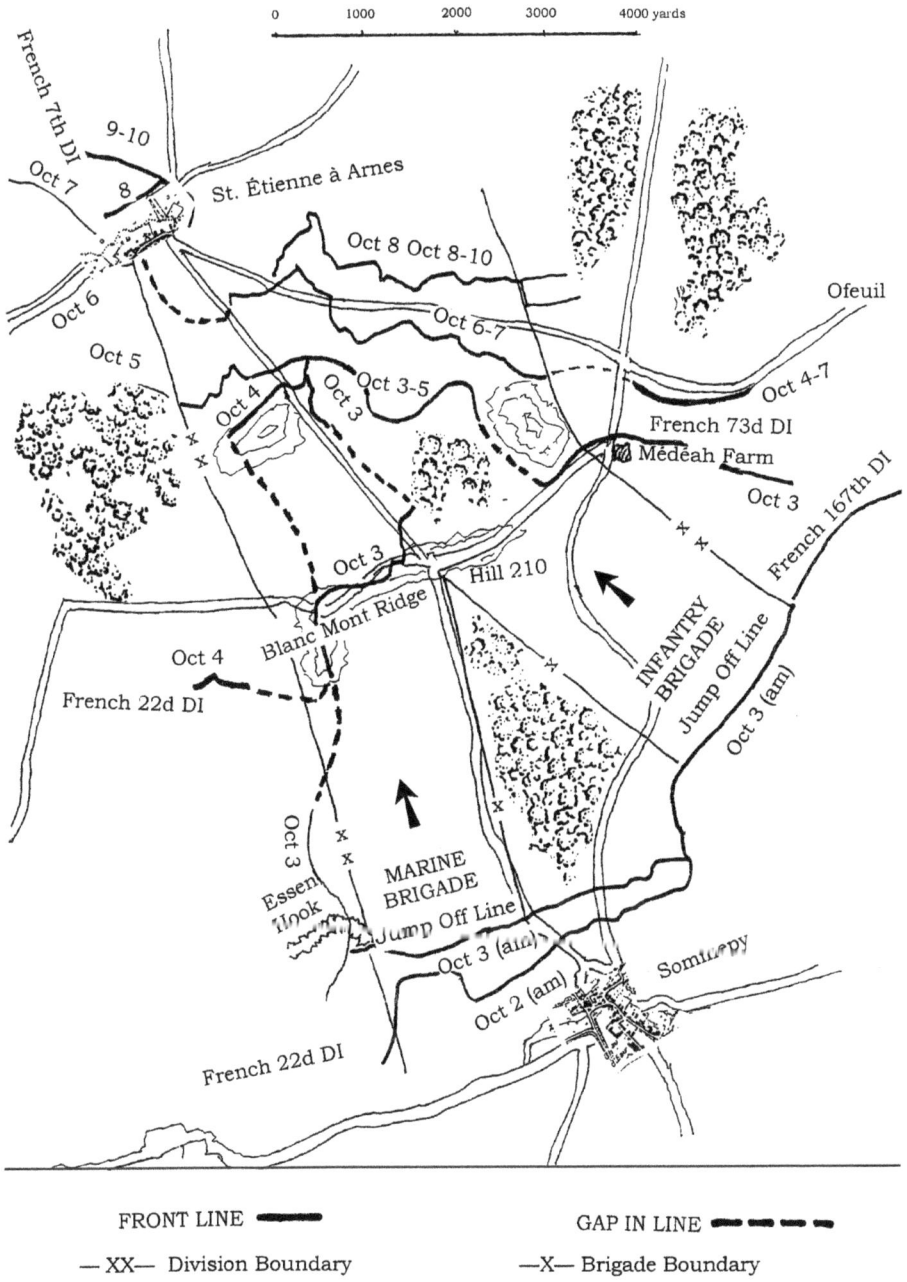

Map 11. 2d Division with the French Fourth Army, October 2–10, 1918.

Their objective was a line of trenches lying about 600 yards southeast of St. Étienne. They were only about a mile forward and not near enough to St. Étienne because the going had been rough and the Marines of the 5th Regiment were somewhat scattered. The left, as we know, was still not covered by the French and the Germans were firing from that direction upon the 5th located mainly on the road. As they were fired upon, the companies of the 5th had moved to their left to engage the enemy. Despite all this, Division headquarters was convinced that their two brigades would put finish to the Germans on the morrow. How wrong they were.

Things got a little better at the end of the day. Final positions were the 9th Infantry on the far right, not as far forward as the 23d Infantry; the latter were about a half mile south of St. Étienne with flanks mainly exposed to the Germans; the 5th Marines held mainly the road and not as far forward as the 23d Infantry; the 6th Marines moved some companies forward to try to relieve the exposed left flank of their comrades of the 5th Marines. The Germans still held the west slopes of Blanc Mont Massif and all the open ground before the 2d Division. Yet, at day's end, the Americans had accomplished what the French had been unable to in nearly four years. The hilltop had been taken and the Germans had been forced to fall back a considerable distance. Now it was just a matter of time before the entire high ground fell to the victors, but the number of casualties would ruin the 2d Division.

After taking the Blanc Mont Massif, this is what the troops saw of their next target, St. Etienne.

Friday 4 October

At 0600 the 5th Marines advanced up the road toward St. Étienne, Larsen's 3/5 in front followed by 2/5 and lastly, 1/5. As the enemy concentrated on the marching column, 2/5 moved off the road to the left of 3/5, which still moved forward on the road. Hamilton's 1/5 moved toward the left beyond 2/5, thereupon receiving most of the German fire. Enemy fire from both machine guns and artillery was devastating. The French still hadn't moved forward to cover that left flank and the enemy made the Americans pay dearly for every inch of ground bought. The 5th regimental history was vague in details but the author expressed the "official" position thus: "October 4th was the bitterest single day of fighting that the Fifth Regiment experienced during the whole war. The advance that day was over difficult terrain in the face of the densest barrage of shell and machine gun fire that the Marines ever had to face. The left flank was continually exposed and the advancing waves were exposed to a merciless enfilading fire." Then he added Lejeune's later comment: "To be able to say when the war is finished, 'I belonged to the 2d Division, I fought with it at the Battle of Blanc Mont Ridge,' will be the highest honor that can come to any man." The regiment was literally destroyed. Hamilton's 1/5 took most of the hits, being on the far left, advancing without any flank cover or support. Messersmith's 2/5 took some heavy hits as well and had a few bad moments that are described elsewhere.[29] Participants, including Elton Mackin (the author of *Suddenly We Didn't Want to Die*, later proclaimed the Germans sucked them into "The Box" and "barely one hundred survived." Both 1/5 and 2/5 managed to fall back on the road, with the 23d Infantry helping to support them. A fine accolade from the authors of the 18th Co.'s history is reprinted here:

> It is no more than just to mention here the part the 23rd Infantry played in the fight. They were on our right flank and but for them I fear there would have been but very few Marines left to tell the story. Always they can be depended upon to gain their objective and hold it no matter what the cost. And the 23rd Infantry suffered heavily, but nevertheless they stuck to their work and held off repeated attempts to counterattack, thus making it possible for us to connect up with them and render assistance if needed.[30]

For all intents and purposes, the 5th Marines were finished. The remnants of 1/5 added up to an inconsequential 156 officers and men, including the walking wounded, about ten percent of what they began the day with. The regiment would not be called upon for the balance of the period the division was in the sector. Lee's 6th Marines, with 6th MG Bn's support, would have to carry the work of the 4th Brigade until the 10th of October. During this day, 43 men of the 5th Marines were awarded DSCs and it would be near impossible to recount them all here. Although not nearly as many were issued to each of the other three regiments, there were so many the same can be said. So many awards to so many heroes.

In the meantime, the 3d Brigade and the 6th Marines had kept busy. The Germans had launched an attack early that morning upon 2/9 (Lt. Col. Alfred C. Arnold*), which felt the brunt of it. It continued for several hours but Arnold and his men persevered. At noon the 23d Infantry leading and the 9th in support attempted an advance to coincide with the 5th Marines. With their flanks in the air, and subjected to intense fire from all angles, they were soon brought to a standstill.

The 73d French DI had strenuously but unsuccessfully attempted to come up on the 3d Brigade's right. The 22d French DI, which had replaced the 21st DI, on the 4th Brigade's left, had drifted toward the west and, though they advanced, still provided no flank support for the 4th Brigade. Therefore, for now, the 2d Division was still out front with no flanking cover. Blanc Mont was still partially occupied, in dugouts, and on the west slope by the enemy, who had to be cleared out of there before an advance upon St. Étienne could successfully proceed.

Major George K. Shuler, CO, 3/6, reconnoitered the western end of the ridge and called in artillery to precede his attack. Late that afternoon the guns fired and the 6th Marines made their move. But the support from the 22d French DI was not adequate and the attack was broken up with considerable loss to the 6th Marines. At midnight the situation in the 3d Brigade was essentially the same as it had been 24 hours earlier.

Saturday 5 October

On the 4th and 5th of October, two privates of the 12th Field Artillery, Harley S. Edwards* and Russell Moran,* remained on duty for fourteen hours, repairing telephone lines, in a stretch 300 yards in length, which were continually being disrupted by intense shell-fire. Twenty times they were cut, and each time Edwards and Moran would go out and make necessary repairs so their battery could continue its work.

Field Order 38 issued at 0400 directed the division to "continue" its advance toward Machault–Cauroy, the former village located about five miles further northeast of St. Étienne. The attack was not to take place, however, until the French came abreast on both flanks. Meanwhile, at 0615, 3/6 advanced on the western slopes, three companies in line (97th, 82d and 83d with the 84th in support) capturing a machine gun nest and making contact with the French 22d DI. In taking the last holdouts on the Blanc Mont Massif the battalion captured four officers, 269 prisoners, 80 machine guns, and a substantial number of mortars. No Marine casualties were sustained.[31]

At 0845 an order was issued which stated that the 6th would be prepared to pass through the 5th in the following order: "Bull" Williams and 2/6 in the lead, Shuler with 3/6 next, and Barker with 1/6 last. In a telephone conversa-

A captured German bunker on the Blanc Mont Massif.

tion at 1250, Williams was directed to move out: "Advance to St. Étienne, keeping liaison with the French on our left and the 3d Brigade on our right.... Halt at St. Étienne and await orders." At about 1500 the 6th moved forward to attack the ridge southeast of St. Étienne. They passed through the 5th Marines at about 1630 and soon 2/6 had also been greatly depleted by casualties, having less than 300 effectives on a front at least a mile in width. On the right a battalion CO of the 23d Infantry strongly advised 1st Lt John A. West* of the 79th Co. to not attempt a further advance because of the numerous machine gun nests lying before them. His own command had already been shattered trying to take the positions. West ignored the words of wisdom, led his company forward and was carried from the field severely wounded.

The 6th had stopped their advance about a mile and a half southeast of St. Étienne, where they dug in. Though they weren't entirely successful, the uncommitted elements of the 4th Brigade came up to protect the left flank of the 23d Infantry, which was still protruding into the enemies lines. The 3d Brigade received no orders to advance on that day as the French had not yet come abreast of them.

Sunday 6 October

The previous evening, an agreement was entered into between Col. Harry Lee of the 6th Marines and Col. Edward R. Stone of the 23d Infantry to launch a combined attack. The morning of the 6th, at 0630, an attack was made upon a machine gun nest southeast of St. Étienne by 3/6 and 2/23 with a platoon of the 2d Engineers attached to cut wire. According to the regimental history, 3/6 suffered at least 40 percent casualties. Heavy resistance brought up three companies of 1/23 to fill the gap developed between the two assaulting battalions, with the 4th company sent in on the right flank. Then Companies L and M of 3/23 were sent in as further support at 0800. The objective was taken at 0930.

At 0900 Col. George W. Stuart was ordered to push his 9th Infantry forward in order to make contact with the French 73d DI. Whereupon 2/9 advanced two companies forward to a line south of the St. Étienne–Orfeuil road. In so doing they established contact with the French just northwest of Médéah Farm.

On the extreme left of the division, 2/6 withdrew under orders when 1/6 moved up and took over the left. The latter was, however, unable to make contact with the 22d French DI, which had managed to move its right flank up to the southern edge of St. Étienne. At 1500 the French 62d RI pulled out of the town leaving the left flank of the 6th Marines once again in the air. Contact was eventually established between the two regiments later that evening. The French had reentered the town in the early evening and the French CO, in righteous indignation, was demanding that the 6th Marines close up to protect his right flank.

General Naulin had been quite apprehensive about the lack of progress by the French on the right and had requested Lejeune "not to hesitate to use his reserves on the flank." On this day, the first elements of the 36th "Cowboy" Division showed up and were placed at the disposition of the 2d Division.[32] On the night of 6–7 October, the 71st Infantry Brigade took over the front line but each brigade of the 2d Division was ordered to leave one battalion plus machine guns and auxiliary weapons in line to support the newcomers. The 23d Infantry was relieved and retired to Pylone Hill but 2/9 remained where they had been to their right. Later it was decided to leave the entire 6th Regiment in line until further notice, with the "Cowboys" to assume command of the front line at 0300.[33]

As veterans usually do, it wasn't long before the doughboys and Marines were conning the newcomers out of some of their most valuable material. The Browning Automatic Rifle was brand new and the cowboys had it. But as soon as the 2d Division grunts got a look at it, they soon convinced the cowboys that it was a loser and "with great reluctance" traded their Chauchats for the BAR. They would, however, be forced to return the BARs to their original owners when the "trades" became known to the officers.

Monday 7 October

At 1130 the French requested that the 2d Division, which was still maintaining overall responsibility for the sector, establish liaison with them in the southeastern outskirts of St. Étienne. One/6 had remained all night in the woods south of the town and they provided part of a patrol that entered the town that morning. During the day the French advanced northwest but the Germans still held St. Étienne. During the day many conflicting reports put the French in the town, out of the town, in the town, and out of the town. Possibly that was a true estimate of the events. About 1150 a patrol of the 6th Marines was fired upon from a cemetery on the eastern edge of the town. Corporal Charles W. Garr,* D Co., 2d Engineers, advancing ahead of the infantry, reconnoitered the town of St. Étienne, then returned through heavy artillery and machine gun fire from both armies to bring valuable information. General Naulin, who had planned to have the 2d Division, with the newly arrived troops of the 36th Division, attack on this day, changed his mind. Lejeune had helped him decide that way by pointing out that the troops were exhausted, and needed rest and an advance on the 8th would not be possible.

Further reports from the 6th Marines that afternoon put the estimated 200 Germans infiltrating back into the town with more seen coming over a hill. French XXI Corps believed the French still occupied the town and requested that the 2d Division relieve them. In fact the Germans still held the town and the French had a very precarious hold on the western edge. Continued reports during the afternoon put a very active enemy northeast of the town; they were massing in the woods and their artillery was pushed forward. It appeared to Corps Headquarters that the Germans were going to make a stand along the ridge line toward Semide, about 10 miles to the northeast.

That evening 1/6 was ordered to occupy trenches about 700 yards south of St. Étienne to fill the gap between the troops on Hill 160. Otherwise, the two divisions were sorting out their places in line during the 7th.

Tuesday 8 October

Orders for an attack this day had already been formulated on the Sixth of October. The 2d Division command (Lejeune) was still authorized to direct the 36th Division and orders were issued for the 71st Brigade to attack on the division front. Their purpose was to take the high ground two miles north of St. Étienne. The French 7th DI, which had relieved the 22d DI, was directing its movement toward Cauroy. That would place it slightly west of Machault, which lay within the approach path of the Americans. The 73d DI would take Bemont Chateau, which would help to narrow the American's pathway, then all three units would advance, with the 2d Division taking Machault.

The 71st Brigade's flanks would be protected by elements of the 2d Division. The 4th Machine Gun Battalion, with 2/9, were to keep liaison with the 73d DI on the right, which they did, becoming heavily involved in the fighting advance. The other liaison was 1/6 in the west. The rest of the 2d Division would remain in reserve though its artillery would perform valuable services

Following Blanc Mont, this is all that remained of the officers of the 2d Bn, 6th Marines.

for the 36th Division. This was, however, to be, essentially, a 36th Division affair.

Nevertheless, 1st Sgt. Charles F. Sigg,* of A Co., 2d Ammunition Train, kept his several trucks loaded with shells for the 2d Artillery Brigade in a place close by them, even though enemy shells were exploding all about them. A native of Germany, Sigg performed this task so well it caused no interruption in the artillery's firing pattern.

This being a history of the 2d Division will preclude providing a detailed description of the day, but, in a nutshell, the 71st Brigade had a very hard day. The Germans fought back and made it very tough going for the brigade. The 142d Infantry managed to retire back to Hill 160, which was still being held by 3/6, and the German counterattack on it was repulsed. Remaining on the hill that night, the 142d was secure. A later report stated that the 71st Brigade had been "roughly handled in its first active service."[34] Things weren't going well for the 36th Division. That day their losses amounted to 75 officers and 1,314 enlisted men. The brigade commander began having doubts about the ability of his men to hold on without bringing up the 72d Brigade and 131st Machine Gun Battalion to support him. Lejeune agreed and passed it up to Corps. Because the 71st did not advance and the Germans didn't counterattack the request was not fulfilled. Both units remained where they were and 71st Brigade, with stalwart support from 3/6, survived the night intact.

During the day the 76th Co., 1/6, had entered St. Étienne, moved through the town to the north, and being pressured by the enemy, had retired back to the town and held it during the night. Captain Macon Overton,* a hero of several battles, managed his company well. They survived a night of continual attacks, two of which were extremely serious. In the meantime, E Co., 2d Engineers, was sent forward to support the 76th Company.

General Lejeune gave verbal instructions to all 2d Division units to discontinue any reliefs until further notice and ordered that the 23d Infantry should go back on line, whereupon the 23d took up positions behind the 141st and 142d Infantry on the St. Étienne–Orfeuil Road. At 2130 the Engineers were called upon to provide three companies, A, B, and C, to relieve 2/9 as right flank guard between the 141st Infantry and the French on their right.

Wednesday 9 to Friday 11 October

Over the three day period, Sgt. 1st Cl William Sarti,* of A Co., 2d Engineers, even though wounded, as were his platoon leader and platoon sergeant and both out of action, kept his platoon together. He brought the men to their new position under heavy fire without losing a man.

Captain Maurice Pincoffs,* of the 2d Sanitary Train, after the lines had been withdrawn, voluntarily crossed an open field under heavy fire to a small wooded area in which a number of wounded men of the division lay wounded. He dressed their wounds and directed their evacuation without further casualties. Army and navy medical personnel were always on the job and provided the most "modern" techniques and care then available.

Marine private Dean F. Smiley,* in the 75th Co., 1/6, single-handed rushed a machine gun nest, killing three of the occupants and capturing the remainder. While engaged in bringing his captives to the rear he was killed by hostile artillery fire. He was awarded a DSC and, unusual for a private, was also awarded a DSM, both posthumously. The battle for the high ground was fought and won by the men of the 2d Division, but by this date their work had concluded; now it was up to the 36th Division to carry the line to its ultimate objective, the Aisne River line. The 73d Machine Gun Co., 6th Marines, plus E Co. of the Engineers, and the entire 2d Artillery Brigade,[35] were allocated as support for the "cowboys." But the rest of the 2d Division were no longer a factor in the ongoing fighting. They were relieved, other than the components mentioned, and command passed to the 36th Division at 1000 on 10 October. The aforementioned 2d Division units remained in line with the 36th Division until 28 October. Basically the remnants of the 2d Division remained in this area until 14 October. The 4th Marine Brigade was assigned duty with the

Reserve of the Fourth French Army. It was then, on 19 October, placed at the disposal of the French IX Corps to relieve the French 73d DI near Attigny. The plan changed and on the night of 23–24 October the entire 4th Brigade returned to the 2d Division.[36]

Saturday 12 October

Maj. Edwin H. Brainard,* USMC, the commanding officer of 1/15, earned a Navy Cross for his fine work during the entire period of the battle for Blanc Mont, 2 to 12 October: "He commanded his group in perfect manner, not hesitating to move it forward through a violent artillery fire, and executing under all circumstances accurate and effective fire on the enemy positions."

By the 7th and 8th of October, the French on both flanks were, finally, in line with the 2d Division. On the left, in liaison with the Marine Brigade (occasionally) were four divisions. On 1–3 October, the 21st DI, were relieved the latter day by the 170th DI, which in turn was relieved later that day by the 22d DI which was relieved by the 7th DI on October 7. On the right flank, the 3d Brigade was in liaison with the 67th DI between 2 and 3 October; on the 4th the 73d DI relieved them and on 5 October the 170th DI relieved them. On the 7th of October the French 346th DI was the right liaison for the 71st Infantry Brigade, 36th Division.

The Second Division suffered a total of 4,832 casualties, attached units another 1,506. The 5th Marines, especially the 1st Battalion,[37] was devastated. That regiment was pulled out of the line on 5 October and remained behind the lines with no further commitment until the Meuse River campaign, nearly a month in the future, and only after receiving numerous replacements. But, during the several days they were active, the regiment captured 62 DSCs/NCs and that is a record.

The Division began the battle with 26,897 effectives and on 31 October, after replacements, it had 26,146. The Division earned more DSCs (229) during their seven day ordeal at Blanc Mont than its next nearest "rival," Belleau Wood (for 184 medals in 30 days). Because of the enormity of those numbers, it has been decided, as at Belleau Wood, to select and mention just a few instances and recipients. The greater percentage were taken in the first several days, especially on the 3rd and 4th of October. Of a Navy Medical Service total of 83 major awards received during the war, 36 were received at Blanc Mont. As John W. Thomason, Jr., later wrote in *Salt Winds and Gobi Dust*, "We were shot to pieces in the Champagne — I never enjoyed the war afterward."

9

MEUSE–ARGONNE

Marshal Foch, with the supporting hand of FM Haig, convinced Gen. Pershing that the Americans should join in an assault by the entire allied/associated forces upon the Hindenburg Line, the most important German defense system. Under French pressure, Haig had finally decided to attack and Foch wasn't about to allow that miraculous event to slip away unfulfilled. Pershing argued about the massive American efforts that went into planning for and preparations made for this assault and was permitted to continue his plan for an "all–American" attack upon the St. Mihiel salient. He must, however, move his army north within a few days to participate with the French in a drive northward, notably about the 15th or 16th of September. The time constraint, with the St. Mihiel attack going forward on 12 September, was, as Pershing said, impossible to meet. Pershing and Foch argued and both became angry to a grievous level.

Finally, it was determined that the American forces must be in place to begin an assault between the 20th and 25th of September. The original St. Mihiel attack was planned for about the 10th of the month but didn't actually come off until the 12th. Even that would barely allow Pershing a week to complete and terminate the attack at the salient and less than a couple of days to get 14 or more divisions into line for the next attack at the Argonne.[1]

As it turned out, the Americans created their own miracle and did manage to get north of Verdun and the First Army into formation for launching their attack on 26 September. There were 14 American divisions, nine in line in three corps, and, located behind the nine on line, three in army reserve.

In order to create this "miracle" Pershing was forced to utilize brand-new, recently arrived, relatively untrained divisions without essential support units, especially artillery, to create the First Army. There were so many divisions available that a Second Army (Maj. Gen. Robert L. Bullard) was created. Those necessaries, field artillery and ammunition, would be supplied by the French. The initial attacks did not go well; in fact, the Americans were badly hurt. Their right flank consisted of two French DI east of the Marne River and the Fourth French Army to their west. That was where the attack upon Blanc Mont would be taking place during early October.

There was to be one more major attack by the First Army, after a brief respite, now to be led by Lt. Gen. Hunter Liggett. That would come off on 14 October and last until the 16th, with very modest success and many more casualties. We will dispense with further description of the events of September and October, except to add that the American forces were, generally, untrained, poorly led, and, as could be expected, slaughtered in their earliest attacks.[2] The German defenses were solid and had been well prepared for some years. To a biased observer, they seemed better prepared along this southeastern line than elsewhere.

Following their assignment with the French Army in the Blanc Mont campaign, Maj. Gen. Lejeune tells us that when he spoke with the Brig. Gen. Hugh A. Drum, Chief of Staff, First Army on 24 October, he was advised that the 2d Division was being situated with the First Army. It was to be the point of the wedge in the next "Great Attack." Drum further indicated that the division was "given that post of honor and the whole Army relied on them to bring the stalemate to an end by breaking through the center of the German Army and thereby forcing it to retreat to the east bank of the Meuse."[3] The 2d Division was assigned duty with the V Corps, U.S. Army, commanded by Maj. Gen. Charles P. Summerall.[4] Upon receiving word of this assignment the division began preparing for what they would be doing in the next few weeks. Summerall's V Corps' responsibility during the coming attack would be along the west side of the Meuse River. The attack was scheduled for 1 November and the 2d Division would jump off from a spot between two villages, Landres-et-St. George and St. George.[5] Replacements had been coming in regularly and the division was now nearly at full strength, though, as could be expected, not thoroughly trained.

The German army was well aware that something "big" was about to happen but uncertain as to where and when. They had been watching the changes and noting the various divisional patches in the area. General von Gallwitz would write an account of the Meuse Argonne battle ten years later for a publication in 1929.[6] He said, "That *famous American crack unit, the 2d Division*, withdrew from opposite Army Unit C and was now reported to be near Montfaucon" (emphasis added), indicating that the 2d Division had earned a place in the annals of the German army. He was, however, incorrect about its location.

Their right liaison would be the 89th Division (Maj. Gen. William M. Wright), composed of draftees from the Plains states. Though only in France since early June, they had participated at St. Mihiel and then in the October operations. They would prove to be a valuable flank unit for the 2d Division.[7] The left liaison would be the 80th Division (Maj. Gen. Adelbert Cronkite) of I Corps, which arrived in France in early June and was assigned to the British army for "training," essentially serving with them at the Somme, until Pershing demanded the return of his divisions for the Meuse Argonne offensive.[8]

The 80th participated in the September–October operations in the Meuse-Argonne. They rested for a few weeks and were then recalled for the 1 November operation, which would require the finesse of an experienced division to keep up with a superb combat division like the 2d Division. This would, at times, be a problem for both divisions.

The 2d Division arrived at its assigned post on 31 October and plans were made for the forthcoming attack. It was decided that the 4th Brigade would jumpoff in a column of battalions, the 3d Brigade following, until the second day when the 3d would move through and take up the lead. The brigades would be in a similar formation, a line of regiments and each in a line of battalions. The front was 2½ miles wide with two regiments occupying it, the 6th Marines (Lee) on the left and the 5th Marines (Feland) to their right. The jump-off time on 1 November was slated to be 0500, later changed to 0530. Unlike previous events, when 1 November arrived, both regiments were in place on high ground located just south of the Landres-et-St. Georges–St. Georges road.

Friday 1 November

On the left was 1/6 (Barker*) followed by 3/6 (Shuler) in support and last was 2/6 (Williams) as reserve. On the right was 1/5 (Hamilton) followed by 2/5 (Dunbeck) in support with 3/5 (Larsen) as reserve. Besides Division, Corps and army artillery, three additional artillery brigades would support the advance. They were guns from the two divisions in reserve, the 1st Division (Regular) and the 42d National Guard Division. Firing would commence and be two hours long in preparation. That would be followed by a barrage for ten minutes, which would then advance slowly so that the infantry might follow it closely. The 2d Brigade of artillery, to keep within close contact with the infantry, was to advance their guns by battalion during the attack. In addition to those units already described, a squadron and a half of planes would provide close air support, and 15 Renault tanks would accompany the infantry. The infantry's objective was the Freya position on Barricourt Ridge, with exploitation beyond the ridge to Nouart.

The day arrived and it was cold and cloudy with expected seasonal fog morning and night. Artillery did its duty, firing from roughly 0300 to 0500 and, according to the history of 1/5, "was highly effective."[9] After this the 5th Marines moved out, two companies (49th and 66th) followed by two companies (17th and 67th). On the left 1/6 led with the 74th Co. (Hermle) on the right and the 76th on the left (Overton), followed by the 75th Co. (Capt. Harold D. Shannon) in support. The 95th was serving with Stowell's mini-battalion. Each battalion was accompanied by a machine gun company. They had already participated in the firing and then collected their guns to join with their comrades in the "Big Parade," through the fields, down onto the road then down into the

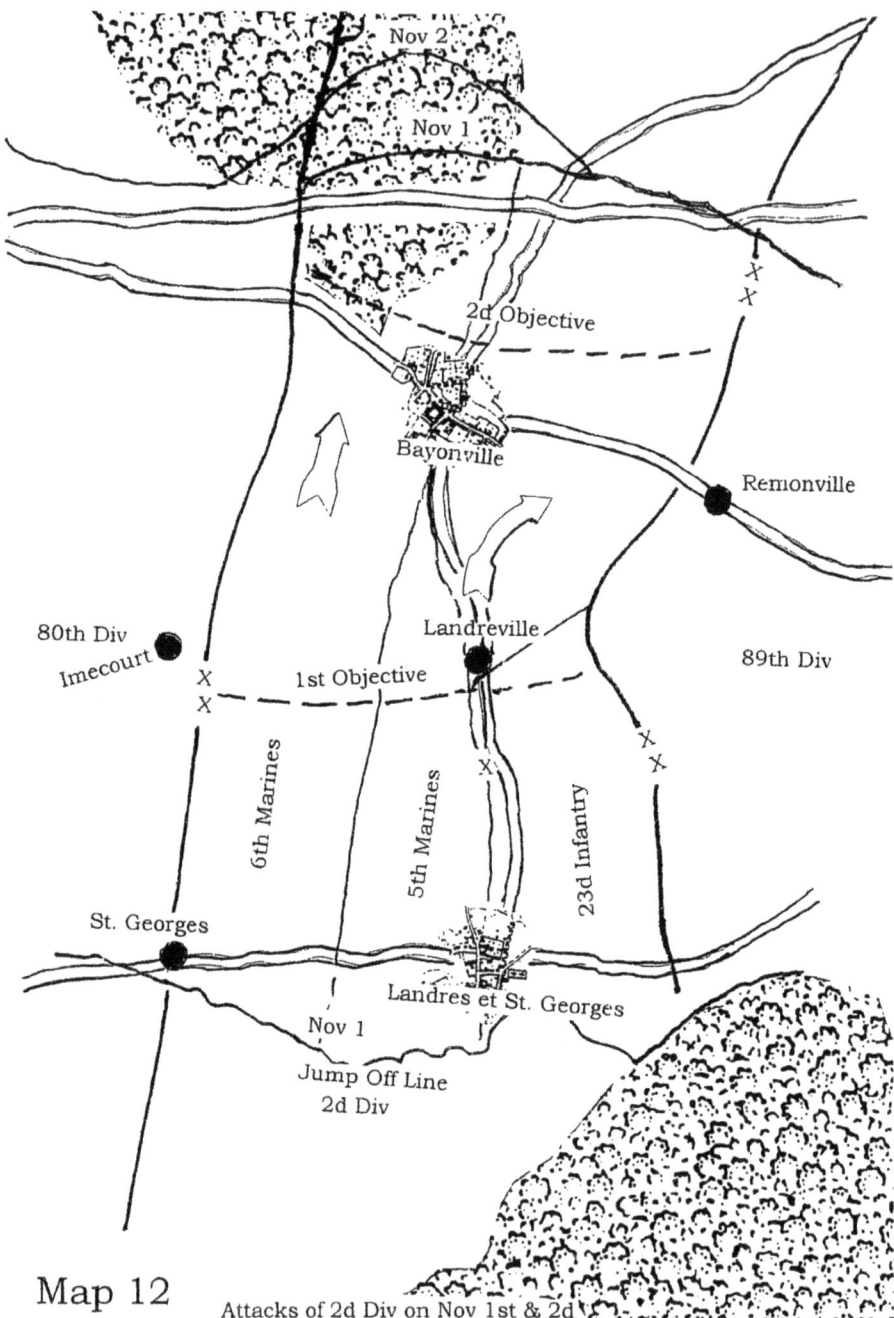

Map 12 Attacks of 2d Div on Nov 1st & 2d

1 November

ravine,[10] then up a steep hill under some modest enemy machine gun fire. The history of the 6th Marines spelled out what the terrain was like: "The terrain was rolling, broken by an occasional patch of woods, consisting mostly of stunted trees and underbrush. The enemy had artillery in many of the small ravines which passes through this sector."[11]

A special attack by the 23d Infantry on the right flank (at Landres-et-St. Georges) required a quick penetration. The attack was into a shallow but wide formation of Germans. Col. Stone put 3/23 (Capt. George A. Shipley*) on the right and 1/23 (Lt. Col. Edmund L. Zane) on the left with two machine gun companies and 2/23 in support. They were rapidly successful. Sergeant Colin B. Joe,* of Co. K, was active immediately. Joe went forward alone when he saw that his company was being held up by two machine guns, knocked out both and captured 9 prisoners. Company C's 1st Sgt, Joseph A. Beaudette,* also single-handedly, attacked a machine gun nest and with his pistol killed the seven German crew members. Arthur C. Cole,* a 1st Lt. of the regiment, led his men forward into a machine gun nest, then he, armed with a rifle, flanked another gun and captured same. Leading his men they attacked another series of machine guns, which resulted in the capture of several more and about 40 German crew members. One other sergeant, Clark T. McCormick,* of Co. L, led his men forward, taking 12 prisoners and two machine guns. It wasn't only the squad and platoon leaders taking courageous action; Capt. Shipley was as active as all the rest of his battalion. With a rifle, he led an assault upon another nest, taking the gun and 28 prisoners. He was further lauded for his additional activities during the rest of the campaign. By 0800 the finely honed and led 23d had taken their objectives. Then the 5th Marines extended their front to the right as they advanced.

Troops of the three regiments soon cleared out the defending Germans in both villages and the 5th and 6th Marines went forward still in the division's advance. The 6th Marines, however, were having a bad time. German counter-battery fire did a job on them and Lee was advised that in the early hours their losses totaled at least 100 men killed and wounded. It was the leading 74th Co. on the right and the 76th Co. on the left which were taking the losses. They were followed in support by the 75th Co., which was also being hit hard. Major George Stowell and his 95th Co. were still assigned to liaison duty on the left flank with the 80th Division.[12]

Barker's 1/6 was doing well considering it was being hurt, but when it was held up at barbed wire, Pvt. David T. Depue,* 76th Co., made a decision to get even or at least balance out some of the battering they were taking. He grabbed a Chauchat from a deceased comrade and rushed forward, charging through the cut wire, firing as he ran, though hit and knocked down twice. He got up, continued forward and, with his ammo gone, belted the occupants of the nest with the rifle's butt. When his platoon made it forward they found Depue dead but with that troublesome German machine gun out of action. A sergeant of his company, William H. Faga,* already a recipient of a DSC at Soissons, earned an oak-leaf cluster for refusing to be evacuated for his severe wounds when he saw that both officers of his platoon had already been taken off the field as casualties. Returning to the lines he then led his command for the balance of the successful attack. Sergeant Frank J. Simon,* also a member of the 76th Company, with two other Marines, as advancing with a tank when the other two were wounded, as was the tanker and Simon. However, the latter continued on alone, capturing 6 Germans and the machine gun nest that had caused the casualties. Captain Macon C. Overton,* the skipper of the 76th, had been killed early while leading his splendid company, earning an oak leaf cluster to his DSC earned at Blanc Mont.[13]

The 95th Co. of the mini-battalion had its own hero that day. Sergeant Frank F. Geiger* displayed unusual coolness and courage while leading his platoon against several machine gun nests but when they were unable to continue he went against several himself, until, while charging one of them unaided, he was wounded. Captain Leo D. Hermle* of the 74th Co., seeing another company having difficulty at St. Georges, led a platoon forward and surrounded a large number of Germans, capturing 155 prisoners and 17 machine guns. Then, he and the 74th Co. moved forward, taking the town of St. Georges and many more machine gun positions. Although painfully wounded, Hermle refused to be parted from his men and remained on the line for two more days until forced by wounds to retire. Besides a DSC he also was awarded a DSM, two Silver Star citations and several French awards. Another man of the 74th, Sgt. Fred M. Marlowe,* assumed command of his section when his platoon sergeant was incapacitated. When his line was held up, Marlowe took two other Marines and together they assaulted a machine gun nest, putting it out of action. That capture caused all the other nests and gunners to surrender and freed up the advancing Marines from enfilading fire.

At 0800 Hamilton's 1/5 was still leading and reported taking a heavy loss of five officers but "few enlisted men." They were on the 1st Objective at 0830 and had captured an estimated 500 prisoners. Hamilton had been moving so rapidly 1/5 had also managed to overtake a battery of German "77's," capturing the guns and crew members. The Third Battalion, Fifth Marines, reported "prisoners coming in continually now." At about 0830 Dunbeck, and 2/5, leapfrogged 1/5 in the lead. Larsen's 3/5 took second place and Hamilton went into the reserve position. This was at a line running from east to west through the northern edge of the Bois l'Epasse.

The Germans continued fighting back, especially at Landreville. One hundred prisoners and a large number of machine guns were taken there. An enemy shell landed in the midst of a platoon commanded by Sgt. Vernon J. Crossen* of the 18th Co. taking out a sizeable number of his men. He managed to reorganize and lead them for the next few days, until he was killed on 4 November. Meanwhile, when his 51st Co's' advance was held up, 1st Lt Robert L.

Montague* successfully led his men in a flanking movement against a withering machine gun fire and artillery bombardment, knocking out several nests.

The fighting became fierce before Landreville but Montague and his men entered the village and soon cleared it and captured an estimated 150 Germans.[14] In the meantime, the 5th Marines' right flank had been exposed and they had been forced in that direction to fight the enemy. The Marines were now a little more than a mile shy of Bayonville, their next objective. A former marine gunner, 1st Lt Charles D. Baylis, led his 55th Company in a flanking movement driving the enemy from Hill 299. At 1140 the regiment reported entering the "Arbre de Remonville" on the hill and were on the 89th Division's sector line. They reported having captured "approximately 30 machine guns, one battery of '8' and about twelve '6' inch guns." The enemy dead included 30 German officers and NCOs. Captain Charley Dunbeck and his lads in 2/5 continued moving forward. Passing through Bayonville they reached their second objective, in the ravine lying about a half mile further north. There they rested for about forty minutes and were leap-frogged by Larsen and 3/5 which assumed the lead position. They were followed into support by Hamilton's 1/5 when Dunbeck went into reserve.

Meanwhile in the 6th Marines, 3/6 took the lead at 0800, with 2/6 in support, and 1/6 in reserve. At 0814 Shuler sent Lee a message that he had reached the first objective with few casualties. On the way forward four men of the 82d Co., Cpl George W. Schreech,* and Pvts Clarence Troup,* Charles S. Gibson,* and William A. Kreuzman* went forward to reconnoiter. They went down into a ravine and found it loaded with enemy machine guns and artillery and brought back several prisoners and much important information for Maj. Shuler. The attack halted for forty minutes while the troops caught their breath. At this point, Shuler assigned three French tanks to the 83d Co. (Capt. Alfred H. Noble), and the tanks moved forward with the next advance. After resting, 3/6 again took the lead at 0900 until they reached the day's second objective. At 1100 Shuler reported holding Chennery (in the sector of the 80th Division) and Bayonville, and his men had taken 100 prisoners and six "88's" (German artillery). He also told Lee the woods "north of the second objective should be well shelled." At Chennery, Noble's company, with tanks leading, flanked and captured a battery of 4 enemy "77's," including an officer and 75 men, which had been direct-firing into 3/6. Private Demarr E. Myers,* of the 84th Co. (Capt. Arnold W. Jacobsen), with another Marine (unnamed) had advanced before their regiment and captured 5 machine guns and fourteen German prisoners.

About noontime, 3/6 reached their second objective and took a rest period. The balance of nearby enemy were seen making for the sector of the 80th Division. Major Ernest Williams and 2/6, at 1450, now took the lead with 1/6 moving up as their support and 3/6 went into reserve. Passing the second objective, 2/6 (Williams) continued advancing in that part of the 80th Division's sector until reaching the southern portion of the Bois de la Folie. While the battalion was so engaged, Captain Kirt Green, skipper of the 80th Co., was killed in action. At approximately 1515 Williams and his battalion had taken the third objective and stopped. His right was resting on Hill 313 and his left at Fontaine des Parades. Williams sent Capt. Gardiner W. Hawkins and the 79th Co. to reconnoiter into Bois de la Folie. His job was to maintain contact with the enemy and exploit as far into the wood as he could, thereby keeping the Germans on the run and not likely to counterattack that night.

Meanwhile, the 80th Division had been having some serious trouble, and Stowell and his men had difficulty in keeping liaison between them and the 6th Marines. At Imecourt, the Marines were forced to take over a small portion of the 80th's sector. At about that point, Germans on the west bank of the Sivry River, unmolested by troops of the 80th Division, worked over the exposed left flank of the 6th Marines. The 80th Division would generally cease forward motion at Imecourt though later in the day they would send elements forward as far as Chennery. The two units met at that town at 1730.

Larsen reported to Feland at 1430 that 3/5 had taken the third objective, including Hill 300, which lay about a mile southwest of Barricourt, which reposed in the 89th Division's sector. Larsen mentioned that his patrols had moved forward without serious confrontation with the Germans but that "our" artillery had dropped a few rounds short. The division had been moving much faster than anyone had expected. He also reported that the 6th Marines and the 89th Division were keeping abreast of 3/5. At 1900, Feland advised Larsen to send out strong patrols, in cooperation with the 6th Marines, around "Magenta Fme," which lay about a half mile further north. In so doing, 3/5 rested at a point just beyond Hill 300.

Meanwhile, that morning, as the Marine Brigade pressed forward, the 9th Infantry followed up in their tracks and found that not all the Germans were dead. Their artillery was busy shelling the rear areas and causing casualties to the infantry. As they went over the top, Sergeant Carl Tawater,* leading the Stokes Mortar section of Hdqs Co., was wounded along with several of his men when a shell landed among them. He, however, saw to it that the wounded were taken care of and then led the balance of his men forward, remaining all day with his platoon despite his painful wound. Otherwise, history clearly states that the 9th Infantry had a reasonably safe and sane day.

The Division had performed wonders that day and would rest, sort of, with their left flank (6th Marines) in the southern portion of the Bois de la Folie. The 5th Marines held the crossroads running between Barricourt on the right and Buzancy on the left. That night and the following day were spent in tightening up the various formations which had tended to become scattered. The men also developed security for the area that had already been taken.

Saturday 2 November

Mostly the troops rested. Yet the 6th Marines, especially 1/6, kept quite busy with the Germans still in the southern portion of the Bois de la Folie. However, 2/6 was not sitting on their laurels. The 79th Co. (Hawkins) was pushed forward to the northeastern edge of the wood while the 96th Co. (1st Lt Clifton B. Cates) was being held up on the west flank by machine guns and one-pounder fire.

Fighting in and around Chennery, which lies just a bit south and west of Bayonville, was tedious and dangerous. Pvt. George H. Croll,* of the 83d Co., entered three dugouts in a period of an hour, and captured a total of 34 of the enemy. One of his officers, 1st Lt. Neil F. Dougherty,* led his platoon against the enemy's artillery emplacement and through skillful maneuvering managed to capture the 10 guns, 5 machine guns and their 42 crew members.[15] Later that day, 2d Lt Claude B. Taugher,* also in the 83d Co., led his men into the village of Bayonville and surrounded German dugouts before they had a chance to escape or organize an effective resistance. He and his men captured 61 of the enemy and, even though he had been wounded in the ankle, Taugher refused to be evacuated.

During the advance in the Meuse River campaign, the troops took advantage of any dugout the Germans had evacuated.

During the day, Col. James C. Rhea returned and reassumed command of the 3d Brigade, and Col. Robert O. Van Horn went back to the 9th Infantry. Soon after orders were received from V Corps for the 9th to move through the 4th Brigade and jumpoff at 0530 on 3 November. They were to assume the Division lead and continue the advance to the Fosse-Nouart line. The position was about a half mile ahead of where the 4th Brigade was then located. The wooded ground before the Marines being too tough to advance through from a daylight jump-off, a decision was made to instead advance that night. So, at 1830 hours, under cover of darkness, the regiment, in a column of battalions (1st, 2d, and 3d), moved forward.

Commanding the advance party, 1st Lt. Charles Hutchings, Jr.,* A Co., 9th Infantry, ran into some enemy in the woods at about midnight. Their mortars and machine guns pinned his platoon down. Hutchings went forward alone to make a personal reconnaissance and when it was completed went back to his command with nine prisoners and valuable information. Company B's 2d Lt. Clarence G. Elmer* volunteered to lead a party from his company to enfilade an enemy artillery battery causing the 9th considerable casualties. They were successful and drove the gunners from their weapons. All night the 9th continued to run into some enemy resistance, which they effectively pushed aside, and arrived at the exploitation line the next morning.

Sunday 3 November

The 23d Infantry, in the Bois de la Folie, had already taken the road for Fosse that morning. The 9th moved by road from Bayonville, then northeast on the Buzancy–Nouart highway. The 3d Brigade was ordered to take up a line of regiments on the Nouart-Fosse line. The 23d on the left and the 9th on the right. Before them lay some severe obstacles, especially and immediately before the 23rd. There was action by the enemy rear guard everywhere and they would be fight desperately. Various possibilities for the brigade were considered. To minimize the expected casualties even night moves were considered. But that would result in small contests with overall casualties probably exceeding what was desired so a morning advance was finally agreed upon.

The first movement was by 1/9 (Maj. d'Alary Fechet), which at 0615 formed for an attack on the heights about a kilometer west of the village of Nouart. The 2d and 3d battalions were in support and reserve, respectively. At 0650 the advance was continued and the ridge southeast of Vaux-en-Dieulet, known as Hill 308, was reached at 0900. Company L, 3/9, liaison company with the 89th Division, moved into Nouart at about 0700, meeting with slight resistance and capturing some prisoners.

By 1030 the 9th had moved forward to a position about a half mile south of Beval and the ridge running to their right in the Bois de Belval, where they

9. Meuse-Argonne

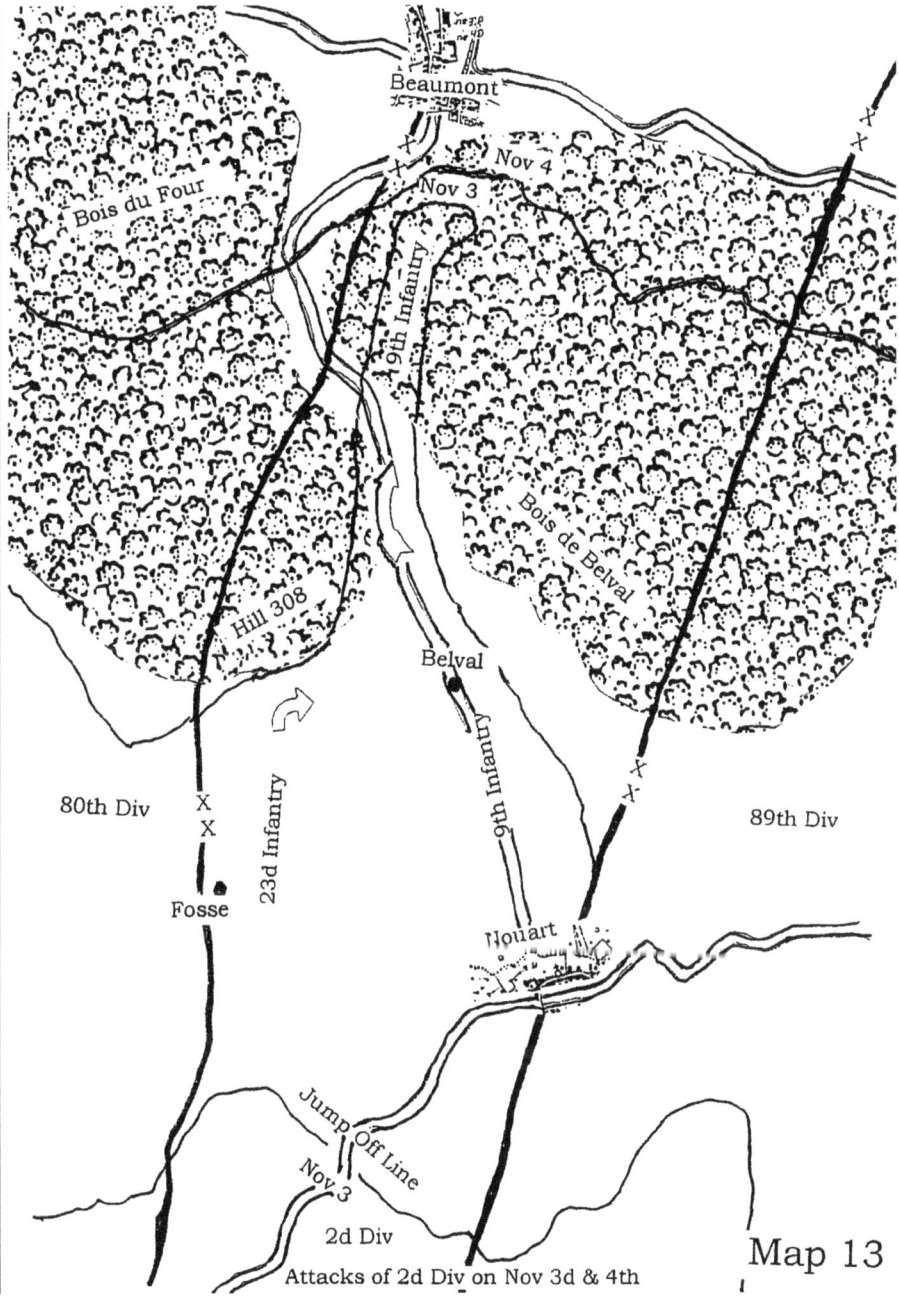

Map 13. 3 to 4 November

met further resistance. Company B ran into trouble at Le Champy Haut, finding the enemy too strong for further progress at that point. Major James H. Day, with 2/9, came up on both flanks but even that additional strength was not sufficient to break through the German line. At this point, 3/9 (Maj. Ladislav T. Janda[16]) came up as further support. Nevertheless, after suffering severe casualties, the regiment was forced to settle down and dig in. On the right flank, the 89th Division made it to a position slightly in the front of the 2d Division, but stopped and they too dug in.

On the left, 1/23 (Zane) started through the Bois de la Folie at midnight and by daybreak were about a half mile north of the woods. By 0900 they had taken the Chateau Belval but soon after were being held up by artillery and machine gun fire from the nearby Bois de Belval. During that time liaison was established with the forward elements of the 9th Infantry. The 80th Division was slightly behind the 23d at noon and, possibly exhausted, didn't try to go any further that day.

At 1400 orders were issued from Division headquarters directing an advance to Beaumont. Artillery prepared the ground for an advance until 1430 at which time the two infantry regiments were each to send a battalion forward to carry out the prescribed operation. They, supported by artillery, were to push through the woods before them and secure a position in the vicinity of Beaumont. The two regiments were to flow northward in parallel on two roads. Later it was discovered that only the road to be used by the 9th Infantry was adaptable so the 23d Infantry was ordered to fall in behind the 9th. The 9th regimental staff decided the 9th Infantry would, in a column of twos, proceed right up the road toward Beaumont. They wouldn't go off road unless conditions forced them to. Conditions that night appeared to prohibit the Germans from making preparations for a counterattack, so the 9th Infantry went ahead and just did it and were successful. Audacity wins out every time.

The 3d Battalion, 9th Infantry, led off, followed briefly by 2/5 (Dunbeck), which joined from Division reserve. A selection of soldiers and Marines that spoke German were at the point as the column moved north on the road. At a point just north of Beval, Dunbeck and his men remained behind and the 23d Infantry moved into their place behind the 9th Infantry. Each time the column encountered resistance the point stayed in place and strong patrols worked both flanks. That method proved successful and the column continued moving forward without serious delay. According to Captain Hilton, CO of the 9th Infantry's machine gun company, each time the column would come upon an encampment of Germans they would engage in a "lively firefight." He further wrote that "the Germans were so surprised and confused that they didn't put up much of a fight."[17]

At midnight the column was nearly a half mile north of La Tuilerie Farm and not far south of Beaumont, their objective.[18] Leading the advance elements of the division, 2d Lt. Harry S. Smith,* platoon leader in Company I, 3/9, had reduced several enemy strong points near the Tuilerie Farm, captured 50 prisoners and much material. This led to the ultimate capture of the farm, which housed the enemy's staff, and helped the regiment to safely establish itself at the end of the day deep into enemy held territory. Near Tuilerie Farm, just about on the line dividing the 89th and 2d Division's sectors, Pvt. John Grundy,* of K Company, 3/9, made his way toward the front to his platoon leader, who had been badly wounded. After dressing his wounds, and seeing that the medics took care of the lieutenant, Grundy again made his way forward. His next acts were to provide liaison between the various platoons of Company K, keeping them apprised of the divergence in each to the others, until he too was badly wounded. Both 3/9 and 2/9 were in the advanced positions that night while 1/9 was in support.

The 23d Infantry had followed the leaders in the following formation: 2/23 (Miller), 3/23 (Shipley), and 1/23 (Zane). They placed their leading battalion at the Beauséjour Farm, which was located in the sector of the 80th Division. Neither of the flanking divisions, 80th and 89th, was able to keep liaison with the 2d Division that evening and as the 2d Division settled down for the evening each flank was exposed to the enemy. Late that day, all C Co. officers were killed or wounded and 1st Sgt. Joseph A. Beaudette[19] assumed command and led C Co. successfully for the next few days. Meanwhile, PFC Louis Mazzoni,* of the 23d MG Co, crawled forward and around some German soldiers until, at their rear, he attacked, killing one and taking the rest prisoner. Five Corps had issued orders at 1530 for the 1st Division to relieve both the 2d Division and the 89th. However, no actual changes were made and the lines remained as before. That night the Germans before them were ordered to reform on the high ground just south of Beaumont and to prepare to defend the town.

Monday 4 November

That morning the 9th Infantry was basically in the same positions as the night before; 2/9 on the left and 3/9 on the right with 1/9 in support. Dunbeck's 2/5 was on line to the right in the vicinity of the Ferme de Belle Tour, which was a few hundred yards south of the 9th Infantry's position and well into the 89th Division's sector. The 23d Infantry's positions were as follows: 2/23 leading with 3/23 behind them and 1/23 farther back in reserve, along a line equidistant with 2/5 but on the far left. Therefore, on this day the division was in a nearly arrowhead position, with both flanks refused. That night, a mechanic in Co. D., 1/23, Pvt. Arthur Lay,* was passing through the enemy lines with messages and came up a small group of Germans. He captured eight of them, including two officers then marched them back nearly four miles. With little rest, for the rest of the day he continued to carry further messages through artillery and machine gun fire and while so engaged he brought back a wounded comrade to a dressing station. Another hero, PFC George B. Statham,* of the 23d MG Co., maintained his machine gun most of that night by himself, all his comrades having been killed or wounded. While so engaged he managed with direct fire to put out of action an enemy gun nest, but he was soon killed by the enemy rifle fire.

This day the 9th Infantry would pay for being way out front. Orders came down from Division at 0830 for the regiment to move forward against the ridge southeast of Beaumont and reconnoiter crossings of the Meuse, and the 23d was to push forward to the left flank of the 9th. Shortly before noon the advance began, right to left, with Major Day's 2/9 and Janda's 3/9 in line. Day's men, especially, took a bad beating and were forced to retire as was Janda's battalion, after also sustaining heavy casualties. Frechet's 1/9 was also involved. One of his men, Pvt. John Capezio,* Co. D, led a squad in a flank attack on a machine gun nest which was holding up his company. His coolness provided the ultimate success and the squad captured the guns and entire crews.

Meanwhile V Corps planners were engaged in fanciful future progress for the 2d Division. They had visions of pushing the Germans back even to Mouzon, on the Meuse, about five miles further north. It would be nearly a week before the 2d Division (6th Marines) would get to that point. In the meantime the 1st Division was ordered to assemble in the rear of the 2d Division and to await further orders. It was planned to move the 1st Division forward on the left flank to take Mouzon.

The Marines had orders to send 3/5 (Larsen) to Dunbeck's right flank. For various reasons Larsen was unable to arrive at that point but did take up positions behind 2/5. Meanwhile 1/5 (Hamilton) halted on a ridge a bit more than a mile south of Dunbeck's position.

That night the 9th held its position but just before midnight the 23d moved out to their right, through the 9th Infantry positions in a two battalion front. Patrols from the 5th Marines made contact with their counterparts from the 89th Division but a two mile gap still existed between their organized lines. On the left side, the 80th Division had moved forward but there was still a breach of at least 500 feet between them and the 9th Infantry. In the meantime the German army had already planned and made further withdrawals during the early hours of 5 November.

Tuesday 5 November

The 23d Infantry continued moving forward. In the early morning hours 2/23 (Miller) took the woods east and southeast of the town of Beaumont. The 80th Division helped and by dawn the town was mopped up. Shipley's 3/23 went after the village of Létanne and took that by 0530. During this encounter, Sgt. Colin B. Joe, whom we met on 1 November,[20] single-handedly attacked three machine gun nests, being severely wounded in that action. Two battalions were on line and another in support after successfully spreading from a point about 1,700 yards east of Beaumont to Hill 241, where the regiment placed an outpost. The top of Hill 241 was sharply above the curve of the Meuse River and allowed visibility in nearly every direction, especially overlooking the ground still "owned" by the Germans.

In the meantime, the 9th Infantry were being kept busy. Near Tuilerie Farm, 1st Lt William H. Carrier,* while in the process of moving towards the battalion's flank, had received word that the flank company was without officers and hard pressed. He made his way with four guides across an open field covered by enemy artillery and machine gun fire. The four guides were hit and out, and Carrier had numerous holes in his uniform. However, he wasn't to be dissuaded and made his way to the company, reorganized it and was credited with saving the situation.

By noon the division's artillery support was reduced to just the 2d Brigade, the other support units devolving back to their own divisions. Some of the infantry of both brigades were engaged in reconnoitering the river for crossing sites. The 4th Brigade, located just to the right of the 3d and slightly further back, were ordered to mop up the Forêt de Jaulnay, located about a mile south of the town of Pouilly, well into the sector of the 89th Division. They were also ordered to reconnoiter for river crossings nearby and prepare machine

A shattered French village along the Meuse River.

gun positions. The Infantry Brigade was issued orders to reconnoiter to its front to determine the feasibility of crossing west of Pouilly. The 5th Marines were ordered to occupy the ridge a mile south of Pouilly, but the 89th had already occupied it with two battalions. The two divisions were obviously becoming mixed up.

Five Corps sent orders to Lejeune at 1930 to clean up the woods north of La Sartelle Farm and seize the bridges over the Meuse that night. La Sartelle Farm is located in the Bois de l'Hospice, opposite where the eventual Marine crossing of the Meuse would take place. There weren't any bridges in that immediate area,[21] but there was one from Mouzon east across the river. That would eventually be "awarded" to the 6th Marines.

Second Division issued orders at 2230 announcing that the 1st Division was moving through the 2d and 80th Divisions in the direction of the line running from Mouzon to Yoncq. The latter lies west, almost equidistant from Beaumont and Villemontry, and is not on our maps. During this period, however, the 2d Division would continue to retain a foothold on the Meuse River banks. Henceforth, its main job was to protect the right flank of the 1st Division. At this time, midnight, the venerable 23d Infantry was still out front with liaison with the 89th Division along the river, south of Pouilly, and the 80th on the Beaumont—Yoncq road.

Wednesday 6 November

Third Brigade issued orders to its 9th Infantry at 1240 in the morning to form up for an advance northward. At 0300 the 9th began moving, in the following formation: 1/9 (Fechet), 2/9 (Day), and in reserve, 3/9 (Janda). Upon reaching La Sartelle Farm, 1/9 took up positions on the ridge facing the river, while 2/9 continued onward just past them, also taking posts on that ridge. The Third Bn. remained in reserve in the Bois du Fond de Limon. Meanwhile the 1st Division was making for Mouzon, at about noontime reaching the heights above the town. Afterward, they were reassigned to advance upon Sedan, to which, at 1400, they began their move.[22] Mouzon still lay in the custody of the German army.

Meanwhile, the space between the 77th Division on the west (the 1st Division's replacement) and the 2d Division, now at Villemontry, was not occupied by U.S. troops, leaving a large gap between them. Five Corps, however, decided to issue orders for the 2d Division to also march on Sedan. At 1800 they directed the 2d Division to assemble to the right of the 1st Division. Their orders were for the 4th Marine Brigade to gather to the right of the Infantry in readiness to march at 0800 on 7 November. The Marines went into bivouac a mile and a half southwest of Beaumont while the infantry remained at their posts, the 23d at Beaumont and the 9th along the river line.

Thursday 7 November

Once again V Corps changed its collective mind, issuing orders for the 2d Division to remain in place holding the line from Létanne to Mouzon, inclusive. The 89th Division would take positions to the east of Létanne. Adjustments were made early that morning with the 9th Infantry ordered to occupy both Villemontry and Mouzon; 3/9 was directed to take the forward positions at Mouzon, protecting the bridge and defending against an enemy penetration or destruction. Meanwhile, the 89th Division assumed control of positions initially taken by the 23d Infantry. Patrol activity by the Infantry Brigade was constant during the day and artillery fire was laid upon points across the river from which German machine gun and artillery fire emitted.

Friday 8 November

This was a quiet day for the 2d Division. The only activity during this day was plans and efforts to effect a passage across the Meuse. Meanwhile, under cover of the brigade's machine guns, the 23d Infantry tried repairing the bridge at Létanne. At 1520 the 23d reported it passable but no one volunteered to find out what was on the other side. At Mouzon, the Germans poured oil on the river, firing it and lighting the bridge area near that town. Janda's 3/9 (Cos. I and L) was assigned the task of cleaning up the German machine guns in Mouzon and making sure the bridge there was taken so a crossing would be feasible on 9 November. At 2130, M Co., supported by L Co., attempted to cross the partially demolished bridge but it was in such bad shape the attempt was called off. With that, the battalion units were withdrawn and returned to Villemontry. Although the Infantry Brigade continued making low-level efforts to cross, Division reassigned that role and sector to the Marine Brigade.

At 2215, V Corps ordered Division to put patrols across the river by boat that night. Additionally it further instructed Division to be prepared to seize the heights northeast of Mouzon. Division engineers were to put a pontoon bridge at Mouzon for one regiment of infantry. Meanwhile, at Létanne, the 89th Division was ordered by V Corps to also put across a pontoon bridge at which one battalion from each division would cross and take the opposite heights.

In order to cross the river, 4th Brigade had ordered the 6th Marines forward to the Bois de l'Hospice in preparation, while the 5th Marines were to hold themselves at the woods near La Thibaudine Farm. The order sent by Division earlier in the afternoon caused the latter order to be ignored and the 4th Brigade was to be ready to cross on the night of 9–10 November. A major change was that the 5th Marines were to advance to the Bois de l'Hospice and the 6th

Marines to instead occupy the La Thibaudine Farm area. The 89th Division remained where it was during the day and night.

Saturday 9 November

Lining the road westward out of Mouzon lies the village of La Faubourg, which had been occupied by 3/9 since the day before. At 0200 on this morning they were ordered to clear out in order to avoid anticipated enemy shelling. Only I Co. provided outpost guards while K Co. moved back to Villemontry, where they would remain. Company L remained within the village until dark when they moved to the Bois du Fond de Limon which lies a bare hundred feet west of the Bois de l'Hospice. Plans to move the 23d Infantry across the river at Mouzon were dropped. In the meantime the 1st Bn., 2d Engineers, were engaged in building bridges.

Orders were issued for the Marines to cross the river at 1800, but this was postponed on account of the lack of bridging material. Otherwise, the Division remained relatively inactive.

Sunday 10 November

Preparations for the crossing of the Meuse continued all day. At 1400 the Marine Brigade issued orders for the 6th Marines, reinforced by 3/5, to cross the river north of Mouzon on two footbridges, after an artillery preparation on and about Mouzon, and seize Hill 336 and Hill 354, south to north. One battalion of the 5th Marines (2/5, Dunbeck), in conjunction with one battalion from the 89th Division (2/356), was to be ready that evening to cross the river. Opposite the Bois de l'Hospice, there were to be two foot bridges, and on the east shore they would seize the Bois d'Alma-Gisors, the Bois des Flaviers, and the high ground between those woods, all of which were heavily occupied by well-entrenched German infantry, artillery, and machine guns. Orders established the operation to begin at 2130.

Major George Hamilton, and 1/5, were ordered, at 1815, to hold themselves in readiness to support the 6th Marines in their effort to cross the river at Mouzon. Alternately, they were to also be ready to support 2/5 at their crossing point. The orders to the 6th Marines were hurriedly issued and Maj. Shuler, to command the operation, didn't receive them until 1730. Nevertheless, within ten minutes the Marines were on their way to Mouzon. When they came closer to Mouzon they found that the enemy artillery were demolishing the approach roads and the column was forced to detour around to the northwest.

At 2230, when the 6th Marines arrived at the rail yards north of the town, they found that only one bridge had been built and was ready to be positioned.

9. Meuse-Argonne 175

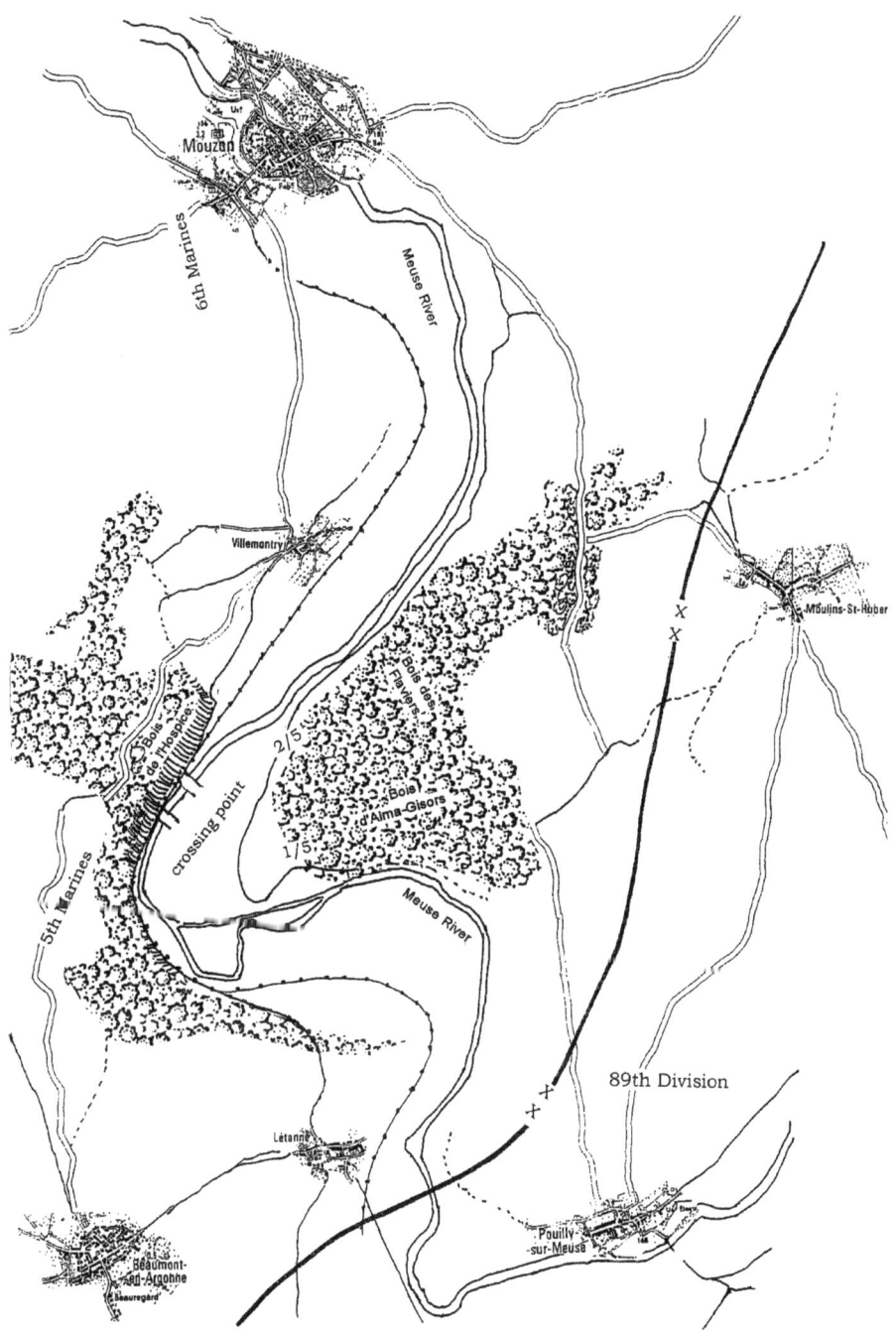

Map 14. Crossing of the Meuse, 10-11 November 1918.

A view looking southeast toward the village of Mouzon.

The Germans had discovered the 2d Engineers and the potential crossing sites were being pounded by their artillery and machine guns. A detail from the 6th Marines was ordered to assist the engineers in the completion of the second bridge but it wasn't available for crossing until 0400 on 11 November. Major Shuler decided (and later was castigated for his decision) not to attempt the crossing at that time and withdrew the regiment, thereby saving many lives. Back to the Bois du Fond de Limon they went since there was no adequate cover in the Mouzon area from the continuing German shelling.

Down the river the 2d Engineers, supported by two companies from 2/9, were busy trying to move the bridges built near Létanne into place opposite the Bois de l'Hospice. By 2000 the 1st and 2d Bns. of the 5th Marines had moved into place on the heights in the same woods. As previously planned, 2/5 and 2/356 were to make the crossing, one on each bridge, with 1/5 supporting both with rifle and machine gun fire. The 89th Division's battalion had come, however, under heavy enemy shelling, had already taken huge casualties, and was not able to move. So 1/5 was instead selected to be their substitute. It was now to be Hamilton and Dunbeck, two of the Corps' brightest and nearly fearless fighting men. Both battalions were up to par, with mostly new replacements. No matter how horrendous the situation, the Marines would cross, and take the eastern shoreline.

The following is an excellent description of how not to fight a war when the enemy is unbroken and an Armistice would be signed on the following morning. The American leadership was well aware of the difficulties inherent in this attack and of the forthcoming end of the war, but from V Corps down, it was go regardless of the anticipated cost.

Various descriptions explain what happened that night. One memoir, by Elton Mackin, told his side of the story: "They lied to us that night. Some were bitter at the thought of it. Was this the confidence we'd earned along the road from June? It may have been since we had so many men who still had a hope of living. Some of us were not long on the front. It was a patent, flimsy lie. Old hands among us knew the difference at once and were prepared for anything. 'We're to move a lot of ammunition over to the 89th, to the right of us'—or so the story ran. There was also talk of an Armistice on the morrow."[23] He added, "The fellows didn't really want to fight again." Even so, some of those making decisions, not on the front lines, of course, wanted it done.[24]

The Germans began shelling the Marines as they moved down a ravine toward the river. Many men fell before even reaching the bridge. One/5 would go over first. It took the men until 2230 before they could make it across and in so doing they left about 90 percent of the battalion in and around the river. On the east shore, one hundred Marines, now reduced to company size, dug in as best they could under continuing severe artillery and machine gun fire.[25]

Dunbeck's 2/5 were held up a short period by an accident on their bridge. Charley, his real first name, spoke to his men prior to crossing. He said, "Men, I'm going across that river, and I expect you to go with me." No Marine could let that pass; as expected, they all went. By 2330 they too were across, or at least, the remnants were. Two/5 moved northeast along the riverbank to attempt to connect with the 6th Marines, who were expected to be across the river further north. As we know, because of the humane courage of Maj. Shuler, the 6th never made it across.

Meanwhile, the remaining members of 1/5 pushed across the flats, driving German infantry and machine guns from their path. Germans had provided considerable opposition so the Marines hadn't made much progress, and both battalion's flanks were exposed. The 89th Division had managed to cross the river down near Pouilly and were also barely holding on.

The heroes are so numerous and the descriptions of their deeds are so similar that just a few names will be entered here. Gunnery Sergeant Samuel Clarkston,* of the 8th Machine Gun Co., supporting 1/5, managed with his one remaining gun to establish a stronghold on the east bank from which he inflicted huge losses upon the enemy. Three members of the 55th Co., Capt. Samuel C. Cumming, skipper, were awarded medals. Private John S. Haney* went up towards the Bois de Flaviers and knocked out several machine guns that were harassing his company, while Sgt. Tony Kane,* who would also be awarded an oak leaf cluster for his bravery at Belleau Wood on 11 June, was awarded his second DSC because he was across the river early on and knocked out several machine guns which were tearing his company apart as they crossed. One additional 55th Co. man, Pvt. Wilbert W. Sinclair,* was another who made it across the river early on and made sure that the machine guns he found weren't on the loose, knocking out two of them all by himself. One officer, 1st Lt Ralph M. Wilcox* of the 17th Co., the left flank of 1/5, pushed through an enemy outpost line, driving back the occupants in the midst of an artillery and machine gun barrage. This tied in both 1/5 and 2/5, which were desperately in need of an association at that point.

Monday 11 November

Somehow, the remnants of the two battalions managed to sustain themselves and retain their forward positions throughout the balance of the night. They were later supported by 2/356 and in turn 1/9 followed by Co. D, 5th Machine Gun Bn., all of which came across the remaining bridge material during the early morning hours. Fechet's Co. D, of 1/9, moved toward Pouilly but found that a battalion from the 355th Infantry, 89th Division had already occupied it. On this day, before the eleventh hour, the several army regiments would push forward and take positions that the greatly reduced Marines were incapable of carrying out.

Hamilton and his men, about 100 in all, pushed forward in the early morning and by 1100, The Hour, had gained and occupied Sénégal Farm ridge. Dunbeck and 2/5 had pushed northeast and had taken numerous villages and farms. One company of 1/5, (66th, Capt. Robert Blake) was at Moulins–St. Hubert, the farthest advance of any AEF unit into enemy held territory.[26] During the morning Larsen and 3/5 came across the river and relieved 1/9 in the Bois d'Alma-Gisors, then in support of the 5th Marines.

Interestingly, hostilities did not automatically cease at 1100 on this front. Word of the armistice had failed to reach these advanced units in time. When word reached them, the Americans are reported to have just laid down and tried to sleep. The Germans, after more than four years of this agony, did manage to celebrate, but just a bit. Otherwise, when it happened, it was mostly All Quiet on the Western Front.

The 2d Division generally remained in the area they occupied until relieved by the 77th Division on 14 November. Then the Division assembled near the town of Pouilly to begin their march into Germany the following day.

The Second Division suffered a total of 3,314 casualties, attached units another 61. The division began the battle with 26,146 effectives and on 30 November, after replacements, it had 26,036.

10

OCCUPATION OF GERMANY AND RETURN HOME

The war was barely over when the designated troops were marched from France, through Belgium and Luxembourg, and into their specific occupation zone across the Rhine River. On 17 November the 2d Division began its movement. The march wasn't easy for the exhausted troops. The allies (French and British) and associates (the U.S.) were anxious to get into the German territory before the former enemy realized what was planned for them, which was certainly nothing like the terms they expected, those based upon President Woodrow Wilson's fourteen points.[1]

Based upon the articles of the armistice, the German army had begun their withdrawal from the occupied zones at once. The allies and Americans allowed a couple of days in order to provide a semblance of a neutral zone between them. For the 2d Division, it was just as well. The weather and enemy action had produced a Division far less ready for additional trouble than some of the lesser tried units. Influenza, then rampant in the world, was, and had been, causing nearly as many casualties as enemy shells. The actual American occupation force was composed of six divisions in a newly formed Third Army (Maj. Gen. Joseph T. Dickman). The 2d Division was selected for this additional honor and was assigned to III Corps (Maj. Gen. John L. Hines). Six days were allotted for the trip with one day for rest. After receiving much new clothing and especially new shoes, which didn't fit, making the march a bit difficult,[2] some of the Marines were back into their uniforms, which made them happy.[3]

The march was through recently enemy occupied territory and the residents of each country were along the route to warmly receive their deliverers. Scenery in these lands, not torn apart as was France, was a pleasant change. The weather was cold but dry and the roads free from snow or other impediments, which helped make the march less difficult than it might have been. The occupying forces were to cross the border no sooner than 1 December and for a few days, especially around Thanksgiving (28 November), they just sat and waited. During this period of no movement, a number of DSCs were pinned on in a rather elaborate ceremony, which pleased some of the men.

The Americans were headed for the Coblenz area as their zone of occupation. The French were further south and the British further north. Connection between the three would be made once the Rhine River was crossed. Second Division headquarters went first to Mettendorf, then to Rittersdorf, and finally to Prüm, where they remained for three days while the infantry units expanded into the nearby hills. The roads were wet and very slippery, and very hard to climb, especially for the motor vehicles. However, everyone noted that the German inhabitants were reasonably docile, showing no obvious hostile feelings to the conquerors.

Still headed for the Rhine, the Division continued its marching until 13 December when the river was finally crossed. Headquarters of the 2d Division was established at Heddesdorf, a suburb of Neuwied. This then was where the American occupation zone would be. Each of the allies, British and French, also set up each of their zones in a semicircle, as did the Americans. The 32d Division was positioned at the center at the outer ring, the 1st Division at the right and the 2d Division at the left. The 4th Brigade was at the left of the Division frontage, with headquarters at Niederbieber; the 3d Brigade was to the right, grouped around Bendorf. These were not expected to be final, and the river was to be part of the Division's responsibility, so that still had to be worked out.

Potential trouble from the still organized German army was anticipated, especially as unfavorable (to the Germans) changes to the terms became obvious to all. Guards were posted at all bridges, at least until the end of the year. In January 1919, orders were issued prescribing what each unit would do in the event of a surprise attack; the counterattack, and the possible advance deeper into Germany were covered. The 4th Brigade and 15th FA were charged with the defense of the outpost zone with the balance of the division in corps reserve. In the event of an advance the 1st and 32d divisions would go forward with the 2d and 42d divisions in the second line. Hostilities had been suspended, but not necessarily terminated.

Once these security measures had been put into place, the Division went back to training. Then recreation including sports followed. Education was another factor for the troops of which many took advantage. Later, some efforts were made to provide higher education, including furnishing college level courses. There was even an "AEF University" established at Beaune, France, mail order for most Americans. Then, of course, there were many parades and ceremonies, too many for the now laid back troops. Living was now mostly with the inhabitants and numerous interactions between the civilians and troops. Pershing and his staff were not happy that the Americans were becoming quite friendly with the former enemy. Orders prohibiting "close interaction" were issued and, for the most part, ignored.

10. Occupation of Germany and Return Home

In the German occupation this portrait was taken of the survivors of the 79th Co, 2/6.

All the while, the occupiers became the government and even junior officers had certain responsibilities that exceeded, generally, their training or expertise. However, most seemed to learn on the job and become reasonably good at it. Mostly, the officials formerly running the communities were retained in their posts and worked well with the Americans.

In May the Germans refused to accept the harsh terms imposed by the French and British. By 17 June the 2d Division was organized to proceed further into Germany to battle any German forces thrown against them. However, the already dismantled German army was in no condition to battle the enemies now concentrated within their country. Their faith in the promise of Wilson's Fourteen Points had effectively disemboweled them. Twenty plus years later the Germans would retaliate and everyone would suffer.

Meanwhile, lots of useless and useful activity took place. One of the least serious was the formation of a ceremonial regiment, known as the Composite Regiment, composed of officers and men from each combat division of the AEF. The 2d Division provided at least two companies composed of veterans of the two brigades. This unit was formed to accompany the CG, AEF, and to parade in Paris, London, New York and Washington, D.C.

Another formation, pulled together from various units in Europe, was called the Schleswig–Holstein Battalion. It included about 26 officers with 700

Top: The Fifth Marines parading in Washington, D.C., August, 1918. *Bottom:* The Sixth Marines parading in Washington, D.C., August, 1918.

men from various units, and it was to remain in Europe for possible operations in connection with a plebiscite to be held to determine which nation that territory would become, German or Danish.

The 2d Division was finally approved to return to the United States. Units moved from their stations in groups. Eventually, from July to mid–August 1919, the 2d Division arrived in the U.S. and managed a long-overdue parade in New York City (8 August), followed by another in Washington, D.C.

The U.S. Marines were transferred from the U.S. Army, back to naval service, on 8 August 1919 and paraded in D.C. as such on 12 August 1919. Their main base, temporarily, would be at Quantico in Virginia.

The U.S. Army, like the U.S. Marines, discharged their "emergency personnel" (draftees and volunteers) within a few days and the remnants of the Division returned to Camp Travis, Texas (also known as Fort Sam Houston), which would be their permanent station.

The war was over.

Appendix A: Pedigree of the Division and Its Units

In 1914 the United States Army was ordered to "keep the fighting south of the Rio Grande."[1] In order to comply, the chief of staff, Maj. Gen. Leonard Wood, authorized the activation of the Second Division. Yet there had been several forerunners to that designation. The first appears to have been the unit commanded by Gen. Henry W. Lawton in Cuba which was in the successful attack upon El Caney on 1 July 1898. Later that year, the named division was now in the Philippines, under Maj. Gen. Arthur MacArthur. On 13 August the 2d Division became part of VIII Corps and was placed north of the Pasig River. The division, heavily composed of various state volunteer units, remained, with the Philippine Expeditionary Force under MacArthur's successful command, for the fighting around Manila. MacArthur began tactically using the only railroad line in the Philippines. It ran between Manila and Dagupan on Lingayen Gulf and was the best supply route in central Luzon. He had a special armored train built for his advances into the countryside. Well into November 1899, it was used to spring upon rebel groups anywhere in the vicinity. The balance of the period was devoted more to guerrilla warfare and the tactics being used were out of date. Maj. Gen. Elwell S. Otis, commanding all U.S. forces in the islands, assigned the division, now composed of 16 regiments, to garrison duty in 117 towns and villages along the 150 miles of railroad tracks from Dagupan to Manila. At this point the division ceased to exist in its earlier format. Otis was recalled to the United States on 5 May 1900 and MacArthur, leaving the division command, assumed his role.

In 1914, Wood's new division was composed of three brigades with a total of ten regiments of infantry, the Sixth Cavalry Regiment, the Fourth Field Artillery Regiment, an engineer battalion, and a signal corps company, as well as an ambulance company and field hospital plus headquarters and service troops. It totaled 11,000 effectives and was considered to be an apt response to

Mexican guerrilla activity. The first site chosen for deployment was at Texas City, but because of the unhealthy conditions at the former, it was later moved nearer Galveston Bay. Col. Robert Lee Bullard was temporarily assigned command of the 4th Brigade until the arrival of Brig. Gen. Clarence R. Edwards, the designated commander.[2]

During the period, until August 1915, the division remained pretty much in various camps, including several at Texas City. The commander, Maj. Gen. J. Franklin Bell, who had replaced Brig. Gen. Frederick Funston,[3] drove the command incessantly: drill, drill and more drill. Training was his forte. And the 2d Division lost nothing by it and became the best organization the U.S. Army possessed. Even the officers were elated by the improvements rendered the division. Unfortunately, on 17 August 1915 a hurricane badly disrupted the area and disturbed the entire 2d Division structure. By now the Mexican mess was solved to President Wilson's satisfaction and the army had only to determine where to disperse each of the units. Effectively, the 2d Division was once again reduced to nothing in the U.S. Army's Order of Battle.

Organization

The 2d Division, Regular Army, was officially authorized by the U.S. Army War Department chief of staff, Maj. Gen. Tasker H. Bliss, on 22 September 1917. The order further stated:

> The War Department directs the organization of the 2d Div, Regular Army. The Div includes troops of the United States Marine Corps which are at Quantico or already in France, and units of the Regular Army stationed at Chickamauga Park, El Paso, Gettysburg, Governors Island, Philadelphia, Syracuse, Fts Benjamin Harrison, Ethan Allen, Myer, Oglethorpe, Riley, Sam Houston, and Camps Robinson and Vail as well as others en route to, or already in, Europe.[4]

Upon completion of the organization, the 2d Division, Regular, would be composed of:

Division Headquarters and Headquarters Troop.
Third Brigade: 9th and 23d Infantry, 5th Machine Gun Battalion.
Fourth Brigade: 5th and 6th Marines, 6th Machine Gun Battalion (Marines).
Second Field Artillery Brigade: 12th and 15th Field Artillery (75mm guns), 17th Field Artillery (155mm howitzers), 2d Trench Mortar Battery.
Divisional Troops: 4th Machine Gun Battalion, 2d Engineers, 1st Field Signal Battalion.
Trains: 2d Train Headquarters and Military Police, 2d Ammunition Train, 2d Supply Train, 2d Engineer Train, 2d Sanitary Train (Ambulance Companies and Field Hospitals 1, 15, 16, and 23).
Other Units: 2d Mobile Ordnance Repair Unit, Mobile Veterinary Section No. 2, Motor Transport Corps Service Park Units 303–363, Salvage Squad No.

2, Sales Commissary Unit No. 1, Detachment Postal Service A.P.O. 710, Railhead Detachment, Clothing and Bath Unit 320-17, Laundry Unit 326, and Bakery Unit 319.

Army Units Lineage

The **Headquarters Troop** was organized in the summer of 1917 at Fort Ethan Allen, Vermont, by details from the 2d Cavalry.

The **Ninth Infantry** was organized in 1855, though they also claimed origins from January 1799 in Burlington, Vermont. There had been earlier regiments bearing the same number, but these passed out of existence and have no connection with the Ninth we are interested in. The regiment was sent to the Pacific Coast via the Isthmus of Panama immediately upon organization, the regiment served in the west until 1892, and took an active part in numerous Indian campaigns. After the Civil War it was reinforced by consolidation with the 27th Infantry (originally formed as the 2d Battalion, 18th Infantry), which had been in active service throughout the war. Needless to say, this unit had no connection with the 18th or 27th Infantry that followed.

In 1892 the Ninth went to Madison Barracks, New York, where for the first time in its existence it had an eastern station and knew complete peace. In 1898 it went to Cuba as a part of the Fifth Army Corps, and took part in the Santiago Campaign. Returning to the United States, it was ordered to the Philippine Islands, then in a state of insurrection. After arduous service there it went to China in 1900 as a part of the international force formed to relieve the legations in Peking, then besieged by the Boxers. On July 13 it took part in the attack upon Tientsin, where it lost 95 men out of 700 engaged, but won its regimental motto, "Keep up the fire," the last words of Colonel Emerson Liscum as he fell mortally wounded. It joined in the march for the relief of Peking, and was present at the storming of that city.

In 1901 it returned to the Philippines, and was active in the guerrilla warfare in the Visayan Islands south of Luzon. At Balangiga, on the island of Samar, "C" Company was almost annihilated; all the officers were killed, but the senior sergeant brought off the remnant of thirty men. After a return to the United States and another tour in the Philippines, the regiment went to Texas, where it was located in 1917. Its battle honors, up to that time, were:

Indian Wars: Washington, 1856, 1858; Wyoming, 1866, 1867; Little Big Horn.
Civil War: Mississippi, 1862; Kentucky, 1862; Murfreesboro, Tennessee, 1863;
    Chickamauga, Chattanooga, Georgia, 1864; Atlanta.
Spanish-American War: Santiago.
Philippine Insurrection: San Isidro; Luzon, 1899, 1900; Zapote River; Tarlac;
    Samar, 1901.
China Relief Expedition: Tientsin; Yang Tsun; Peking.

The **Twenty-third Infantry** was organized in 1861, as the 2d Battalion Fourteenth Infantry. The regiments of the group formed at this time never operated as tactical bodies, but each battalion served as an independent unit, much like a British battalion. In 1866 this existing fact was recognized by constituting each such battalion a separate regiment; and the one now of interest was designated as the 23d Infantry. This regiment had no connection with earlier regiments bearing either number, nor with the present Fourteenth Infantry.

It served in the Army of the Potomac during the Civil War. In the summer of 1865 it went by way of the Isthmus of Panama to San Francisco, and the companies were scattered in numerous posts on the Pacific Coast. Their service was active, exploration and Indian fighting from Oregon to Arizona, and here the reorganization was made. The duty of the regiment remained unchanged. Hardly a monthly return for the next ten years fails to show marching and scouting in the Indian country, and about half of them show hostile contact, ranging from minor incidents to serious combat. In 1898 the regiment embarked for the Philippines, having been again reorganized into three battalions. Two battalions arrived in time to take part in the capture of Manila. During the insurrection, in 1899 and 1900, the regiment was widely scattered, parts of it having service in Luzon, in the central islands of Cebu and Leyte, and among the Moros of the extreme south, in Jolo and Mindanao.

It returned to the United States in 1900, but in 1902 began another tour in the Philippines, going by way of Suez. It was again stationed in Mindanao, where the service was very active. It took a prominent part in the expeditions into the interior, both to the great Lake Lanao upland country and up the Rio Grande valley. From 1905 to 1908 there was another brief visit to civilization, with stations in New York State, then Mindanao and Jolo again in 1908 and 1909. The regiment then returned home, and in 1917 it was stationed in Texas. Its battle honors then were:

Indian Wars: Arizona, 1866; Idaho, 1868; Little Big Horn.
Civil War: Peninsula; Manassas; Antietam; Fredericksburg; Chancellorsville; Gettysburg; Virginia, 1863; Wilderness; Spotsylvania; Cold Harbor; Petersburg.
Spanish-American War: Manila.
Philippine Insurrection: Manila; Malolos.

The **Second Engineers** traces its origin to 1846, when an engineer company was organized for the Mexican War. It served also in the Mormon Expedition of 1858, and, expanded into a battalion, was with the Army of the Potomac throughout the Civil War. Parts of the battalion served at Santiago in 1898, in the Philippines and in China. Further expansion was made from time to time, and in 1916 the 2d Battalion of Engineers became an independent regiment, the 2d Engineers.

It was then at Colonia Dublan, Mexico, as part of the Pershing expedition against Villa; so the regiment has the distinction of having been formed on foreign soil. When the United States entered the war with Germany, it was at El Paso, Texas. Its battle honors were:

Civil War: Peninsula; Antietam; Fredericksburg; Chancellorsville; Virginia, 1863; Wilderness; Spotsylvania; Cold Harbor; Petersburg; Appomattox.
Spanish-American War: Santiago.
Philippine Insurrection.

The **Twelfth Field Artillery** was formed in June 1917 at St. Asaph's, near Alexandria, Virginia, by details from the 3d FA at Fort Myer, also in Virginia. That month the **Fifteenth FA** at Syracuse, New York, was created from the 4th FA, the **Seventeenth FA** at Camp Robinson, Sparta, Wisconsin, from the 8th FA, and the **Second Trench Mortar Battery** at Gettysburg was assembled by transfer of individuals from various regular regiments. None had served previously with those designated numbers and consequently all were new formations.

The **Fourth** and **Fifth Machine Gun Battalions** were similarly formed, by individual personnel transfers rather than from established units. The 2d Division's own 4th Machine Gun Battalion had an unusual beginning. It was formed in Syracuse, New York, from volunteers gleaned from the 48th Infantry, then in residence, and draftees, most of whom seemed to be recent immigrants from Europe. Syracuse was the home of the laudable Lewis Machine Gun factory and many of the gunners from the division were trained there.

The **First Field Signal Battalion** was formed in 1916, by consolidation of two independent signal companies (Company E, formed in 1899, and Company I, in 1904), both of which had served in the Philippines and in Cuba. In 1917 an additional company was added.

Of the train units, only the **First Field Hospital** and the **First Ambulance Company** existed in 1917. All other units were formed by details from various sources, mostly at Chickamauga. Most personnel were inducted for the term of the war from civilian hospitals, a few of which were university based research institutes.

The army units of the Division are thus seen to fall into three classes: (a) old regiments, reduced by drafts to form new ones, and again recruited up; (b) new regiments formed upon a solid nucleus transferred from some parent organization; and (c) new ones formed by transfer of small groups from several old ones. Evidently the first class was the most fortunate; the third class the least so, for these units possessed no framework to start with, and had only the intangible spirit of the Regular to help them.

Marine Corps Units Lineage

In 1917 the U.S. Marine Corps was possibly in better shape to go to war than was the U.S. Army. By that it is meant that they had been "chasing bandits" all over the Caribbean, in the Philippines, in China, and any place they could take their Springfield .03's. Hardly a year had gone by that Marines were not fighting with someone, somewhere. Initially they could and did put together a regiment, the 5th, to ship over and be among the "First to Fight" in France, only they weren't. We will get to that part of our story in its proper place.

The **Fifth Regiment, Marines,** was formed in April 1914 to intervene in, and when necessary fight, inhabitants of various Latin American states. This was to enable President Wilson to teach these backward people to "to elect honest men." He was unhappy with most of those elected, or nonelected, political officials south of our border, consequently Marines were busy during the period. This regiment survived for a brief period, serving at Vera Cruz, Mexico, in 1914; there were additional problems in Haiti and its sister nation, Santo Domingo, but the regiment was disbanded on 24 December 1914, although several of its companies were transferred to East Coast duty stations.

After war with Germany was declared, on 19 May 1917, Josephus Daniels, secretary of the navy, offered the war department a regiment of Marines for service in France. Since the Marine Corps already had four regiments on active service, the resurrected one was designated the Fifth. Complications aside, the regiment was shipped to France via navy transport ships in June 1917, then as part of the 1st Division (Regulars).

The **6th Regiment, Marines,** was formed at Quantico in August 1917. Initially there was no guarantee that this regiment would be accepted by Headquarters, AEF The Marine commandant, Major General George Barnett, was only "speculating" that they eventually would. It would take a much longer period to transfer this regiment to France. In fact, it went by battalions stretching over a period from October 1917 until the last element arrived in France in February 1918.

The **6th Machine Gun Battalion** was formed on 17 August 1917 at Quantico on orders from Major General Commandant George Barnett. The formation was originally designated the **1st Machine Gun Battalion** but title was changed in France on 15 January 1918 by General Order No. 4, 2d Division, to the number **Six**.[5] It too had been organized based upon Gen. Barnett's expectation that, once another Marine regiment was accepted for service in France, a machine gun battalion would be required to create a brigade. His ultimate plan was to create a Marine division, which never came to fruition.[6]

Originally, however, the staff of the AEF had no idea what to do with an independent regiment of Marines (the Fifth) which had arrived on 27 June 1917. For a while it was attached to the 1st Division but the four required regiments were intact and the fifth "wheel" wasn't part of their story. Then someone figured out they needed guards and longshoremen where ships were unloading, so why not utilize men trained for that kind of work. So Pershing assigned the regiment to a bunch of odd jobs which, it is safe to say, the Marines hated (and possibly also the entire U.S. Army as well). It wasn't until later in the year that the Marines managed to hook up with their own breed. But they too were immediately put to work like their brethren of the 5th and if memoirs are any indication of their attitude they too were furious.

The final piece to complete the brigade was the 6th Machine Gun Battalion, only at the time it was the designated the First Provisional Machine Gun Battalion, with headquarters staff and but two of the four companies required. There would be some adjustments before the 4th Brigade was complete and ready for combat service.

Sailing Schedule

The 3d Brigade of Infantry, then known as the 1st Provisional Brigade, would sail sooner than their comrades of the 4th Brigade, except for the 5th Regiment of Marines, already in France with the First Division. Half of the 9th Infantry sailed on 7 September 1917 and the second half on 18 September 1917 from Hoboken and New York. The first group landed at St. Nazaire on 20 September. The other portion landed at Liverpool, England, on 3 October. The 23d Infantry, which also sailed on 7 September from Hoboken, arrived intact at St. Nazaire on 20 September.

Third Brigade's 5th Machine Gun Battalion (formed in August 1917 as a Provisional MG Bn) sailed on 18 September from New York and arrived on 5 October at Le Havre. As early as 11 August, the brigade had already been officially assigned as part of the 2d Division. In fact, the War Department had considered the idea of assembling infantry from army units around the eastern part of the nation as the division's second brigade, but decided to utilize U.S. Marines instead, resulting in the Ninth Infantry, the 23d Infantry, the Fifth Machine Gun Battalion and the 2d Engineers all arriving in France during the month of September.

The Fifth Marine Regiment sailed from New York, arriving at St. Nazaire, France, between 26 June and 2 July 1917. As we know, in the interim they became laborers.

The Sixth Marine Regiment had a very complicated schedule. The 1st Battalion sailed earliest, under Major John A. Hughes' command, and arrived at St. Nazaire on 5 October 1917. They too became laborers, like the other Marines in France. The 3d Battalion, 6th Marines (for ease we will call them simply "Marines" from here on), under the command of Major Berton W. Sibley was next to arrive at Brest on 12 November. That battalion received the same treatment as its predecessors: labor. Major Thomas Holcomb's battalion, 2/6, managed to avoid the unpleasant duties inflicted upon their Marine comrades. When they arrived and debarked at St. Nazaire on 8 February 1918, they were at once shipped east to a training camp to join the balance of their brigade, now in training.

The two companies of the 1st Machine Gun Battalion arrived at St. Nazaire on 28 December 1917. Of course they would later become the four company 6th MG Bn.

The balance of the division sailed from different ports at different times. The 2d Engineers sailed on 10 September, from Hoboken, New Jersey, and, via Glasgow, Scotland, arrived at Le Havre, France, on 6 October.

Three field hospitals and ambulance companies moved across the Atlantic in November and December as follows: On 24 November 1917, Field Hospital 1 and Ambulance Company 1 left El Paso, Texas, and sailed on 5 December from Hoboken, landing on 22 December at St. Nazaire; on 1 December, Field Hospital 15 and Ambulance Company 15 left Fort Benjamin Harrison, Indianapolis, Indiana, sailed on 4 December from Hoboken, and arrived at Brest on 21 December; Field Hospital 23 and Ambulance Company 23 moved from Ft. Oglethorpe, Georgia, sailing on 5 December from Hoboken, and arriving at St. Nazaire on 22 December.

On 12 December the enlisted personnel for Divisional Headquarters and Headquarters, 2d FA Brigade, sailed from Hoboken, and arrived at Brest on 27 December; the 15th FA sailed from New York and arrived on 25 December at Liverpool, England. On 13 December the 17th FA sailed from Hoboken and arrived at Brest on 28 December. Both the 4th Machine Gun Battalion (Divisional), and the newly organized 2d Trench Mortar Battery, moved from Gettysburg on 15 December to Camp Merritt, New Jersey. From there they moved to and embarked from Portland, Maine, on 24 December, arriving at Liverpool on 8 January. Only the 12th FA was delayed in sailing for France. They wouldn't leave the United States until January 1918.

Other organizations of the division left the U.S. in late December and arrived in Europe during January 1918. Principally they were the various trains: 2d Ammunition Train, 2d Supply Train, First Field Battalion, Signal Corps, 2d Military Police, and Motor Transport Corps all arriving, usually, late in January. The 12th FA finally assembled in France on 31 January 1918. It was the last major arrival. All divisional units would begin their training period and most were selected for initial training in trenches beginning in mid–March with the French army near Verdun.

Appendix B:
Second Division Register

Time and Place of Organization

Division organized at Bourmont, France, on 26 October 1917.

Subdivisions

Infantry

3d Infantry Brigade: 9th Regiment, 23d Regiment, 5th Machine Gun Battalion
4th Marine Brigade: 5th Marine Regiment, 6th Marine Regiment, 6th Machine Gun Battalion.
Divisional MG Bn, 4th Machine Gun Battalion

Artillery

2d Field Artillery Brigade: 12th Field Artillery, 15th Field Artillery, 17th Field Artillery, 2d Trench Mortar Battery

Engineers

2d Engineer Regiment

Signal Corps

Field Signal Battalion

Trains

2d Train Hdqs and Military Police
2d Ammunition Train
2d Supply Train
2d Engineer Train
2d Sanitary Train

Miscellaneous

Headquarters Troop
2d Mobile Ordnance Repair Shop
Mobile Veterinary Section No. 2
Motor Transport Corps
Service Park Units 303 and 363
Salvage Squad No. 2
Commissary Unit No. 1
P.E.S. det. A.P.O. 710
Railhead Detachment
Clothing and Bath Unit No. 320*
Mobile Laundry Unit No. 326*
Bakery Unit No 311*
Delousing and Bath Unit No. 17*

Commanding Generals

Brig. Gen. Charles A. Doyen, USMC from 26 Oct 1917
Maj. Gen. Omar Bundy, NA from 8 Nov 1917
Maj. Gen. James G. Harbord, NA from 15 Jul 1918
Maj. Gen. John A. Lejeune, USMC from 29 Jul 1918

*These units joined Division after its arrival in Germany.

Chiefs of Staff

Col. Preston Brown, 6 Apr 18–18 Sep 18

Col. James C. Rhea, 19 Sep 18–1 Nov 18

Col. Hu B. Myers, 2 Nov 18 to date.

Dates of Arrival in France

3d Brig. Infantry: Sep to Oct 1917
4th Brig. Marines: Jun 1917 to Jan 18
2d Brig. Field Artillery: Dec 1917 to Jan 18
Trains and other troops: Oct 1917 to Jan 18

Training Periods

Subordinate units assembled in Bourmont area for intensive training in Jan 1918 and continued to 14 Mar 1918. Robert Espagne area 11 May to 20 May 18. Gisors, Chaumout-en-Vexin area 21 May to 31 May 18. Colombey-les-Belles area 18 Aug to 1 Sep 18.

Verdun Sector
15 Mar to 13 May 18

Division occupied Toulon and Troyon sectors in conjunction with the French. A German raid in force was made against the 3d Bn, 9th Infantry, on 13 April 18. This was the largest demonstration made against American troops up to this time. The 9th Infantry took many prisoners and inflicted heavy casualties on the Germans.

Aisne-Marne Defensive
(Chateau Thierry)
31 May to 5 Jun 18

The Division moved by camion to an area northeast of Meaux and took up a position across the Paris-Metz highway west of Chateau Thierry 31 May 18. The German advance on Paris was stopped and the enemy thrown back during this operation, which lasted until 6 Jun 18.

Chateau Thierry Sector
6 Jun to 9 Jul 18

Almost continuous fighting marked the 2d Division's stay in this sector. During this time the Belleau Woods and the villages of Bouresches and Vaux were captured. Casualties were heavy, but the American army demonstrated its ability to successfully meet in battle the best of German troops.

Aisne-Marne Offensive
(Soissons)
18 July to 19 Jul 18

Attacked as part of the 20th Army Corps (French) near Soissons on the western side of the salient the Germans had pushed down to the Marne. Captured Beaurepaire Farm, Vauxcastille, Vierzy and advanced to Tigny.

Marbache Sector
12 Aug to 16 Aug 18

Quiet sector on Moselle River. No action except for numerous patrols.

St. Mihiel Offensive
12 Sep to 16 Sep 18

Went into the line near Limey, night of 9 Sep 10 Sep 18; attacked with 1st American Army 12 Sep18, captured Thiaucourt, Xammes and Jaulny, advanced to the vicinity of Rembercourt. Relieved 16 Sep 18. Took many prisoners, losses slight. Attack made in accordance with plans perfected in training area.

Meuse-Argonne Offensive
(Champagne)
1 Oct to 10 Oct 18

Moved from Mairy-sur-Marne to Suippes-Souain Area. Went into front line under 21st Corps (French) October 1, 1918, near Somme-Py. Cleaned up Essen Trench. Jumped off 3 Oct 18, and advanced to Medeah Ferme, Blanc Mont Ridge Road. Captured the strong enemy position of Blanc Mont and town of St. Étienne. American losses were severe. Relieved by 36th Division, U.S., 10 Oct 18, and moved to rest area near Somme Suippes.

Meuse-Argonne Offensive
1 Nov to 11 Nov 18

Marched to 1st American Army area 22 to 25 Oct 18. Relieved 42d Division in line near Landres-et-St. Georges, night of 30/31 Oct. Attacked 1 Nov 18, advanced to Corps Objective. Captured Landres-et-St. Georges, St. George, Landreville and Bayonville; continued the advance for several days and captured Fosse, Nouart, Letanne and Beaumont. Crossed the Meuse the night of 10/11 Nov 18, and were fighting east of the river when the armistice went into effect.

A total of 319 officers and 9,972 men, who were present with the Division on March 15, 1918, were present for duty on this date.

Remained in the Beaumont-Pouilly Area refitting until 17 Nov 18.

March to the Rhine

Marched at 0500 on 17 Nov 18; crossed the American front line, advanced through Belgium and Luxembourg and entered Germany 1 Dec 18. Reached the Rhine in the vicinity of Remagen and crossed this river 13 Dec 18. Occupied area No. 2 of the American Sector of the Coblenz Bridgehead and established headquarters at Heddesdorf.

Accomplishments in the Field

Kilometers advanced against opposition — 62.

German Prisoners Captured

Officers	Men	Total
288	11738	12026

Materiel Captured

Heavy Artillery	Light Artillery	Trench Mortars	Machine Guns[1]	Anti Tank Guns	Rifles
74	269	58	1350	8	1000

Decorations Awarded

Medal of Honor — 13
Distinguished Service Crosses — 675
Distinguished Service Medals — 10
Belgian Crosses — 6
Legion of Honor (French) Officers — 17
Medaille Militaire (French) Men — 42
Croix de Guerre (French) — 2,740
Croce di Guera (Italian) — 15
Knight of Order of Crown of Italy Officer — 1
Citations for Distinguished Gallantry — 795

American Citations

2d Division — G.O. 112, G.H.Q., AEF, 9 Jul 18.
2d Division — G.O. 9, Hdqs 111, A.C., 25 Jul 18.
2d Division — G.O. 26, Hq. V.A.C., 20 Nov 18.
2d Division — G.O. 232, G.H.Q., AEF, 19 Dec 18.
2d Division — G.O. 233, G.H.Q., AEF, 26 Dec 18.

French Army Citations

Division units
4th MG Bn 18 Jul 18.
2d Regiment Engineers 18 Jul 18.
2d Regiment Engineers 3 Oct 18.
3d Brigade
Co. I, 9th Regiment, 14 Apr 18.
Co. L, 9th Regiment, 14 Apr 18.
4th Pl., Co. K, 9th Regiment, 14 Apr 18.
Co. F, 9th Regiment 6–7 Jun 18.
Co. G, 9th Regiment 6–7 Jun 18.
9th Regiment 18 Jul 18.
23d Regiment 18 Jul 18.
9th Regiment 3 Oct 18.
23d Regiment 3 Oct 18.

5th MG Bn 18 Jul 18.
4th Brigade (Marine)
2 to 13 Jun 18.
5th Regiment Marines
6th Regiment Marines
6th MG Bn Marines
5th Regiment Marines 18 Jul 18.
6th Regiment Marines 18 Jul 18.
6th MG Bn Marines 18 Jul 18.
5th Regiment Marines 3 Oct 18.
6th Regiment Marines 3 Oct 18.
2d Artillery Brigade
12th FA Regiment 18 Jul 18.
15th FA Regiment 18 Jul 18.
17th FA Regiment 18 Jul 18.
Battery D, 17th FA 18 Jul 18.

Division Casualties

	Killed & Died	Severely Wounded	Slightly Wounded	Gassed	Missing	Total
Officers	189	113	393	70	0	765
Men	4,988	4,888	3,565	2,662	328	25,224

Third Infantry Brigade: Time and Place of Organization

31 August 1917, Syracuse, NY, then called 1st Provisional Brigade, or the Syracuse Brigade.

Subdivisions

Ninth Infantry Regiment, Twenty-Third Infantry Regiment, 5th Machine Gun Battalion.

Names of Commanding Officers

Col. Harry R. Lee, 21 Sep 17 to 10 Oct 17.
Col. Walter K. Wright, 10 Oct 17 to 16 Feb 18.
Brig. Gen. Peter Murray 16 Feb 18 to 7 May 18.
Brig. Gen. Edward M. Lewis, 7 May 18 to 15 Jul 18.
Brig. Gen. Hanson E. Ely, 15 Jul 18 to 17 Oct 18.
Col. Robert O. Van Horn, 17 Oct 18 to 2 Nov 18.
Col. James C. Rhea, 2 Nov 18 to 23 Nov 18.
Brig. Gen. Charles E. Kilbourne, 23 Nov 18 to 24 Feb 19.
Brig. Gen. Thomas W. Darrah, 24 Feb 19 to 31 Mar 19.
Col. Robert O. Van Horn, 31 Mar 19 to 9 Jun 19.
Col. Milo C. Corey, 9 Jun 19 to 23 Jun 19.
Brig. Gen. Paul B. Malone, 23 Jun 19 to date.

Date of Arrival in France

20 September 1917 to 6 October 1917.

Training Periods

Between 1 and 9 October 1917, the Brigade was assembled in the Bourmont Area. By the middle of November only 4 rifle companies were left in the 23d Infantry and 6 in the Ninth, the others having been sent to the S.O.S.,[2] to be used as labor troops. These troops had no further training until they returned to the Brigade in January. About the 15th of January, 1918, a period of intensive training was begun which continued up until the troops went into the line, 9 May to 20 May at Bar-le-Duc. On 20 May a movement by train lasting two days was begun to an area north of Paris. Intensive training was continued.

Verdun Sector

In March orders were received directing the movement of the Brigade to sector on the western side of St. Mihiel Salient. The movement was begun on 13 March. Brigade headquarters was established at Troyon. The first troops entered the lines on the night of 17/18 March 1918. The first engagement with the enemy occurred on the night of 18/19 March. The enemy attempted a raid on the 23d Infantry trenches but did not succeed in reaching them. A Brigade sector was formed on 24 April, the Brigade functioning as a Brigade of the 52d French Division. The tour of duty as a whole was very quiet in this sector with the exception of the night of 13/14 April, when the enemy attempted a large raid in the sector occupied by the 9th Infantry. It was a victory for the Americans as [they] not only drove the enemy off but captured more and killed a larger number than they lost.

Chateau Thierry Sector

On 18 July, [sic]³ Brigade attacked and drove the enemy from Chateau Thierry Sector, and eventually took up an organized line on 6 June, and remained in this sector until July, being relieved from the front lines on the night of 9 July by the 51st Brigade, 26th Division. During this period troops were under continuous artillery and machine gun fire. On 1 July a battalion of the 9th and one of the 23d Infantry, in a perfect attack, captured Vaux and La Roche woods. On 16 July troops moved by bus to the vicinity of Villers Cotterets woods.

Aisne Marne Offensive

On 18 July Brigade attacked and drove the enemy from Beaurepaire Ferme, Vauxcastille, captured the town of Vierzy and established a line in advance of the town which they held until relieved by a French division on the night of 19/20 July.

Marbache Sector

Upon relief, the Brigade was moved to the vicinity of Pierrefonds on 20 July, thence to Ormoy-Villers on 21/22 July, remaining there until 28 July when the Brigade was moved to Nancy. On the night of 6/7 August troops relieved a French division in the Pont-a-Mousson Sector. A Brigade of the 82d Division relieved the Brigade on the night of 13/14 August. Troops proceeded upon relief to the vicinity of Colombey-les Belles.

St. Mihiel Offensive

On 2 September troops began a movement towards the line and on the morning of 12 September attacked from the front of Limey; in a rapid advance they captured Thiaucourt, Xammes and Jaulny, and established lines in advance of these towns which they held until relieved by 4th Brigade.

Meuse-Argonne Offensive (Champagne)

Night of 15/16 September troops were moved to the Ansauville Area. On 20 September movement was made to the Toul Area, a further move by train was made 25 September to the Chalons Area. On 30 September troops were moved by bus to the vicinity of Suippes. On the morning of 3 October, the Brigade, as part of the French 4th Army, attacked north of Somme-Py, capturing Blanc Mont Ridge in concert with Fourth Brigade. The line was eventually advanced one kilometer east of St. Étienne where the Brigade was relieved by the 71st Brigade of the 36th Division on the night of 9/10 October. Troops upon relief proceeded to the Chalons Area.

Meuse Argonne Offensive

Movement to the front began on 21 October. On 1 November one regiment of the Brigade attacked in conjunction with the 4th Brigade. Night of 2/3 November, 3d Brigade relieved the 4th Brigade and on morning of 3 November, attacked and drove the enemy from Fosse, Nouart, Belval and Le Champey Bas. Night of 3/4 November, a night advance was made to the open ground north of Belval woods, capturing Tuillerie Ferme and Beausejour Ferme. A further advance was made on the night of 4/5 November, the towns of Beaumont and Letanne being mopped up at daybreak. The west bank of the Meuse was held until the night of 10/11 November when a battalion of the 9th Infantry crossed the Meuse after the 4th Brigade and established itself on the high ground across the River.

March to the Rhine

On 17 November, march to the Rhine began. On 13 December, crossed Rhine and became reserve of 3d U.S. Army Corps occupying Coblenz bridgehead.

Ninth Infantry Regiment: Time and Place of Organization

January 1799, Burlington, Vermont.

Names of Commanding Officers

Col. Leroy S. Upton, 1 Jun 18 to 25 Jul 18.
Lt. Col. Edward R. Stone, 26 Jul 18 to 30 Aug 18.
Col. George W. Stuart, 31 Aug 18 to 15 Oct 18.
Maj. Hanford MacNider, 15 Oct 18 to 2 Oct 18.
Lt. Col. Milo C. Corey, 25 Oct 18 to 2 Nov 18.
Col. Robert O. Van Horn, 3 Nov 18 to 5 Apr 19.
Col. Alfred C. Arnold, 5 Apr 19 to date.

Date of Arrival in France

20 September 1917, St. Nazaire.

Training Periods

Bourmont Area during winter 1917–1918; Bar-le-Duc training Area 6 May to 20 May 18; Chaumont-en-Vexin Area, 20–30 May 18; Colombey-les-Belles Area, 16 Aug to 1 Sep 18.

Verdun Sector

Held Subsector Rouvrois, 18 Mar to 19 May; Second Battalion Subsector Mont-Sus-les-Cotes, 6 to 12 May 18.

Aisne Marne Defensive (Chateau Thierry)

Went by truck to Chateau Thierry, 31 May.

1 June took over and held Vaux Sector, assisting in stopping Boche drive on Paris.

Advanced lines 6 to 7 June. Held lines and repulsed repeated counterattacks from 1 June to 9 Jul.

Took Vaux 1 Jul.

Left this sector 9 Jul and went to La Barre, Bezu, Chambardie District.

Aisne-Marne Offensive (Soissons)

Went to Villers-Cotterets by truck, 17 Jul.

Took part in attack 18/19 Jul.

20 Jul marched to Levignan.

25 Jul marched to Per-les-Combien.

Entrained for Nancy 31 Jul.

Marched to Quartier-Seille Sector 4 Aug. Marched to Colombey-les-Belle training area 16 Aug.

St. Mihiel Offensive

Went by truck to St. Mihiel Sector, 1 Sep.

Attacked near Limey 12 Sep.

Marched to Tout Rest Area, 20 Sep.

Entrained for Chalons-sur-Marne, 25 Sep.

Argonne-Meuse Offensive (Champagne)

Went by truck to Suippes 30 Sep.

With 6th Marines in attack on Blanc Mont Ridge, 3 Oct, and engaged here until relieved on 9 Oct.

Marched to Courtisel, 14 Oct.

Argonne-Meuse Offensive

Marched to Exermont region 25 Oct.

Leapfrogged Fifth Marines, 2 Nov, advancing until 4 Nov.

Leapfrogged 23d Infantry evening of

5 Nov. Advanced and took up front line position west bank of Meuse from Beaumont to Monzon.

Took part in attack on the night of 10 Nov; crossed Meuse morning of 11 Nov.

March to the Rhine

Billeted in Beaumont until 17 Nov, when march to the Rhine started. Marched through Belgium, Luxembourg and Rhine provinces, arriving at Remagen, 9 Dec.

Engaged in training troops to present time.

Reviewed by General Pershing, 14 Mar 19.

Twenty-Third Infantry Regiment: Time and Place of Organization

Summer of 1917 at Syracuse, NY.

Names of Commanding Officers

Col. Walter K. Wright, 15 Mar 17 to 15 Feb 18.
Col. Paul B. Malone, 15 Feb 18 to 2 Sep 18.
Col. Robert O. Van Horn, 2 Sep 18 to 11 Sep 18.
Col. Edward R. Stone, 11 Sep 18 to 1 Mar 19.
Col. Milo C. Corey, 1 Mar 19 to 15 Jun 19.
Lt. Col. D.W. Spurloch, 15 Jun to 23 Jun 19.
Col. Milo C. Corey, 23 Jun 19 to date.

Date of Arrival in France

20 September 1917.

Training Periods

Intensive training in the vicinity of St. Thiebault and Goncourt until 17 Mar 18; some of the units used as provost and construction detachments. Vicinity of Cheminon-la-Ville and Lisle-en-Rigault, 10 to 20 May, during which time regiment was inspected by General Pershing. On 20 May moved by train and marching to Chaumont-en-Vexin and Trie-la-Ville. Training for large scale operations was vigorously pushed. Plans for the relief of the 1st Division at Cantigny were changed because of the German drive on Paris.

Verdun Sector

On 17 Mar 18, the regiment occupied a subsector near Ranzieres, taking over C.R. Riga from the French. On 28 Mar C.R. Turin was taken over from the French. Subsector Lacroix was occupied 23 Apr, one battalion holding C.R. Chevreuils, and one C.R. Sangliers. The entire period was quiet save for two enemy raids and one raid by [American] forces. Few casualties were suffered.

Aisne-Marne Defensive (Chateau Thierry)

Chateau Thierry area started 31 May. The regiment was thrown into a gap in the French line near Coulombs on 2 Jun. Small enemy attacks were beaten off. On 4 Jun relieved by the French and on 5 Jun, the 1st and 3d battalions took over the line from Bouresches to Le Thiolet, relieving the Marines. These two battalions attacked late in the afternoon 6 Jun, gaining their objective with heavy losses. The regiment retained the portion of the line Bouresches-Le Thiolet (both inclusive) until 9 Jul. The period was one of great activity but the only notable offensive action after 6 Jun was the attack 1 Jul. Our 3d Battalion, attacking with a battalion of the 9th, captured Bois de la Roche and the ground on the left of Vaux.

Aisne-Marne Offensive (Soissons)

On 18 Jul attacked from a position near Longpont. Advance was 9 kilometers. Relieved night 19/20 Jul. Marched to

St. Étienne, thence to Ormoy-Villers. On 30 Jul moved to Nancy.

Marbache Sector

A portion of the line near Pont-a-Mousson was held from 4 to 16 Aug when the regiment moved to Allain to prepare for the St. Mihiel Drive.

St. Mihiel Offensive

The regiment attacked near Limey 12 Sep, advancing 9 kilometers and capturing Thiaucourt. On 14 Sep relieved and moved by easy stages to Camp Lafayette near Souain where it arrived 30 Sep. Colonel Edward R. Stone had assumed command 11 Sep.

Meuse Argonne Offensive (Champagne)

On 3 Oct attacked as part of the 4th French Army — General Gouraud. Supported the 9th to the Medeah Farm Objective and then passed through them, storming the heights southeast of St. Étienne-aux-Arnes. The resistance was strong and the fighting more bitter than in any other engagement. Remained in action until 9 Oct. Relieved by 141st Infantry 9/10 Oct, marched to Camp Noblette near Chalons-sur-Marne, remaining there until 22 Oct, when the regiment moved, by marching, through St. Mennehould and the Argonne to a position in the woods near Exermont.

Meuse-Argonne Offensive

On the night of 31 Oct/1 Nov, relieved the 165th Infantry and attacked at 0530, 1 Nov on a two-kilometer front. Captured Landres-et-St. Georges, Bois de Hazois and Bois l'Epasse. Advancing continuously from November 1st to November 5th, captured Posse, Letanne and Beaumont.

March to the Rhine

The armistice found the regiment in and around Yoneq. Preparations were immediately made for the march to the Rhine. The movement to the Rhine started 16 Nov. Passing through Stenay, Virton, into Belgium, thence through Luxembourg, crossed the Sauer River into Germany at Bollendorf on December 1. On 13 Dec crossed the Rhine at Remagen, and on 20 Dec went into permanent billets at Vallendar, Germany.

Fifth Machine Gun Battalion: Time and Place of Organization

August 1917, Syracuse, NY

Names of Commanding Officers

Maj. Shelby C. Leasure, 14 Aug 17 to 27 Oct 17.

Capt. d'Alary Fechet, 10 Jan 18 to 29 May 18.

Maj. Harry T. Lewis, 29 May 18 to 17 Jan 19.

Capt. George L. Moulton, 17 Jan 19 to 1 Feb 19.

Maj. d'Alary Fechet, 1 Feb 19 to 14 Feb 19.

Maj. A.S. Peake, 14 Feb 19 to present date.

Date of Arrival in France

September 1917.

Training Periods

Assigned to Ninth and Twenty-third Infantry regiments and trained with them in Bourmont area until March 1918. Verdun Sector. The middle of March saw this new-formed battalion as a member of the 3d Brigade leave its training area for actual trench life and warfare in a sector near Verdun. Headquarters was established at Troyon throughout this period from 15 Mar to 20 May. Company C with the 3d Battalion of the 9th Infantry had a taste of real action in a raid by the Germans on Maizey, 13 Apr.

Aisne-Marne Defensive (Chateau Thierry)

Relief and a rest of one week at Longeville, near Bar-le-Duc, was followed by a move by rail to Bouconvillers near Chars in new Division area above Paris. Ordered to entrain at Chars on 31 May and was rushed around the east of Paris to Nanteuil where it detrained. A forced march through and past Meaux brought the battalion into line with the infantry which had come by camion on the front northwest of Chateau Thierry. Battalion headquarters was established at Coupru. Thirty-eight days of trying warfare was followed by one week's rest.

Aisne-Marne Offensive (Soissons)

On 16 Jul began the ride by camions and a forced march to Villers-Cotterets out of which came the attack of 18 Jul. Two hot days of swift action up to and beyond Vierzy on the Plateau of Soissons and the Battalion was again relieved, returning to Bergy, north of Meaux, for a ten day's rest.

Marbache Sector

From Nanteuil-le-Houdin to Nancy by rail, then ten days in a quiet Sector near Pont-a-Mousson, Battalion headquarters being at Ville-au-Val.

St. Mihiel Offensive

The period of 15 to 30 Aug was spent in Camp Bois dé l'Eveque between Toul and Nancy in replacing and training, On 1 Sep the Battalion moved by two easy marches to position in woods south of Limey. On the 12th to 14th it took part in the St. Mihiel action aiding in the capture of Thiaucourt and Jaulny. After relief returned through Limey and marched back to barracks at Toul.

Meuse-Argonne Offensive (Champagne)

On 21 Sep moved by train from Toul to Sogny-aux-Moulins. After a week at this town the Battalion marched to Somme-Suippes and went into the action of 1 to 10 Oct at Somme-Py and Blanc Mont, an action which caused the Battalion the heaviest losses it had yet suffered. From 15 to 24 October a much-needed rest was given the Battalion.

Meuse-Argonne Offensive

On 24 Oct began a three day march ending with Battalion headquarters established at Cbaudron Farm. On 1 Nov began the successful attack through Landres-et-St. George, Bayonville, Nouart and Beaumont, which ended finally with the crossing of the Meuse on the last day of the war.

March to the Rhine

On 17 Nov marked the beginning of the march to the Rhine through Stenay and Montmedy, France, and Vitron and Arlon, Belgium. The last week of November was spent at Haller, Luxembourg. On 1 Dec the Battalion crossed the border into Germany marching north and northeast by way of the Ahr River Valley, coming out upon the Rhine at Sinzig. The Rhine was crossed at Remagen on 13 Dec. Present station, Weitersburg, Germany, was reached 16 Dec 18.

Fourth Marine Brigade: Time and Place of Organization

23 October 1917, Bourmont, France.

Subdivisions

Fifth Marines, Sixth Marines, Sixth Machine Gun Battalion.

Names of Commanding Officers

Brig. Gen. Charles A. Doyen, 23 Oct 17 to 6 May 18.

Brig. Gen. James G. Harbord, N.A., 6 May 18 to 15 Jul 18.

Col. Harry Lee, 15 Jul 18 to 25 Jul 18.

Brig. Gen. John A. Lejeune, 25 Jul 18 to 28 Jul 18.

Brig. Gen. Wendell C. Neville, 28 Jul 18 to present date.

The Brigade was under instruction of the French in the Bourmont training area with Brigade headquarters located at Damblain, remaining there until 14 Mar when it commenced movement into subsectors of the Verdun Front, the first units of the Brigade entering the front line during the night of 16/17 Mar. At, that time Colonel Wendell C. Neville commanded the 5th Regiment, Colonel Albertus W. Catlin commanded the 6th Regiment and Major Edward B. Cole commanded the 6th Machine Gun Battalion. Remained on the Verdun Front until 14 May, where the Brigade proceeded to a training area around Vitry-le-Francois. In the meantime, on 6 May, Brigadier General James G. Harbord assumed command, relieving General Doyen, who had been ordered to the United States. On 19 May, Brigade left that area and proceeded to the area around Gisors and Chaumont-en-Vexin, remaining there until 31 May when the units of the Brigade moved by camions into the sector northwest of Chateau-Thierry, going into line immediately upon its arrival, 1 to 3 Jun. During operations of the Brigade, the companies of the 6th Machine Gun Battalion were usually assigned to battalions of the two regiments.

In action northwest of Chateau Thierry from 1 Jun to 7 Jul 18, during which the Brigade captured Bouresches, Bois de Belleau and Hill 142. Brigade was relieved 7 Jul and took up reserve position behind the lines just occupied until 16 Jul.

Actions Following Chateau-Thierry

South of Soissons 18 to 20 Jul.
Pont-a-Mousson 9 to 18 Aug.
St. Mihiel 13 to 15 Sep.

Champagne

Capturing Mont Blanc [sic] 1 to 9 Oct.

Argonne-Meuse

Including crossing of Meuse 1 to 11 Nov–March to Germany commenced 17 Nov 18. Crossed German frontier 1 Dec. Crossed Rhine 13 Dec. From 14 Dec 18, to date, Occupying "Rhine Sector" of Coblenz Bridgehead Area.

Fifth Regiment, Marines: Time and Place of Organization

The 5th Regiment, United States Marine Corps, was organized during the latter part of May and the first of June 1917. The Headquarters Company, Supply Company, Second and Third Battalions were organized at the Philadelphia Navy Yard and the Third Battalion at Quantico.

Subdivisions

The original company composition of the battalions was as follows: 1st Battalion — 15, 49, 66, 67. 2d Battalion — 23, 43, 51, 55. 3d Battalion — 8, 16, 45, 47. 8th Machine Gun Company.

Base Detachment (Originally for replacements): 7th Company, 17th Company, 18th Company, 20th Company

The final company composition of the battalions was as follows: 1st Battalion — 17, 49, 66, 67. 2d Battalion — 18, 43, 51, 55. 3d Battalion — 16, 20, 45, 47. 8th Machine Gun Company.

Names of Commanding Officers

The late Brigadier General (then Col-

onel) Charles A. Doyen, from time of organization until 1 Nov 1917.
Lt. Col. Hiram I. Bearss, 1 Nov 17 to 1 Jan 18.
Col. Wendell C. Neville, 1 Jan to 17 Jul 18.
Col. Logan Feland, 17 Jul to 21 Mar 19.
Col. Harold O. Snyder, 21 Mar 19 to present date.

Date of Arrival in France

1st Battalion: 26 Jun 17 on USS *De Kalb*.
2d and 3d Battalions: 27 Jun 17 on USS *Henderson*.
Headquarters and Supply companies: 2 Jul 17 on USS *Hancock*.

Training Periods

17 July 17 to 23 Sep 17, at Menancourt and Naix, France. At this time the regiment was attached to the 1st Division.
23 Sep 17 to 13 Mar 18, at Breuvannes and Damblain.
The Third Battalion, which had been doing guard duty at St. Nazaire, rejoined the regiment on 10 Jan 18, and trained at Colombey.

Verdun Sector

Les Eparges Sector (Subsector Montgrimont) 17 Mar 18 to 27 Mar 18.
Verdun Sector, (Subsector Eix-Moulaincourt — Chatillon) 31 Mar 18 to 12 May 18.

Aisne-Marne Defensive (Chateau Thierry)

20 May to 31 May 18. Regimental Headquarters, Headquarters Company, Supply Company, 8th Machine Gun Company and 1st Battalion at Boury-en-Vexin, 2d Battalion at Coureiles, 3d Battalion at Vandancourt.
1 Jun to 5 July 18. Assisted in stopping enemy drive on Paris during first few days of June and assumed the offensive from 6 June 18, retaking two kilometers on a two-kilometer front, while in this sector.

Aisne-Marne Offensive (Soissons)

17 Jul to 21 Jul 18. Attacked near Soissons advancing 8 kilometers and capturing Chaudun.

Marbache Sector

(Subsector Pont-a-Mousson) 16 Aug 18.

St. Mihiel Offensive

12 Sep to 16 Sep 18.

Meuse-Argonne Offensive (Champagne)

1 Oct to 9 Oct 18. Took part in the capture of Mont Blanc [*sic*] and held ground gained causing the enemy to withdraw to the Aisne River.

Meuse-Argonne Offensive

1 Nov to 11 Nov 18. Attacked near Landres-et-St. George and forced bridgehead across Meuse river north of Beaumont, the night before the armistice.

March to the Rhine

17 Nov commenced march to the Rhine River passing through Belgium and Luxembourg. Crossed German frontier on 13 Dec 18, taking up front line sector on northern portion of Bridgehead, which the regiment holds at present date.

Sixth Marines: Time and Place of Organization

1 August 1917, Quantico, Va. (Hq. & Supply Cos.)

Subdivisions

The company composition of the battalions is as follows: 1st Battalion — 74,

75, 76, 95. 2d Battalion — 78, 79, 80, 96. 3d Battalion — 82, 83, 84, 97. 73d Machine Gun Co.

Names of Commanding Officers

Col. Albertus W. Catlin, 17 Aug 17 to 6 Jun 18, when wounded in Belleau Woods.

Lt. Col. Harry Lee, 6 Jun 18 to present date.

Date of Arrival in France

October 25, 1917.

Training Periods

17 Nov 17 to 15 Jan 18, provost and construction duty throughout southern France; Bourmont training area 15 Jan to 14 Mar, intensive warfare training; vicinity of Vitry-le-Frandos, 12 May 18.

Verdun Sector

The regiment moved to the Toulon Sector, a few kilometers southeast of Verdun. The regiment remained in this quiet sector two months, part of which time the regiment and, during the rest of the stay, the division held a sector of its own. The men soon became accustomed to the enemy's shell-fire and gas, and by the middle of May considered themselves veteran soldiers.

Aisne-Marne Defensive (Chateau Thierry)

From 20 to 30 May the regiment was billeted in the region north of Paris in and around the town of Serans, and on 30 May was rushed to Chateau Thierry front to help stop the Boche drive on Paris. The regiment went into positions in support of the French along a line extending from Le Thiolet through Triangle Farm, to Lucy-le-Bocage. The French were exhausted and dropped back of [the American] lines. The Boche made several attempts to drive [the Americans] back but failed. On 6 Jun Colonel Catlin was wounded and Lieut-Colonel Harry Lee assumed command of the regiment. After four weeks of almost continuous fighting this regiment was relieved by the 103d Regiment of the 26th Division on the night of 5/6 July and took up a position along the Army Reserve lines near Bezu-le-Guery.

Aisne-Marne Offensive (Soissons)

On 16 and 17 Jul the regiment moved by camions to the Villers-Cotterets forest south of Soissons. On 18 Jul Foch's great counterattack started. This regiment was in division reserve in the initial attack, but the following day took over a three regiment front and advanced the line a kilometer and a half.

Marbache Sector

Relieved 19 July, and went to the quiet Pont-a-Mousson Sector from 7 to 16 Aug, when it moved to the Colombey-le-Belles area for training.

St Mihiel Offensive

On 2 Sep the regiment started a series of night marches which took it up to the jump-off positions for the St. Mihiel offensive. The attack started at 0500, 12 Sep. This regiment was in support of the 23d Infantry. The troops jumped off from the trenches around Limey and advanced over ten kilometers, taking Thiaucourt and the heights beyond, capturing many prisoners, machine guns and cannon. On the following night the regiment relieved the 23d Infantry and advanced to the Army Line, which it held until relieved on the night of 15/16 Sep, by the 310th Regiment, 78th Division. Upon being relieved the regiment marched to the Foung area, remained there until 27 Sep, then moved by train to towns southeast of Chalons-sur-Marne.

Meuse-Argonne Offensive (Champagne)

Moved into trenches north of

Somme-Py night of 1/2 Oct. Advanced lines 2 Oct preparatory to attack on Blanc Mont. Attacked on 3 Oct, capturing Blanc Mont. Remained in line until night of 9/10 Oct. Fighting was very heavy in this period. Upon relief marched to Chalons area.

Meuse-Argonne Offensive

On 27 Oct the Division was transferred to the First American Army, which was fighting in the Argonne Forest. On the night of 31 Oct this regiment relieved a regiment of the 42d Division in the front line near Sommerance. The attack started at 0530 on the morning of 1 Nov and was entirely successful. The enemy's line was broken, five towns were taken and many prisoners, machine guns and cannon were captured. On the night of 2 Nov, the 3d Brigade passed through the 4th Brigade and continued the advance to the Meuse. On the morning of 11 Nov, when hostilities ceased, this regiment was in support of the 23d Infantry in the Bois-du-Fond d'Almon on the west bank of the Meuse.

March to the Rhine

Beginning 17 Nov, as part of Column No. 2, 2d Division, took up a twenty-three day march through Belgium, Luxembourg and part of Germany to the Rhine. The route of march was as follows: Puilly — La Forte — Ailon — Useldingen — Speldorf — Waxweiler — Prum — Hillpsheim — Schuld — Abriveiler — Sinzig — Brohl. Crossed the Rhine 13 Dec and three days later took over the left subsector of the Coblenz Bridgehead with regimental headquarters at Leutesdorf and battalions in Honnigen, Rheinbrohl and Leutesdorf. Work was immediately started on the defense of the sector.

Sixth Machine Gun Battalion: Time and Place of Organization

27 August 1917, Quantico, Va., at that time called First Machine Gun Battalion, name being changed upon its arrival in France.

Subdivisions

15th, 23d, 77th, 81st Companies.

Names of Commanding Officers

Maj. Edward B. Cole, until mortally wounded in Belleau Woods, 10 Jun 18.
Capt. Harlan E. Major 10 Jun to 12 Jun 18.
Capt. George H. Osterhout 12 Jun to 20 Jun 18.
Maj. Littleton W.T. Waller, Jr., 20 Jun to 24 Oct 18.
Maj. Matthew H. Kingman 25 Oct 18 to present date.

Training Periods

Battalion disembarked on 31 Dec 17 and entrained for the Bourmont Training Area, arriving at Damblain, Vosges, 3 Jan 18; detrained and took station in Germainvillers, Chaumont-Ville, and Breuvanues. Remained in the Bourmont Training Area until 16 Mar 18, when the battalion moved to a new area.

Verdun Sector

Served in the front line trenches in the Verdun Sector supporting the infantry battalions from 17 Mar to 14 May,

Aisne-Marne Defensive (Chateau Thierry)

Served in the sector northwest of Chateau Thierry and participated in a series of pitched battles with the enemy from 1 Jun to 6 Jul 18.

Aisne-Marne Offensive (Soissons)

Participated in the great Marne offensive of 18 to 20 Jul, near Soissons.

Marbache Sector

Served in the front line trenches at Pont-a-Mousson from 6 Aug to 17 Aug 18.

St. Mihiel Offensive

Participated in the St. Mihiel drive, 12 to 16 Sep 18.

Meuse-Argonne Offensive (Champagne)

Participated in the Champagne offensive and the storming of Blanc Mont Ridge and the capture of the town of St. Étienne from 1 to 10 Oct. Accompanied the Fourth Brigade of Marines on its second trip into the Champagne sector to relieve the 73d French Division in the front line above Leffincourt. The day after arrival at Leffincourt the orders to relieve the French were revoked, and orders issued to rejoin the 2d Division, this from 20 to 23 Oct 18.

Meuse-Argonne Offensive

Participated in the Argonne-Meuse offensive and pursuit from 1 to 11 Nov 18.

March to the Rhine

March to the Rhine from 17 Nov to 9 Dec 18, crossing the Rhine at Remagen, Germany, on 13 Dec 18. With the Army of Occupation on outpost *eine* [one] from 14 Dec 18 to present date.

Second Field Artillery Brigade: Subdivisions

(1) 12th Field Artillery (2) 15th Field Artillery—75mm guns (3) 17th Field Artillery—155mm Howitzers (4) 2d Trench Mortar Battery.

Names of Commanding Officers

Brig. Gen. William L. Kenly, 1 Jan 18 to 1 Feb 18.
Brig. Gen. George Irwin, 1 Feb 18 to 20 Apr 18.
Col. William J. Cruikshank, 5 May to 11 May 18.
Brig. Gen. William Chamberlaine, 11 May to 27 Jun 18.
Brig. Gen. Albert J. Bewley, 27 Jun to 3 Nov 18.
Col. Dan T. Moore, 3 Nov 18 to 13 Feb 19.
Brig. Gen. Manus McCloskey, 13 Feb 19 to present date.

Date of Arrival in France

12th Field Artillery—25 Jan 18.
15th Field Artillery—27 Dec 17.
17th Field Artillery—31 Dec 17.
Second Trench Mortar Battery—10 Jan 18.

Training Periods

With French materiel at Valdahon, France, until entrainment for front, 19 Mar 18; near Chaumont-en-Vexin from 21 May–31 May 18; training and maneuvers from 22 Aug to 4 Sep, in vicinity of Toul.

Verdun Sector

Sector south of Verdun from 24 Mar to 12 May 18, with 33d and 52d French Divisions.

Aisne-Marne Defensive (Chateau Thierry)

Entrainment and forced marches to Cocherel, arriving 1 Jun 18, and took position in line northwest of Chateau Thierry on 3/4 Jun. From 3 Jun to 9 Jul, continually in support of 4th Brigade in Bois de Belleau, and of Third Brigade in all preparation and final attack on Vaux. Relieved by 51st F.A. Brigade.

Aisne-Marne Offensive (Soissons)

Supported attacks of Second Division south of Soissons in the great counter-offensive of 18 Jul. Verte-Feuille Ferme, Vierzy, Tigny and Villemontoire. Remained to support the attacks of the French 32th and 85th Divisions. Relieved 25 Jul. Marched to near St. Soupplets.

Marbache Sector

Entrained 31 Jul for area South of Nancy, near Neuves-Maisons. Near Pont-a-Mousson 9 Aug to 22 Aug, relieving 64th French Division. Relieved by 157th F.A. Brigade and marched to area south of Toul, Bainville.

St. Mihiel Offensive

In line south of Limey, 10 Sep. Supported the attacks of the Second Division 12 Sep on Thiaucourt, Jaulny, Xammes. Relieved 18 Sep and marched to Pagny-sur-Meuse. Entrainment 25 Sep for area south of Chalons-sur-Marne.

Meuse-Argonne Offensive (Champagne)

Took position in line north of Suippes, near Somme-Py, 1 Oct. Supported all October attacks, which brought about the capture of Blanc Mont and St. Étienne. Supported 36th American Division 10 to 27 Oct; German retreat and [American] pursuit to Aisne 11/12 Oct. Dricourt, Vaux-Champagne and Attigny.

Meuse-Argonne Offensive

Marched 27 to 30 Oct to positions north of Exermont in the 5th Army Corps (U.S.) area. Supported infantry advance from Sommerance to Meuse, 1 to 11 Nov. Bayonville, Fosse, Nouart, Beaumont, Mouzon. Relieved 14 Nov by 152d F.A. Brigade.

March to the Rhine

Began 17 Nov furnishing mounted men and accompanying batteries for Columns 1 and 2. The mounted men acted as points for the advance guards in both columns, preceding the infantry. Route: Stenay, Montmedy (France), Virton, Arlon (Belgium), Brouch, Mersch and La Rochette (Luxembourg), through Germany starting December 1 via Mittendorf, Rittersdorf, Prum, Gerolstein, Nieder Ehr, Adenan and Ahrweiler. Across the Rhine to towns along the Eastern bank. Brigade Headquarters at Neuwid, Germany, 13 Dec 18.

Twelfth Field Artillery Regiment: Time and Place of Organization

7 June 1917, St. Asaphs, Va.

Names of Commanding Officers

Col. Manus McCloskey, 12 Jan 18 to 4 Aug 18.
Col. John R. Kelly, 5 Aug 18 to 29 Aug 18.
Lt. Col. John A. Holabird, 30 Aug 18 to 11 Nov 18.
Col. David Mc McKell, 12 Nov 18 to 10 May 19.
Lt. Col. John D. Von Holtzendorff, 10 May 19 to 4 Jun 19.
Col. David Mc McKell, 14 Jun 19 to present date.

Date of Arrival in France

31 January 1918.

Training Periods

Valdahon, under French instructors and with French materiel.

Verdun Sector

Supported different infantry units. Very little activity.

Aisne-Marne Defensive (Chateau Thierry)

After forced marches to Cocherel from Trie Chateau, north of Paris, and from Cocherel to Paris Farm, took position between Paris Farm and La Voie du Chatel on 3 Jun. Supported the Fourth Brigade, 18 to 20 Jul. Remained in line to support esches [Bouresches?] during the month of June. Relieved 10 Jul.

Aisne-Marne Offensive (Soissons)

On 15 Jul began march to Villers Cotteret Forest, traffic congestion making the march difficult. Supported all attacks of the Fourth Brigade, 18 to 20 July 18–20. Remained in line to support French attacks until 25 Jul. Entrained for Nancy area 31 July.

Marbache Sector

In line here 7 to 21 Aug, during which time there was very little activity. Relieved 21/22 Aug by 320th Field Artillery. Marched to Xeuilly 23 Aug, and remained there in training until 3 Sep.

St. Mihiel Offensive

Went into position behind Limey on 11 Sep. First Battalion fired rolling barrage for attack 12 Sep, the Second Battalion following the infantry advance. Positions in rear of Thiaucourt occupied evening of 12 Sep. Remained in support of infantry until relieved by 14th F.A. 17 Sep. Marched to St. Germain-sur-Meuse.

Meuse-Argonne Offensive (Champagne)

Moved to Suippes 25 to 28 Sep, by train and foot. Took positions near Somme-Py night 1/2 Oct. Supported advance of infantry on 3 Oct, when Blanc Mont was captured, then moved behind the ridge to support, attack on St. Étienne-a-Arnes. Supported 36th Division advance to the Aisne 11 to 27 Oct.

Meuse Argonne

Completed march 30 Oct and got in position to support the attack of 1 Nov. Moved forward with infantry each day and supported infantry in crossing of the Meuse, night of 10/11 Nov. Very severe campaign because of bad weather and poor roads.

March to the Rhine

Started march 17 Nov passing through Etalle and Arlon (Belgium), Ermsdorf (Luxembourg), Waxweiler, Prum and Neuenahr, Germany. Final billets, Honningen and Rheinbrohl am Rhein, reached 13 Dec 18.

Fifteenth Field Artillery: Time and Place of Organization

Syracuse, N.Y. 1 June 1917

Commanding Officers

Lt. Col. Thomas E. Merrill, 1 Jun 1917 to 5 May 1918.
Col. Joseph R. Davis, 5 May 18 to 1 Apr 19.
Maj. E.J. Maloy, 1 Apr to 14 Apr 19.
Maj. E. LaRue, 14 Apr to 6 May 19.
Lt. Col. H. Templeton, 19 May to 4 Jun 19.
Col. Joseph R. Davis, 4 Jun 19 to present date.

Date of Arrival in France

27 December 1917.

Training Periods

Equipped with French materiel at Valdahon, France, and trained for two months under French instructors, 30 Dec 17 to 18 Mar 18. Divisional maneuvers at Dellincourt, Oise, from 19 May to 31 May 18.

Verdun Sector

First Battalion in Troyon subsector,

supporting Ninth Infantry. Second Battalion in Rupt subsector, supporting Twenty-third Infantry. Considerable counter preparation fire executed until 10 May.

Aisne Marne Defensive (Chateau Thierry)

Supported attacks of Fifth and Sixth Marines on Bois de Belleau, 6 to 25 Jun. Supported Third Brigade attack on Vaux 1 Jul, firing 6,000 rounds of mustard gas as preliminary preparation. Averaged 3,000 rounds daily during this period. Relieved by a regiment of the Twenty-sixth American Division, 9 Jul.

Aisne Marne Offensive (Soissons)

Assembled in Villers Cotteret Forest for Soissons attack. Fired rolling barrage and advanced in close support of infantry during initial attack of 18 Jul, firing constantly day and night until the morning of 20 Jul, when the division was relieved. Remained in line to support attacks of the French, 20 to 25 Jul.

Marbache Sector

Pont-a-Mousson subsector from 5 to 23 Aug. Very quiet.

St Mihiel Offensive

From position just east of Limey, First Battalion fired rolling barrage, while Second Battalion crossed No Man's Land behind the attacking infantry. After attack had progressed both battalions took up position behind Thiaucourt, 12 Sep 18. Relieved 16/17 Sep.

Meuse Argonne Offensive (Champagne)

Went into position behind Somme-Py 2 Oct. On 3 Oct, fired rolling barrage and advanced to positions north of Somme-Py and two kilometers southeast of Medeah Farm. From 4 to 10 Oct engaged in considerable firing of barrages, zone and harassing fire, and heavy shelling of large German depots and railhead in vicinity of Machault. Regiment supported 36th American Division after relief of 2d Division infantry. Followed advance of 36th Division through Vaux-Champagne, Chufilley, Coulonunes et Marqueny, and Maebault to Aisne River. Relieved, 27/28 Oct.

Argonne Meuse Offensive

Fired many barrages and kept pace with the rapid advance of the infantry 1 to 11 Nov. Occupied various positions near Landres-et-St. George, Landreville, Bayonville, Nouart, Fosse, La Forge Farm, Beaumont and Yoncq. From Yoncq positions fired 7,000 rounds to cover Fourth Brigade crossing of the Meuse, night 10/11 Nov.

March to the Rhine

Marched via Beaumont, Stenay, Montmedy, Virton, Chenois, Christach, Waltbillig, crossing German border 1 Dec. Passed through Eifel and Rhine Province via Neunahr. Crossed Rhine at Remagen 13 Dec, going into permanent billets in Wollendorf-Fahr area.

Seventeenth Field Artillery Regiment: Time and Place of Organization

Camp Robinson, Wisconsin, 11 May 1917.

Names of Commanding Officers

Col. Albert J. Bowley, 17 Jun 17 to 26 Jun 18.

Col. John R. Kelly, 26 Jun 18 to 2 Aug 18.

Lt. Col. Leonard O. Sparks, 2 Aug 18 to 31 Oct 18.

Col. Robert H. Dunlap, U.S.M.C., 31 Oct 18 to 8 Jan 19.

Col. E.R. Warner McCabe, 8 Jan 19 to present date.

Date of Arrival in France
31 December 1917.

Training Periods
Valdahon, France, under French instructors. Work on 155 Howitzers from 3 Jan to 18 Mar 18. Divisional maneuvers near Chambers 27 May 18.

Verdun Sector
Quiet sector near Rupt chosen for regiment's first sector. Batteries went into position 25 Mar, and commenced practice in fire for destruction, harassing fire, counter-battery fire, counter-offensive preparation, and raids.

Aisne-Marne Defensive (Chateau Thierry)
Regiment entrained for Chateau Thierry salient 31 May. Batteries were in position and firing 4 Jun, located directly behind the Bois de Belleau. Here the regiment fired day and night for over a month, helping the infantry take Bois de Belleau, Boursches, Vaux, and Hill 204. Relieved 8 Jul, by 103d Field Artillery of 26th Division.

Aisne Marne Offensive (Soissons)
Regiment commenced march to Villers-Cotteret Forest 14 Jul. Took position and fired barrage for the attack south of Soissons on 18 Jul. Engaged here for one week, moving forward with the infantry. Relieved on 25 Jul, and marched to Plissis-Bellville to entrain for Nancy area.

Marbache Sector
Very quiet sector near Pont-a-Mousson, 6 to 21 Aug. Relieved by 319th F.A. and marched to Mereville for drill, replacements and maneuvers. Moved up 3 Sep to prepare positions for St. Mihiel attack.

St. Mihiel Offensive
Batteries in position near Limey firing according to schedule in first all American attack, 12 Sep 18. All objectives gained in 24 hours, and for a week the regiment busied itself reducing machine gun nests, firing captured guns. Relieved 19 Sep, and marched to Pagny-sur-Meuse for rest.

Meuse Argonne Offensive (Champagne)
Supported infantry in attack on Blanc Mont, 3 Oct. Until 10 Oct supported attacks of 2d Division and then supported 36th Division in pursuit of enemy to the Aisne River. Occupied positions near Vaux-Champagne and Pauvres until relieved 27/28 Oct.

Meuse Argonne Offensive
Fired barrage from positions near Exermont for general attack of 1 Nov. Followed infantry advance until 10 Nov, firing barrage for crossing of Meuse River night of 10/11 Nov. Rested and equipped for march to the Rhine.

March to the Rhine
Began march 17 Nov. Crossed German border 1 Dec, Rhine 14 Dec. Billeted in Bendorf until 5 Feb, when the regiment was motorized and moved to Fortress of Ehrenbreitstein.

Second Regiment of Engineers: Time and Place of Organization
Colonia Dublan, Mexico, 1 August 1916.

Names of Commanding Officers
Col. James P. McIndoe, 1 Jun 17 to 27 Jun 18.
Lt. Col. Carey H. Brown, 28 Jun 18 to 5 Jul 18.
Col. William A. Mitchell, 6 Jul 18 to 21 Oct 18.
Maj. John J.F. Steiner, 22 Oct 18 to 29 Oct 18.

Col. William A. Mitchell, 30 Oct 18 to 11 Nov 18.
Lt. Col. William E.R. Covell, 12 Nov 18 to 3 May 19.
Col. Stuart C. Godfrey, 4 May 19 to present date.

Date of Arrival in France

6 October 1917, via Glascow [sic], Southampton and Le Havre.

Training Period

15 Oct 17 to 1 Jan 18, in American Sector near Toul, engaged in construction work. 1 Jan to 15 Mar 18, in Bourmont training area.

Verdun Sector

Regiment occupied a section of the line continually occupied in the construction of fortifications. On 16 May, the regiment was moved by trucks to a billeting area near Bar-le-Duc. A few days later the entire division moved by rail to the rear of the Beauvais front where it was going to relieve the First Division, but on 30 May orders were received for movement by truck to the Chateau Thierry salient the following morning.

Aisne-Marne Defensive (Chateau Thierry)

On 2 Jun 18, the regiment took up a position in front of Lucy-le-Bocage near the Paris-Metz road. While in this area the regiment was employed as infantry on Hill 142, and in the Bois de Belleau.

Aisne-Marne Offensive (Soissons)

From 18 to 22 Jul the regiment was in the Soissons offensive near Vierzy, where it was again employed as infantry.

Marbache Sector

After Soissons the regiment moved to a rest area near Nancy, where it remained until 7 Aug, when it moved into the line at Pont-a-Mousson. Time in this sector was devoted to the reconstruction of field fortifications.

St. Mihiel Offensive

On 17 Aug, the regiment moved to a training area near Toul, where it remained until it moved forward for the St. Mihiel attack.

Meuse-Argonne Offensive (Champagne)

From 3 to 11 Oct the regiment was used as infantry with the 2d Division. From 11 to 28 Oct the regiment was attached to the 36th Division in the advance to the Aisne River, building roads and furnishing patrols for the 36th.

Meuse-Argonne Offensive

The last offensive, 1 to 11 Nov, the entire regiment was occupied opening roads through St. George and Landre-et-St. George, later keeping forward roads open; a light railway for artillery ammunition was also constructed; two footbridges were thrown across the Meuse River on the night of 10/11 Nov, under heavy artillery and machine gun fire. The infantry crossed over these successfully.

March to the Rhine

After the armistice the regiment marched to the Rhine, where they are billeted in the town of Engers am Rhein. A large amount of construction work in the Division area has been carried on from here.

Fourth Machine Gun Battalion: Time and Place of Organization

Organized 2 October 1917, at Gettysburg, Pa., into a four company Provisional Machine Gun Battalion. Officers and men from 4th, 7th, 58th, 60th and 61st Infantry regiments.

Names of Commanding Officers

Maj. W.E. Mills, 15 Aug 17 to 17 May 18.
Maj. Edmund L. Zane, 17 May 18 to 27 Aug 18.
Maj. Andrew D. Bruce, 27 Aug. 18 to 16 May 18.
Maj. George H. Weems, 16 May 19 to present date.

Date of Arrival in France

Sailed from Portland, Me., for England, 24 Dec 18, arriving at Liverpool, England, 7 Jan 18. Sailed for France via Southampton, Le Havre, arriving at Bourmont, France, 14 Jan.

Training Periods

Bourmont Area, reorganized into Divisional Machine Gun Battalion of two companies, 18 Jan. Bois de l'Eveque area, 15 Aug to 4 Sep 18.

Verdun Sector

In Toulon and Troyon Sectors from 15 Mar to 13 May 18.

Aisne-Marne Defensive (Chateau Thierry)

31 May to 5 Jun, as Division Reserve. 6 Jun to 9 Jul, engaging in successive attacks on north strip of woods in Bois de Belleau with Marines.

Aisne-Marne Offensive (Soissons)

18/19 Jul, attacking with assaulting battalion of 3d Brigade on Vierzy and Bois de Hortense. 30 Jul moved into billets at Fleville, via Nancy and Nanteuil.

Marbache Sector

9 to 16 Aug as Division Reserve.

St. Mihiel Offensive

12 to 16 Sep, engaging in attack, supporting 3d Brigade, 12 Sep, advancing to Thiaucourt. 15 Sep relieved and withdrawn to rest area Camp Roy Meiux-Guy. Marched to Suippes via St. Germain, 27 to 30 Sep.

Meuse Argonne Offensive (Champagne)

1 to 10 Oct, engaged in attack against Blanc Mont Ridge supporting 4th Brigade, 3 Oct. 6 to 10 Oct in front line. positions with 3d Brigade north of Medeah Farm. Relieved and withdrawn to rest area.

Meuse Argonne Offensive

1 to 11 Nov. Advancing to Bayonville, supporting 9th Infantry 1 Nov and to positions 20 meters north of Fosse, supporting 5th Marines 3 Nov. Advanced with front line 3d Brigade through La Tuillerie Farm to positions around Beaumont on the Meuse. 10/11 Nov supporting 4th Brigade in crossing Meuse.

March to the Rhine

Marched from Beaumont 18 Nov, passing through Verneuil-le-Grand, France; Septfontalne, Tuntington, Oberglaback and Nomera, Luxembourg, Kruchten, Phillipsweiler, Dierdorf, Heisdorf, Ober Ehr, Limbaugh, Dumplefeld, Oberwinter, Engers and Irlich, Germany; going into permanent billets in the latter place, 16 Dec 18.

First Field Battalion, Signal Corps: Time and Place of Organization

October 1916. Fort Bliss, Texas. Formed from Field Companies E and I, Signal Corps.

Subdivisions

Radio Company A, Wire Company B, Outpost Company Headquarters and Supply Detachment, Medical Detachment.

Names of Commanding Officers

Capt. Edwin A. Hickman, October 16 to 10 April 17.
Capt. Olney Place, 10 Apr 17 to 25 Jul 17.
Capt. George A. Wieczorek, 25 Jul 17 to 31 Aug 17.
Capt. Octave DeCarre, 31 Aug 17 to 15 Feb 18.
Capt. Clarence L. Adams, 15 Feb 18 to 20 Mar 18.
Maj. Frank K. Chapin, 29 Mar 18 to 8 Aug 18.
Capt. Thomas L. Clark, 8 Aug 18 to 2 Sep 18.
Maj. Charles Murphy, 2 Sep 18 to 15 Nov 18.
Capt. Ira G. Holcomb, 15 Nov 18 to 22 Dec 18.
Maj. Frank K. Chapin, 22 Dec 18 to 24 Dec 18.
Maj. Charles Murphy, 24 Dec 18 to present date.

Date of Arrival in France

12 January 1918, Le Havre. Arrived in Liverpool, England, 7 January 1918.

Training Periods

Bourmont area 20 Jan 18 to 13 Mar 18. Bar-le-Due area, 12 May 18 to 20 May 18. Chaumont-en-Vexin, 20 May 18 to 31 May 18. Colombey-les-Belles, 18 Aug 18 to 2 Sep 18.

Toulon-Troyon Sector, Verdun, France

17 Mar 18 to 2 May 18.
Took over lines of communication from the French. Maintained radio, telegraph and telephone communications 1st, 2d, 3d and 4th platoons of Company C attached to the 9th and 23d Infantry and 5th and 6th Marines, respectively.

Aisne-Marne Defensive (Chateau Thierry)

Went by truck from Chaumont-en-Vexin to May-en-Multien. Marched to Montreuil-aux-Lions, 1 Jun 18. Established and maintained communication within the division until relieved from sector 9 Jul 18. Marched to Chamigny.

Aisne-Marne Offensive (Soissons)

Went to Villers-Cotterets Woods by truck, 17 Jul 18. Established and maintained communications under difficulties during drive until relieved 22 Jul 18. Marched to Nanteuil-le-Hadouin 25 July 18. Entrained for Nancy 31 Jul 18.

Marbache Sector

9 to 17 Aug 18. Proceeded by truck to Marbache, 9 Aug 18. Communication established. Relieved 17 Aug 18. Proceeded by truck train to Colombey-les-Belles.

St. Mihiel Offensive

Marched from Colombey-les-Belles to Ferme d'Allemand. Proceeded by trucks to Bois dit de Rayes 10 Sep 18. Communication established in trench sector, vicinity of Limey. 12 to 16 Sep 18, radio, and telephone communication established and maintained during attacks. Marched to Toul 21 Sep. Entrained for Mairy-sur-Marne 25 Sep.

Argonne-Meuse Offensive (Champagne)

Went by trucks to Suippes, 29 Sep. Marched to Souain 1 Oct. Communication established and maintained on Axis of Liaison during attack, 2 to 10 Oct. Marched to Camp Montpellier 10 Oct. Marched to Ferme de Vadenay 14 Oct. Marched to Herpont 23 Oct.

Argonne-Meuse Offensive

Went by trucks from Herpont, to Les Islettes 25 Oct. To Exermont 27 Oct. Took over lines of communication from 42d Division. 1 Nov communication along Axis of Liaison extended to Landres St. Georges. 2 Nov to Bayonville. 3

Nov to Fosse. From Fosse to banks of Meuse and on night of 10/11 Nov to east bank of Meuse.

March to the Rhine

Left Fosse 17 Nov, marched through France, Belgium, Luxembourg and Rhine Provinces arriving at Neuwied, Germany, 13 Dec 18. Radio, telephone and telegraph communication within the Division established and maintained to date. Training of troops. Reviewed by General Pershing 14 March 19.

Second Supply Train: Time and Place of Organization

1 October 1917, Fort Sam Houston, Texas.

Names of Commanding Officers

Maj. William F. Herringshaw, Cav., 13 Oct 17 to 21 Aug 18.
Maj. Henry N. Manney, Jr., USMC, 21Aug 18 to 3 Apr 19.
Capt. Daniel J. Canty, 3 Apr to 11 Apr 19.
Capt. Gordon H. Steele, 11 Apr 19 to present date.

Date of Arrival in France

29 January 1918, via Liverpool and Winchester, England.

Training Periods

Bourmont area, 14 Feb to 15 Mar 18. Robert Espagne area 15 to 20 May 18. Chaumont-en-Vexin area, 22 to 30 May 1918.

Verdun Sector

Train arrived in this sector on 19 Mar, billeting in St. Andre and Osches. Private Montague S. Hersley, Company A, was killed in a truck accident, being the first casualty in the Train.

Aisne-Marne Defensive (Chateau Thierry)

The Train reached Meaux on 31 May and camped on the edge of this town until 22 Jun when it moved to La Ferte-sous-Jeuarre for the rest of the action.

Aisne-Marne Offensive (Soissons)

During this action the Train encamped in Rouvilla near Crepy-en-Valois from 16 Jul until 21 Jul, when it moved to Brassoir Farm near Pierrefonds. Returned to Rouville 23 Jul. The Train was cited in orders for work in this and the preceding action.

Marbache Sector

The Train was moved to Belleville on 6 Aug, remaining there until 16 Aug.

St. Mihiel Offensive

During this action the Train was encamped south of Toul from 2 Sep to 15 Sep, in the Bois-de-Minorville to 6 Sep in the Bois Andilly until 10 Sep, and in Francheville, until 21 Sep, when it returned to the Toul camp.

Meuse-Argonne Offensive (Champagne)

On 21 Sep, the Train reached l'Epine, moved to Suippes on 4 Oct, and to La Cheppe on 14 Oct. Companies C and F remained in with the 36th Division until 27 Oct.

Meuse-Argonne Offensive

The Train moved to Les Islettes on 24 Oct, and from there to a ridge northeast of Charpentry on 28 Oct. The next move was to a camp north of Very on 31 Oct, and on 7 Nov the Train occupied Landres-et-St. George.

March to the Rhine

On the march to the Rhine the Train passed through Stenay, Longwy, Mersch,

Reisdorf, Nattenheim, Gerolstein, Adenau and Heimersheim, arriving at their final destination Heddesdorf, on 14 Dec.

Second Ammunition Train: Time and Place of Organization

11 October 1917, Chickamauga Park, Ga.

Names of Commanding Officers

Col. Herman A. Sievert, Cav., 11 Oct 17 to 14 Apr 18.
Maj. John C. Fairfax, Inf., 14 Apr 18 to 13 Jun 18.
Col. W.H. Munroe, CAC, 13 Jun 18 to 19 Aug 18.
Col. Richard P. Rifenberick, Jr., Inf., 19 Aug 18 to 5 Feb 19.
Lt. Col. Sparks, 5 Feb 19 to 10 Feb 19.
Maj. L.B. Clapham, Inf., 11 Feb 19 to 19 May 19.
Lt. Col. A.D. Brace, Inf., 19 May 19 to present date.

Date of Arrival in France

30 January 1918, via Liverpool, Winchester and Southampton.

Training Periods

Bourmont area, 2 Feb to 17 Mar 18

Verdun Sector

On 17 Mar, the Train traveled by rail to the Verdun Sector, where training was continued until 13 May. The Horsed Battalion drew its animals and some rolling stock and training was carried on with this equipment. On 13 May, the Train moved overland to the Vaulere district.

Aisne-Marne Defensive (Chateau Thierry)

From 1 Jun to 9 Jul the Train was engaged in the delivery, of ammunition in the Chateau Thierry sector. The Horsed Battalion was camped at Caumont, and the Motor Battalion on the Paris-Metz road.

Aisne-Marne Offensive (Soissons)

On 9 Jul, the Train moved, by marching, to Changis, where it remained until 14 Jul. On 14 Jul it moved to the Soissons district where, from 17 to 25 Jul, it was engaged in carrying wounded and rations, and the delivery of ammunition.

Marbache Sector

The Train remained in rest until 30 Jul when it moved to the Pont-a-Mousson sector. There it was comparatively quiet and the time was spent in cleaning and repairing equipment.

St. Mihiel Offensive

On 4 Sep the Train moved overland to the St. Mihiel front where, from 11 to 21 Sep, it was engaged in delivering rations and ammunition to the front, and carrying wounded to the rear.

Meuse-Argonne Offensive (Champagne)

Moved to the Champagne Front on 27 Sep. Served 2d Division in attack 2 to 10 Oct. 11 to 27 Oct, served 2d Division artillery and 36th Division in the advance to the Aisne.

Meuse-Argonne Offensive

1 to 11 Nov, the Train delivered ammunition to all units of the 2d Division, working under very difficult conditions. The Train was at Fosse when hostilities stopped.

March to the Rhine

Started march 17 Nov, arriving at Beudorf, Germany, on 14 Dec. Moved to permanent billets at Nieder-Bieber on 16 Dec 18.

Second Sanitary Train: Time and Place of Organization

The units composing Train were organized individually 2 Jul to 19 Oct 1917, at Forts Harrison, Riley and Oglethorpe, with following exceptions:
Headquarters on 10 Aug 18, Millery, France.
Medical Supply Unit on 12 May 18, Buerey, France.

Subdivisions

Headquarters.
Field Hospital Section: Headquarters, First, Fifteenth, Sixteenth and Twenty-third Field Hospitals.
Ambulance Section: Headquarters, First, Fifteenth, Sixteenth, and Twenty-third Ambulance Companies.
Medical Supply Unit.

Commanding Officers

Lt. Col. Edgar W. Miller, M.C., Train Commander.
Lt. Col. Henry A. Ingalls, M.C., Director, Field Hospitals, 2 Oct 17 to 2 Dec 18.
Lt. Com. Leslie L. Pratt, M.C., U.S. Navy, 2 to 31 Dec 18.
Maj. Edgar W. Miller, M.C., Director, Ambulance Cos. 22 Nov 17 to 10 Aug 18.
Capt. W.C. Meacham, M.C., 10 Aug. 18 to 31 Dec 18.
1st Lt. A.C. Spencer, S.C., Medical Supply Unit.

Dates of Arrival in France

20/21 Dec 1917. Some units 5 Feb 1917.

Training Periods

Bourmont area, 25 Dec 17 to 15 Mar 18.

Sectors and Offensives

Verdun Sector. 16 Mar to 16 May 16 18.
Aisne-Marne Defensive (Chateau Thierry). 1 Jun to 12 Jul 18.
Aisne-Marne Offensive (Soissons). 15 Jul to 25 Jul 18.
Marbache Sector. 5 to 17 Aug 18.
St. Mihiel Offensive. 12 to 16 Sep 18.
Meuse-Argonne Offensive (Champagne). 2 to 22 Oct 18.
Meuse Argonne Offensive. 1 to 11 Nov 18.

At all of these fronts the Train performed the usual service. The Field Hospitals operated sorting stations, hospitals for the gassed and sick, and a surgical hospital for the seriously wounded. The ambulance companies operated stations for slightly wounded, and dressing stations, besides their ambulance and litterbearer service.

March to the Rhine

Field hospitals alternately operated hospitals for sick, injured, and foot-sore, while on the march. Final destination, Engers am Rhein was reached on 15 Dec 18.

Second Engineer Train: Time and Place of Organization

29 August 1917, Washington, D.C.

Names of Commanding Officers

1st Lt. Frank I. Bowler, 29 Aug 17 to 15 Aug 18.
1st Lt. Eric W. Luster, 15 Aug 18 to 22 Apr 19.
1st Lt. H.S. Barrons, 27 Apr 19 to present date.

Date of Arrival in France

10 November 1917.

Training Periods

Rosieves-sur-Mouzon, 3 Jan to 15 Mar 18. Bois de l'Eveque, 15 Aug to 3 Sep 18.

Verdun Sector

Stationed at Ancemout.

Aisne-Marne Defensive (Chateau Thierry)

Supplied front line troops with engineer tools during the period 2 Jun to 10 Jul 18 in the Chateau Thierry sector.

Aisne-Marne Offensive (Soissons)

On 16 Jul the Train left its station on the Marne to take part in the 18 Jul counter-offensive. Relieved on the night of 19 Jul and moved to Prigny, near Meaux, for rest.

Marbache Sector

On 30 Jul the Train entrained for Nancy. Billeted at Frouard for four days and then moved to the woods, between Dieulouard and Belleville.

St. Mihiel Offensive

Delivered picks, wire cutters, and shovels to the attacking troops on 11 Sep and when the attack started followed the infantry forward, reaching the Bois de Four on 13 Sep. Relieved on 15 Sep and the Train moved back to Toul.

Meuse-Argonne Offensive (Champagne)

Took part in 2d Division attack near Blanc Mont Ridge 2 to 10 October. Remained in with 36th Division until latter part of October.

Meuse-Argonne Offensive

Participated in attack of 1 to 11 Nov. Established dumps at Sommerance and Exermont. Moved forward behind troops, stopping at Landreville, Buzancy and Sommauthe. Located at Beaumount when the armistice went into effect.

March to the Rhine

Passed through towns in France, Belgium, and Luxembourg, and crossed German border on 1 Dec. Reached permanent station Block Heimbach, Germany, on 20 Dec 18.

Motor Transport Corps: Time and Place of Organization

Service Park Unit No. 403, 11 December 1917, Fort Sam Houston, Texas. Service Park Unit No. 363, 15 March 1918, Camp Meigs, Washington, D.C.

Subdivisions

M. T C. Detachment, Headquarters Second Division.
S.P.U. 303. S.P.U. 363.

Names of Commanding Officers

Maj. W.C. Mahoney.
2d Lt. Leonard Vezina, S.P.U. 303.
Capt. Bert. C. Bronson, S.F.U. 363.

Dates of Arrival in France

23 January and 13 April 1918.

Training Periods

Bourmont area from 3 Feb to 16 Mar 18 (S.P.U. 303).

Verdun Sector

S.P.U. 303 served with 2d Division from 19 Mar to 15 May 18. Headquarters at St. Andre. S.P.U. 363 joined at Scrupt latter part of May.

Aisne-Marne Defensive (Chateau Thierry)

Both units served during the entire time the Division was in line here, stationed at La Ferte and Meaux.

Aisne-Marne Offensive (Solssons)

Headquarters south of Soissons 18 to 22 Jul 18.

Marbache Sector

3 to 17 Aug. The shops at this time worked approximately eighteen hours a day.

St. Mihiel Offensive

During the preparation for and execution of this drive the shops were continually moving, 9 to 16 Sep.

Meuse-Argonne Offensive (Champagne)

3 to 24 Oct, with headquarters at Suippes.

Meuse-Argonne Offensive

Exermont to Beaumont between 1 and 11 Nov.

March to the Rhine

Started 21 Nov, four days after the Division. Arrived at present station, Rasselstein, Germany, on 14 Dec.

Second Mobile Ordnance Repair Shop: Time and Place of Organization

13 November 1917, Rock Island Arsenal.

Names of Commanding Officers

Capt. G.D. Sturtevant, 17 Nov 17 to 7 Feb 18.
Capt. F.T. Boyd, 7 Feb to 13 Nov 18.
1st Lt. H.C. Ewers, 13 Nov 18 to 6 May 19.
Capt. C.G. Howe, 6 May 19 to present date.

Training Periods

Trained at La Valdahon, France, with 2d F.A. Brigade, 10 Jan to 15 Mar 18. Some training in machine gun school at Langres.

Date of Arrival in France

27 December 1917.

Accomplishments

The MORS was at all fronts with the Division, busily engaged in the repair of all ordnance. The following is a partial list of the work accomplished while on the active front.

	(Destroyed and Replaced)		
		Enemy	
	Repaired	Fire	Premature
Howitzer 155mm	38	1	0
French 75mm	176	8	11
Hotchkiss Machine Gun	689	replaced	
Replaced Hotchkiss Tripods	140	41	
Chauchats	574	274	
U.S. Rifles	596	809	
Pistols	99	5	

In addition to the above work each 75mm and 155mm was overhauled and readjusted twice. After each major operation all machine guns in the Division were overhauled and new parts substituted when needed.

Besides the regular routine of duties of the shop, a large number of motor vehicles, wagons and carts were repaired. During every engagement the men volunteered to drive the cargo trucks of the organizations between the forward dressing stations and the rear so as to aid in the evacuation of the wounded. Drivers often drove nights and worked during the day.

Divisional Headquarters Troop: Time and Place of Organization

5 October 1917, Fort Ethan Allen, Vt., personnel being picked from Second U.S. Cavalry Regiment.

Names of Commanding Officers

Capt. Walter Goodwin.
Capt. A.T. Colley.
1st Lt. R.E. Symmonds.
Capt. V.E. Pritchard.
Capt. W.F. Daugherty.
Lieut. C.Q. Billyard.
Capt. L. Martin.

Date of Arrival in France

28 December 1917.

Training Periods

Beaumont area, 1 Jan 18 to 15 Mar 18, on garrison duty. Reorganization in Robert-Espagne area, 9/10 May 18.

Verdun Sector

Troop stationed in Ancemont and Somme-Dieu while the Division was in this sector. Furnished dispatch riders and orderlies for the staff.

Aisne-Marne Defensive (Chateau Thierry)

Stationed at Montreuil-aux-Lions. Engaged in guarding and escorting prisoners of war while on this front, 1 Jun to 10 Jul.

Aisne-Marne Offensive (Soissons)

Moved to Villers Cotteret Forest 16 Jul, and during the offensive furnished orderlies and guarded prisoners of war.

St. Mihiel Offensive

Moved to Francheville on 5 Sep, and on 12 Sep moved into the woods near Limey to prepare for the St. Mihiel attack. At this place did MP duty, furnished dispatch riders, and guarded prisoners of war. Arrived at Thiaucourt 14 Sep, and upon relief moved to Toul.

Meuse-Argonne Offensive (Champagne)

On 26 Sep troop left Toul by rail, arriving in the Champagne sector on 30 Sep to operate with the Fourth French Army. Performed usual duties at this front and moved to Camp Mt. Pelier on 13 Oct.

Meuse-Argonne Offensive

Moving through Herport, and Les Islettes, the troop arrived at Charpentry on 28 Oct. Moved to Exermont on 31 Oct. Troop performed the same duties in this as in all previous offensives. Stationed at Fosse when hostilities were suspended.

March to the Rhine

Accompanied Division Headquarters on the march, stopping in the same towns.

Second Military Police: Time and Place of Organization

11 October 1917, Fort Oglethorpe, Ga. Personnel selected from 8th, 11th, and 17th Cavalry regiments, and from the 51st and 56th infantry regiments.

Names of Commanding Officers

Capt. W.L. Roberts, 11 Oct 17 to 19 Aug 18.
Capt. Richard L. Pemberton, 19 Aug 18 to present date.
Provost Marshals:
Maj. H.H. Broadarst, 11 Oct 17 to 18 Jul 18.
Maj. Franklin D. Garrett, USMC, 18 Jul 18 to 30 Oct 18.
Capt. Richard L. Pemberton, 30 Oct 18 to present date.

Date of Arrival in France

30 January 1918, via Liverpool and Le Havre.

Training Period

Bourmont area. 31 Jan to 15 Mar 18.

Verdun Sector

Performed usual military police duties.

Aisne-Marne Defensive (Chateau Thierry)

Relieved from Verdun front and moved to Robert Espagne for a short rest. Moved to Beauvais Sector on 20 May. Left for Chateau Thierry front on 31 May. Stationed at Montreuil-aux Lions, 3 Jun to 10 Jul. Engaged in directing traffic and guarding roads at this front. One man killed and two wounded by shell fire.

Aisne-Marne Offensive (Soissons)

17 July the company moved by camion to the Villers Cotteret Forest. Occupied in breaking traffic congestion.

Marbache Sector

1 August the company entrained at Plissis-Belleville for Nancy, arriving 3 Aug. 9 Aug the company moved to Millery in the Pont-a-Mousson Sector.

St. Mihiel Offensive

A short rest was secured in the Colombey-les-Belles area, 17 Aug to 1 Sep. Movement to the St. Mihiel salient started on 1 Sep and on 10 Sep company headquarters opened at Manonville. Two men were killed and two wounded by enemy shell fire on 11 Sep.

Meuse-Argonne Offensive (Champagne)

After St. Mihiel the company rested in Toul for a week and then moved to the Champagne front, arriving in Suippes 30 Sep. During the Division's attack on Blanc Mont Ridge, the company regulated traffic. One man was killed and six wounded near Somme-Py.

Meuse-Argonne Offensive

For this offensive the company was strengthened by the addition of ten officers and two hundred enlisted men from the Fourth Brigade. Lieut. Fay M. Scott was killed near Fleville on 1 Nov. The company was stationed at Fosse on 11 Nov.

March to the Rhine

Detachments from the company accompanied the advance elements of the Division on the march, controlling traffic and doing guard duty. Arrived at Neuwied, Germany, on 13 Dec, occupying permanent billets in that city. Company scattered throughout the Division area at present, performing general Military Police duties.

APPENDIX C:
MAJOR AWARDS
TO 2D DIVISION PERSONNEL

The Second Division earned more decorations for valor than any other United States division in the American Expeditionary Force.

The awards shown are limited to major decorations, American and French. They are the Medal of Honor, Distinguished Service Cross and (later) Navy Cross, and the Distinguished Service Medal, and from France, the Legion of Honor, and the Medal Militaire. The latter is, as far as I can determine, France's equivalent to the Medal of Honor, and was awarded just to enlisted men and general officers. The Navy Cross was created after the end of the war and was, generally, awarded as a duplicate to the army's DSC citation, but not always. There were instances when the NC didn't follow a DSC. In the naval service, Marines and navy, the NC took precedence over the DSC. Since the entry for "NC, DSC" is almost always for one event, just one event has been listed.

There were also numerous awards made by foreign nations, members of the alliance in the war, to American soldiers, sailors, and Marines. Those nations include Belgium, Italy, Portugal, and Montenegro. The actual status of each award is not known, compared to French awards; therefore they have not been included.

Another American award, created during the war and issued for acts that didn't quite meet the standard for the DSC, was the Silver Star citation. A citation was awarded either by a division or by the AEF. It was later, following the end of the war, when ribbons were issued, worn on the citations like later battle stars. Some men were awarded several Silver Star citations, even five or six. However, in 1933 a medal, the Silver Star medal, was created and in every case one medal was awarded, no matter how many stars, to each recipient. However, at the time of the war, it was not a medal, nor considered a major award. Therefore, none are included in this list. Additionally, if they had been included, the total would be in the thousands. Every member of the Second Division deserved at least one, but the shame is that not all got them.

Secondarily, many persons receiving "major" awards also were awarded one or more Silver Star citations, usually for the same act. They, according to the act creating the medal, were not entitled to a medal. Consequently, it would be very difficult to discern which men later received the medal. There were numerous instances when the Silver Star was awarded when an obvious DSC, or even a later NC, should have been their reward. An eminent example was when Pvt. Henry P. Lenert of the 16th Company, 3/5, brought in (some say) nearly one hundred captured German officers and soldiers and his reward was a Silver Star citation.[1] He got even, though; he was rewarded with a journey to parade in Paris on the 4th of July. Lenert managed to stay in Gay Paree for several weeks before turning himself in.

The individual listings are by name (last, rank, first and middle initial) then the award then the location in brackets. The latter are abbreviated to "TT" for Toul-Toulon; "BW" for Belleau Wood, including Vaux or anyplace in the vicinity; "SO" for Soissons; "SM" for St. Mihiel; "BM" for Blanc Mont; and "MA" for Meuse-Argonne. The number of awards for each is an example of the severity of each engagement. The division served in the Toul-Toulon (Verdun area) for about two months, at Chateau Thierry (Belleau Wood) for one month, at Soissons for two days, at St. Mihiel for about two/three days, at Blanc Mont for at most seven days, and at the Meuse-Argonne for eleven days.

2d Div Hdqs
Albright, Lt. Col. Owen S.   DSM
Beebe, Lt. Col. Royden E.   DSM
Bridges, Col. Charles H.   DSM, LH
Brown, Brig. Gen. Preston   DSM, LH
Bundy, Maj. Gen. Omar   LH
Cole, Maj. Edwin B. USMC   LH
Conger, Col. Arthur L.   DSM
Derby, Lt. Col. Richard, MC   DSM, LH
Hayes, Maj. James H.   DSM
Herbst, Col. George A.   DSM
Keyser, Lt. Col. Ralph S. USMC   DSM, LH [BM]
Lay, Lt. Col. Harry B. USMC   NC [SM]
Lee, Lt. Col. Burton J.   DSM
Lejeune, Maj. Gen. John A. USMC A & N DSM, LH
Matthews, Lt. Col. Hugh USMC   NC, DSM, [TT]   LH [BM]
Montgomery, Col. John C.   DSM
Myers, Col. Hu B.   DSM [BM]
Nelson, Capt. Robert L. USMC   NC [SM-BM-MA]
Rhea, Col. James C.   DSM, LH [BM]
Robinson, Capt. Fielding USMC   LH

4th MG Bn
Aiello, Pvt. Antonio Aco   DSC [SO]
Beeby, Pvt. Henry H. Aco   DSC [SO]
Bruce, Maj. Andrew D.   DSC [SO] LH [BM]
Carrgeorge, Pvt. Socrates Aco   DSC [SO]
Danysch, Sgt. Steve G. Fco   DSC [SO]
DiCarlo, PFC Salvatore Bco   DSC [SO]
Hanna, Pvt. Edward G. Hqs   DSC [BM]
Harris, Sgt. Job R. Bco   DSC [BM]
Hunt, Pvt. Charles H. Hqs   DSC [BM]
Phillips, Pvt. Charles Aco   DSC [SO]
Srygley, 1st Lt. Elam F.   DSC [BM]
Wyatt, Cpl Lindon Bco   DSC [BM]

3d Brig Hdqs
Ely, MG Hanson E.   DSC [SO]
Hall, LC Charles P.   DSC [SO]

9th Infantry
Adams, Pvt. Edward Eco   DSC [BM]
Adams, 2d Lt. John O.   DSC [BM]

Allen, Pvt. William Y. Fco   DSC [BM]
Arnold, Lt. Col. Alfred C. [2] DSC [SM & BM]   LH
Baldwin, PFC Thomas Kco   DSC [SO]
Barrett, 2d Lt. Herbert W.   DSC [BM]
Bart, Pvt. Frank J. Cco   MoH, MM [BM]
Bassett, Cpl. Waldo S. Lco   DSC [SO]
Bellinger, Pvt. Edward A. Fco   DSC [BW]
Blakeman, Sgt. Chester W. Dco   DSC [MA]
Bouton, Maj. Arthur E.   DSC [SO]
Boyle, Sgt. William J. Mgco   DSC [BM]
Bradley, PFC Joseph L. Lco   DSC [BM]
Brewer, Sgt. John B. Kco   DSC [SO]
Brooks, Sgt. Floyd A. Kco   DSC [BM]
Brown, Cpl. Herbert A. Kco   DSC [SO]
Burdett, Capt. William C.   DSC [BM]
Burns, Pvt. Thomas E. Eco   DSC [SO]
Buschman, Sgt. Jerome Gco   DSC [SO]
Campbell, 2d Lt. John A.   DSC [BM]
Capezlo, Cpl. John Dco   DSC [MA]
Cappell, Capt. Marvin   DSC [BM]
Carr, Capt. Warner R.   DSC [BW]
Carrier, 1st Lt. William H.   DSC [MA]
Carter, 2d Lt. Thomas E.   DSC [MA]
Colburn, Capt. Alvin   DSC [BW]
Courtney, Pvt. Arthur M. Dco   DSC [MA]
Cowle, Sgt. James Kco   DSC [MA]
Crompton, Sgt. William H. Med DSC [BM]
Curlee, Cpl. William Fco   DSC [BM]
Denig, Maj. Robert L. USMC   NC, DSC, LH [BM]
Dogress, Pvt. Christian Aco   DSC [BM]
Dupre, Sgt. Harold J. Lco   DSC [BM]
Earle, Cpl. William J. Eco   DSC [BM]
Edwards, 2d Lt. Hugh F.   DSC [BW]
Elmer, 2d Lt. Clarence G. Bco   DSC [MA]
Emery, 1st Lt. Joseph W., Jr.   DSC [BW]
Erkenbrack, Pvt. Harry E. Fco   DSC [BM]
Estep, Pvt. Isaac Cco   DSC [MA]
Foss, Pvt. Saxon C. Fco   DSC [BM]
Fritz, Cpl. Clyde A. Kco   DSC [SO]
Gardner, Pvt. Elmer W. Gco   DSC [SO]

Garside, Pvt. Henry F., Jr. Fco   DSC [MA]
Gelairtch, Pvt. August Lco   DSC [SO]
Gjerstad, Pvt. Gustav Dco   DSC [MA]
Golightly, Sgt. Arthur C. Fco   DSC [MA]
Grundy, Pvt. John Kco   DSC [MA]
Hambrick, Sgt. Gordon A. Kco   DSC, MM [BM]
Harwood, Pvt. Frank M. Dco   DSC [BM]
Hassard, Cpl. Robert J. Eco   DSC, MM [SO]
Helliwell, 1st Lt. Harold B.   DSC [BM]
Hevenor, 1st Lt. Richard S.   LH
Houston, PFC Clyde Mco   DSC, MM [MA]
Howard, 1st Lt. William H.   DSC [SO]
Hunter, Pvt. Jones W. Gco   DSC [BW]
Hutchins, 1st Lt. Charles, Jr.   DSC [MA]
Ives, 1st Lt. Erwin B.   DSC [BM]
Jackson, Sgt. William Bco   DSC [BM]
Jankowski, Sgt. Jan Supply   DSC [BW]
Janssen, Cpl. Rolla Hq   DSC [BM]
Kacprzyki, Pvt. Bronislaw Med   DSC [SM]
Kelly, 1st Lt. Leo B.   DSC [BW]
Kilby, PFC Robert E. Kco   DSC [SM]
Kimball, 1st Lt. Walter G.   DSC [SM]
Klaesi, PFC Arnold Fco   DSC [SO]
Lashiwer, PFC Hyman Mco   DSC [SM]
Launcelot, Sgt. Marc V. Bco   DSC [BM]
Lay, Mechanic Arthur Dco   DSC [MA]
Leonard, 1st Lt. Melvin H.   DSC [SO]
Losco, PFC Patrick Hco   DSC [MA]
Macarovsky, Sgt. Herman Hco   DSC [BM]
MacNider, Capt. Hanford [2]   DSC, LH [BM & MA]
Mangiaracina, Pvt. Frank Fco   DSC [MA]
Mates, Pvt. Harry Hco   DSC, MM [BM]
Mattfeldt, 1st Lt. Clyburn O.   DSC [SM]
Mazurkevczk, Pvt. Stanley Mco   DSC [SM]

McVicker, PFC Franklin D. Aco   DSC [BW]
Mebriski, Cpl. Michael Ico   DSC [SM]
Menges, Pvt. Ben H. Hqs   DSC [BM]
Michaels, 1st Lt. Emmett C.   DSC, LH [BM & SM]
Minelga, Pvt. Frank   Eco   DSC [BM]
Mleak, Pvt. Joseph D.   Eco   MM
Morgan, Cpl. John H. Dco   DSC [BM]
Myers, 1st Lt. Charles   DSC [BW]
Norton, Pvt. Earl D.   Hco   DSC [BW]
Ofler, Sgt. George H.   Fco   DSC [BW]
O'Rourke, Pvt. John P.   Med   DSC [BM]
Osborne, Cpl. Harry   Fco   DSC [BM]
Owens, Sgt. Gilbert   Mco   DSC [BM]
Parker, 1st Lt. George E., Jr.   DSC [BM]
Parker, Pvt. John A.   Gco   DSC [BM]
Payne, PFC Earle C.   Med   DSC [BM]
Pedro, Pvt. Jerome C. Hqs   DSC [BM]
Perkaus, Sgt. Frank Supply   DSC [SO]
Peterson, Pvt. Helmer Eco   DSC [BM]
Platner, Capt. Aaron A.   DSC [BM]
Plummer, Pvt. George Lco   DSC [SO]
Robertson, 2d Lt. Archibald G.   DSC [SM]
Rockwell, Pvt. John C. Gco   DSC, MM [SO]
Rockwell, Pvt. William F. Gco   DSC [SO]
Ryan, Cpl. Oscar H.   Kco   DSC [MA]
Sanders, Cpl. Nathan P. Lco   DSC [SO] MM [BM]
Schmitz, Pvt. Charles Ico   DSC [TT]
Schkoda, Bugl Thomas Mgco   DSC [BM]
Seastrand, Pvt. Einer W.   Med   DSC [BM]
Shamanski, PFC Walter A. Hqs   DCS [BW]
Shimanoski, Pvt. Alfred Gco   DSC [SO]
Sikivica, Pvt. Pit   Dco   DSC [BM]
Simpson, Sgt. John B. Ico   DSC [SO]
Sloan, Pvt. Ozro L. Cco   DSC [SM]
Smith, Pvt. Fred E. Kco   DSC [MA]
Smith, 2d Lt. Harry S.   DSC [MA]
Smith, Sgt. Millard Kco   DSC [MA]
Smith, Cpl. Thomas J. Hco   DSC [BW]
Smith, Pvt. Warren C. Lco   MM
Smith, 1st Lt. Willard L.   DSC [MA]
Speer, Capt. Charles E.   DSC [SO]
Spencer, 1st Sgt. Gilbert A. Lco   DSC [SO]
Starkey, 1st Lt. Joseph W.   DSC, LH [BM]
Statham, PFC George B. Mgco   DSC [MA]
Steiner, Sgt. George C. Cco   DSC [BM]
Steininger, Pvt. Roy H.   Med   DSC [BM]
Stewart, Cpl. Bert L. Mco   DSC [BM]
Stone, Col. Edward R.   DSM
Tawater, Sgt. Carl Hqs   DSC [MA]
Taylor, Capt. John L.   DSC [SO]
Thompson, Pvt. Simon M. Fco   DSC [BM]
Ticknor, Cpl. Arthur J. Ico   DSC [SO]
Tierce, Pvt. William A. Dco   DSC [SM]
Toblini, Pvt. Andy Fco   DSC [BM]
Tomlinson, Mech. Raymond W. Hco   DSC [BW]
Upton, Col. Leroy S.   DSC, DSM [SO]
Van Horn, Col. Robert O.   DSM [MA]
Viera, PFC Henry Mco   DSC [SO]
Wagner, Pvt. Tony Mco   DSC [SM]
Wall, Pvt. Walter W. Eco   DSC [SO]
Waters, Cpl. Floyd E. Hqs   DSC [MA]
Weems, Capt. George H.   DSC [BW]
Wendels, Pvt. Anthonia Kco   DSC, MM [SO]
Williams, PFC Frank G. Hqs   DSC [BM]
Williams, PFC Mack H. Mco   DSC [BM]
Woods, 1st Lt. Lambert A.   DSC [BW]
Woodward, Capt. Dudley W.   DSC, LH [SO]
Worthen, Mech. William M. Mco DSC [BM]
Worthington, Capt. Henry H.   DSC [TT]
Zambryski, Pvt. Alexander Mco [2] DSC [MA]
Zeiler, Cpl. Elmer   Fco   DSC [BM]

23d Infantry

Alekno, Pvt. Frank Bco   DSC [TT]

Major Awards to 2d Division Personnel

Babst, Chaplain Julius J. [2] DSC [BW & BM]
Bay, Cpl. Roland W. Cco   DSC [BM]
Beard, PFC Edwin L. Mco   DSC [BW]
Beaudette, 1st Sgt. Joseph A. Cco   DSC [MA]
Callard, Pvt. Arthur Aco   DSC [BM]
Canavan, PFC Patrick Med   DSC [BM]
Caygill, 1st Lt. Harry W.   LH
Cole, 1st Lt. Arthur C.   DSC [MA]
Cook, Maj. Fred A.   DSC [BM]
Cullen, Pvt. Frank J. Gco   MM
DeMay, Pvt. Joseph Lco   DSC [BW]
Doyle, Cpl. John J. Cco   DSC, MM [BM]
Eaton, Capt. Starr S.   DSC [BW]
Elliott, Maj. Charles B.   DSC, LH [BW]
Farkas, Sgt. Joe F. Eco   DSC [SM]
Fechet, Maj. d'Alary   DSC, LH [SO]
Fuller, 2d Lt. Kenneth E.   DSC [SO]
Furbush, 1st Lt. George W., Jr.   DSC [BW]
Gallagher, Cpl. John G. Eco   MM
Galloway, 1st Lt. Justin P.   DSC [BW]
Genest, Mech. Paul P. Lco   DSC [BW]
Gibson, Capt. Herbert D.   DSC [BM]
Goltra, 1st Lt. Isaac V.   DSC [BW]
Gorman, Cpl. James A. Gco   DSC [BM]
Green, Capt. James G., Jr.   DSC [BW]
Griffen, 1st Lt. Martin G.   DSC [BM]
Hamilton, 1st Lt. Otho   DSC [BM]
Hansen, Cpl. Herman L. Aco   DSC [BM]
Hardy, Sgt. Leslie   Bco   DSC [BW]
Heath, Cpl. Floyd E. Cco   DSC [BM]
Heimerdinger, 2d Lt. Charles   DSC [MA]
Hildreth, Capt. Richard P.   DSC [MA]
Joe, Sgt. Colin B. Kco   DSC [MA]
Kane, Pvt. Charles J. Ico   DSC [BW]
Kibler, 1st Lt. John T.   DSC [BM]
Korgis, Sgt. Hercules L. Eco   DSC [BM]
Legassy, Pvt. Napoleon Kco   DSC [BM]
Liebsch, 1st Sgt. Otto Fco   MM
Lonadler, Pvt. Jules Lco   DSC [MA]
Longfield, Cpl. Simon E. Dco   DSC [BW]
Lotz, Cpl. John D. Mco   DSC [BM]
Luzi, Pvt. Luzius Mco   DSC [BW]
Malone, Col. Paul B.   DSC, DSM [SO]
Martin, Capt. Claude A.   DSC [BW]
Mathis, 1st Lt. John D.   DSC [BW]
Mazzoni, PFC Louis Mgc   DSC [MA]
McCarthy, Pvt. William E. Hco   DSC [BW]
McCormick, Sgt. Clark T. Lco   DSC [MA]
McGay, 2d Lt. George H.   DSC [SM]
McKenna, Cpl. Patrick Lco   DSC [BW]
McLawhon, Sadlr. Lewis B. Mgc   DSC [BW]
Menge, PFC William M. Med   DSC [BM]
Menter, Pvt. Linus H. Med   DSC [BM]
Meyering, 1st Lt. William D.   DSC [TT]
Mikos, Cpl. John J. Med   DSC [BM]
Mitchell, Capt. Clarence   DSC [MA]
Mitchell, 2d Lt. John E.   DSC [BM]
Molloy, 1st Lt. Joseph A.   DSC [SO]
Moore, Capt. Charles E.   DSC [BW]
Morningstar, Sgt. Leroy Med   DSC [BW]
Mulhall, Sgt. Henry L. Gco   DSC [BM]
O'Brien, Cpl. John R. Bco   MM
Oldynski, PFC Charles Hco   DSC [BM]
Otto, 1st Lt. Andrew C., Jr.   DSC [SO]
Patrick, Chaplain William E.   DSC [MA]
Phelan, Cpl. Edward F. Eco   DSC [SO]
Reeve, 1st Lt. Charles B.   DSC [BM]
Reynolds, Capt. William G.   DSC, LH [BM]
Richman, Pvt. Henry C. Mco   DSC [BW]
Sharp, 1st Lt. James H.   DSC [BM]
Sheeran, 1st Lt. James J.   DSC [BW]
Shepherd, Capt. Grant   DSC [BW]
Shimanowich, Pvt. Alex Lco   DSC [BW]
Shipley, Capt. George A.   DSC [MA]
Shumate, PFC John W. Mco   DSC [BW]
Siers, Pvt. Frank Mco   DSC [BW]
Sinatra, Pvt. Marion Kco   DSC [BW]

Stavrum, 1st Lt. Edwin R.   DSC [BW]
Stone, Col. Edward R.   DSC, LH [BM]
Strickland, Sgt. Albert B. Hco   DSC [SO]
Sullivan, PFC Dan W. Mgco   DSC [BW]
Swarts, 1st Lt. Ralph E.   DSC [BM]
Sybert, PFC Clarence Mco   DSC [MA]
Tarter, Sgt. Charles M. Ico   DSC [BW]
Taylor, 2d Lt. Thomas J.   DSC [MA]
Thabert, PFC William F. Kco   DSC [BM]
Thomas, Bugl. Everett Ico   DSC [BW]
Thompson, Capt. Henry L.   DSC [MA]
Turano, Pvt. John Ico   DSC [BW]
Waddill, Maj. Edmund C.   DSC [BW]
Wetherell, Cpl. Frederick Gco   MM [SO]
Whitaker, Cpl. Jesse Lco   DSC [BM]
White, 2d Lt. Donald W.   DSC [MA]
Youngdahl, Capt. Oskar E.   DSC [BM]
Zane, LC Edmund L.   DSC, LH [BM]

5th MG BN

Berry, 2d Lt. Benjamin I.   DSC [BM]
Blaknee, 1st Sgt. Faun. Bco   DSC [BM]
Cain, Sgt. James S. Cco   DSC [BM]
Chapman, Capt. Eldridge G.   DSC [SM]
Claflin, Sgt. James A. Med   DSC [SM]
Clark, Cpl. Patrick J. Cco   DSC [SM]
Henricksen, Pvt. Hans Aco   DSC [MA]
Hovatter, Pvt. Everett E. Med   DSC [BM]
Lewis, Maj. Harry T.   LH
Mazkwaz, Cpl. Louis.   DSC [BM]
Pistikoudis, Cpl. Theodore   DSC [BW]
Stevens, 2d Lt. Harry A. Cco   DSC [BM]
Swanson, Cpl. Clayton E. Aco   DSC [BM]
Vercoe, Pvt. Stanley Med   DSC [SM]
Wozniak, Pvt. Anthony Bco   DSC [BM]

4th Brig Hdqs [Marines]

Dietrich, 1st Lt. Carl   NC
Galliford, Capt. Walter T.   NC
Geary, Sgt. Maj. William J.   DSC [BW]

Harbord, MG James G., USA   A & N DSM [BW]
McNair, Chaplain James D.   NC [BW]
Seigrist, Sgt. Maj. Hobart A.   NC [BW]
Van Amburg, Cpl. Hugh C.   NC, DSC [SO]
Wilson, 1st Lt. Wilson   NC

5th Marines

Alexander, Cpl. Merl C.   NC, DSC [BW]
Auer, Cpl. Charles   NC, DSC [BW]
Baker, Sgt. Harry I.   NC, DSC [BM]
Baker, Pvt. Joseph M.   NC, DSC [BW]
Barczykowski, Pvt. Frank J.   NC [BW], NC DSC [SO]
Barnhart, Sgt. Frank A.   NC, DSC [BM]
Barron, Pvt. William L.   NC, DSC [BW]
Barrows, Pvt. Albert E.   NC, DSC [BW]
Batson, 1st Lt. Albert P.   NC, DSC [BW]
Beauchamp, Capt. Felix   NC, DSC, LH [BM]
Becker, 1st Lt. Fred H., USA   DSC [SO]
Bell, Sgt. Joe   NC, DSC [BW]
Bernier, Gy Sgt. Oliver D.   NC, DSC [BW]
Bernstein, Cpl. David   NC, DSC [BM]
Berry, Maj. Benjamin S.   NC, DSC, LH [BW]
Blake, 1st Lt. Robert   NC, DSC [BW]
Blachfield, Capt. John   NC, DSC [BW]
Bounday, Pvt. Robert   NC, DSC [BM]
Brady, Chaplain John J.   NC, DSC [BW]
Brautigan, Pvt. George F.   NC, DSC [BW]
Bridgford, Pvt. John V.   NC, DSC [MA]
Brown, Pvt. Dilmus   NC, DSC [BW]
Broxup, Pvt. John   NC, DSC [BM]
Budde, Pvt. George W.   NC, DSC [MA]
Buford, Gy Sgt. David L.   NC, DSC [BW]
Campbell, Sgt. William E.   NC, DSC [BM]

Carbary, Gy Sgt. James   NC, DSC [BW]
Carhart, 2d Lt. Joseph B.   NC, DSC [SO]
Carter, Sgt. Joe   NC, DSC [SO]
Casey, Sgt. John   NC, DSC [BW]
Christiansen, Pvt. Leroy C.   NC, DSC [BM]
Clark, Pvt. James L.   NC, DSC [BW]
Clarkston, Gy Sgt. Samuel   NC, DSC [MA]
Colvin, Pvt. David P.   NC, DSC [BW]
Cook, Gy Sgt. Walter   NC, DSC [BM]
Cooper, Pvt. Oscar M.   NC, DSC [BM]
Corbett, 1st Sgt. Murl   NC, DSC [BW]
Cornell, Capt. Percy   NC, DSC [BM]
Courtney, Sgt. James   NC, DSC [BM]
Coverdell, 2d Lt. Vern A.   NC, DSC [BM]
Crepeau, Pvt. Louis J.   NC, DSC [BW]
Cronin, Sgt. Raymond P.   NC, DSC [BW]
Crossen, Sgt. Vernon J.   NC, DSC [MA]
Crowther, 1st Lt. Orlando C.   NC, DSC [BW]
Cukela, Sgt. Louis   MoH, MM, LH [SO]
Culnan, Sgt. John H.   NC, DSC [BW]
De Carre, Capt. Alphonse   NC, DSC, LH [BW]
Devlin, Pvt. Bert W.   NC, DSC [BM]
Dockx, Cpl. Francis J.   NC, DSC [BW]
Doody, Cpl. John   NC, DSC [SO]
Dunbeck, Capt. Charley   NC, DSC [BW]
Ellis, Lt. Col. Earl H.   NC
Engel, Sgt. William F.   NC, DSC [BM]
Fay, Capt. John H.   NC, DSC [BW]
Feigle, Sgt. William M.   NC, DSC [MA]
Feland, Lt. Col. Logan   DSC, A & N DSM, LH [BW]
Ferguson, Cpl. William J.   NC, DSC [MA]
Fischer, Cpl. Robert McG.   NC, DSC [BW]
Flynn, Gy Sgt. Francis J.   NC, DSC [BW]
Fox, Sgt. Daniel R.   NC, DSC [BM]
Fox, Pvt. Wade E.   NC, DSC [BM]
Frazier, 2d Lt. Walter D.   NC, DSC [BW]
Funk, Pvt. Peter   NC, DSC [BM]
Geer, Cpl. Prentice S.   NC, DSC [BW]
Gest, Pvt. Sydney G.   DSC [BW]
Gibbons, Sgt. James J.   NC, DSC [BW]
Gilbert, Pvt. Leslie T.   NC, DSC [BM]
Gladstone, Pvt. Leo   DSC [BW]
Glendenning, 1st Lt. Henry P.   NC, DSC [BM]
Godbey, Cpl. Arnold D.   NC, DSC [BW]
Grant, 1st Sgt. John   NC, DSC [BW]
Griffen, Cpl. William L.   NC, DSC [BW]
Gustafson, Sgt. John A.   NC, DSC [BW]
Hagan, 1st Lt. John A.   DSC [BW]
Hamilton, Maj. George W.   NC, [2] DSC [BW]
Haney, Pvt. John   NC, DSC [MA]
Hansen, Cpl. William   NC, DSC [BW]
Hardiman, Pvt. Michael J.   NC, DSC [BM]
Heckman, 2d Lt. Jacob C.   NC, DSC [BW]
Hewitt, Cpl. Charles W.   NC, DSC [BW]
Higginson, 1st Sgt. William   NC, DSC [BW]
Higley, Pvt. Robert F.   NC, DSC [BW]
Hiller, Cpl. Walter S.   NC, DSC [BW]
Hirst, Pvt. Samuel C.   NC, DSC [BM]
Hoffman, Gy Sgt. Charles F.   MoH, MM [BW]
Hope, Capt. Edward B.   NC, DSC [BW]
Hopta, Cpl. Joseph L.   NC, DSC [SO] MM [MA]
Hughes, Cpl. John D.   NC, DSC [BM]
Hulbert, MarGun Henry L.   NC, DSC [BW]
Hunt, Capt. Leroy P.   NC, DSC [BM]
Hunter, 1st Sgt. Daniel A.   NC, DSC [BW]
Hurley, Pvt. Paul T.   NC, DSC [SO]
Inman, Sgt. Leon W.   NC, DSC [BM]

Israel, 2d Lt. Frederick   NC, DSC [BM]
Johnson, 2d Lt. Gillis A.   NC, DSC [BM]
Jordan, Cpl. Jack   NC, DSC [BM]
Justensen, Pvt. William A.   NC, DSC [SO]
Kanes, Sgt. Tony W.   NC, DSC, MM [MA]
Kaulsky, Pvt. Frank   NC, DSC [BM]
Keller, Sgt. Theodore   NC, DSC [MA]
Kelly, 1st Lt. Francis J., Jr.   NC, DSC [BM]
Keyser, Maj. Ralph S.   NC [BW]
Kness, Pvt. Karl F.   NC, DSC [BM]
Kocak, Sgt. Matej   A & N MoH, MM [SO]
Korman, Pvt. Frank A.   NC, DSC [BM]
Kukoski, Pvt. John   NC, DSC [BW]
Larsen, Maj. Henry L.   NC [BW]
Lee, Cpl. Will   NC, DSC [BM]
Legendre, 2d Lt. James H.   NC, DSC [BW]
Lienhard, 2d Lt. Jacob   NC, DSC [BM]
Leitner, Pvt. Aloysius   NC, DSC [BW]
Lindgren, 2d Lt. Edward E.   NC, DSC [BM]
Locke, Cpl. Karl W.   NC, DSC [BW]
Lukins, Sgt. Fred T.   NC, DSC [BW]
Luloff, Pvt. Zalme   NC, DSC [BM]
Lyng, 2d Lt. Arthur E.   NC, DSC [BM]
Lyster, Pvt. Wayne G.   NC, DSC [BM]
Mackin, PFC Elton E.   NC, DSC [BM]
Madsen, 1st Sgt. Edmund T.   MM [BW]
Markley, 1st Sgt. George   NC, DSC [BM]
Martin, Pvt. Oscar E.   DSC [BW]
Mathias, Pvt. Jean   NC, DSC [BW]
McCoy, Pvt. Charles T.   NC, DSC [BM]
McCoy, Capt. James   NC, DSC [BW]
McIntyre, Pvt. William   NC, DSC [SO]
Melcher, Cpl. Edward J.   NC, DSC [BW]
Messinger, Pvt. Elias J.   NC, DSC [SO]
Miles, 2d Lt. Thomas H.   NC, DSC [BW]
Miller, Pvt. Thomas A. O.   NC, DSC [BM]
Mincey, Cpl. George A.   NC, DSC [BW]
Montag, Cpl. Bernard W.   NC, DSC [SO]
Morse, Maj. Edmond H.   NC
Moseley, Capt. Gaines   NC, DSC [BM]
Murray, Capt. Charles I.   NC, DSC [BW]
Naegle, Pvt. Hans M.   NC, DSC [MA]
Neville, BG Wendell C.   A & N DSM, LH
Norstrand, Sgt. Maj. Carl J.   NC, DSC [BW]
O'Brien, Pvt. John F.   NC, DSC [SO]
Olds, Sgt. Arthur   NC, DSC [BM]
Otto, Cpl. William H.   NC, DSC [BW]
Park, Chaplain Albert N.   NC [BM]
Parmley, Sgt. William B.   NC, DSC [BW]
Peterson, 2d Lt. William C, USA   DSC [BW]
Pilcher, Sgt. Luther W.   NC, DSC [BW]
Pitts, Cpl. Robert C.   NC, DSC [BW]
Platt, Cpl. Chester E.   NC, DSC [BW]
Platt, 1st Lt. Jonas H.   NC, DSC [BW]
Puryear, Maj. Bennet, Jr.   NC [TT]
Rea, 2d Lt. Leonard E.   NC, DSC [BM]
Reath, Sgt. Thomas E.   NC, DSC [BW]
Regan, Cpl. Gerald V.   NC, DSC [BM]
Richmond, Cpl. Charles H.   NC, DSC [BM]
Richmond, Pvt. Clarence L.   NC, DSC [BM]
Rindeau, Gy Sgt. Arthur J.   NC, DSC [BW]
Roberts, Pvt. James H.   NC, DSC [SO]
Rockey, Capt. Keller E.   NC, DSC [BW]
Rodgers, Sgt. John W.   NC, DSC [BW]
Rodgers, Gy Sgt. Martis S.   NC, DSC [BM]
Ryan, Cpl. John E.   NC, DSC [BM]
Schiani, Pvt. Alfred   NC, DSC [BW]
Schwab, Sgt. Vincent M.   NC, DSC [BW]
Scott, Gy Sgt. Milton R.   NC, DSC [BM]
Seitz, Pvt. Lester E.   NC, DSC [BM]
Shearer, Maj. Maurice E.   NC, DSC, LH [BW]
Sherman, Sgt. Stephen G.   NC, DSC [BW]

Shepherd, Capt. Lemuel C.   NC, DSC [BW]
Showers, Pvt. William L.   NC, DSC [BM]
Sieg, Pvt. Robert E.   NC, DSC [BM]
Silverthorn, 1st Lt. Merwin H.   NC, DSC [BM]
Simpson, Pvt. Roy H.   NC, DSC [BW]
Sinclair, Pvt. Wilbert W.   NC, DSC [MA]
Slover, Cpl. Robert   NC, DSC [BM]
Smith, Pvt. John F.   NC, DSC [BM]
Somers, 2d Lt. Vernon L.   NC, DSC [BW]
Stensson, Pvt. Carl H.   NC, DSC [BM]
Stockton, 1st Lt. James R.   DSC [BM]
Strain, Cpl. Benjamin T.   NC, DSC [BW]
Sweet, Gy Sgt. Walter   NC, DSC [BW]
Synnott, 2d Lt. Joseph A.   NC, DSC [BW]
Taubert, Pvt. Albert A.   NC, DSC, MM [SO]
Tharau, Gy Sgt. Herman   NC, DSC, MM [SO]
Thayer, 1st Lt. Sydney, Jr.   NC, DSC [MA]
Thomas, 2d Lt. Fred   [2] DSC [BW & BM] NDSM [BM]
Thomason, 1st Lt. John W., Jr.   NC [SO]
Thompson, Pvt. John W.   NC, DSC [BM]
Todd, Gy Sgt. Harold   NC, DSC [BW]
Townsend, 1st Lt. George L.   NC [MA]
Turrill, LC Julius S.   NC, DSC, LH [BW]
Van Deusen, Sgt. Robert R.   NC, DSC [BM]
Vierbuchen, Sgt. William J.   NC, DSC [BW]
Vollmer, Pvt. Frank D.   NC, DSC [BM]
Walter, Pvt. Stephen M.   NC, DSC [BM]
Wass, Capt. Lester S.   NC, DSC [BW & SO]
Wear, Cpl. Eugene W.   NC, DSC [BW]
Werner, Sgt. Bernard   NC, DSC [BW]
West, Sgt. Henry B.   NC, DSC [BW]
Westergren, Pvt. Harry O.   NC, DSC [BM]
Whitehead, Capt. Frank   NC, DSC [BM]
Wilcox, 1st Lt. Ralph McM.   NC, DSC [MA]
Willmot, Gy Sgt. William H.   NC, DSC [MA]
Winchenbaugh, Cpl. Wolcott   NC, DSC [TT}
Wise, Col. Frederick M.   ADSM, LH [BW]
Wodarezyk, Gy Sgt. Michael   MM [BW]
Womack, Pvt. John H.   NC, DSC [MA]
Wood, Pvt. Dolph   NC, DSC, MM [SO]
Yarborough, 1st Lt. George H., Jr.   NC, DSC [BW]
Zinner, 2d Lt. Fred J.   NC, DSC [BM]

6th Marines

Adams, 1st Lt. James P.   NC, DSC [BM]
Alsup, Pvt. Julian W.   NC, DSC [BM]
Anderson, Pvt. Carter L.   NC, DSC [BM]
Aselton, Pvt. Ernest K.   NC, DSC [BM]
Axton, Pvt. Andrew K.   NC, DSC [BW]
Barker, Maj. Frederick A.   NC [MA]
Becker, Trpt. Vernon P.   NC [SM]
Beird, Pvt. Roy H.   NC, DSC [BM]
Belfry, Sgt. Earl   NC, DSC [BW]
Bogan, Sgt. Henry S.   DSC, NDSM [SM]
Bonneville, Pvt. Marion S.   DSC [BW]
Boone, Cpl. Raymond W.   NC, DSC [BW]
Brandon, Pvt. Clyde   NC, DSC [BM]
Broberg, Pvt. Carl   NC, DSC [BM]
Brooks, Cpl. Charles W.   NC, DSC [BW]
Brooks, Pvt. Elbert E.   NC, DSC [BW]
Burnes, Capt. John F.   NC, DSC [BW]
Carter, Pvt. James W.   NC, DSC [BW]
Cates, 1st Lt. Clifton B.   NC, [2] DSC, LH [BW]
Catlin, Col. Albertus W.   LH
Chandler, 1st Lt. Henry E.   NC, DSC [SM]

Chase, Cpl. Roy W.   NC, DSC [BW]
Chatman, Pvt. Grover M.   NC, DSC, MM [SM]
Child, Cpl. Howard J.   NC, DSC [BW]
Clark, Pvt. Chalmers   NC, DSC [BM]
Cogswell, 1st Lt. Julius C.   NC, DSC [BW]
Cone, Cpl. Ben   NC, DSC [BW]
Cook, Pvt. Howard C.   NC, DSC [SM]
Cornell, MarGun Walter R.   NC, DSC [BW]
Croll, Pvt. George H.   NC, DSC [MA]
Daly, 1st Sgt. Daniel   NC, DSC, MM [BW]
Darche, Chaplain Harris A.   NC [BW]
Dargis, Cpl. Joseph A.   NC, DSC [BW]
Dennis, 1st Lt. Clarence A.   NC, DSC [BW]
Depue, Pvt. David T.   NC, DSC [MA]
Donaghue, Sgt. Robert H.   NC, DSC [BW]
Dougherty, 1st Lt. Neil F.   NC, DSC [MA]
Duncan, Capt. Donald F.   NC, DSC [BW]
Dunlavy, Pvt. Herbert D.   NC, DSC [BW]
Eddy, 2d Lt. Henry L. USA   DSC [BW]
Eddy, 2d Lt. William A.   NC, DSC [BW]
Evans, LC Frank E.   NC [BW]
Faga, Cpl. William H.   DSC [SO] NC, DSC [MA]
Farrant, Sgt. Oliver C.   NC, DSC [SO]
Fleitz, Pvt. Morris F.   NC, DSC [BW]
Fletcher, Cpl. Harry B.   NC, DSC [BW]
Flocken, Pvt. John B.   NC, DSC [BW]
Fowler, 2d Lt. Edward C.   NC, DSC [BM]
Frank, Sgt. George P.   NC, DSC [BW]
Frye, Pvt. John G.   NC, DSC [BM]
Fuller, Capt. Edward C.   NC, BSC [BW]
Furr, Pvt. Walter E.   NC, DSC, MM [SO]
Garges, Cpl. Joseph A.   DSC [BW]
Geiger, Sgt. Frank F.   NC, DSC [MA]
Gibson, Pvt. Charles S.   NC, DSC [MA]

Gibson, Cpl. Raymond   NC, DSC [BW]
Glucksman, Pvt. Samuel   NC, DSC [BM]
Groff, Gy Sgt. John   NC, DSC [BW]
Hamlin, Cpl. Vincent R.   MM [SO]
Hanson, Cpl. Raymond W.   NC [SO]
Haws, Pvt. Edward H.   NC, DSC [BM]
Hermle, 1st Lt. Leo D.   DSC, NDSM, LH [MA]
Hill, Cpl. Fred W.   NC, DSC [BW]
Holcomb, LC Thomas   NC, LH [BW]
Houchins, Sgt. Lyle C.   NC, DSC [SM]
Huffstater, Pvt. Leon D.   NC, DSC [BW]
Hughes, LC John A.   NC [BW]
Hurley, 1st Lt. Philip H., USA   DSC [BW]
Ingalls, Cpl. John J.   NC, DSC [BW]
Johnston, 2d Lt. Scott M.   NC, DSC [SO]
Jordan, Pvt. Richard O.   NC, DSC [BM]
Kelly, Pvt. John J.   A & N MoH, MM [BM]
Kidder, 2d Lt. Hugh B.   NC, DSC [BM]
Kruezman, Pvt. William A.   NC, DSC [MA]
Lee, LC Harry   A & N DSM, LH
Lindsey, Pvt. Clinton S.   NC, DSC [BW]
Loomis, Cpl. Casey V.   NC, DSC [SM]
Lotspiech, Pvt. Orr V.   NC, DSC MM [SO]
Marlowe, Sgt. Fred M.   NC, DSC [MA]
Marshall, 2d Lt. Ralph W.   NC, DSC [BW]
McHenry, 1st Lt. John   NC [BM] DSC [SO & BM]
McKinney, Sgt. Darel J.   NC, DSC [BW]
McLeod, Pvt. Herman   NC, DSC [BW]
Meyer, Pvt. Albert   NC, DSC [SM]
Miller, Pvt. Hugh S.   NC, DSC [BW]
Mills, Pvt. Bruce H.   NC, DSC [BM]
Moore, 2d Lt. William B.   NC, DSC [BW]
Moorland, Cpl. Oscar   NC, DSC [BM]

Myers, Pvt. DeMarr E. NC, DSC [MA]
Nagazyna, Gy Sgt. John J. NC, DSC, MM [SO]
Noble, 1st Lt. Alfred H. NC, DSC [BW]
Nutting, Pvt. Lester H. NC, DSC [SM]
O'Kelley, Sgt. Grover C. NC, DSC [BW]
Overton, 2d Lt. John NC, DSC [SO]
Overton, Capt. Macon C. NC, [2] DSC [BM & MA]
Parker, Cpl. Donald M. NC, DSC [SM]
Pruitt, Cpl. John H. A & N MoH [BM]
Quick, Sgt. Maj. John H. NC, DSC [BW]
Randles, Cpl. Harold J. NC, DSC [BW]
Reeves, Cpl. Roy R. NC, DSC [BM]
Roberts, 1st Lt. Charles D. NC, DSC [BW]
Robertson, 1st Lt. James F. NC, DSC [BW]
Robinson, 2d Lt. Caldwell C. NC, DSC [BW]
Rockwell, Pvt. Mearl C. NC, DSC [SO]
Schneider, 1st Lt. John G. NC, DSC [MA]
Schreech, Cpl. George W. NC, DSC [MA]
Sellers, 1st Lt. James McB. NC, DSC [BW]
Sexton, Pvt. Fred L. NC, DSC [SO]
Sheaff, Cpl. Donald R. NC, DSC [BW]
Shepherd, Pvt. Royal H. C. NC, DSC [SO]
Shuler, Maj. George K. A & N DSM, [SM] LH [BM]
Sibley, Maj. Berton W. NC [BW]
Simmons, Pvt. Samuel S. NC, DSC, MM [BM]
Simon, Sgt. Frank J. NC, DSC [MA]
Skaggs, Cpl. William H. NC [SO]
Smiley, Pvt. Dean F. DSC, NDSM [BM]
Smith, Capt. Dwight F. NC, DSC [BW]
Sockham, Gy Sgt. Fred W. N MoH [BW]

Spaulding, Cpl. David F. NC, DSC [BW]
Stair, Pvt. Willet A. NC, DSC [SO]
Taugher, 2d Lt. Claude B. NC, DSC [MA]
Thrasher, Pvt. Dana B. NC, DSC [SO]
Tilghman, Cpl. Allen B. NC, DSC [BW]
Timmerman, 2d Lt. Louis F., Jr. NC, DSC [BW]
Timothy, 2d Lt. James S., USA DSC [BW]
Troup, Pvt. Clarence D. NC, DSC [MA]
Ulrich, Gy Sgt. William NC, DSC [SM]
Vial, Cpl. Frank A. NC, DSC [BW]
Viera, Pvt. Joe N. NC, DSC [BM]
Wallace, 1st Lt. William F. NC, DSC [BM]
West, 2d Lt. John A. NC, DSC [BM]
Wheeler, 1st Lt. Frederick C. NC, DSC [BW]
Williams, Maj. Ernest C. NC [BM]
Wilmer, Maj. Pere NC [SO]
Wollert, Cpl. Edward J. NC, DSC [SM]
Worrell, Pvt. John NC, DSC [BW]
Zane, Capt. Randolph NC, DSC [BW]

6th MG Bn

Bald, Cpl. Edward NC, DSC [BM]
Bleasdale, 1st Lt. Victor F. NC, DSC [BM]
Bower, 2d Lt. George NC, DSC [SM]
Brummett, Pvt. James R. NC, DSC [SM]
Butterfield, Cpl. Olin J. NC, DSC [BM]
Cole, Maj. Edward B. NC, DSC [BW]
Cole, Pvt. James E. NC, DSC [MA]
Crabbe, Pvt. Thomas P. NC, DSC [BM]
Dillon, Pvt. John E. NC, DSC [MA]
Fury, Sgt. William H. NC, DSC [BW]
Haefliger, Pvt. Fred NC, DSC [BM]
Hart, 1st Lt. Jack S. NC, DSC [SM]
Hoffman, Pvt. Leonard L. NC, DSC [BM]

McNulty, 1st Sgt. John   NC, DSC [BM]
Montague, Capt. Robert M.   NC, DSC [MA]
Moran, Pvt. Patrick J.   NC, DSC, MM [SM]
Multer, Pvt. Walton L.   NC, DSC [BM]
Olsen, Pvt. Joseph E.   NC, DSC [BM]
Pauley, Pvt. Willard E.   NC, DSC [BW]
Porter, Pvt. Ernest W.   NC, DSC [SM]
Pretty, Pvt. James L.   NC, DSC [BW]
Ream, Pvt. Bertram L.   NC, DSC [BW]
Slyke, Sgt. Alfred G.   NC, DSC [BM]
Spencer, Pvt. Ernest   NC, DSC [SM]
Syverson, Pvt. Grannis L.   NC, DSC [BM]
Voorhees, Pvt. George C.   NC, DSC [BM]
Waller, Maj. Littleton W.T., Jr.   NC, LH
Widdifield, 2d Lt. Cecil J.   NC, DSC [BM]
Wincenciak, Sgt. William   NC, DSC [BM]

Navy Medical Corps

Bailey, Phm3 George W.   DSC [BM]
Balch, Phm1 John M.   N MoH, DSC [SO]
Ball, Phm2 Ernest B.   NC, DSC [BM]
Barber, Phm3 Wayne   NC [BM]
Barker, Phm3 Leonard M.   NC [SO]
Barrett, Phm3 Alfred A.   NC [BM]
Bear, Hap1 Absalom F.   DSC [BM]
Bennett, Hap1 Morton L.   NC [SM]
Bird, Phm1 Francis M.   DSC [BM]
Boone, LCmd Joel T.   N MoH [SO] DSC [BW]
Bowman, Phm2 Alvin L.   NC, DSC [MA]
Bracken, Phm2 William J.   NC [BM]
Brogden, Phm3 Ronald R.   NC, DSC [SM]
Brown, Phm3 Raymor R.   NC [BM]
Brumbeloe, Phm3 Algernon T.   NC [BW]
Cochrane, Cpm Robert S.   DSC [BM]
Crosby, Cmd Paul T.   NC [BW]
Dessez, Cmd Paul T.   NC, DSC [BW]
Dickinson, Lt. Dwight, Jr.   NC, DSC [BM]
Farwell, Cmd. Wrey G.   NC, DSC [BW]
Fitzsimmons, Phm3 Frank L.   NC [MA]
Gates, CPhm Horatio D.   NC [SO]
Gill, Lt. William T., Jr.   NC, DSC SO]
Goodwin, Phm3 Oscar S.   NC [SM]
Grantham, Hap1 James H.   NC [MA]
Greer, Phm3 William B.   NC [BM]
Grimland, Lt. Gordon L.   NC [SM]
Henderson, Phm3 Ernest L.   NC [BM]
Herrman, Hap1 Bernard W.   NC [SM]
Hook, Lt. Frederick R.   NC, DSC [BM]
Hull, Hap1 Roy E.   NC [BM]
Jamison, Phm1 Roland R.   DSC [BM]
Jarvis, Cpm Harry W.   NC [SO]
Jennison, Phm2 Charles S.   NC, DSC [BM]
Johnson, Hap1 Joseph S.   NC [BW]
Kaga, Phm1 Raymond   NC [SM]
King, Lt. Ogden D.   NC, DSC [BW]
Kingsbury, Hap1 Karl O.   DSC [TT]
Kinkle, Phm3 Clyde A.   NC [SO]
Lawler, Cmd Robert J.   NC [BM]
Layton, Hap1 Lester K.   NC [SO]
Lewis, Phm2 Spencer J.   NC [BM]
Litchfield, Phm3 John R.   NC, DSC [SM]
Lyle, LCmd Alexander G.   N MoH [TT]
Mack, LCmd Cornelius H.   NC [SO]
Manning, Hap1 James E.   NC, DSC [SM]
Martin, Hap2 Hal E.   NC [BM]
McKenney, Phm2 Leroy N.   NC [SO]
Medkirk, CPhm Forest T.   NC [SO]
Messanelli, Phm2 Ray A.   DSC [BM]
Michael, LCmd William H.   NC, DSC [BW]
Moll, Phm2 Joseph J.   NC [MA]
Moring, Lt. Travis S.   NC [BM]
Muller, Phm2 Ekard   NC [BM]
Nolan, Phm3 Vincent A.   DSC [BM]
Nolte, Phm1 William V.   DSC [BM]
Osborne, Lt. Weedon E.   N MoH, DSC [BW]
Peterson, Phm3 George I.   DSC [BM
Petty, Lt. Orlando H.   N MoH, DSC [BW]

Major Awards to 2d Division Personnel

Pilkerton, Phm3 Oliver W. NC [SO]
Pratt, LCmd Lester, L. NC, DSC [BW]
Pratt, Lt. Malcolm L. NC [BW]
Raume, Phm1 John DSC [BM]
Reed, Phm2 Eugene B. DSC [BM]
Reister, Phm2 Junius E. NC [BW]
Roberts, Phm3 Harold C. NC [BW]
Rodemich, Phm3 Lorraine F. NC [SO]
Rogers, Phm2 Benjamin F. DSC [BM]
Russell, Phm2 Thomas N. NC, DSC [BM]
Shea, Lt. Richard O'B. NC, DSC [BW]
Simmer, Phm1 Tony NC [TT]
Smith, Phm1 Thomas R. NC [BM]
Stamps, Cpm Bernice B. DSC [SM]
Strott, Cpm George G. NC [BW]
Taylor, Hap1 Guss L. NC [BW]
Taylor, Phm2 Leslie R. NC [MA]
Templeton, Phm1 Percy V. NC [BM]
Thompson, Hap1 Buford G. NC [BM]
Tousic, Cphm Frank DSC [BM]
Whalen, Hap1 LaVeque L. NC [SO]
Wiley, Phm3 Harry K. NC [BM]
Witt, Phm3 George D. DSC [BM]
Yates, Phm3 Frank R. DSC [BM]

2d Art Brig Hdqs

Bowley, Brig. Gen. Albert J. DSM [BW]
Burr, Maj. William E. LH
Chamberlaine, BG William LH
McCloskey, BG Manus DSC [BW]

12th FA

Calvin, Capt. Henry L. DSC [SO]
Carton, Sgt. Charles A. DSC [BM]
Cross, Cpl. Herbert A. DSC [SM]
Edwards, Pvt. Harley S. Bco DSC [BM]
Ellest, Pvt. Monroe Eco DSC [SM]
Forsyth, PFC Matthew W., Jr. Eco DSC [SM]
Geyer, Pvt. Robert E. Eco DSC [SM]
Gillotti, Pvt. Angelo Eco DSC [SM]
Green, Sgt. Donald F. Eco DSC [SM]
Hendricks, 1st Lt. Henry N. DSC [BM]
Holabird, LC John A. DSM
Hood, Capt. Robert B. DSC [SM]

Moran, Pvt. Russell J. Eco DSC [BM]
Settle, PFC Frank J. Eco DSC [SM]

Thomas, Sgt. Carr M. Aco DSC [BW]

15th FA

Brainard, Maj. Edwin H. USMC NC [BM]
Cunningham, Capt. Oliver B. DSC [SO]
Davis, Col. Joseph R. DSM [BW] LH [BM]
Kean, 1st Lt. Robert W. DSC [SO]
Overmeyer, Cpl. George J. Hqs DSC [BW]
Van de Graff, Coleman H. DSC [SO]

17th FA

Borgardt, 2d Lt. Charles F. DSC [BW]
Dunlap, Col. Robert H. USMC NC [MA]
Hubbard, Capt. Willis W. DSC [SM]
Kelly, Col. John R. LH
McKendry, Pvt. Stewart J. Eco DSC [BW]
Reinhart, Maj. Stanley E. DSM

2d Engineers

Bartlett, Pvt. Elmer E., Jr. Cco DSC [BM]
Benjamin, 1st Lt. Ray M. DSC [BM]
Berlander, Sgt. Albert M. Dco DSC [BM]
Blust, Pvt. Paul E. Cco DSC [BM]
Boyd, Pvt. Layton A. Med DSC [BM]
Byrd, 1st Sgt. Mack C. Dco DSC [BW]
Cope, Cpl. Onal M. Cco DSC [BW]
Doogs, Pvt. John A. Cco DSC [BM]
Gallo, Sgt. Joseph Aco DSC [BW]
Garr, Cpl. Charles W. Dco DSC [BM]
Goodrich, Pvt. Louis A. Aco DSC [BW]
Gustafson, PFC Carl B. Cco DSC [BM]
Holt, Pvt. Jefferson Med DSC [BW]
Levan, Cpl. Simpson Aco DSC [BW]
Miller, 2d Lt. John C. DSC [BW]
Mitchell, Col. William A. DSM, LH
Molesberry, 1st Lt. Howard C. DSC [BW]
O'Brien, Sgt. John J. Dco DSC [BM]

Raffington, Pvt. Charles S. Med DSC [BW]
Reid, Pvt. Allison W. Aco   DSC [BM]
Sanders, Sgt. Joseph D. Dco   DSC [BW]
Sarti, Sgt. William Aco   DSC [BM]
Saunders, Cpl. Thomas D. Aco   DSC [SM]
Shepard, PFC Erwin E. Cco   DSC [BM]
Snow, Maj. William A.   DSC [BW]
Spafford, 1st Lt. James H.   DSC [BM]
Stefmel, Sgt. William J. Dco   DSC [BW]
Steiner, Maj. John J.F.   DSC [BM]
Wilkerson, Pvt. Alfred Bco   DSC [SO]

1st Signal Bn

Hart, 1st Lt. John A., USA   NC [SO]

2d Ammunition Train

Sigg, 1st Sgt. Charles F. Aco   DSC [BM]
Walters, Sgt. Arthur L. Bco   DSC [MA]

2d Sanitary Train

Pincoffs, Capt. Maurice C.   DSC [BM]

15th Ambulance Co

Harkenrider, Pvt. Louis H. USA   DSC [BW]

2d Div Hdqs

France   17
St. Mihiel   2
Blanc Mont   3

4th MG Bn

Soissons   7
Blanc Mont   6

3d Brig Hdqs

Soissons   2

9th Infantry

France   2
Toul-Toulon   2
Vaux-Belleau   17
Soissons   29
St. Mihiel   12
Blanc Mont   56
Meuse   28

23d Infantry

France   4
Toul-Toulon   2
Vaux-Belleau   34
Soissons   10
St. Mihiel   2
Blanc Mont   34
Meuse   15

5th MG Bn

France   1
Vaux-Belleau   1
St. Mihiel   4
Blanc Mont   8
Meuse   1

4th Brig Hdqs

France   3
Belleau Wood   4
Soissons   2

5th Marines

Toul-Toulon   1
Belleau Wood   61
Soissons   21
Blanc Mont   50
Meuse-Argonne   15

6th Marines

Belleau Wood   43
Soissons   15
St. Mihiel   12
Blanc Mont   25
Meuse-Argonne   12

6th MG Bn

Belleau Wood   5
St. Mihiel   5
Blanc Mont   12
Meuse-Argonne   2

Navy Medical

Toul-Toulon   3
Belleau Wood   19
Soissons   15
St. Mihiel   9

Blanc Mont 35
Meuse-Argonne 5

Totals

France 27
Toul-Toulon 8

Belleau Wood 184
Soissons 99
St. Mihiel 46
Blanc Mont 229
Meuse-Argonne 78

CHAPTER NOTES

Preface

1. George B. Clark, *Devil Dogs. Fighting Marines of World War I* (Novato, CA: Presidio Press, 1998).

Introduction

1. G.S. Viereck, ed., *As They Saw Us: Foch, Ludendorff and Other Leaders Write Our War History* (Garden City, NY: Doubleday, Doran, 1929), 35–36.
2. Ibid., 40.
3. Ibid., 112.
4. Ibid., 141. He forgot that Upton was CO of the 9th Infantry, and Malone CO of the 23d Infantry.
5. Ibid., pg 162.
6. In the recent past Russia had not stood by Serbia against Austria-Hungary in a confrontation. That was when they were getting over their 1905 defeat by Japan and suffering a revolution that same year. This time, the officials in Moscow believed that they must stand and be counted if their position of power in the Balkans was not to suffer further degradation.
7. The figures quoted totaled about a half million French casualties for the period from August through December 1914.
8. Of much greater interest to the British was the fact that Germany was building a modern super navy to protect its mercantile shipping. Almost worse, they had taken a heavy toll on British exports.
9. There were people who intimated that if the Allies lost the war, the many loans made by the House of Morgan and a few other banking firms in New York might be lost.

Chapter 1

1. This later became a separate machine gun battalion but with the addition of two more companies and support services. The regimental machine gun company would remain in place.
2. That, of course, presumed that the officers would be capable of handling more men. The end result proved that assumption would not be achievable in every situation.

Chapter 2

1. This was the first U.S. Marine officer to command a division ever, in any war.
2. The regiment had been formed, primarily, from men with experiences in Haiti and Santo Domingo.
3. Bernard McCrossen, *Diary of the Machine Gun Company, 23rd Infantry, Second Division, 1917–1919* (Vallender-Rhine: Hartmann, 1919), 32.
4. Although Col. Fritz Wise mentioned this fact in the summer the Marines had both French and British training officers on hand. According to him, "The British at that time were crazy about the bayonet. They knew it was going to win the war. The French were equally obsessed with the grenade. They knew it was going to end the war." Quoted in James Hallas, *Doughboy War* (Boulder, CO: Lynne Rienner, 2000), 53.
5. Robert Winthrop Kean, *Dear Mar-*

raine, *1917–1919*, (N.p.: Self-published, 1969), 55.

6. In actual fact, it was Captain André Laffargue, a French officer, who initially conceived the concept the Germans adapted. The French and British ignored the ideas and suffered consequently. They came around when it became obvious that they must.

7. Bearss was known affectionately for many years in both the Army and Marine Corps as "Hiking Hiram." He would later lead the 102d Infantry in some of its bloodiest battles in the war. See George B. Clark, *Hiram Iddings Bearss, U.S. Marine Corps: Biography of a World War I Hero* (Jefferson, NC: McFarland & Company, 2005).

Chapter 3

1. Toulon is a great French naval base on the southeast coast along the Mediterranean Sea. The name of the wartime sector was usually shortened to "Toul" because it wasn't far from a city of that name.

2. Located about 2½ miles below Souilly, then a rail center.

3. Bernard McCrossen, *Diary of the Machine Gun Company, 23rd Infantry, Second Division, 1917–1919* (Vallendar-Rhine: Hartmann, 1919).

4. Harry Collins, *The War Diary of Corporal Harry Collins* (Pike, NH: The Brass Hat, 1996). Found at Blanc Mont hillside on 3 October in the deceased Collins' pocket. Whoever found it sent the diary to his mother.

5. Martin Gus Gulberg, *A War Diary* (Chicago: Drake Press, 1927).

6. Robert Winthrop Kean, *Dear Marraine, 1917–1919* (N.p.: Self-published, 1969).

7. Reis-El Bara, Henry J. Stewart and Glen G. Stewart, *The 3rd Battalion 17th F.A. in 1918* (Coblenz: H.L. Scheid, c. 1919). This is very confusing. The alpha designation of E and F are the 2d battery.

8. *From Robinson to the Rhine: Battery "A" 17th Field Artillery, 1917–1918–1919* (Coblenz: Kindt & Meinardus Nachf P. Straub, c.1919). Unlike the 12th and 15th FA, the 17th had 155mm heavy artillery.

9. Moses Taylor is not in the 2d Division history, "Roll of Honor." However, he is listed in the 9th Infantry's unit history.

10. Oliver Lyman Spaulding and John Womack Wright, *The Second Division American Expeditionary Force in France, 1917–1919* (NY: Hillman, 1937) 241.

11. Warren R. Jackson, George B. Clark, eds., *His Time in Hell: A Texas Marine in France* (Novato, CA: Presidio Press, 2001).

12. Spaulding and Wright, 246.

13. Generally speaking, the company commanders were frequently former NCOs who, through years of experience, almost always took care of their own needs first. However, many others of them proved that NCOs could be superior company officers when given the opportunity. Generally they were a mixed bag, but the latter group was much more prevalent.

14. Major Robert E. Adams, CO of 1/6, was soon after transferred to the command of 3/38, 3d Division.

15. Mention of the unit being utilized could not be located; primarily it was to function in a trench environment.

16. The training and resultant attitude of the trainees is described in the chapter titled "Training."

17. Over sixty junior U.S. Army officers served in the Marine Brigade in the three earliest battles. They did their duty exceptionally well and should be remembered. For details see G.B. Clark, *A List of Officers of the 4th Marine Brigade* (Pike, NH: The Brass Hat, 1992).

18. This was the last time the 2d Division, and most of the American divisions except those serving with the British army up north, served in trenches. Pershing had rightly decided that his AEF would fight the war moving. Mistakes were made, but not as many or at so high a price as to the Allies and Germans early in the war.

19. Quoted in Spaulding and Wright, 26.

20. *Records of the Second Division (Regular)*, vol. 1, *Field Orders, 1918–1919*.

Chapter 4

1. The town of Chateau Thierry would soon be, at this period, defended by the newly arrived 7th Motorized Battalion of the 3d Division (Regulars) and some

French colonial troops. It also gave its name to the entire sector in which the one-month battle was fought between several French infantry divisions and the 2d and 3d American divisions against numerous German divisions. That battle will be forever known in American parlance as Belleau Wood, but it also included activities in and around the entire area and units other than U.S. Marines, though the latter are usually identified when that name is applied. This, unfortunately, caused much anger among U.S. Army regulars who felt ignored even though they played an invaluable part in the overall struggle.

2. The word denotes a type of French bus.

3. William A. Mitchell, *The Official History of the Second Regiment of Engineers and Second Engineer Train, United States Army, in the World War* (San Antonio: San Antonio Print Co., 1920).

4. There were also natives of Madagascar and various other people from then French Indo-China.

5. The two zones would, in reality, be reversed. Third Brigade would be where the Fourth was scheduled to be and vice versa. This would entirely change the history of the world, at least insofar as the two brigades' attitudes toward each other were concerned.

6. According to the unit history Gen. Henri J.E. Gouraud, CG, the XXI Corps had issued orders for the first arrival to take up positions from the villages of Monneaux, opposite Hill 204, now loaded with Germans, south to Bonneil, covering a good eight miles with two battalions. Gouraud expected three battalions to be on line, but that wouldn't have left any reserves.

7. Listed on contemporary maps as Bois de la Clerembauts. See Clark, *Devil Dogs*.

8. "Morris" Shearer had relieved Adams in command of 2/6 at Toul, and was temporarily in command of 1/6, while Major John "Johnny the Hard" Hughes, was away at school. Hughes would return and resume command in a week. Shearer would eventually command 3/5 to the end of this campaign.

9. Listed on contemporary maps as Bois de Champillon. See Clark, *Devil Dogs*.

10. Aulnois is quite a distance westward from the Monneaux-Bonniel line, perhaps two miles or a bit more.

11. Elliott E. Cooke, "We Can Take It" and "We Attack," *Infantry Journal* (July and August 1937). Reproduced by The Brass Hat in one volume, circa 1992.

12. Gulberg, *A War Diary*, 24.

13. Shearer was not truly on Hill 142, but a ridge in St. Martin's Wood, which was to the east of Hill 142.

14. Turrill had two of his companies diverted, the 17th and 66th, to serve with Wise's battalion.

15. Emphasis in the original.

16. The battalion would remain pretty much before Montreuil until 18 June when Zane was directed to relieve a company of the 6th MG Bn in Belleau Wood. It appears that Bundy and Brown had made the decision to preserve one of their three machine gun battalions intact.

17. I believe Harbord made a mistake and have never seen that remark emanating from anyone in the 6th Marines. Possibly it did happen but was not noted to any great extent.

18. The 3d Division's 7th Infantry would be sent into Belleau Wood to relieve the 5th and 6th Marines in mid-June. Otherwise, the 3d Division would remain pretty much along the Marne River, to the east of Chateau Thierry until their time came in mid-July. Then they clobbered a major German crossing of the Marne River.

19. First Lt. Lemuel C. Shepherd, Jr., would earn a DSC and later an NC for his heroics this day. He would become a division commander in World War II and would be USMC commandant during the Korean War.

20. Harbord and Pershing were rather close personal friends and it was primarily because of this relationship that Harbord won command of the 4th Brigade upon the relief of Charles Doyen. (My opinions are seen in note 24.)

21. The Journal of Operations gives 0500 as the time of the attack but the

French went off at 0345 and 1/5 went at the same time.

22. I believe the other officer, from the 67th Company, was 2d Lt. Thomas A. Goodwin, USA, who remained with the company until after the battle at Soissons, when he transferred to the 23rd Infantry.

23. His real name was Ernest Janson. For some reason when he enlisted he selected Charles Hoffman as his *nom de guerre*.

24. I hold Harbord primarily responsible for the losses that day. That does not exclude some of the senior Marine officers who were also relatively incapable of handling large formations of men under conditions of which they were completely ignorant and for which they were mentally unequipped. In fact, no officer of the entire AEF was fully prepared. To perhaps obtain a better concept of what happened to the Marine Brigade at Belleau Wood, a reading of this author's *Devil Dogs*, published by Presidio Press and still in print, might be helpful. Three/5 was wiped out, 1/5 and 3/6 were in shambles, and 2/6 lost most of two companies. Figuratively, Harbord and his subordinates managed, in one day, to destroy four Marine battalions of over 1,200 officers and men each.

25. George V. Gordon, *Leathernecks and Doughboys* (Pike, NH: The Brass Hat, 1996), 58–59.

26. Berry would continue to remain a Marine for many years to come.

27. That report also angered many soldiers and has since caused terrible animosity between both groups.

28. From a report written by Riffle many years later, kindly provided by his son.

29. I do not wish to contradict the colonel, but the 17th FA reported having over 1,400 rounds available that evening and the 15th at least 335 rounds per gun. There is no report available from the 12th FA until July but most likely they had available a similar number of rounds.

30. Robert Kean refers to this lack in *Dear Marraine* on page 102.

31. In checking all volumes of the 2d Division Records and the regiment's own history, I found little of substance to report on 6 June other than what is shown. Apparently Malone's 23d should also have been "resting."

32. This was later revised upward for the 4th Brigade to 31 officers and 1,056 men killed, wounded and missing, from Spaulding's 2d Division History, on page 54. the figure was revised to 1,492 total in the 1944 publication of the *2d Division Summary of Operations*, p. 23, but that was for three days, 6–9 June. However, the 7th to the 9th of June were not as active for the 4th Brigade as the 6th of June had been.

33. Arnold was quite a guy and was awarded one DSC at Blanc Mont and an oak leaf cluster for St. Mihiel. He was another enlisted man who made good.

34. *Records of the Second Division*, vol. 5.

35. *2d Summary of Operations*, 15.

36. Harbord frequently bypassed superiors to send direct orders to their subordinates.

37. *Records*, vol. 6.

38. What Harbord was saying was that the Americans lacked sufficient training and what they had received had been from those who had suffered the losses.

39. For some reason, the *2d Division Summary* goes astray on this date, showing the attack as being on 11 June, rather than the correct 10 June. It would remain incorrectly dated in those records for some time to come.

40. He reported three casualties coming across. In actuality, Hughes' orders were to have moved quite a way up into the woods to the "X-Line," which was about halfway up, but he had then barely entered the woods and was not as far in as Sibley had been. This would cause a load of confusion, death and destruction, and much unhappiness later.

41. At 0745 Hughes gave PC coordinates of "176.0–260.9," which was at the very bottom of the woods. Coordinates of the X-line were 176.0–261.7, close to a half mile difference. For some reason no one seemed to read the coordinates carefully. Division history calls it "400 yards."

42. Capt. Major would be killed in action on 15 June 1918.

43. If there was a response to this ques-

tion, this author has been unable to locate same.

44. *Records*, vol. 6.

45. My copy of the famous and rarely seen *The United States Army 2d Division Northwest of Chateau Thierry* by J.W. Thomason has handwritten entries by Harbord, Wise and Capt. William R. Mathews, complaining about the others and especially Harbord's orders to Wise. (This author's revised edition of Thomason's work was published in 2006 by McFarland & Company.) Both Marines insist that an earlier order, No. 83, directed Wise to go in at those coordinates. There is no number 83 to be found. Harbord insisted the number was "3." It appears he was correct.

46. Hughes, an eminent field officer, was greatly criticized for this period. Several Marines later wrote a less than complimentary critique of 1/6's performance at Belleau Wood. Wise, furious in his memoir, made no bones about his feelings. In fairness, Hughes was suffering greatly from gas, which would drive him out of the Corps in 1919.

47. Grand-nephew of the famous author.

48. It might be apocryphal, but Connor supposedly later apologized for his callous response. That didn't help the Marines.

49. Actually, Anderson would be basically a bystander because his regiment was taken control of by Col. Wendell Neville, who remained at his PC. Logan Feland, the man on the site, would be the actual controller.

50. This was possibly why Wise, who visited his wife in Paris in July, responded to her query, "How are the Marines?" with "There aren't any Marines left."

51. *Second Division Records*, vol. 5.

52. Malone was an 1894 West Point graduate and an honor graduate of the School of the Line and later of the Staff College. He retired a brigadier general in 1919 and earned the DSM. His son, of the same name, would follow him into the army.

53. The incoming Marines gave the men of 1/7 a verbal bad time about losing ground, which they had to retake. This they would also relay onto infantry of the 26th Division when they came in to relieve the 2d Division in July. The men of the "YD" had no idea what the Marines were getting at (personal information from this author's uncle, who was there at the time).

54. Upon Pershing's arrival in France he was assigned to be Pershing's aide. He was a direct descendent of the Marquis de Lafayette and, because of that relationship, an American citizen and a member of the American Order of the Cincinnati.

55. Wise had an altercation with Harbord, consequently he was "transferred" to the School of the Line at Langres. He would be back in July, but very briefly. See Clark, *Devil Dogs*, for details.

56. The 7th Infantry returned to the control of the 3d Division.

57. I have not been able to find the often quoted statement, "Woods now entirely U.S.M.C.," anywhere in the official records. No doubt the official document was taken by someone who was aware of its historic importance. This quotation is the closest to it that I could find.

58. Lenert was decorated and then went to Paris where he went AWOL to celebrate.

59. The book was published in 1937. The official 1944 *Summary of Operations, 2d Division,* changes those to losses of 465 killed and 2,113 wounded, a considerable difference. Total losses to the 23d were 1,466 and to the 9th they were 1,117. Losses to the 4th Brigade, same source, were 636 killed and 3,466 wounded. The 5th suffered 2,157 and the 6th, 1,945. The machine gun battalion casualties: 5th, 162 and the 6th, 196.

60. Yet German intelligence passed along the information, during the night, that an attack was expected. After that lengthy barrage it would appear that something was coming. It seemed to be common knowledge among the civilians of Chateau Thierry, who were talking about the forthcoming assault.

61. This author could locate no message confirming that the two companies ever made the connection.

62. Earlier, the great von Hindenburg essentially told an American reporter the

Chapter 5

1. Betz is located almost directly north of Meaux and about twenty miles southwest of the attack zone.
2. Commonly known among the French as the "butcher" for his wastage of men.
3. Lee was retroactively promoted to colonel effective 1 July 1918. Neville, who was slated to move up to brigade command, had taken ill following the end of the Belleau Wood campaign and was resting in a Paris hospital.
4. James G. Harbord, *Leaves from a War Diary* (NY: Dodd Mead and Company, 1925), 318–19.
5. Viereck, *As They Saw Us,* 157.
6. Cooke, "We Can Take It" and "We Attack," 22.
7. When Ely was told that Upton was in a fit of depression he told Upton to "shape up or ship out," or words to that effect. Later Ely was complimentary to Upton and for the record.
8. Extract from Johnson and Hillman, *Soissons 1918,* 64.
9. The original article appeared in several 1937 issues of the venerable *Infantry Journal.*
10. Kean, *Dear Marraine,* 148. There is no mention of the unit or name.
11. He was killed in action at Blanc Mont on that most disastrous date, 4 October 1918.
12. They were Sgt. Jerome Buschman and privates John Rockwell, William F. Rockwell, Alfred Shimanoski, and Watzlaw Viniarsky. All earned a DSC for their courage.
13. The latter portion of the quote was not within Turrill's operation report, but taken from material provided by a 1/5 runner, PFC Elton E. Mackin, who was standing nearby. Other reports, like Cooke's memoir, gave the dialog as much lower keyed, but essentially the same.
14. Keyser had less than 120 officers and men, about 10 percent, left. First Lt. Samuel C. Cummings said he heard later that there was but one officer and twenty-nine men left of the 51st Co., out of the original 8 officers and 250 men, when they reached the end of the day.
15. That flank was still "up in the air," as the military would describe it. The Moroccans still had not come up to provide a left flank cover for the 2d Division (6th Marines).
16. Denig, who had been CO of 1/30, 3d Division, was along as an observer with 2/6 and had served briefly with the 5th Marines at Belleau Wood. He would be assigned to command 3/9 at Blanc Mont and would remain a Marine postwar. Eventually he became a brigadier general and director of public relations for the Corps during World War II.
17. Kemper F. Cowing and Courtney R. Cooper, *"Dear Folks at Home": The Glorious Story of the United States Marines in France as Told in Their Letters from the Battlefield* (Boston: Houghton Mifflin, 1919), 253.
18. *History of the 74th Company, 6th Regiment,* n.d. (reprint), 7.
19. *A History of the 80th Company, Sixth Marines,* n.d. (reprint), 4–5.
20. *Seventy-eighth Company, Sixth Marines,* n.d. (reprint), 4.
21. Joseph E. Rendinell and George Pattullo, *One Man's War: The Diary of a Leatherneck* (New York: Sears and Co., 1928), 153.
22. *A Brief History of the Sixth Regiment, U.S. Marine Corps, July, 1917–December, 1918,* n.d. (reprint), 14.
23. Viereck, *As They Saw Us,* 161.
24. Harbord was a reasonably good administrator but mostly a rather poor field commander. He literally destroyed the Marine Brigade on 6 June and certainly was not there when needed by the 2d Division at Soissons. His complaints are a weak excuse for not being more proactive with the French.
25. He has been, by some historians, acclaimed as the first Marine to command a division. That is not true; Brig. Gen. Charles Doyen assumed command of the

2d Division in October 1917, remaining so until the arrival of Bundy in November.
26. Johnson and Hillman, *Soissons 1918*, 114. Johnson or Hillman, referring to the Vietnam War use of the term "body count" for total success, was being facetious, of course.

Chapter 6

1. It is the generally accepted conclusion that Pershing decided that he would accept a Marine commanding a U.S. Army division, but would not accept an entirely Marine division. Therefore, to quiet the Marine commandant, George Barnett, Lejeune was the new CG of the 2d Division.
2. According to the 2d Division Syllabi, Kelly, previously CO of the 17th, was in command of the 12th until 29 August, and Holabird replaced him. Lt. Col. Leonard C. Sparks assumed command of the 17th on 2 August and retained it until 31 October.
3. Both patrol reports were taken from *Records, Second Division*, vol. 7, n.d.
4. Kean, *Dear Marraine*, 171.
5. When Maj. Gen. Commandant Barnett urged the secretary of war to accept Marines as part of the AEF, he was informed that the army command didn't believe that the Marines could supply sufficient manpower to keep the unit viable in combat. Barnett, of course, told them the Marines could and would. There were numerous reasons why the replacement situation was having serious problems, but eventually Barnett managed to sort it all out and more Marines began coming to Europe soon afterward.
6. Warren R. Jackson, *His Time in Hell*, ed. George B. Clark (Novato: Presidio, 2001), 158–59.
7. Division history cites the visit as being by both Liggett, CG, I Corps, and Maj. Gen. Joseph T. Dickman, CG, IV Corps.

Chapter 7

1. Sgt. Bernard J. McCrossen diary, Machine Gun Company, 23d Infantry.

2. Denig had a distinguished career. During this war he had already served with the 5th Marines, led a battalion of the 6th Marines at Soissons, and would continue to lead 3/9 until wounded during the capture of Médéah Farm on Blanc Mont Ridge. There, for his courage and ability, he was the recipient of numerous prestigious decorations, including the Navy Cross and DSC.
3. Essentially their 102d Infantry, led by another U.S. Marine, Col. Hiram I. Bearss, would push through the German army without firing a shot, and reach the middle of the salient in a few hours, thereby cutting off the retreat of numerous German units. They would be met, coming from the opposite direction, by the 1st U.S. Division at Vigneulles.
4. Actually, because of the large numbers involved, they believed it to be a French preparation. The Germans were still unaware that great numbers of American troops had been pouring into France during the previous few months. To stifle growing morale problems, they ignored the fact that ships with American troops were getting through their submarine cordon. By now there were close to 2,000,000 American troops in France.
5. Elton E. Mackin, *Suddenly We Didn't Want to Die: Memoirs of a World War I Marine* (Novato: Presidio Press, 1993), 141.
6. The artillery preparation was, according to all available accounts, the heaviest that anyone had experienced so far. Perhaps they had to conserve their shells for whatever might come in the next few days.
7. There is a great conflict in time for this support. The operations report (vol. 7) for the 5th Marines states that the relief was sent forward at 0300 on 13 September. But a field message (vol. 5) from Feland to Neville, dated 12 September and timed at 2130, reported that Shearer had already sent the two companies forward to Col. Stuart on 12 September.
8. Kelly would be awarded three Silver Star citations at St. Mihiel and even though when the going got rough he was always "leading," his many tribulations with legal matters kept him a private, and broke, all during the war.

Chapter 8

1. French army leadership had already suffered a major mutiny in the bloody failure of the spring offensive of 1917 and was doing everything possible to avoid a like situation in 1918. Therefore, it had been decided by them that they would (finally) conserve French blood and let the other contestants shoulder a major portion of the aggressiveness required to defeat the Germans. "Let George do it," was the new theory, and the AEF was "George."

2. Foch had requested three divisions but Pershing cried poor and instead offered two.

3. John A. Lejeune, *Reminiscences of a Marine* (Philadelphia: Dorrance, 1930), 337. Gouraud pointed to his anchor collar insignia, which indicated that it was for colonial infantry, of which he had been a part in his early service years. The colonials were part of the French navy. The French navy also had (perhaps still have) Marines operating from warships.

4. Ibid., 340.
5. Ibid., 342.
6. Ibid.
7. Ibid., 343.

8. This move was probably another gimmick used by Foch to give Lejeune the impression that his division was indeed being broken up. It certainly helped to convince Lejeune.

9. Ernst Otto, *The Battle at Blanc Mont (October 2 to October 10, 1918)* (Annapolis: U.S. Naval Institute Press, 1930), 8.

10. Ibid.

11. McClellan, "The Battle of Blanc Mont Ridge," *Marine Corps Gazette*. 7, no. 1 (March 1922): 6–7.

12. The luck of the draw. Just as it had been at Belleau Wood, the Marine Brigade drew what was to be the most difficult assignment: the Blanc Mont Massif.

13. *Marine Corps Gazette*. Op. cit., 8.
14. Lejeune, 346–347.
15. Ibid., 349.

16. *Records of the Second Division*, vol. 5. Memo was issued by Lt. Col. Earl H. Ellis, USMC, Division Adjutant (hereinafter *Records*).

17. Otto, 8.

18. Ibid., 11. In the translated version, they utilized the American style of unit identification.

19. Ibid. At this stage most of the description covers the front of the 3d Brigade and the French II Corps, but not yet the 4th Brigade.

20. Once the battle started, the commanding officer of all the machine gun battalions, AEF, had little control over his command after dispersing his companies among the line battalions. His was, more or less, an administrative function during combat.

21. Spaulding and Wright, *The Second Division American Expeditionary Force in France, 1917–1919*, Hilton diary, 279.

22. Diary of Pvt John A. Hughes, Battery C, 15th FA. He was writing about the preparation, not the rolling barrage which began at 0545 that morning.

23. The Monograph No. 9, published in 1921, identifies the division as the 67th. The maps accompanying the *2d Division Summary of Operations in the World War* clearly identify it as the 167th DI, as does the text, published in 1944.

24. Diary of Hilton, dated 3 October 1918. The official Monograph No. 9, prepared by the Historical Branch, War Plans Division, General Staff clearly states on page 10, "Casualties were few." The preparers probably weren't there but Hilton was. Yet it is the only place I have seen that critique of the 167th DI, which seemed, otherwise, to have performed as required.

25. Monograph No. 9 states "5th Marines," but Barker was CO of 1/6 and they were leading the 4th Brigade that morning. Error in No. 9, on page 10.

26. Kelly was a character. He had already earned several Silver Star citations, and a Croix de Guerre Bronze at Belleau Wood. In addition to his MoH he would also be awarded a Médaille Militaire and two Croix de Guerre, a Palm and Bronze, plus an Italian War Cross and Montenegrin Silver Medal of Valor.

27. Sellers was never one to ignore writing up award citations for his men. They performed at a high level and he cited them every chance he could.

28. Diary of Cpl John E. Aasland, 55th Co, 2/5, dated October Third.
29. For additional details read Clark, *Devil Dogs,* on pages 322–324.
30. Harry B. Field and Henry G. James, *Over the Top with the 18th Company, 5th Regiment, U.S. Marines: A History* (Rodenbach, Germany, 1919?), 26.
31. At least so the records recite, but it sounds incredulous.
32. This was the other American division promised to the French.
33. The actual relief and subsequent rearrangement of the 2d Division regiments is a matter of discord among several government sources, none of which are in agreement. I have used what seems most likely to be correct. In fact, the neophyte 36th Division was more or less thrown into the battle to relieve the shattered infantry of the 3d and 4th brigades and they did marvelously well. The 2d Division took the unassailable Blanc Mont Massif but were not in any condition to do more. The ground was level, the enemy shot to pieces, and the "cowboys" took the rest of it, going all the way to the Aisne River.
34. Blanc Mont, Monograph No. 9, June 1921, 25.
35. The later divisions being brought to France were basically all infantry so support services for each had to be obtained elsewhere. Consequently, since the 36th had no artillery available on hand, the 2d Artillery Brigade remained with the 36th until they reached the Aisne River line.
36. I have been unable to determine the reasoning behind this unusual, to say the least, French directive. The Brigade was in terrible shape and probably couldn't, at that time, be of any service even in a support function.
37. The total number of 1/5 Marines still able to move (some walking wounded) was 156 officers and men out of an approximate 1,200 to 1,300. The other two battalions were badly hurt, but not quite that badly. It has been calculated that 4 October was the worst day for the U.S. Marines in any war they had been in, that is until 20 November 1943, at Tarawa, which was close.

Chapter 9

1. This prohibited the plan to proceed forward and take Metz, thereby interrupting all traffic then supplying that fortified city. As James Hallas expressed in his book *Squandered Victory,* without proceeding on to take Metz, the reduction of the St. Mihiel salient was a wasted effort. .
2. Their excessive casualties later created a sensible backlash against the Franco-British insistence on early American participation. Some latter day historians have not seemed to take that into consideration when panning the American involvement in the Meuse-Argonne Campaign. Bad planning on the part of the American staffs also helped.
3. Lejeune. Page 371.
4. Summerall, a reasonably effective general, was not the most popular leader in the AEF. In fact, to many of the officers and men he was downright intemperate. It was the luck of the draw that the division would get him instead of Maj. Gen. John L. Hines, CG of III Corps, or Maj. Gen. Joseph T. Dickman, CG of I Corps, both reliable, competent officers, with responsible dispositions.
5. Villages so close together that no one could say which town they lived in. French spelling was *Landres-et-St. George* (according to the map) for the larger town on the right. St. Georges for the smaller village on the left.
6. Appearing in George S. Viereck, editor. *As They Saw Us.* NY, 1929. Page 245.
7. The 89th would, like the 2d, go directly north. The River Marne would curve to the westward before the 89th and the 89th was to then cross the Marne at that point and proceed north on the eastern side. The 2d would have the Marne as its right flank and plans were made for it to also cross over and join the 89th on the eastern side. When the time came, both plans went haywire.
8. Which Haig, after demanding American sharing in the attack to help protect his right flank, was angry and hostile to Pershing for wanting his "loaned" divisions returned. Haig had a use for them; possibly to lead off the British advance?

9. *History of the First Battalion, 5th Regiment, U.S. Marines, June 1917 — August 1919.* Published and distributed from profits of Battalion Exchange (n.p., n.d.), 19.
10. Personal observation on site.
11. *A Brief History of the Sixth Regiment, U.S. Marine Corps, July, 1917 — December, 1918* (n.p. [Quantico], n.d. [c. 1919]), 29.
12. Stowell, a solid citizen, was leading a so-called mini-battalion composed of his company, another from the 319th Infantry, 80th Div., and a platoon from the 73d MG Company. Their responsibility was to maintain liaison between the 80th and 2d divisions.
13. Captain Overton was another great loss to the Corps.
14. The Marines later complained that the German machine gunners firing upon the advancing 2d Bn were flying a Red Cross flag from a window they were located in.
15. He has a living relative, Joe Goren, who is pulling together a memoir of that fighting machine.
16. Janda is an interesting individual. He appears in the regiment's history as a lieutenant, captain and major. One wonders if he did, in fact, progress that rapidly.
17. Diary of Captain R.C. Hilton, 283 in the *History of the Second Division.*
18. Located just about where the head of the column shows on the map as "Nov 3."
19. See also Beaudette's actions on 1 November, above.
20. Joe was awarded a Distinguished Service Cross for his combined heroics on the 1st and 5th.
21. This statement is continued in the records but it wasn't until the night of 10–11 November that the 2d Engineers created two pontoon type wooden bridges for the 5th Marines to cross. I, along with a number of friends, have scouted that area and found only the remnants of those pontoon bridges, and no others.
22. The following produced a very peculiar situation, which caused serious repercussions within the U.S. Army and created hostilities and personal enmities which lasted until another war. The 1st Division's leadership was at the very heart of the matter.
23. Mackin, *Suddenly We Didn't Want to Die,* 251.
24. After modest investigation, it appears as though that ruling came down from AEF, perhaps originating with Foch and company. No one seemed to have the courage and decency to refuse the orders.
25. The enemy didn't make any effort to "dig them out." No doubt their leadership wasn't going to unnecessarily lose anymore men to a war already over.
26. There is an interesting sidelight to this. The only unit that didn't reflect the Armistice at 1100 was the 66th Company, which was far ahead (at the personal request of Dunbeck) out looking for missing Marines of 2/5. They came upon German troops celebrating in Moulins-St. Herbert and only then realized the war was over.

Chapter 10

1. Wilson's terms were reasonable; however, the other "victorious" participants had different ideas. Ultimately, Germany's hatred for the harsh conditions that prevailed was the primary cause of World War II.
2. They were English made and with different lasts, which style caused many foot problems.
3. It is a little known fact that the Marines were assigned U.S. Army uniforms when their uniforms began to wear out in the spring of 1918.

Appendix A

1. This was relating to the April 1914 landing at Vera Cruz, Mexico, by the U.S. naval forces, Marines and sailors. It was even then planned that the U.S. Army would replace the sailors, but the Marines would remain.
2. Bullard would later command the 1st Infantry Division in France. Edwards would command the 26th Division in France. The 4th Brigade would then still be

part of the 2d Division but composed of Marines.

3. After he had been sent to Vera Cruz to command the army and Marines, both of which still occupied the town.

4. *Order of Battle of the United States Land Forces in the World War, American Expeditionary Forces: Divisions*, vol. 2 (Washington, D.C.: Center of Military History, United States Army, 1988), 25.

5. No doubt because the Division already had a 4th MG Bn (Divisional) and a 5th MG Bn assigned to the 3d Brigade. Numerically, it made sense.

6. The second brigade, the 5th, was created for that ethereal, never to be seen Marine division, with two infantry regiments, the 11th and 13th (Voodoo), and the 5th Machine Gun Battalion, all of which arrived in France. Unfortunately, they were sidetracked to work mostly as laborers, and to protect AEF Headquarters, and some to be replacements for the 4th Brigade casualties.

Appendix B

1. Many machine guns captured at St. Mihiel were not counted and are not counted in this total.

2. Services of Supply.

3. Date is in the original but it is obviously grossly incorrect. The next entry for Soissons begins with the same words and is correct. The first words would be incorrect unless they referred to approximately 1 July 1918. It was, however, the 26th Division that eventually drove the Germans from the Sector, on or about the 18th of July.

Appendix C

1. Sgt. Alvin York received the Medal of Honor for bringing in, with the assistance of 8 other men who I believe received nothing, one hundred thirty-two Germans.

BIBLIOGRAPHY

United States Government Publications

American Battle Monuments Commission. *American Armies and Battlefields in Europe.* Washington, D.C.: U.S. Government Printing Office, 1938.
Annual Report of the Secretary of War, 1919. Washington, D.C.: U.S. Government Printing Office, 1919.
McClellan, Edwin N. *The United States Marine Corps in the World War.* Washington, D.C.: U.S. Government Printing Office, 1920.
Navy Yearbook, 1920 and 1921. Washington, D.C.: U.S. Government Printing Office, 1922.
U.S. Navy. *Annual Report of the Secretary of the Navy for the Fiscal Years 1918–1919–1920.* Washington, D.C.: 1918, 1919, 1920.
_____. *Annual Reports of the Navy Department for the Fiscal Years 1917–1920.* Washington, D.C.: U.S. Government Printing Office, 1918–1921.
U.S. Army. *Records of the Second Division (Regular).* 10 vols. Washington, D.C.: The Army War College, 1927

Personal Papers and Unpublished Memoirs

Barnett, George. "Soldier and Sailor Too." N.p., n.d. [1923?].
Bellamy, David. "Personal Diary, 23 October 1917–22 August 1919." N.p., n.d.
Cordes, Onnie J. "The Immortal Division." N.p., n.d.
Draucker, James H. "Telling It Like It Was." N.p., n.d. (entries from 6 April 1917 to August 1919).
Moore, William B. Letters to his mother, dated 31 March 1918 through August 1919.
Paris, Gus. "Hold Every Inch of Ground." Owensboro, KY: n.d.
Soares, Denzil I. "Diary of Pvt. Denzil I. Soares, April 1918–April 1919, U.S.M.C." N.p., n.d.
Thomas, Eugene R. Letters to his mother, beginning on "Mother's Day" 1918.
Thompson, Troy T. "Private Edward Clyde Thompson: A Marine's Accounting of World War I." N.p., n.d. (circa 2003).
Zischke, Peter H. "Recollections of My Father, Herman A. Zischke." Orinda, CA: 2004.

Books

Akers, Herbert H. *History of the Third Battalion, Sixth Regiment, U.S. Marines.* Hillsdale, Michigan: Akers, MacRitchie and Hurlburt, 1919.
American Battle Monument Commission. *2d Division Summary of Operations in the World War.* Washington: D.C.: U.S. Government Printing Office, 1944.

Americans Defending Democracy: Our Soldiers' Own Stories. New York: World's War Stories, 1919.
Andriot, Captain R. *Belleau Wood and the American Army*. Translated by W. B. Fitts. Washington, D.C.: Belleau Wood Memorial Association, n.d.
Anon. *Decorations, United States Army, 1862—1926*. Washington, D.C.: War Department, Office of the Adjutant General, 1927.
_____. *From Robinson to the Rhine: Battery "A," 17th Field Artillery, 1917–1918–1919*. N.p., n.d.
_____. *The Ninth U.S. Infantry in the World War*. Neuwid am Main: Louis Heusersche Buckdruckerei, 1919.
_____. *Second Division Memorial Day, June 2nd, 1919, 75th Company, 6th Regiment, U.S. Marines*. Reprint, Pike, NH: The Brass Hat, 1995.
_____. *The Second Division, Syllabi of the Histories of Regiments and Separate Organizations*. Coblenz, Germany: Coblenzer Volkszeitung, 1919.
_____. *Where the Marines Fought in France*. Chicago: Park and Antrim, n.d. [1919?].
Asprey, Robert B. *At Belleau Wood*. New York: G.P. Putnam, 1965.
Bellamy, David. *History of the Third Battalion, Sixth Regiment, U.S. Marines*. Pike: The Brass Hat, 2000.
Blakeney, Jane. *Heroes: U.S. Marine Corps, 1861–1955*. Washington, D.C.: 1957.
Brannen, Carl Andrew. *Over There: A Marine in the Great War*. Edited by Rolfe L. Hillman, Jr., and Peter F. Owen, with an afterword by J.P. Brannen. College Station: Texas A & M University Press, 1996.
Brown, Ronald J. *A Few Good Men: The Story of the Fighting Fifth Marines*. Novato, CA: Presidio Press, 2001.
Brown, William. *The Adventures of an American Doughboy*. Tacoma: Smith-Kinney, n.d. (circa 1919).
Carter, William A. *The Tale of a Devil Dog*. Washington, D.C.: Canteen Press, 1920.
Catlin, Albertus W. *With the Help of God and a Few Marines*. New York: Doubleday, 1919.
Clark, George B., ed. *A Brief History of the Sixth Regiment, U.S. Marine Corps, July, 1917–December, 1918*. Reprint, Pike, NH: The Brass Hat, 1992.
_____. *Citations and Awards to Members of the 4th Marine Brigade*. Pike, NH: The Brass Hat, 1992.
_____. *Devil Dogs: Fighting Marines of World War I*. Novato, CA: Presidio Press, 1999.
_____. *Hiram Iddings Bearss, U.S. Marine Corps: Biography of a World War I Hero*. Jefferson, NC: McFarland, 2005.
_____, ed. *History of the Fifth Regiment Marines (May 1917–December 31, 1918)*. Reprint, Pike, NH: The Brass Hat, 1995.
_____. *The History of the Third Battalion 5th Marines, 1917–1918*. Pike, NH: The Brass Hat, 1995.
_____. *A List of Officers of the 4th Marine Brigade*. Revised ed. Pike, NH: The Brass Hat, 2001.
_____, ed. *Major Awards to U.S. Marines in World War One*. Reprint, Pike, NH: The Brass Hat, 1992.
_____, ed. *United States Marine Corps Medal of Honor Recipients*. Jefferson, NC: McFarland, 2005.
Collins, Harry. *The War Diary of Corporal Harry Collins*. With David Fisher and George B. Clark. Reprint, Pike, NH: The Brass Hat, 1996.
Cooke, Colonel Elliot D. *"We Can Take It, We Attack": Americans vs. Germans*. Reprint of 2 vols. in 1, Pike, NH: The Brass Hat, 1992. First published in 1936.
Cowing, Kemper F., and Courtney R. Cooper. *"Dear Folks at Home": The Glorious Story of the United States Marines in France as Told in Their Letters from the Battlefield*. Boston: Houghton Mifflin, 1919.
Curtis, Thomas J., and Lothar R. Long. *History of the Sixth Machine Gun Battalion*.

Reprint, Pike, NH: The Brass Hat, 1992.
Daniels, Josephus. *The Cabinet Diaries of Josephus Daniels, 1913–1921.* Lincoln: University of Nebraska Press, 1963.
Derby, Richard. *"Wade in, Sanitary!": The Story of a Division Surgeon in France.* New York: G.P. Putnam, 1919.
Donaldson, G.H., and W. Jenkins, *Seventy-eighth Company, Sixth Marines, Second Division Army of Occupation.* Reprint, Pike, NH: The Brass Hat, 1994.
Field, Harry B., and Henry G. James. *Over the Top with the 18th Company, 5th Regiment, U.S. Marines: A History.* Rodenbach, Germany, [1919?].
Finney, Ben. *Once a Marine, Always a Marine.* NY: Crown, 1977.
Fleming, Charles A. *Quantico: Crossroads of the Corps.* Washington, D.C.: Headquarters, U.S. Marine Corps, 1978.
General Headquarters, American Expeditionary Forces. *Citation Orders 1 through 10, 3 June 1919 — 31 August 1920.* France and Washington, D.C.
Gordon, George V. *Leathernecks and Doughboys.* 1927. Reprint, Pike, NH: The Brass Hat, 1996.
Gulberg, Martin G. *A War Diary.* Reprint, Pike, NH: The Brass Hat,1989. First published in 1927.
Hallas, James H., ed. *Doughboy War: The American Expeditionary Force in World War I.* Boulder, CO: Lynne Rienner, 2000.
_____. *Squandered Victory: The American First Army at St. Mihiel.* Westport, CT: Praeger, 1995.
Hamilton, Craig, and Louise Corbin. *Echoes from Over There.* New York: Soldier's, 1919.
Harbord, James G. *Leaves from a War Diary.* New York: Dodd Mead, 1925.
Headquarters, Second Division, American Expeditionary Forces. *General Order 40, July 5, 1918; G.O. 44, July 12, 1918; G.O. 88, December 31, 1918.*
Hemrick, Levi. *Once a Marine.* New York: Carlton Press, 1968.
Jackson, Warren R. *His Time in Hell: A Texas Marine in France.* Edited by George B. Clark. Novato: Presidio Press, 2001.
Johnson, Douglas V., II, and Rolfe L. Hillman, Jr. *Soissons 1918.* College Station: Texas A&M University Press, 1999.
Jones, William K. *A Brief History of the 6th Marines.* Washington, D.C.: Headquarters, U.S.M.C., 1987.
Kean, Robert Winthrop. *Dear Marraine, 1917–1919.* Privately published, 1969.
Kerrigan, Evans E. *American War Medals and Decorations.* New York: Viking Press, 1971.
Lejeune, John A. *Reminiscences of a Marine.* Philadelphia: Dorrance, 1930.
Macgillivray, George C., and George B. Clark, eds. *A History of the 80th Company, Sixth Marines.* Reprint, Pike, NH: The Brass Hat, 1991.
Mackin, Elton B. *Suddenly We Didn't Want to Die.* Edited by George B. Clark. Novato, CA: Presidio Press, 1993.
March, William [pseud.]. *Company K.* New York: Harrison Smith and Robert Haas, 1933.
McCahill, William P. *The Marine Corps Reserve, 1916–1966.* Washington, D.C.: U.S. Government Printing Office, 1966.
McClellan, Edwin N. *The United States Marine Corps in the World War.* Washington, D.C.: U.S. Government Printing Office, 1920.
McCrossen, Bernard J. *Diary of the Machine Gun Company, 23rd Infantry, Second Division, 1917–1919.* Vallender-Rhine: Hartmann Brothers, 1919.
Michelin. *The Americans in the Great War: Illustrated Guides to the Battlefields.* 3 vols. France: Michelin, 1920.
Millett, Allan R. *In Many a Strife: General Gerald C. Thomas and the U.S. Marine Corps, 1917–1956.* Annapolis: Naval Institute Press, 1993.

Mitchell, William A. *The Official History of the Second Regiment of Engineers and Second Engineer Train, United States Army, in the World War.* San Antonio: San Antonio Print Company, 1920.
Morgan, Daniel E. *When the World Went Mad.* Reprint, Pike, NH: The Brass Hat, 1992. First published in1931.
Morrey, Willard I. *History of the 96th Company, 2d Battalion, Sixth Regiment, United States Marine Corps.* Washington, D.C.: Headquarters, U.S. Marine Corps, 1967.
Otto, Ernst. *The Battle at Blanc Mont.* Annapolis: U.S. Naval Institute Press, 1930.
Pattullo, George. *Hellwood.* Philadelphia: Curtis, 1918.
_____. *Horrors of Moonlight.* New York: private printing, 1939.
Reis-El Bara, Henry J., and Glen G. Stewart. *The 3rd Battalion, 17th FA, in 1918.* Coblenz: H.L. Scheid, n.d. (circa 1919).
Rendinell, Joseph E., and George Pattullo. *One Man's War: The Diary of a Leatherneck.* New York: J.H. Sears, 1928.
Scanlon, William T. *God Have Mercy on Us!* Boston: Houghton Mifflin, 1929.
Sellers, James M. *World War I Memoirs of Lieutenant Colonel James McBrayer Sellers, USMC.* Pike, NH: The Brass Hat, 1997.
Smith, Scott D. *Awards of the French Croix de Guerre to Marines during the World War.* Twenty-nine Palms, CA: n.d. (circa 1995).
Spaulding, Oliver Lyman, and John Womack Wright. *The Second Division American Expeditionary Force in France, 1917–1919.* NY: Hillman Press for the Second Division Association, 1937.
Stringer, Harry R., ed. *Heroes All!* Washington, D.C.: Fassett, 1919.
_____. *The Navy Book of Distinguished Service.* Washington, D.C.: Fassett, n.d. (circa 1921).
Strott, George G. *History of Medical Personnel of the United States Navy, Sixth Regiment, Marine Corps, American Expeditionary Forces in World War 1917–1918.* Reprint, Pike, NH: The Brass Hat, 1995.
Thomason, John W., Jr. *Fix Bayonets!* New York: Scribner's, 1925.
_____. *The United States Army Second Division Northwest of Chateau Thierry in World War I.* Edited by George B. Clark. Jefferson, NC: McFarland, 2006. First published Washington, D.C.: National War College, 1928.
U.S. Marine Corps. *History of the First Battalion, 5th Regiment, U. S. Marines, 1919.* Reprint, Foster, RI: The Brass Hat, 1980.
_____. *History of the Second Battalion, 5th Regiment, U.S. Marines.* Reprint, Foster, RI: The Brass Hat, 1980.
_____. *History of the Second Battalion, Fifth Marines.* Quantico: Marine Barracks, 1938.
_____. *History of the Sixth Regiment, U.S. Marines.* Tientsin, China, 1928.
_____. *History of the Third Battalion, Sixth Marines.* N.p., n.d.
_____. *74th Company, 6th Regiment, Second Division, A.E.F.* Reprint, Pike, NH: The Brass Hat, 1994.
U.S. Navy. *Medal of Honor, 1861–1949.* N.p., n.d. (circa1950).
Vandoren, Lucien H. *A Brief History of the Second Battalion, Sixth Regiment, U.S. Marine Corps, during the Period June 1st to August 10th, 1918.* Reprint, Pike, NH: The Brass Hat, 1995.
Venzon, Anne Cipriano, ed. *The United States in the First World War: An Encyclopedia.* New York: Garland, 1995.
Viereck, George Sylvester, ed. *As They Saw Us: Foch, Ludendorff and Other Leaders Write Our War History.* Garden City, NY: Doubleday, Doran, 1929.
Wise, Frederic M., and Meigs O. Frost. *A Marine Tells It to You.* New York: J.H. Sears, 1929.

Articles

Clark, George B. "Medal of Honor Marine: John Joseph Kelly." *Leatherneck,* November 1998, 40–47.

Daugherty, Leo J., III. "General Thomas Holcomb (1879–1965)." *Marine Corps Gazette.* August 1997, 88.

Hillman, Rolfe L., II. "Second to None: The Indianheads." *Proceedings* (Annapolis: U.S. Naval Institute), November 1987, 57–61.

Thomas, Gerald C. "Battalion Command 'Over There': The Fifth Marines, 1917–1918." *Marine Corps Gazette.* Pages 112 & 106.

_____. *The Sixth Marines, 1917–1918.* Same as above but with only nine officers. Pages 88 & 78.

_____. *The Sixth Machine Gun Battalion.* Same but with three officers. Pages 96 & 82.

_____. *Regimental Command "Over There" 1917–1918.* Same with six officers. Pages 87 & 81.

INDEX

Adams, Lt. Col. John P. 77, 81
Aiello, Pvt. Antonio 110
Alband, Lt. 28
Allen, Pvt. William Y. 144
Alsup, Pvt. Julian W. 144
Anderson, Cpl. Frank W. 28
Anderson, Col. Thomas M., Jr. 76, 77

Armies, American:
AEF Headquarters (Chaumont) 14, 17, 86, 96, 116, 181
3d Composite Regiment 181
Schleswig-Holstein Bn 181
1st Army 119–20, 122, 133, 157–58
2d Army 157
I Corps 39, 117, 118, 158
III Corps 113
IV Corps 96, 118
V Corps 158, 170, 172–73, 177
VI Corps 96
IX Corps 113

1st Division 2, 9, 10, 15, 21, 35, 37, 93, 96, 111, 113–14, 119, 121, 170, 180
1st Regiment of Engineers 21
18th Infantry 101

2d Division (Second to None) 3, 9, 10, 12, 14, 15, *passim* 180–83; awards 221–235; pedigree 185–192; register 193–220
1st Field Signal Bn 47, 53
2d Regiment of Engineers 13, 14, 20–21, 39, 40, 45, 46, 50, 53, 54, 64, 72, 73, 96, 98, 107, 115, 126, 152–53, 155, 174, 176
1st Bn (1/2) 21, 24, 45, 174
A Co. 45, 61, 87, 126, 155
B Co. 45, 59, 64, 65, 87, 155
C Co. 44, 45, 155
2d Bn (2/2) 24, 45

D Co. 24, 45, 53, 54, 87, 153
E Co. 45, 54, 83, 155
F Co. 45, 54
4th Machine Gun Bn 12, 47, 48, 83, 104, 110
A Co. 110, 153
B Co. 83, 104, 106
2d Ammunition Train 154
Co. A 154
2d Military Police 13
2d Sanitary Train 13, 155

2d Artillery Brigade 12, 48, 50, 65, 67, 71–72, 84, 88, 113, 115, 120, 122, 126, 127, 132, 143, 154–55, 168, 171
12th Artillery Regiment (75mm Guns) 12, 13, 17, 33, 48, 50, 71–72, 114, 146
1st Bn (1/12) 25
2d Bn (2/12) 25
Battery E 122
15th Artillery Regiment (75mm Guns 12, 13, 17, 24, 33, 48, 50, 57, 103, 111, 114–15, 146, 180
1st Bn (1/15) 25, 156
2d Bn (2/15) 25
17th Artillery Regiment (155mm Guns) 12, 16, 33, 48, 50, 88
1st Bn (1/17) 25, 48
2d Bn (2/17) 25
Battery A 24, 35
2d Bn 24
Battery D 24
Battery E 24,
Battery F 24
3d Bn (3/17) 24
2d Trench Mortar Battery 25

3d Brigade 2, 7, 25, 49, 50, 65, 73, 84, 87–88, 90, 91, 97, 98, 104, 113, 114, 119,

255

126, 128, 137–38, 142–43, 150–51, 156, 159, 166, 171, 172, 180
9th Infantry 2, 14, 19, 25, 26, 32, 33, 42, 44, 47, 50, 51, 52, 63–64, 71, 73, 74, 76, 81, 82, 84, 85, 87–88, 98–99, 101, 106, 112–14, 117, 122, 125–26, 128, 141–42, 146, 150, 152, 164, 166–69, 171–73
Headquarters Co. 164
1st Bn (1/9) 20, 44, 45, 51, 76, 90, 101, 120, 123–24, 126, 142–43, 166, 169–70, 172–73, 178
A Co. 143, 166
B Co. 124, 143, 166–68
C Co. 90, 125, 143
D Co. 178
2d Bn (2/9) 14, 27, 44, 53, 63, 65, 87, 101, 103, 105–6, 114–15, 120, 123–24, 126, 142–44, 150, 152–53, 155, 166, 169–70, 172
D Co. 124, 170
E Co. 103
F Co. 88, 114, 144
G Co. 105, 114
3d Bn (3/9) 14, 19–20, 32, 42, 44, 87, 101–3, 106, 120, 122, 123, 126, 128, 142–43, 166, 168–70, 172–74
I Co. 32, 44, 120, 168, 173–74
K Co. 44, 103, 105, 128, 169
L Co. 32, 44, 166, 173–74
M Co. 44, 102, 122, 173
9th Machine Gun Co. 27, 87, 141, 143, 168
23d Infantry 2, 7, 14, 15, 26, 31, 32, 40, 42, 44, 46, 48, 50, 52, 53, 57, 62–65, 73, 74, 77, 82, 83, 84–85, 87, 88, 90, 98–99, 102–7, 111, 113–15, 123, 128, 142–44, 146, 149–51, 161, 166, 168–70, 172–74
1st Bn (1/23) 23, 45, 46, 62–63, 81, 99, 121, 124, 125, 146, 152, 161, 168–69
A Co. 23, 125
C Co. 124, 161
2d Bn (2/23) 45, 47, 49, 50, 86, 99, 104, 121, 125, 161, 169–70
C Co. 169
D Co. 169
E Co. 105, 125
3d Bn (3/23) 46, 47, 62–64, 74, 79, 85–86, 87, 90, 121, 125, 152, 161, 169–70
I Co. 78–80
K Co. 62–63, 80, 161
L Co. 152, 161
M Co. 23, 28, 63, 81, 152
23d Machine Gun Co. 15, 23, 38, 42, 48, 104–5, 169

5th Machine Gun Bn 12, 44–48, 87–88, 124, 127, 178
A Co. 87
D Co. 88, 178

4th (Marine) Brigade 1, 2, 7, 14, 20, 27, 45, 49, 50, 51, 64, 70–73, 75–76, 86, 87, 91, 95, 97, 113–114, 119, 126, 128, 135, 137–41, 149–51, 155–56, 159, 166, 171–73, 180
5th (Marines) Regiment 9, 10, 14, 15, 26, 27, 33, 49, 50, 52–53, 74, 83–84, 98–100, 102, 113, 120, 123, 125–26, 128, 137, 139, 145–46, 148–50, 156, 159, 161, 163–64, 173–74, 176
1st Bn (1/5) 40, 44, 46–48, 50, 51, 53, 54, 64, 74–75, 79, 100–1, 103–4, 106, 121, 128, 141–42, 146, 149, 156, 159, 162–63, 170
17th Co. 48, 50, 54, 56–57, 64, 101, 142, 159, 174, 176–78
49th Co. 48, 54–57, 159
66th Co. 48, 50, 54–57, 103, 159, 178
67th Co. 14, 54–57, 159
2d Bn (2/5) 46–51, 55, 64, 70–72, 75, 77, 79, 83, 98, 100–05, 114, 121, 126, 128, 141, 149, 159, 162–63, 168–70, 174, 176–77
18th Co. 29, 33, 45, 107, 149, 162
43d Co. 70, 107
51st Co. 49, 54–56, 70, 107, 162
55th Co. 98, 101, 107, 126, 128, 163, 177–78
3d Bn (3/5) 40, 46, 51, 53, 56–58, 68, 73, 75, 77, 82–86, 98, 121, 128, 141, 146, 149, 159, 162–64, 170, 178
16th Co. 58, 64, 83, 85, 125, 127
20th Co. 58, 59, 82–84, 125, 127
45th Co. 58, 64, 125, 127, 129
47th Co. 58–59, 75, 84–85, 125, 127, 129
8th Machine Gun Co. 14, 49, 106, 141, 177
6th (Marines) Regiment 27, 33, 42–48, 50–51, 53–54, 65, 74, 84, 86, 107–12, 113, 114, 116, 122, 128, 137, 139–41, 144, 146, 148, 151–55, 159, 161, 164–65, 173–74
1st Bn (1/6) 31, 43, 45–46, 50–51, 53, 67–68, 74, 77, 86, 109, 116, 122, 128, 130, 132, 141, 150, 152–53, 155, 159, 161, 163, 165
74th Co. 31, 109, 129–30, 159, 162
75th Co. 130, 155, 159, 161–62
76th Co. 67, 70, 129, 155, 159, 161–62
95th Co. 75, 116, 159, 161–62
2d Bn (2/6) 43, 51, 53, 62, 65, 67–68, 74, 77, 79, 86, 109–11, 122, 128–32, 141, 144, 150–51, 159, 163, 165
78th Co. 62, 74, 109–10, 131, 139, 144

Index

79th Co. 60, 61, 109, 131, 151, 164–65
80th Co. 60, 65, 109, 130, 164
96th Co. 46, 60, 107, 132, 165
3d Bn (3/6) 30, 44, 49–50, 53, 57, 59, 61, 65, 68, 77, 84, 86, 110, 122, 128–29, 141, 150, 154–55, 159, 163
82d Co. 23, 49, 50, 65–66, 129, 150, 163
83d Co. 44, 50, 61, 84, 129, 150, 163, 165
84th Co. 49, 61, 110, 129, 150, 163
97th Co. 22, 49, 110, 129, 150
73d Machine Gun Co. 49, 50, 58, 130, 141, 155
6th Machine Gun Bn 12, 39, 44, 46, 48, 49, 56, 68, 71, 82, 98, 104, 107, 114–15, 137, 141, 145, 149
15th Co. 56, 69, 104, 141
23d Co. 59, 64, 78, 82, 83, 115, 141
77th Co. 58, 62, 83, 141
81st Co. 56–58, 130, 141
Navy Medical Detachment 13, 156

3d Division 5, 51, 63, 75, 96
7th Infantry 76–84
1st Bn (1/7) 77, 81–82
3d Bn (3/7) 82
30th Infantry 51, 63
7th Motorized Machine Gun Bn 5

5th Division 113, 118–19, 124, 126
20th Field Artillery 126–27
Battery E. 126
10th Brigade 113

26th Division 2, 6, 9, 10, 15, 91, 93, 119, 122
51st Brigade 91
52d Brigade 91

29th Division 113
57th Brigade 113

32d Division 180

36th Division 133, 152–54
71st Brigade 152–54
142d Infantry 154
72d Brigade 154
131st Machine Gun Bn 154

42d Division 2, 9, 119, 159, 180

77th Division 114, 172, 178
152d Field Artillery Brigade 114
78th Division 132
309th Infantry 132

310th Infantry 132

80th Division 158, 161, 164, 168–69, 172

82d Division 114, 115, 119
325th Infantry 114, 115

89th Division 118, 119, 121, 125, 128, 158, 163, 166, 168–69, 171–72, 174, 178
177th Brigade 125
353d Infantry 125
355th Infantry 178
356th Infantry 174, 176
2d Bn (2/356) 174, 176, 178
90th Division 118, 119

Armies, French:
Second Army 18, 24
Fourth Army 133–35
Sixth Army 39, 85, 86
Eighth Army 24, 113
Tenth Army 95, 97
II Corps 138
III Corps 82, 85, 87
VII Corps 40
X Corps 22, 25, 26
XI Corps 135, 137
XX Corps 97
XXI Corps 40, 53, 75, 82, 133, 135–38
XXXII Corps 113
XXXVIII Corps 87
7th DI 153, 156
10th Colonial DI 51, 63, 86, 101, 111
21st DI 137–42, 144, 150, 156
22d DI 150, 153
26th DI 121
28th DI 145
33d DI 22, 25
34th DI 22, 25, 26th
38th DI 102
39th DI 86, 87, 121
43d DI 42, 46–49, 51, 86
51st DI 26
52d DI 22, 25
58th DI 111
61st DI 136, 145
67th DI 156
73d DI 150, 153, 156
131st DI 26
167th DI 42, 51–53, 143
170th DI 137, 156
115th Infantry 56
153d Infantry 90
174th Infantry 77

Index

Armies, German:
Sturmtruppen 31, 32, 33
12th Saxon Corps 135
3d Guard DI 138
Guard Fusilier Infantry 138–39
7th DI 135, 138
14th Reserve DI 135
15th Bavarian DI 138, 146
31st Infantry 146
42d DI 138
51st Ersatz DI 138
170th DI 143
199th DI 138–39
200th DI 135, 138
203d DI 138
406th Infantry 138
409th Infantry 138
410th Infantry 138
232d DI 77
237th DI 75
47th Infantry 63
401st Infantry 89
444th Infantry 77

Arnold, Maj Alfred C. 63, 64, 87, 142, 150

Baker, Col. Chauncey B. 11
Baker, Secretary of War Newton 9
Ballard, Pvt. 83
Barcsykowski, Pvt. Frank 101
Barker, Maj. Frederick 122, 128–29, 140, 144, 161
Barnett, MGC George 68, 111
Bart, Pvt. Frank J. 143
Bartlett, Maj. Harry G. 20
Battles (other than 2d Division): Cantigny 10, 35, 37; Seicheprey 10
Baylis, 1st Lt. Charles D. 163
Beall, Capt. Russell 81
Bearss, Maj. Hiram I. 20, 32, 33, 96
Beaudette, 1st Sgt. Joseph A. 161, 169
Beeby, Pvt. Albert E. 110
Beird, Pvt. Roy H. 144
Berry, Maj. Benjamin 47, 51, 53, 56, 57, 58, 61
Bessell, Lt. Col. William W. 39, 40, 50
Blake, Capt. Robert 178
Blanc Mont (Blanc Mont Ridge, Essen Hook, Médéah Farm, Orfeuil, St Étienne, Somme-Py) 133–156, 157
Bliss, Maj. Gen. Tasker 11, 92
Bourne, Capt. Louis M., Jr. 129
Bouton, Maj. Arthur E. 87, 88, 101

Bowen, Maj. George C. 81, 120
Bowley, Col. Albert J. 16, 88, 95, 113, 126
Brainard, Maj. Edwin H. 156
Brewer, Sgt. John B. 105
Bridges, Col. Charles H. 35
Brogan, Sgt. Henry S. 131
Brown, Lt. Col. Carey H. 83
Brown, Cpl. Herbert A. 105–6
Brown, Col. Preston 35, 36, 37, 39, 40, 45, 53, 54, 63, 73, 79, 97, 116
Buford, Gy. Sgt. David I. 46
Bullard, Maj. Gen. Robert Lee 113, 157
Bundy, Maj. Gen. Omar 5, 10, 14, 20, 36, 37, 49–50, 53, 69, 70, 73, 75–76, 79, 82, 96
Burlingame, Capt. Claude 124–25
Butterfield, Cpl. Olin J. 145

Capezio, Pvt. John 170
Carrier, 1st Lt. William H. 171
Case, Capt. Philip T. 58, 125
Cates, 2d Lt. Clifton B. 60, 61, 165
Catlin, Col. Albertus 27, 44, 49, 61, 109
Cauldwell, Capt. Oscar R. 46
Chamberlaine, Col. William 35, 48, 49, 62, 84
Chandler, 1st Lt. Henry E. 130
Chapman, Capt. Eldridge G. 124
Chateau Thierry (Belleau, Belleau Wood, Bussiares, Hill 142, Lucy-le-Bocage, Torcy, Triangle Farm, Vaux) 2, 5, 37–94, 96, 156
Chatman, Pvt. Grover N. 130
Clafin, Sgt. James A. 127
Clark, Pvt. Patrick J. 127
Clarkston, Gy. Sgt. Samuel 177
Coffenburg, Capt. Bailey 60, 130
Cole, 1st Lt. Arthur C. 161
Cole, Maj. Edward B. 44, 68
Collins, Cpl. Harry 23
Conachy, Capt. Peter 58, 125
Conger, Col. Arthur L. 96
Connor, Brig. Gen. Fox 51, 70, 73
Cooke, 1st Lt. Elliott W. 45, 98, 101
Corbin, Capt. William O. 49
Craig, Brig. Gen. Malin 39
Croll, Pvt. George H. 165
Cronkite, Maj. Gen. Adelbert 158
Crossen, Sgt. Vernon J. 162
Crowther, 1st Lt. Orlando 54, 55
Cruikshank, Col. William M. 35
Cukela, Sgt. Louis 103
Cumming, Capt. Samuel C. 177
Curlee, Cpl. William 144

Daly, Gy. Sgt. Daniel J. 61
Danley, Pvt. Lester L. 115
Davis, Lt. Col. Joseph R. 35, 48, 57
Day, Maj. James H. 168, 170, 172
DeChambrun, Col. Jacques A. Fr 82
Dégoutte, Gen. Jean M. Fr 75, 92
Denig, Maj. Robert L. 109, 120, 122, 126, 142
Depue, Pvt. David T. 161
DiCarlo, PFC Salvatore 104
Dickman, Maj. Gen. Joseph T. 113, 179
Dobiez, Pvt. Stanley 23
Dobson, 1st Lt. William A. 125
Dockx, Cpl. Francis J. 46
Donohue, Cpl. Patrick P. 61
Dougherty, 1st Lt. Neil F. 165
Doyen, Brig. Gen. Charles A. 5, 14, 29, 34, 35
Doyle, Pvt. John J. 125
Drum, Brig. Gen. Hugh A. 12, 158
Duchêne, Gen. Denis. Fr 39, 40, 75
Duckham, 1st Lt. William 58
Dunbeck, Capt. Charley 70, 159, 162–63, 168–70, 174, 176–77
Duncan, Capt. Donald F. 60

Eaton, Capt. Starr S. 80
Edwards, Maj. Gen. Clarence 7
Edwards, Pvt. Harley 150
Ellet, Pvt. Monroe 122
Elliott, Maj. Charles B. 46, 47, 62–63, 73, 79–81, 87–90
Elmer, 2d Lt. Clarence G. 166
Ely, Brig. Gen. Hanson 99, 104, 106, 113, 139, 141, 143
Evans, Maj. Frank E. 65–66, 73

Faga, Sgt. William H. 162
Farkas, Sgt. Joe 125
Fay, Capt. John 106
Fechet, Maj. d'Alary 105, 166, 170, 172, 178
Feland, Lt Col. Logan 14, 56, 75, 77, 96, 99–100, 113, 115, 127, 159, 164
Field, Cpl. Harry B. 29
Foch, Marshal Ferdinand. Fr 19, 49, 133, 157
Foley, Capt. Frank C. 120
Forsyth, PFC Matthew W., Jr. 122
Fox, Maj. Milo P. 64
Fritz, Cpl. Clyde A. 103

Ganoe, Sgt. Arthur R. 109
Garr, Cpl. Charles W. 153
Gaston, Maj. Jesse 77

Geiger, Sgt. Frank F. 162
Gérard, Maj. Gen. Augustin G.A. Fr 113
Geyer, Pvt. Robert E. 122
Gibbons, Floyd. Am 61
Gibson, Pvt. Charles S. 163
Gillotti, Pvt. Angelo 122
Goodwin, PhM3d Oscar S. USN 129
Gordon, 2d Lt. George V. 58
Gouraud, Gen. Henri J.E. Fr 134–35
Graham, Sgt. Walter F. 24
Grant, Lt. Col. Walter S. 51
Green, Sgt. Donald F. 122
Green, Capt. James O. (Joe) 28, 79, 81
Green, Capt. Kirt 164
Greenwood, Pvt. Thomas A., Jr. 24
Griffen, 1st Lt. Martin J. 125
Grimland, Lt. Gordon A. USN 129
Grundy, Pvt. John 169
Gulberg, Sgt. Martin G. 23, 28, 45

Haefliger, Pvt. Fred 145
Haig, Field Marshal Douglas. Br 19, 25, 157
Hall, Capt. Farragut F. 121
Hamilton, Capt. George 54, 55, 56, 57; Major 141, 149, 159, 162–63, 170, 174, 176, 178
Haney, Pvt. John S. 177
Harbord, Brig. Gen. James G. 15, 35, 43, 48–59, 67, 68–77, 83–86, 96–99, 105, 111, 113
Hart, 1st Lt. Jack S. 130–31
Hassard, Cpl. Robert 103
Hawkins, Maj. 114–15
Hawkins, Capt. Gardiner W. 164–65
Hellé, Gen. Joseph. Fr 7, 98, 111
Herbst, Lt. Col. George A. 96
Hermle, 1st Lt. Leo D. 159, 162
Herrman, Hap1st Bernard W. USN 129
Hezzelwood, 2d Lt. George W. 115
Hilton, Capt. Roy C. 27, 141, 143–44, 168
Hines, Maj. Gen. John L. 179
Hirschauer, Gen. Auguste. Fr 25
Hoffman, Gy. Sgt. Charles F. 55–56
Holabird, Lt. Col. John A. 114
Holcomb, Maj. Thomas 43, 67, 74–75, 77, 86, 95, 108–9, 116, 140
Hood, Capt. Robert B. 122
Houchins, Cpl. Lyle C. 130
Hughes, Maj. John A. 67, 68, 70, 72–73, 77, 108–10
Hunt, Capt. LeRoy 101, 142
Hurley, Capt. Patrick J. 77
Hutchings, 1st Lt. Charles, Jr. 166

260 Index

Irwin, Col. George LeR. 35

Jackson, Cpl. Warren R. 28, 68
Jacobsen, Capt. Arnold W. 163
Janda, Maj. Ladislav T. 168, 170, 172–73
Joe, Sgt. Colin B. 161, 170
Joffre, Marshal Joseph J. Fr 9
Johnston, Capt. James H. 129
Jordan, Pvt. Richard O. 144

Kacprzyzki, Pvt. Bronislaw 122
Kane, Sgt. Tony 178
Karstaedt, Capt. Frederick W. 61
Kean, 1st Lt. Robert 17, 24, 103, 111, 115
Kelly, Pvt. John J. 131, 144
Kelly, Col. John R. 114
Kennedy, 1st Lt. Alexander, Jr. 64
Keyser, Maj. Ralph S. 83, 85, 98, 100, 104–5, 107
Kibler, 1st Lt. John T. 125
Kidder, 2d Lt. Hugh 140
Kilby, PFC Robert E.L. 128
Kimball, 1st Lt. Walter J. 124
Kocak, Sgt. Matej 103
Kreuzman, Pvt. William A. 163

Lange, Capt. Otto F. 32
Larsen, Capt. Henry L. 58, 67; Major 141, 159, 162–64, 170, 178
Lashiwer, PFC Hyman 122
Lay, Pvt. Arthur 169
Lay, Lt. Col. Harry 141
LeBrun, Gen. Fr 82
Lee, Lt. Col. Harry 61, 68, 75, 95, 96, 108, 113, 129, 139, 141, 149, 151, 159, 163
Lejeune, Maj. Gen. John A. 111, 113, 116, 134–35, 139–40, 149, 153–55, 158
Lenert, Pvt. Henry P. 86
Lewis, Maj. Gen. Edward M. 7, 29, 49, 73, 88–89
Lewis, Maj. Harry T. 45
Liggett, Maj. Gen. Hunter 91, 116, 158
Litchfield, Phm3d John R. USN 130
Livingston, Maj. John G. 47
Lloyd, Capt. Egbert T. 65
Lockwood, Pvt. Wilbur E. 125
Loomis, Cpl. Casey V. 130
Ludendorf, Gen. Erich von. Gr 6

Mackin, PFC Elton 149, 177
Major, Capt. Harlan E. 69, 71
Malloy, 2d Lt. Joseph A. 107
Malone, Col. Paul B. 7, 27, 31, 44–49, 57, 61–68, 72–74, 77–81, 88, 99, 102–3, 113

Mangin, Gen. Charles. Fr 7, 95, 97, 98
Manning, Phm3d James E. USN 130
Marbache (Colombey, Mousson, Seille River) 113–117
Marlowe, Sgt. Fred M. 162
Martin, Maj. George W. 129
Mattfeldt, Capt. 1st Lt. Clyburn O. 126
Mazurkevczk, Pvt. Stanley 122
Mazzoni, PFC Louis 169
McCloskey, Col. Manus 114
McCormick, Sgt. Clark T. 161
McCrossen, Sgt. Bernard 15, 23, 27–28, 38, 48
McCune, Sgt. Karl 128
McEvoy, Capt. Thomas T. 129
McGay, 2d Lt. George H. 124
McIndoe, Col. James F. 96
Mebreski, Cpl. Michell 120
Merrill, Lt. Col. Thomas 35
Messersmith, Maj. Robert 121, 126, 128, 141
Meuse-Argonne (Beaumont, Landre-et-St. Georges, Létanne, Moulins Mouzon, Villemontry-Yoncq) 25, 157–178
Meyer, Pvt. Albert 131
Meyerling, 1st Lt. William D. 30
Meyers, Pvt. Demarr E. 163
Michel, Gen. Victor. Fr 44–47
Miller, Maj. 169–70
Mills, Pvt. Bruce H. 144
Mitchell, Col. William A. 96
Montague, 1st Lt. Robert L. 162–63
Moore, Capt. Charles E. 78, 80, 82
Moran, Pvt. Patrick J. 130–31
Moran, Pvt. Russell 150
Murray, Brig. Gen. Peter 29, 35

Naulin, Gen. Stanislas. Fr 75, 82, 136, 138–39, 152–53
Neville, Gen. Robert G. Fr 8, 27
Neville, Col. Wendell C. 45–49, 56, 57, 72–77, 83, 84–85
Noble, 1st Lt. Alfred H. 61, 129; Capt. 163
Nutting, Pvt. Lester H. 132

O'Leary, Lt. Col. Arthur J. 128
Osborne, Cpl. Harry 144
Osterhout, Capt. George H. 71, 82
Overton, 2d Lt. John 109
Overton, 1st Lt. Macon 70, 129, 155, 159, 162

Parker, Pvt. Donald M. 130

Parker, 1st Lt. George E. 114
Passaga, Maj. Gen. Fénelon F.G. Fr 113
Peck, Capt. DeWitt 126
Pennington, Pvt. 83
Pershing, Gen. John J. 7, 9, 10, 16, 18, passim 182
Pétain, Marshal Henri-Phillipe. Fr 16, 40, 49, 135
Peters, Pvt. Andy 75
Peyton, Maj. 121, 125
Phelan, Cpl. Edward F. 105
Phillips, Pvt. Charles 106, 110
Pincoffs, Capt. Maurice 155
Platner, Capt. Aaron A. 142, 143
Platt, Capt. Richard N. 58, 83, 125
Poe, 2d Lt. Edgar Allen 73
Pruitt, Cpl. John H. 144

Quinn, Sgt. 115

Rendinell, Cpl. Joseph 22, 29, 30, 110
Rhea, Col. James C. 134, 141, 143, 166
Richardson, 2d Lt. Stephen M. 114
Riffie, Pvt. Raymond T. 61, 110
Robertson, 1st Lt. James F. 61

St. Mihiel (Jaulny, Limey, Rembercourt, Thiacourt) 24, 25, 118–32, 157
Sarti, Sgt. 1st Cl William 155
Saunders, Cpl. Thomas D. 126
Savatier, Gen. Eugène. Fr 7, 34
Schmitz, Pvt. Charles 32
Schreech, Cpl. George W. 163
Scllero, Capt. James McB. 144
Settle, PFC Frank J. 122
Shannon, Capt. Harold D. 159
Shearer, Maj. Maurice 43–46, 67, 68, 73, 84–85, 121, 125–28
Sheridan, Gy. Sgt. Aloysius P. 60
Shiel, Capt. Robert H. 129
Shipley, Capt. George A. 161, 169–70
Shuler, Maj. George K. 141, 150, 159, 163, 174–77
Sibley, Maj. Berton W. 44, 53, 59, 61, 64–67, 73, 74, 83, 108–9, 122, 128–29
Sigg, 1st Sgt. Charles F. 154
Silverthorn, Sgt. Merwin H. 59, 82
Simon, Sgt. Frank 162
Sinclair, Pvt. Wilbert W. 178
Smiley, Pvt. Dean F. 155
Smith, 2d Lt. Harry S. 168
Smith, Maj. Holland McT. 34
Smith, Capt. Mark 110
Soissons (Beaurepaire, Chaudun, Fôret de Retz, Maison Neuve, Vauxcastille, Vierzy) 95–112
Speer, Capt. Charles 101
Stallings, 1st Lt. Laurence T. 75
Statham, PFC George B. 170
Stokley, 1st Lt. Robert G. 81
Stone, Col. Edward R. 113, 142, 151, 161
Stowell, Capt. George A. 67, 68, 159, 161, 164
Stuart, Col. George W. 113, 125, 127, 141, 152
Summerall, Maj. Gen. Charles P. 158
Sundval, 2d Lt. August L. 33
Sweeny, Cpl. William A. 30
Syverson, Pvt. Grannis L. 145
Szopinski, Cpl. Roman J. 24

Taugher, 2d Lt. Claude B. 165
Tawater, Sgt. Carl 164
Taylor, 2d Lt. Moses E. 27
Tebbetts, Col. Harry F. 35
Thomason, Capt. John W., Jr. 99, 156
Tierce, Pvt. William A. 124
Toblini, Pvt. Andy 144
Toulon (Toul, Verdun) 21, 22, 24, 25, 31
Turrill, Maj. Julius S. 44–48, 50, 54, 56–57, 79, 98, 100, 104, 106, 121

Ulrich, Gy. Sgt. William 130
Upton, Col. Leroy 7, 27, 32, 43, 47, 71, 81, 89–90, 99, 102, 106–7, 113

Valentine, Capt. Frank C. 80
Van Horn, Col. Robert O. 166
Von Gallwitz, Gen. May. Gr 158
Von Nidda, Gen. Krug. Gr 135

Waddill, Maj. Edmund C. 61, 62–63, 73, 74, 81, 121, 124
Wagner, Pvt. Tony 122
Waller, Maj. Littleton W.T., Jr. 82, 141
West, 1st Lt. John A. 151
White, 2d Lt. Richard R. 125
Whitley, Maj. Franklin L. 47, 90
Wilcox, 1st Lt. Ralph 178
Wilkerson, Pvt. Alfred 126
Wilkinson, 2d Lt. Arthur 142
Williams, Maj. Ernest C. 122, 128–29, 144, 150–51, 163–64
Williams, Capt. Lloyd W. 49, 56, 70
Wilmer, Maj. Pere 109
Wilson, Pres. Thomas Woodrow 9, 179
Winans, Capt. Roswell 56, 64
Winchenbaugh, Cpl. Wolcott. Am 33

Wise, Lt. Col. Frederick M. 34, 46, 48, 51, 71–72, 75, 77, 83, 115
Wollert, Cpl. Edward J. 131
Wood, Lt. 115
Worthington, Capt. Henry H. 32, 101
Wright, Maj. Gen. William M. 158

Young, Pvt. George L. 82

Yowell, Capt. Robert 58, 83, 84, 125
Zane, Maj. Edmund L. 47, 161, 169
Zane, Capt. Randolph T. 60, 61, 65
Zeiler, Cpl. Elmer 144
Zwicky, 1st Lt. William H. 76

www.ingramcontent.com/pod-product-compliance
Ingram Content Group UK Ltd.
Pitfield, Milton Keynes, MK11 3LW, UK
UKHW041933140426
5217IPUK00014B/458